D0204918

ESTHETICS
CONTEMPORARY

ESTHETICS CONTEMPORARY

edited by RICHARD KOSTELANETZ

 Prometheus Books
1203 Kensington Avenue,
Buffalo, New York 14215

Especially for
Mary Emma Harris

079925

Published 1978 by Prometheus Books
1203 Kensington Avenue, Buffalo, New York 14215

Library of Congress Catalog Number: 77-73848
ISBN 0-87975-105-3

Printed in the United States of America

Epigraphs

Aesthetics ... aims primarily at a *theoretical understanding of the arts and related modes of behavior and experience.* As distinct from specialized studies of a single art, aesthetics deals with *all the arts* ... Aesthetics differs from art *history* in organizing its materials more in theoretical than in chronological order. It classifies its data and conclusions mainly according to general concepts of recurrent types, tendencies, and relationships.—Thomas Munro, "The Morphology of Art as a Branch of Aesthetics" (1954).

The avant-garde of today has definitely eroded the fundamentals of aesthetics which had seemed so firm for many centuries. I shall not urge that the transmitted aesthetics is certain to survive; it may well be that we will pass through a period of crisis and that at the other side a new continuum of the arts with a considerable shift of emphases will emerge. ... Some scholars have forecast the death of art itself. This obituary seems wrongly conceived; and yet, there is *an end to plausibility for certain definitional ideas* of the traits of art.—Stefan Morawski, *Inquiries into the Fundamentals of Aesthetics* (1974).

All the arts derive from the same and unique root.

Consequently, all the arts are identical.

—Wassily Kandinsky, "Concrete Art" (1938).

The imagination (as a productive faculty of cognition) is a powerful agent for creating, as it were, a second nature out of the material supplied to it by actual nature.—Immanuel Kant, *Critique of Judgment* (1790).

Epigraphs

The starting point for all systems of aesthetics must be the personal experience of a peculiar emotion. The objects which provide this emotion we call works of art. All sensitive people agree that there is a peculiar emotion provoked by works of art . . . . This emotion is called the aesthetic emotion. —Clive Bell, *Art* (1913).

The artist's effort, always and everywhere, is to attain a fresh mode of cognition. At the same time he struggles to disembarrass himself of procedures which force him to say things that are either commonplace or false. —Donald Barthelme, "After Joyce" (1964).

The Minimalists appear to have realized, finally, that the far-out in itself has to be the far-out as end in itself, and that this means the furthest-out and nothing short of that. They appear also to have realized that the most original and furthest-out art of the last hundred years always arrived looking at first as though it had parted company with everything previously known as art. In other words, the furthest-out usually lay on the borderline between art and non-art.—Clement Greenberg, "The Recentness of Sculpture" (1967).

What kind of love or grief is there in [a work of art]? I don't understand, in a painting, the love of anything except the love of painting itself. If there is agony, other than the agony of painting, I don't know exactly what kind of agony that would be.—Ad Reinhardt, in a symposium (1951).

Modern art divides the public into two classes, those who understand it, and those who do not understand it—that is to say, those who are artists and those who are not. The new art is an artistic art.—José Ortega y Gasset, "The Dehumanization of Art" (1925).

But one thing has not changed: the relation of any new art—while it is new—to its own moment; or, to put it the other way around: every moment during the past hundred years has had an outrageous art of its own, so that every generation, from Courbet down, has had a crack at the discomfort to be had from modern art.—Leo Steinberg, "Contemporary Art and the Plight of its Public" (1962).

There has always been, and still is, a great gulf between philosophical esthetics and the arts themselves. A person may study the former for years in an American philosophy department, without having to examine a single work of art. As in Europe, esthetics here usually has emphasized highly general problems concerning the nature of art, beauty, and esthetic value. Esthetics of this narrow, traditional sort has always failed to interest many college students, or to satisfy the inquiring layman. They find in it, not a unifying approach to the arts—but another highly specialized little subject, off in a corner by itself, devoted to endless debate over small technicalities.

Contents

Contents

Contents

Preface

The remarks of an artist, a moralist or a churchman are sometimes as significant in revealing the implicity aesthetic assumptions of an age as are the more high-powered and recondite formulations of the philosophers.

—Harold Osborne, *Aesthetics and Art Theory* (1970).

Esthetics is our word for the philosophy of art, which is to say, abstract thought that defines artistic experience in general terms meant to have comprehensive relevance. Esthetics characterizes the broadest, most encompassing view of art. Though dependent upon a tradition of deduced principles, esthetic thinking also has an inductive empirical dimension. Thus, as the arts have changed in time, so has and must esthetic thought; for the esthetics of a particular period both reflects and illuminates the predominant art of that era. Our perception of art, like our perception of reality, must continually be updated.

There is no question that most esthetic notions based on Renaissance art, say, are irrelevant to modern work; but only now is it becoming clear that an esthetics founded upon artistic modernism may, in crucial respects, be similarly obsolete before contemporary art. Hypotheses of "expression" or "representation," for instance, have little relevance to that advanced art since 1959 (a crucial date) which is considered important. No esthetic think-

13

ing aspiring to genuine pertinence can afford to wallow in issues that have been surpassed; ostriches cannot move forward while their heads are buried in the sand.

It is indicative that academic estheticians tend, in my observation, either to ignore post-1960 art entirely, or to use old-fashioned criteria to dismiss nearly all of it, or more modestly, to recognize the need for a new esthetics they are unable to provide. On the other hand, critics concentrating on a particular art generally lack the interdisciplinary integrating capacities that distinguish the best esthetic thinking from unsystematic and/or specialized perceptions. For these reasons, most texts and anthologies of esthetics published in recent years tend to reflect a frustrating ignorance of the most significant contemporary art, while *criticism* of this new art rarely provides more general esthetic truths.

Nevertheless, some critics, historians and artists have published suggestive statements that realize, sometimes inadvertently, both the comprehensive perspectives of esthetic thinking and a clear understanding of contemporary art. Some of these ideas simply define common qualities of initially independent developments, while others have perhaps influenced the creation of art. Though many contributors to this book may lack the credentials (or blessings) of professional estheticians, all exemplify the standards and purposes of their intellectual tradition.

Its strict sense of contemporaneity notwithstanding, this anthology intends to be eclectic—heeding no orthodoxies, establishing no hierarchies, and flattering no parochial coteries. Some of the contributors no doubt disagree with others (or with me, and vice versa). By presenting a wide range of current issues, this book aims to open discussion, rather than close it off; one implicit theme is different ways of talking about contemporary art. Still, I should acknowledge that my own sense of contemporary importance reflects particular discriminations made in my prior critical books on contemporary art and literature—*The Theatre of Mixed Means* (1968), *The End of Intelligent Writing* (1974), *Twenties in the Sixties* (1978)—and in several anthologies I have edited on experimental art, futuristic social thought, and criticism. My selections also reflect Anglo-American standards of critical veracity. Indicatively, there is little in this book with which I totally disagree, and even less that I find totally incomprehensible. My introduction is a critical-historical survey of post-World War II esthetic thinking in America; it aims to provide background to subsequent contributions.

Since this book is produced in the United States, and its contributors are, like the avant-gardes in all arts, mostly American, I have personally favored the U.S. spelling of *esthetics*, nonetheless respecting the European orthography of others. In principle, I have avoided recycling otherwise appropriate essays that are conveniently available elsewhere (for example, Susan Sontag's "The Aesthetics of Silence"). Every effort has been made to verify the spelling of all proper names and to trace the ownership of all copyrighted material, in addition to making full acknowledgment of the latter's use. If any error or omission has occurred, it will be corrected in subsequent editions, providing that appropriate notification is submitted in writing to the author.

I am grateful to Paul Kurtz of Prometheus Books for contracting this long-fomenting collection, and to Elizabeth King, and Rita Wilson for their editorial and production work. I wish to thank the contributors and/or their publishers for granting permissions to reprint their works. Regina N. Cohen helped me with preliminary research, and Mary Emma Harris has aided me in several ways—among them, the completion of this book. The dedication is a partial measure of my gratitude.

Part One

Richard Kostelanetz

Contemporary American Esthetics

Aesthetics, or the science of art . . . is only the progressive systematiza-
tion, always renewed and always renewing, of the problems arising from
time to time out of reflection upon art.
    —Benedetto Croce, "Aesthetics," *Encyclopedia Britannica* (1929).

The questions of esthetics are unchanging—the definition of art (as distinct from non-art or sub-art), the function of art, the types of art, the genesis
of art, the effects of art, the relation of art to society and history, the criteria
of critical evaluation, the processes of perception, and the generic characteristics of superior works. As esthetic thinking deals with properties common
and yet peculiar to all things called "art," the philosophy of art, in contrast to
"criticism," offers statements which are relevant to more than one art, if not
fundamental to the arts in general—the presuppositions being, first, that the
various arts are more interrelated than not and, second, that common artistic
assumptions are more significant than differences in content and materials.
Esthetics is, by definition, primarily concerned with "fine art," if not with
only the very best art; and although the philosophy of art customarily
depends upon the established hierarchies of critical reputation for its choice
of individual examples, esthetics provides more foundation for critical practice than the latter offers the former. Concomitant esthetic concerns include

Reprinted from *Sun & Moon*, I/4 (1977), by permission of the author. Originally drafted in 1970.
Copyright © 1977 by Richard Kostelanetz.

19

the nature of badness and/or vulgarity in art, and the question of whether art is, or should be, primarily the imitation of nature, the expression of self, or wholly the creation of imagination; for these are issues that are most definitively considered with reference to all of the arts.

Esthetics is more self-reflective than criticism, as well as more dispassionate about particular art forms or works; for it evinces not only a breadth of interest that is ideally all-encompassing but also an objective distance from individual artists, certain styles, internecine disputes and fluctuating hierarchies of reputation. Different esthetic philosophies emphasize different issues, as their basic choices often, on one hand, reflect prior metaphysical or epistemological assumptions (which may not always be explicit) and, on the other, determine their approach to remaining esthetic issues. Whereas the aim of science is systematic structure, the philosophy of art, even at its finest, is a set of related propositions. Esthetic thinking also tends to be more prescriptive than other branches of philosophy, ethics of course excluded; the American philosopher Charles S. Pierce called esthetics "the basic normative science."

Esthetics has evolved as both a branch of philosophy (that currently has slight eminence within the American academic profession) and a collection of theoretical reflections by artists and critics, both making explicit those encompassing generalizations that are merely implicit in individual works, so that esthetic thought tends to come either from professional philosophers with an interest in art or from artists and critics with aspirations to philosophy. For these reasons, esthetics is not exclusively the domain of self-avowed estheticians, as the epithet is implicitly honorific, characterizing first, a certain way of thinking about art and, then, a level of both perspective and generalization that distinguishes true esthetic ideas from mere criticism about art. Since major theories of art emphasize not just different fundamental questions but different dimensions of artistic practice—the creation of art, say, rather than its perception; or evaluation, rather than generic forms—esthetic philosophies generally do not possess sufficient common touchstones to invite easy comparison with each other. A further presupposition holds that art is a particular kind of discourse, differing from both expository argument and verifiable demonstration; it is best regarded as a second nature, so to speak, which is distinct from primary nature.

The answers to the classic esthetic questions change in time, particularly as the success of a persuasive new style in art renders many old answers dubious, if not ludicrous. Everyone familiar with current art would find obsolete the favorite nineteenth century categories of the sublime, the tragic, the comic and the picturesque, all of which were derived from a theory of literary and artistic kinds. The reason is simply that those qualities, so conspicuous in much nineteenth century work, are just not particularly prominent in recent art. As Benedetto Croce wrote in 1929, "The chief problem of our time, to be overcome by esthetics, is connected with the [current] crisis in art and in judgments upon art produced by the romantic period"; and it is a modern truth that the same art which seemed incomprehensibly innovative to one generation is likely to strike succeeding generations as all too familiar. Indeed, a great change in art, as in our own time, challenges the old esthetic principles and raises a demand for new formulations that bring traditional preoccupations abreast of new experience; one result of every decisive revolution in art should be a comparable revolution in esthetic thinking.

American esthetics between the world wars focus, d upon three large themes—the eternal characteristics of realized art, the nature of subjective processes in artistic creation, and art's social relevance. The first concern unifies, in retrospective intellectual history, estheticians as otherwise contrary as the neo-Aristotelians, with their emphasis upon the resolution of linear forms, and the New Critics, who claimed to derive esthetic criteria (as well as critical methods) that were valid for all literature and, by implication, for all art too. A statement typical of the time (although its author's principal theory of art as wish-fulfillment put him outside of these two schools) was DeWitt H. Parker's assertion, in *The Analysis of Art* (1924), that "the general characteristics of esthetic form" could be reduced to six simple principles: "The principle of organic unity, or unity in variety, as it has been called; the principle of the theme; the principle of thematic variation; balance; the principle of hierarchy; and evolution." Pursuing this concern with unifying structure, Parker followed Aristotle in defining "organic unity [as] the master principle of esthetic form; all the other principles serve it," so that, here and elsewhere, the quest for unifying esthetic principles inspired an emphasis upon internal artistic unities. Even an esthetician-critic as instinctively eccentric as Kenneth Burke made his major theme the insidiously unifying impact of realized artistic forms.

Another school of American esthetics, influenced by the Italian philosopher Benedetto Croce (and to a lesser extent by Henri Bergson), emphasized intuition, as opposed to intellect, in an expressionistic theory of art. This had much in common with yet another theory which was derived from the impact of Freudian psychology upon esthetic thinking—regarding all works as expressions (and, thus, symbolic revelations) of the submerged, nonrational psychic constitution of its creator. However, both the Crocean and the Freudian positions were ultimately neither objective nor systematic enough to forge philosophical statements with more profundity than obvious platitude.

21

And although the Freudian position often informed illuminating literary criticism, its descriptions of creative processes remained too abstract and mechanical—too divorced from the real problems of artistic choice and construction. (The European origins and dissemination of these traditions perhaps explains why Jean-Paul Sartre's esthetics, say, or Theodor Adorno's, also seem so similarly abstract and amorphous.) Moreover, the decidedly objectivist, self-effacing character of nearly all contemporary arts, especially since 1959, makes expressionist theories appear even more irrelevant.

It was characteristic of John Dewey, in contrast, to be less concerned with the creation of art, or even with George Santayana's earlier emphasis upon esthetic pleasure, than with the audience's experience of serious art. In his single most influential esthetic text, indicatively entitled *Art as Experience* (1934), Dewey first characterized the pattern of human experience and perception—intrinsically unending, yet full of short-term conclusions. He then defined art's function as the coherent organization of experience, which is to say the creation of conclusions. This definition leads Dewey to suggest that the materials available to art can include anything in the world, and then that any practical or intellectual activity, "provided that it is integrated and moved by its own urge to fulfillment, will have esthetic quality." It follows that all successful art is "clearly conceived and consistently ordered," no matter the quality of the medium's surface; for in true esthetic perception, "A beholder must *create* his own experience." (This emphasis upon the experience of art identified what became known as contextualist esthetics; its primary exponents have been Stephen C. Pepper and Irwin Edman.)

As persuasive as Dewey was in characterizing ideal esthetic experience, his book resembles much of his other philosophy (as well as Emerson's and Thoreau's before him) in casting essentially normative statements in a descriptive, matter-of-fact style. Secondly, the persuasiveness of his position is somewhat undermined by Dewey's evident ignorance of individual works of art and his equally evident insensitivity to issues of artistic quality. Finally, this emphasis upon the audience's experience becomes outright subjectivism in Curt John Ducasse's eccentric but influential *The Philosophy of Art* (1929), which holds that esthetic value depends upon individual experience and, thus, that works of art cannot be objectively compared to each other. It is scarcely surprising that those philosophers and critics regarding art as the diametric opposite of science should advocate a contrary intellectual methodology as more appropriate to esthetic discussion.

In the decade after the Second World War, no philosophy of art seemed more dominant in America than that expounded by Susanne K. Langer, first in *Philosophy in a New Key* (1942), and then in her most sustained esthetic exposition, *Feeling and Form* (1953). Her theory of art as symbolic representation is indebted to the German philosopher Ernest Cassirer, for symbolism became Langer's "new key" for generating philosophical answers. "The edifice of human knowledge," she wrote in the earlier book, "stands before us, not as a vast collection of sense reports, but as a structure of *facts that are symbols* and *laws that have their meanings.*" The words of human language she regarded as one strain of symbolic activity; the nondiscursive material of the nonliterary arts became another. Both of them, she said, are devoted to "the creation of forms symbolic of human feeling," and a symbol is, in Langer's definition, "any device whereby we are enabled to make an abstraction." Thus, to answer the question of how artistic order is created, Langer suggests that the artist endeavors to create unique symbolic structures that nonetheless present "semblances" of familiar feelings—a creative process that, as Langer describes it, scarcely draws upon unconscious materials. "The function of art," she writes, "is the symbolic expression not of the artist's actual emotions, but of his knowledge of emotions." If the symbolic presentation is true to the form of a certain feeling, then this formal abstraction will not only give esthetic pleasure by itself; it will also function to instigate that particular feeling in the spectator.

The intellectual achievement of Langer's esthetics is a richly supported theory of art-as-emotion which avoids traditional schemes of expression and individual personality on one hand, and explicit universal myth on the other. One evident presupposition is that the ulterior meaning of nonlinguistic forms can be universally understood; in truth, however, cultural anthropology documents this last assumption as needlessly naive—the color white, for instance, suggesting to Eskimos feelings quite different from those it inspires in Bushmen. A more critical limitation of Langer's esthetics is the general sense that her ideas best characterize American art that was prominent in the 1930s and 1940s—the representational music of Aaron Copland, the programmatic dance of Martha Graham, the poetry of T. S. Eliot, and post-cubist abstract painting. The sensitive historian of esthetics, Thomas Munro, observed in 1950 that "symbols and symbolism" was then the dominant esthetic concept. (Similarly, one reason for the influence of gestalt psychology at that time was that it rationalized the perception of abstract painting.) Instead, the most significant art since 1960, in America and elsewhere, is by contrast so consciously constructivist and nonreferential that no symbolic translations are intended.

Indeed, a conspicuous lack of contemporary relevance continues to plague nearly all recent writing by American academic estheticians, most of whom appear more concerned with understanding and interpreting classic

RICHARD KOSTELANETZ

doctrines, and many of whom let their apparent ignorance of recent art slide into an unashamed hostility that fans the fires of philistinism. Even worse, as the British philosopher Richard Wollheim noted, "The great difficulty in any modern book of esthetics is to find anything to criticize. For by and large what is not unintelligible is truism." Anyone reading academic estheticians in bulk discovers that they rarely confront the major contemporary questions, and, if then, rarely decisively enough; and this general vagueness leads to further platitudinousness in their specific discussions. Perhaps one reason why they continually complain about being misunderstood, even by their professional peers, is that their initial expositions are so frequently unclear. Then too, they often make a point of emphasizing "value" or evaluation (as supposedly untemporal and, thus, a philosophical specialty); but this emphasis, like that upon "beauty," serves in practice to introduce precisely those archaic standards that modernist art tries to surpass. As values, both artistic and humane, do indeed change in time, evaluation remains among the less enlightening approaches to any new art (or to any unfamiliar experience, for that matter). New art, in contrast, customarily denies platitude and previous standards of excellence; it challenges accepted esthetic assumptions (particularly those separating art from non-art); it must be apprehended accurately before it is judged. Similarly, it is extreme works, rather than conventional ones, which prompt esthetic reawakening. With the acceptance of a radically different art comes the need to reinterpret, if not recreate, esthetic philosophy.

The truth is that just as so much consequential contemporary sociology comes from writers outside the official profession, so the esthetic philosophy more appropriate to our time has been forged largely by artists and critics. This shift in origins comes not without shortcomings, of course. Whereas deductive estheticians tend to presume that their theories are relevant to all art, the artist or critic, customarily working inductively, makes no pretense of moving beyond his primary enthusiasms. Concomitantly, artists and even critics inevitably adopt an approach whose initial scope is much narrower than Langer's, say, or Dewey's; they do not feel the academic obligation to acknowledge prominent previous alternative theories before presenting their own. Indicatively, they find definition more essential than evaluation, and the qualities of "significance" or "interest" more laudatory than, say, "beauty." Thirdly, artists and critics tend to be more intimately familiar with the extreme artistic endeavors that pose the most radical challenges to a de facto philosophy of art. *These* up-to-date, inductive estheticians, at their best, forge generalizations relevant not just to one art but contemporary arts as a whole; and in the sum of their particular perspectives

24

is perhaps a comprehensive esthetic philosophy that, except for minor divergences, would have fairly general contemporary relevance—at least to advanced American art since 1959.

One of the first American books to deal comprehensively, if not prophetically, with distinctively contemporary arts was L. Moholy-Nagy's *Vision in Motion* (1947). Its author, born in Hungary in 1895, became successively a painter and photographer in post-World War I Berlin, a teacher at the Weimar Bauhaus, a filmmaker, a designer, a sculptor, and much else. A refugee from Hitler's Germany, he emigrated first to London and then to Chicago in 1937 to head the New Bauhaus, which later became the Institute of Design (itself subsequently incorporated into the Illinois Institute of Technology). Published just after Moholy-Nagy's premature death in 1946, *Vision in Motion* draws upon its author's incomparably various artistic experience, in order to outline his innovative (and influential) program for artistic education. More importantly, as a participant-observer in the revolutions of modern art, Moholy-Nagy personally understood its radical break with past art; as an intellectual, he acknowledged the need for a new esthetics.

In the unprecedented activities of modern art, he found two encompassing tendencies—kinesis and arts-between-old-arts. The first revolutionary development—art that moves—he traced back to cubism and its innovation of systemic multiple perspective realized within a single plane; so that one change in the visual arts, for instance, was a decisive evolution from "fixed perspective to 'vision in motion' [of] seeing a constantly changing moving field of mutual relationships." This leads, of course, to mobile sculpture (in which Moholy-Nagy himself was a pioneer creator) and even to cinema, where the form of cinematic montage with multiple perspective represents a formally analogous extension of cubism. In all modern art, Moholy-Nagy finds "space-time" or "vision in motion," which he ultimately regards as "a new dynamic and kinetic existence free from the static, fixed framework of the past," and this art demands, in turn, unprecedented kinds of esthetic perception. Moholy-Nagy's generalization is, of course, as perspicacious for contemporary painterly arts as post-ballet modern dance; and the simultaneously multiple perspective of cubistic visual space has formal analogies with, among other phenomena, the aural experience of post-Schoenbergian serial music.

On the second point of arts-between-old-arts, Moholy-Nagy offers a discussion of sculpture, for instance, which acknowledges that an Alexander Calder mobile possessing negligible weight, kinetic form and virtual (imagined) volume is not sculpture in the traditional sense, but something else—a hybrid of sculpture and theater; and recognitions like this lead him to an acknowledgment of an increased diversity of artistic types. A next step is his acceptance of the unprecedented perceptual experiences instigated by the new art forms. Indeed, precisely because his esthetic thinking is so free of a priori limitations (upon artistic forms, or systems of meaning), Moholy-Nagy can offer persuasive rationalizations for freedoms already forged in art. Underlying this acceptance is, nonetheless, a strong sense of the particular integrity and capabilities both of each traditional artistic medium and of each new inter-medium as well; so that just as an artist would be ill-advised to do in one form what could better succeed in another, so a critic should not judge a painting or a Calder mobile with criteria more relevant to literature.

To explain the evolution of art, especially stylistic change (which remains the basic evolutionary unit), Moholy-Nagy introduces a theme previously unknown in American esthetics (which has tended to avoid the issues of artistic genesis and transformation). This new kind of sociological explanation, which can be called technological determinism, deals with the impact of crucial machinery upon the creative sensibility. The modern end of the Renaissance mode of representational space, where a scene is portrayed "from an *unchangeable*, fixed point following the rules of the vanishing-point perspective," is attributed to "speeding on the roads and circling in the skies. . . . The man at the wheel sees persons and objects in quick succession, in permanent motion." If technology transforms the sensibilities of both perceivers and creators, it follows that art created after the dissemination of radios and then television would differ from earlier art, and these differences would in turn reflect those new technologies. (This theme was to be more prominently developed in the sixties by Marshall McLuhan.)

Moholy-Nagy also regards technology as crucially changing the sum of materials available to artists and thus, again in turn, influencing stylistic development. For instance, the innovative design of even something as mundane as a chair reveals an indebtedness to "electricity, the gasoline and diesel engines, the airplanes, motion pictures, color photography, radio, metallurgy, new alloys, plastics, laminated materials. . . ." One obvious extension of this principle holds that electronic sound-generation not only creates an audibly different music but that the mere existence of electronically-assisted sound would also affect musical works that are composed entirely by nonelectronic means. In addition, as technology continues to develop new forms, so will art, in turn, reflect new techniques. Extending this sense of history to politics, Moholy-Nagy suggests that changes in creativity and technology—in both mind and matter—must necessarily precede transformations in society.

No American has done more to forge an esthetics for post-World War II advanced art than John Cage, perhaps because no other avant-garde artist or critic has so persistently insisted that radical developments in his own initial specialty—in this case, the composition of music—are generatively relevant to other arts. Typically, those ideas suggesting esthetic respeculation have been scattered through Cage's numerous lectures and interviews, his innumerable conversations both private and public, and the essays and texts he collected into three books of miscellaneous writings—*Silence* (1961), *A Year from Monday* (1967), and *M.* (1973). His esthetic philosophy is also articulated, largely by resonant implication, in his musical works. Cage's purpose could be defined as opening all esthetic activity to creative processes and perceptual experience unknown before; so that he came to regard as most laudable those contemporary works that represent a purposeful violation of old artistic ideas. "Art, if you want a definition of it," he wrote, "is criminal action, because it conforms to no rules." In order to transcend ingrained convention Cage frequently exhibits a dialectical intelligence that asserts that art might be the opposite of everything it once was; yet by making diametrically contrary esthetic statements, Cage thus makes possible a range of intermediate syntheses. For example, if the aim of art was once the fabrication of a presentation that is as various and interesting as possible, Cage proposes creating something with minimal surface variety and little immediate interest, even espousing outright repetition and, thus, boredom as not only perceptually engrossing but fertilely inspiring ("The way to get ideas is to do something boring"):

> In Zen they say: If something is boring after two minutes, try it for four. If still boring, try it for eight, sixteen, thirty-two, and so on. Eventually one discovers that it's not boring but very interesting.

(This concern with repetition to cunning excess is also found in the works of Gertrude Stein, who was probably the most consequential precursor of radical American esthetics.) Cage's ideas have come to rationalize, for both better and worse, all in contemporary art that extends itself in time and space far more than was previously acceptable.

If past art aimed to display an artist's esthetic consciousness and the work's essential organization, Cage advocates the use of procedures that would both minimize the artist's taste and induce structural disorganization. In the case of music this principle informs Cage's invention of the prepared piano, where the strings' original pitches and timbres are radically changed. Cage then devised chance operations for "composing" or writing out a score, so that traditional structures would assuredly be avoided; and then came the use of live-time machines, such as a turned-on radio with spinning dials, so that the sounds emitted could not be predicted in advance. All these rejections of previous constraints also function, intentionally and intelligently, to free artistic creation from personal control and, therefore, the resulting work from both conventions and cliché. It follows that, in sharp contrast to previous composers, Cage intends to avoid giving his performer-collaborators a score that is too specific. He thereby allows them far more freedom of individual action than earlier musicians had. Indeed, he has followed his self-withdrawal logic to this radical esthetic definition: "Art instead of being an object made by one person is a process set in motion by a group of people." This esthetic theme of art as process, rather than product, also had immense influence upon painting and sculpture (even in different styles), as well as dance and intermedia, all through the sixties and seventies.

In the end, Cage favors not artistic improvisation, which depends too much upon acquired habits and, thus, conventions, but artistic indeterminacy—the creation of conditions or ground rules that force artists to work in unusual ways, which are in turn likely to produce unexpected, unpredictable results. Indeed, precisely in his preference for extreme originality and complex *acoherence,* coupled with his contempt for familiar objects and experiences, does Cage himself deny the absolute, indiscriminative licence implied by his philosophy. His self-denying principles notwithstanding, Cage in practice usually retains some authority (invariably revealing ingenious and tasteful choices) over the frame of activity, thereby insuring, paradoxically, an art of *purposeful purposelessness,* as distinct from purposeless purposelessness. Indeed, the key to his artistic intelligence is precisely the imposition of general constraints that allow, if not induce, a paradoxically circumscribed range of specified freedoms.

The artistic result of Cage's strategy of freedom within subtle constraints has usually been fields of disordered activities that are formally beyond collage, which is merely a juxtaposition of several dissimilars. Instead, Cage realizes a far more multiple mélange that is without symbolic references, without a formal center, without distinct beginnings or ends, thus suggesting unfinishedness. He regards such willful disorder as naturalistic—as an "imitation of nature in her manner of operation." More specifically, he initiates an ongoing event that is as formally nonclimactic and internally repetitive as nature herself usually is; and this conclusion explodes the art-life dichotomy, as well as the hierarchical structuring, that were both sacred to traditional esthetics.

Precisely because Cage's ideas rationalized works of art that a previous age (and archaic critics) would have found hopelessly chaotic (or in violation of old rules), he came to insist that audiences accept disorder—in this case, atonal and astructural sound; so that in the course of reflecting the philosophic influence of Zen Buddhism, he asserts that not only must people perceive everything, but we must accept everything we perceive. However, this assertion too remains a dialectical antithesis in Cage's ironically systematic, ironically extreme but highly suggestive esthetics.

It should not be forgotten that the alarm over "disintegration of form" on the part of conservative critics such as Erich Kahler, expressed in his 1969 book of that title, actually indicates their own inability to grasp alternative formal structures (if not an experiential ignorance of what they condemn); for in fact, true formlessness in any created object or experience is impossible. Anything that can be characterized in one way rather than another, as resembling one thing rather than another thing, has, by that act of definition, a perceptible form. In the nonhierarchical evenness or pure formal diffuseness that is characteristic of Cage's own best art is a kind of definable unity that, needless to say, is not emphasized in his philosophy of art.

Another Cagean strategy has been the creation of artworks or events that, though superficially trivial, have great resonance as implied philosophical statements. In his *4'33"* (1952), for instance, an eminent pianist sits at his instrument and makes no audible pianistic sound for four minutes and thirty-three seconds. Nothing happens, in a superficial sense; yet by making no sound in a context where sound is expected, the piece implies that in the "silence" is the work's sound—or more precisely, in all the random, surely atonal and unstructured ambient noises audibly within the frame of *4' 33"* is the "music." Thus, the esthetic point, by inference, is that art consists of all the sensory phenomena that one chooses to perceive. The next inference holds that normal life is rich in art or esthetic experiences that are continually available to the spectator who attunes or focuses his sensory equipment.

Cage's idea of art as anything that generates esthetic experience curiously carries John Dewey's thinking to a logical extreme, as do Cage's notions of art as revealing experiential reality and of the beholder as necessarily creating his own experience. In addition, *4' 33"* for all of its radicalness reveals a debt to Marcel Duchamp, whose great original idea consisted of imposing, by means of art rather than argument, esthetic value on things that were not initially, or previously, endowed with artistic status.

The radical gesture in Cage's esthetics lies in his justifying the creation and acceptance of perceptual disorder. Somewhat similar concerns inform Morse Peckham's highly original and provocative essay, *Man's Rage for Chaos* (1965), which is indicatively subtitled, *Biology, Behavior, and the Arts.* Drawing upon a scholarly background in English literature and cultural history, its author suggests that, though man craves order in his life, esthetic experience "serves to break up orientations, to weaken and frustrate the tyrannous drive to order, to prepare the individual to observe what the orientation tells him is irrelevant, but what may well be highly relevant." This emphasis upon the individual's experience of art, as well as the method of deducing artistic value from an idealization of perceptual processes, also resembles John Dewey (who likewise confessed to more interest in behavior than art); but quite contrary to Dewey, who wanted art to provide artistic order for the sake of common experience, Peckham takes the radical tack of advocating artistic disorder on humane grounds. "Art is the reinforcement of the capacity to endure disorientation," his book concludes, "so that man may endure exposing himself to the tensions and problems of the real world. . . . Art is rehearsal for the orientation which makes innovation possible." By implication, then, the new forms of "disordered" art better prepare our perceptual equipment to comprehend the unprecedented structures of contemporary life; but in philosophical contrast to Cage, Peckham advocates disorder with respect to previous art (or conventions), not in imitation of lifelike processes.

Peckham is by training a scholar-critic of literature; Cage, initially a creator, finally in more arts than music. Another philosopher of the new art was at his professional beginnings a painter who also took degrees in philosophy and art history; so that Allan Kaprow's most important text, *Assemblage, Environments & Happenings* (1966, though first drafted and circulated several years before) exhibits a participant-observer's synthesis of both involvement and distance—and an intelligent awareness of both personal experience and esthetic issues. A sometime composition student of John Cage, Kaprow assimilated his teacher's passion for stretching both the creative imagination and the receptive sensibility. Indicatively, he first became known for advocating, in his essay "The Legacy of Jackson Pollock" (1958), the use of all possible materials and "unheard-of happenings and events" in the processes and preoccupations of painting—a position ultimately traceable to Marcel Duchamp, with a nod to Cage. Kaprow's book outlines an evolution, in part his own, from collaged paintings to assemblages (or three dimensional collage) to environments (or artistically enclosed spaces), and finally to a mixed means performance art that he characterized in retrospect as "a collage of events in certain spans of time and in certain spaces." In short, Kaprow follows Moholy-Nagy in advocating the rejection of conventional barriers between the arts; and like Cage, Kaprow challenges the traditional distinction between art and life. In Kaprow's thinking, the latter position demands, first of all, the strict elimination, in one's artistic practice, of the materials, actions, and themes indigenous to earlier arts:

> A picture, a piece of music, a poem, a drama, each confined within its
> respective frame, fixed number of measures, stanzas, and stages, however great
> they may be in their own right, simply will not allow for breaking the barrier be-
> tween art and life. And this is what the objective is.

Indeed, the new art Kaprow invented, to which he gave the unfortunately
catchy name of "a happening," is perhaps the closest that art has yet come to
meshing with life (and reducing the psychic distance of traditional esthetic
experience), while yet retaining a distinct artistic, nonlife identity. The
crucial point for the philosophy of art lay in the fact that a true happening—
a performance occurring outside a theatrical setting, completely open (or un-
fixed) in both time and space, and involving everyone who happens to be
within its frame of activity—was by intention as unpredictable, as impermanent, and as changing as life itself. Nonetheless, the endeavor still satisfied an old definition of art as reflecting more or less deliberate operations—
in this case, the scenario of roughly outlined activities that the happenings-
artist provided in advance to his prospective collaborators.

"At present," Kaprow's book concludes, "any avant-garde is primarily a
philosophical quest and a finding of truths, rather than purely an esthetic
activity." Thus, whereas Cage offered an esthetic for unpredictability (and
the acceptance of happenstance), Kaprow forged instead a philosophy advocating impermanence on one hand, and art independent of any objective
forms on the other. "Once, the task of the artist was to make good art," he
wrote in a manifesto first published in 1966, "now it is to avoid making art of
any kind." What, then, is the "artist" to do? Kaprow's answer was *anything*,
regardless of exhibited craftsmanship or permanence, yet with both the
intention of uniqueness and the awareness that his or her doings would
probably be recognized as artistic endeavor.

> The decision to be an artist thus assumes both the existence of a unique activity
> and an endless series of deeds which deny it. . . . Anything I say, do, notice, or
> think, is art—whether or not desired—because everyone else aware of what is
> occuring today will probably (not possibly) say it is, or think of it as art at some
> time or other.

Kaprow's ideas, along with such examples of inferential art as Cage's *4'33''*,
forge an idealist philosophy of art, which bases significance primarily upon
perception and contextual awareness rather than the art object. Several
radical implications of this view were suggestively developed by another

artist-critic, Michael Kirby, first in *Happenings* (1965), and then in essays, especially "The Aesthetics of the Avant-Garde," that he collected in *The Art of Time* (1969).

The contemporary impact of epistemological empiricism, as well as analytic philosophy, inspires the ideal of a rigorously empirical esthetics. Such a discipline would be capable of clearly distinguishing analytic elucidation from evaluation, and then of making precisely accurate statements which, as a prime criterion of acceptability, could be verified, in roughly similar form, by every equally knowledgeable observer. Of course, such empirical esthetics would become valuable only to the extent that the commentaries of its exponents moved beyond inarguable facts and superficial descriptions to more profound critical illuminations which would, nonetheless, exhibit a logical consistency, a linguistic precision and a verifiable accuracy that were previously unknown in discourse about art. In a retrospective summary written in 1951, of a program first presented in his earlier essay "Scientific Method in Esthetics" (1928), Thomas Munro championed "a scientific, naturalistic approach to aesthetics: one which should be broadly experimental and empirical, but not limited to quantitative measurement; utilizing the insights of art criticism and philosophy as hypotheses, but deriving objective data from two main sources—the analysis and history of form in the arts, and psychological studies of the production, appreciation, and teaching of the arts." However, as Munro himself is a prodigiously thorough scholar and decisive theorist, his own major contributions have been not a philosophy of art but exhaustive and definitive studies of, first, the categories of artistic endeavor, *The Arts and Their Interrelations* (1949), and then historiographical theories of *Evolution and Art* (1963). (One result of analytic philosophy alone—especially Ludwig Wittgenstein's influence—has been an academic concern with the language of art and literary criticism.)

Among the more eccentrically suggestive, and yet patently unsuccessful American attempts at an empirical theory of artistic value were the foolishly simplistic algebraic formulas that the Harvard mathematician George Birkhoff proposed in his *Aesthetic Measure* (1933): $M = O/C$ where, "within each class of aesthetic objects," M equals esthetic measure, O is order, and C is complexity. However, one problem with this "quantitative index of [art objects'] comparative esthetic effectiveness" is that it offered no empirical method for specifying the exact degree of each factor in the equation—for verifiably quantifying the components. A second problem with Birkhoff's formula is that it measures unity in variety, which is at best only one of several dimensions of artistic value. Such deductive theorizing, in contrast to the inductive generalizations more appropriate to science, prompted

Thomas Munro himself to comment in 1946 that quantitative esthetics so far "has dealt less with works of art than with preferences for various arbitrary, simplified linear shapes, color combinations, and tone-combinations."

Beyond that, the new, post-World War II scientific hypotheses of communication—information theory and cybernetics—both suggest schemes of esthetic understanding. The first, for example, promises a quantitative measure of the experience flowing from a work of art to its receptor—not the content of these transmitted messages, but the size of its channel, the amount of communication precisely measured in "bits," and its quality in terms of essential information versus redundancy. Though several writers, John R. Pierce, Leonard Meyer and Lejaren Hiller among them, have attempted to derive esthetic hypotheses from information theory, no new major philosophy of art has yet emerged. Cybernetics, which emphasizes responsiveness within a closed system, offers ideas less relevant to static art than to that new art form which emerged in the sixties: responsive kinetic environments; but here too, esthetic theory is more nascent than mature. There is no doubt that a truly persuasive empirical esthetics would represent a great intellectual advance, especially with an artistic generation less eager than its predecessor to rescue art from science; and the result might well supercede previous esthetics much as physics replaced some terrains of metaphysics. While the inadequacies of the forays so far suggest that the procedures used to encapsulate primary physical nature may have little relevance to the artifacts of secondary nature, the philosophy of art probably could profit from emulating the rigor, objectivity, and decisiveness of scientific discourse.

A continuing, but somewhat peripheral concern of recent American esthetics has been the difference between art and sub-art. The latter is not synonymous with *non-art* or *anti-art*, both of which are by now thought to be historically relative terms (last year's "anti-art" often becoming tomorrow's convention). Rather, the term *sub-art* refers to that kind of commercialized popular or mass art that became prominent in the nineteenth century and, thanks to advertising and mass-merchandizing, increasingly pervasive in the twentieth. One of the first major analyses of sub-art came from the critic Clement Greenberg (himself an able advocate of modernism in all culture), whose 1939 essay, "Avant-Garde and Kitsch," made decisive distinctions that influenced future esthetic discussion. True arts, in his view, "derive their chief inspiration from the medium they work in" and an awareness of artistic history, while kitsch is subservient both to established artistic formulas and, usually, to the prospect of an imminent sale. Different in intention and intrinsic nature, kitsch and art also vary in effect. Innovative art at first strikes its spectator as puzzling, if not inscrutable, inevitably creating its own audience of admirers, while kitsch exploits stereotyped understanding for a pre-conditioned public, dealing finally in "the lowest common denominators of experience." In contrast to kitsch, which cultivates the *effects* of art (and often programs an unmistakable response), avant-garde art, as noted already, defines its integrity by a capacity for genuine surprise. Greenberg continues, "Avant-garde culture is the imitation of imitating," as "its best artists are artist's artists, its best poets, poet's poets." The difference between kitsch and avant-garde (synonymous in Greenberg's mind with all that remains relevant in contemporary culture) is so great that they have nothing in common beyond cultural ancestry and superficial mediumistic resemblances.

> Kitsch is mechanical and operates by formulas. Kitsch is vicarious experience and faked sensations. Kitsch changes according to style, but remains always the same. Kitsch is the epitome of all that is spurious in the life of our time.

The social origins of kitsch, in Greenberg's view, lie not in capitalism per se, as most "left" critics charged, but in modern industrial society, which on one hand induces mass-merchandizing of all objects that could be manufactured in unlimited numbers and, on the other, creates the "urban masses" who become the most eager consumers of kitsch. The Soviet Union, he hastens to point out, suffers as much kitsch as the U.S.

The issue of mass culture continues to preoccupy many American intellectuals, scarcely a few of whom were also as attuned to genuine art as Greenberg. (Most of them, one suspected, studied tripe because they preferred it to art, or at least found kitsch more susceptible to critical analysis.) Whereas the sociologist customarily studies kitsch's relationship to its audience, esthetic discussion emphasizes its intrinsic nature and purpose; and while critical and moral reasoning could separate one kind of kitsch from another, the esthetic point remained: that kitsch is not art but sub-art. The first real contribution after Greenberg's formulation came from Marshall McLuhan in *The Mechanical Bride*, written during the War but not published until 1951. Here McLuhan examines mass-cultural artifacts with a critical sensibility honed on the close rhetorical analysis of English literature. This approach enabled him to perceive that the representational discontinuity distinguishing modernist painting and literature also characterizes, for example, the newspaper's front page with its discontinuous field of unrelated articles, oversized headlines, and occasional captioned pictures:

> It is on its technical and mechanical side that the front page is linked to the techniques of modern science and art. Discontinuity is in different ways a basic concept of both quantum and relativity physics. . . . Notoriously, it is the visual technique of Picasso, the literary technique of James Joyce.

The Mechanical Bride broached two esthetic themes that McLuhan developed more prominently in his later works: that this discontinuity reflects the impact of electronic information technology (such as, in the example at hand, the wire news service) and that, differences in quality notwithstanding, "The great work of a period has much in common with the poorest work." All this insight into mass culture does not prevent McLuhan from proposing a necessary measure for distinguishing art from kitsch. "How heavy a demand does it make on the intelligence? How inclusive a consciousness does it focus?" (The "pop" paintings of the sixties, it should be noted, do not invalidate this distinction; for though the artist appropriated subject matter drawn from kitsch, the best works turn this mundane material to highly sophisticated and uncommon ends.)

Nothing indicates more conclusively the obsolescence of traditional esthetics than the irrelevance of its favorite terms; and as such earlier phrases as *beauty* and *aesthetic distance* lose their currency, the times become ripe for a new esthetic philosophy. Much of this opportunity has been assumed, albeit circuitously, by artists and critics; so that by now, at least in America, a substantial intellectual structure can inform intuitive and/or sensory sympathy for the new art. The result has been a perceptual emphasis that ultimately underscores a highly idealist (and almost solipsistic) philosophy of art, which encompasses such radical propositions as Marshall McLuhan's "Art is anything you [the artist] can get away with," and Cage's hypothesis that art is anywhere, and everywhere that the spectator wishes to perceive it. ("Theater takes place all the time, wherever one is. And Art simply facilitates persuading one this is the case.")

The new esthetics has, it is true, won more acceptance from artists than literary people, but the revolutions of modernism have always first occurred in the nonliterary arts. Nonetheless, ignorance of these ideas, like responses proclaiming "hoax" and/or "not art," will usually serve to identify a commentator as fundamentally philistine, no matter how well "educated" he superficially seems. Only this new esthetics, rather than an older one, can assimilate the artistic innovations of the past two decades—not just mixed-means events, artistic machines, and kinetic environments, but also conceptual art, experimental literature and works revealing the impact of new technologies of mental change. Contemporary art is, in truth, "the only art we have"; and as it continually changes, so there is an unending need for an esthetic philosophy that is, as Croce put it, "always renewed and always renewing."

Michael Kirby

The Aesthetics of the Avant-Garde

There are those who say that the term *avant-garde* is obsolete, that it is no longer useful, that an art fitting the term no longer exists. This view is based on the proposition that an avant-garde artist is, by definition, one who is so far "ahead of his time" that his work is not accepted by society. Thus Cubism, the *Fauves,* Dada, and so forth were avant-garde at the time of their origins but are no longer, and, because the products of contemporary artists are generally accepted by the art world and at least a certain significant portion of the concerned public, there is no true avant-garde today.

If we follow strictly the definition I have sketched, there is certainly some truth in this conclusion. The public at large still rejects avant-garde work. Its tastes continue to cling to social realism in drama, representationalism in painting and sculpture, and the diatonic scale in music. But, except perhaps for theatre, there is a wide acceptance of avant-garde attitudes among those who are actively involved with the arts. I know only three or four artists who might in any way be considered to be important who are not able to show their work regularly at an established gallery. Whether this contemporary acceptance of art is due to the socially "safe" quality of the work or to the greatly increased number of dealers, art publications, and educated members of the potential art public is not the question. It is true that the present social context of artistic creation is significantly more permissive and accepting

Reprinted from *The Art of Time* (Dutton, 1969), by permission of the author. Copyright © 1969 by Michael Kirby.

than it was when the term *avant-garde* was first coined.[1] But since there does not seem to be a more fitting word to stand for the type of art with which I am concerned, I continue to use *avant-garde*, although perhaps with some slight modification of meaning.

For one thing, *avant-garde* may still be used to describe those works of the late nineteenth and earlier twentieth centuries that did take some time to be accepted by society. Just as there is still usefulness in the names of the various movements of which it was composed, one may continue to refer to work as *avant-garde* even after is has become a basic element in most surveys of art history. In this sense, *avant-garde* becomes almost synonymous with *modern art*, although *contemporary art* would be a much larger category including artists of quite different and more traditional persuasions.

While the term *modern art* is flat and bland, however, *avant-garde* refers specifically to a concern with the historical *directionality* of art. An advance guard implies a rear guard or at least the main body of troops following behind. It is this attitude or belief in the directionality of art that is of primary importance. Some artists may accept the limits of art as defined, as known, as given; others may attempt to alter, expand, or escape from the stylistic aesthetic rules passed on to them by the culture. This impulse to redefine, to contradict, to continue the sensed directionality of art as far as they are able, is independent of success. The fact that an artist does not actually succeed in adding anything of importance to the historical development of art does not, in this sense, make the term *avant-garde* inapplicable. It is his intent or desire that is enough to separate him from those who do not share his goals and beliefs.

Nor is the acceptance or rejection of an artist's work by society sufficient grounds to determine correct use of the term. Directionality, or a belief in and concern with directionality, depends upon the creator and not upon the attitudes of society. Thus it is possible to say, without any contradiction in terms, that contemporary avant-garde art is generally accepted by society while that earlier work in which the beliefs were first manifested was not.

[On the negative side, there is a glamorous and romantic aura surrounding the French term that I do not intend to exploit in my usage. In many cases, this nostalgic romanticism seems to be the reason for the denial of its applicability to contemporary artists. What might be called *the Van Gogh syndrome* reasons that if an artist has not suffered, he cannot be of any worth; therefore, if society accepts the work without first punishing the creator with its rejection, the art is necessarily inferior. This is one way to "prove" the insignificance of work one does not like and to protect memories of the Good Old Days when artists, all of whom lived in garrets, were great, persecuted, heroic, and tormented.]

At any rate, it is quite obvious that standard aesthetic theory has little or no relevance to the art of the avant-garde. By *aesthetic theory* I do not mean art criticism, the discussion of styles of art, or the evaluation of particular works. This type of thought, much of it provided by the artists themselves, is quite abundant and, frequently, to the point. But present philosophical investigation and discussion of the broad principles of artistic appreciation are inadequate in the light of avant-garde work. It is this very inadequacy that gives rise to the use of such terms as *anti-art* and *non-art* when discussing the avant-garde. Since the work does not fit traditional explanations and codifications of the aesthetic experience, some new category is invented for it. Extant philosophical principles are protected by the too simple expedient of refusing to admit that the troublesome material falls into the same category as that which has already been used as the basis of long-held internally consistent theories.

The investigation by philosophy of the aesthetic experience must come after the fact, however. It cannot arbitrarily limit the area of investigation in order to arrive at results that it desires. Unless aesthetics explains the perception of all of art, it is of little intellectual or practical worth. Theory cannot contradict practice, and the total available data must fit the theories or the theories must be changed. For this reason, it is imperative to reexamine, reevaluate, and modify basic aesthetic theory in light of the avant-garde. This effort, when complete and detailed, should provide not only an aesthetic of the avant-garde but aesthetics that are based on, and applicable to, all art.

In discussing the inadequacy of "traditional aesthetics," I am not necessarily referring to the theories of any specific philosopher or philosophers but to what appear to be commonly held beliefs about the aesthetic experience. These general beliefs are given cogent shape by any number of theoretical writers, of course, but it is not my intent to criticize any one of them in detail. In most cases, such as that of empathy theory, it is not a question of abandoning the construct completely but of realizing that it has limited rather than universal application. Since existing theories were based upon particular works, they still retain limited validity in reference to those works, even though they cannot be given the fundamental pertinence that they claim.

To a certain extent, since it tends to determine and channel perceptions, such a new theory becomes polemical and didactic. As I have said, however, the promulgation of particular value judgments is not the intent of this essay, and we are not directly concerned here with appreciation and evaluation. It should not be surprising that even the artists who are involved with the avant-garde do not agree among themselves about the artistic worth of particular pieces. (I can think of only two artists whose work as a whole has achieved an even approximately unanimous acceptance, for however brief a time, among my many friends and acquaintances who are artists.) From the sociopsychological point of view, anyone's reaction to a work of art is as "true" and "valid" as anyone else's, and it is too easy to see such critical discussion as the elevation of one person's experience at the expense of another's. We are concerned here with theories of art in general rather than with the details of appreciation of any one art.

But the avant-garde still stirs strong negative emotions, and many people (like John Simon, who states dramatically that "This may be the dark night of the arts") seem to reject modern art *in toto*. On this level contentiousness may be involved, and a new aesthetic adequately encompassing the products of the avant-garde should permit values of that work to be seen more easily by those who were previously unable to do so. I certainly do not mean to claim, however, that anyone or everyone who accepts the avant-garde must, should, or does accept my formulations.

The term *avant-garde* does not, in itself, denote value. Avant-garde work per se is neither good nor bad. If we attempt to distance ourselves from the effect involved in the question, it would be logical to assume that the objective quality—if such a term has any meaning—or usual experience of avant-garde works would fall along a normal distribution curve with most of the pieces being "average" with quite small percentages registering as "near perfect" or "totally inadequate." The subjective reaction to this distribution might alter the labeling in more emotional directions, but this kind of distinction is not the purpose of the type of aesthetic theory with which we are concerned.

It is sufficient for our purposes to recognize that a significant number of sufficiently normal people derive what they report to be intense aesthetic experiences from avant-garde work. This is a sociological fact. If these experiences cannot be explained by traditional aesthetic theory, modifications in that theory must be made to elucidate the general principles involved in the entire range of aesthetic experience.

1. When discussing aesthetics, one is expected to begin with a definition of the word *art*. The problem is clear: to provide a definition broad enough to include all that is considered art while clearly differentiating it from all that is not art. As has already been suggested, the question of definition would seem to be particularly important when considering avant-garde work,

which is continually attempting to redefine the limits of art itself.

One useful definition is that which describes a work of art as *a man-made thing which has no objective practical or functional purpose.* It is obvious that only man creates art: It is not a natural occurrence, nor is it produced by animals.

Of course, this definition allows doodles, jewelry, fireworks, decoration, cartoons, and many other functionless creations to be called *art.* Is there any reason to be concerned, however, if a definition does not categorically separate rock gardens and fountains from sculpture? If more subtle distinctions are needed, subcategories such as *commercial art, popular art, fine art,* and so forth may be employed. After all, *art* is a word of neutral value. It does not mean that the particular work of art is either good or bad; a doodle may be merely considered *bad art* rather than being excluded from the category of *art.*

But this is not the way we think when we say something is "not art." Being a work of art somehow seems important to us: Art is more worthwhile than non-art. Thus we deny the appellation *art* to anything that seems to us unimportant, trivial, or insignificant, whether it is a doodle or an avant-garde painting. This subjective personal reaction is, of course, what art is all about, but it cannot be used as a basis for definition, since there will never be any universal agreement on what is important or unimportant, significant or trivial. Personal taste is no grounds for determining what is, or is not, art.

This is really the problem that the concept of *fine art* attempts to solve: some art, that to which we are almost always referring when we use the word, is sensed to be of an entirely different order. Since we wish to consider only this type of creation, we may define a work of art as *a man-made thing of no objective practical or functional purpose that is intended to have aesthetic importance or significance.* In other words, since it is commonly accepted that art is important, man-made, and functionless, a thing is a work of art if it is intended as art.

This intent to achieve aesthetic importance or significance is entirely the concern of the creator, and the standards involved are his alone. Intention is not decided or determined by the observer. This limits the range of things with which we are concerned: Its creator does not claim significance for a doodle, but everything that is implicitly or explicitly proposed as significant art by an artist must be considered as art, whether or not we ourselves evaluate it as significant.

Thus, furniture, silverware, automobiles, rockets, and so forth are not art, even if we look at them as if they had no purpose. The observer does not convert something that has a practical purpose into a work of art merely by changing his attitude toward it. Duchamp did demonstrate with his "ready-mades," however, that a functional thing may become a work of art by being made functionless and placed in the context of art. It is not the physical characteristics or sensory impact of a man-made thing that determines whether or not it is art, but a factor that exists only in cognition: its purpose. This emphasis on the subjective aspects of experience rather than on the objective physical characteristics of the thing experienced will be a consistent concern of this essay.

As I pointed out a moment ago, status as art does not mean that the work is good art. A claim of importance does not mean that a thing is important. But it does differentiate the work from all those that make no such claim, limiting the field without recourse to personal judgment and giving us a starting point for a study of aesthetics. This study can be seen as little more than an explanation of the experiential context within which a work justifies or fails to justify its claim to importance and significance.

In one meaning of the word, *aesthetics* may be considered as the "philosophy of the beautiful," but the relationship of beauty and art now appears to be a thoroughly inconsistent one. Not all art is beautiful, nor is the presence of beauty enough to designate a creation as a work of art. To my mind, *beauty* has become a debased and almost meaningless word. One reason for this is that, although the experience of beauty is an entirely subjective thing, the implications of the word, strangely enough, have tended to become objective. Everyone knows that a sunset *is* beautiful. If I say to you, "She is a beautiful girl," it may not indicate any emotional reaction to the girl on my part but merely that I recognize the fact that her appearance falls within those clear limits of beauty that you and everyone else in our culture will recognize. This objectification may add to the reliability of communication, but it makes the word *beauty* trite and banal, hardly representative of the characteristics of the aesthetic experience that we wish to designate.

It could be said that flowers or a sunset are seen as beautiful because of their subtlety, variety, and intensity of color; an overcast sky at evening would not be beautiful because it lacked this kind of perceptual excitement. This view of beauty emphasizes the pleasure and appeal of pure sensory stimulation for its own sake. Although the appeal of art has traditionally been "for its own sake," it is precisely this view of aesthetic experience that I will argue against. Applied to art, this definition of beauty supports entertainment, excitement, titillation, and sensory pleasure as central values. Although useful as a contrast conception against which the basic nature of art may be seen, a purely sensory concept of beauty does not adequately explain the aesthetic experience.

In actuality, an overcast sky at evening might appear much more beautiful than the most elaborate sunset to a farmer, for example, whose crops were in desperate need of rain. Even though we have defined art as being nonutilitarian, this practical sense of the word *beauty* does, I think, have some pertinence to the aesthetic experience, and I will return to it later. It suggests, for one thing, that the experience of a thing—in this case, the clouds—depends upon the total historical/personal context.

Since everyone knows that a sunset is beautiful, the implication, when applying the word to art, is that the aesthetic experience should be of the same sort. But exactly the opposite is true. The aesthetic experience is of an entirely different kind or order from the experience of nature. Although the perceptual mechanisms are identical, the results of the perception of art and non-art are not the same: It is these very differences that we want to study.

Thus the primary reason for rejecting the term *beauty* as of key importance in understanding the aesthetic experience is its common association with sensory pleasure. I am not sure that pleasure of any kind is a necessary aspect of the perception of art, even when the work is rated positively. In other words, it is conceivable that a piece can be seen as significant and meaningful without the viewer feeling pleasure.

Although I consider the nature of the aesthetic experience to be spiritual, I do not wish to argue the specific point here. Let us say that art seems to be a spiritual matter: It conveys the *feeling* that it functions at a basic level of existence. But spiritual experiences are not always pleasant ones, and St. John of the Cross, for example, suffered his "dark night of the soul." Art that is disturbing, disorienting, or repulsive can, theoretically, also be important and meaningful. At any rate, I think it best to consider pleasure, especially sensory pleasure, as merely a possible adjunct to the aesthetic experience. The creation of beauty and pleasure certainly do not define it.

One reason for the confusion of beauty in nature with what I will call, for the moment, "beauty in art" lies in the intensity of both experiences. Although introspective reporting remains a poor tool, it is all we have, and all subjective statements about art agree on an intensity of experience that distinguishes "good" art from "bad." But what is it that is felt intensely? Distinctions disappear and quantity tends to replace identity. Keats was apparently feeling this when he wrote his famous, "Beauty is truth, truth beauty." The subjective reaction to what is perceived as a truth can have great intensity, as can the reaction to the perception of beauty, although in neither case is the intensity a necessary or defining characteristic. When truth or beauty are perceived without this intensity of experience, they can be distinguished quite easily, but this is not true in their heightened states, when they are "all ye know on earth, and all ye need to know." This same kind of blurring of distinctions by heightened affect may explain the tendency to suppose that intense aesthetic experience is equivalent to the reaction to natural beauty.

Thus the key word in aesthetic theory is not *beauty*, as has been suggested by traditional aesthetics, but *significance*. The feeling or perception of significance may be mislabeled as *beauty*, but the two are not the same. Let me emphasize that I am speaking now about significance as a *quality of perception* and not as a cognitive factor. Of course it may also exist as a cognitive element in the same way that beauty may be understood and known rather than felt, but it is significance as a quality of perception that can be seen as explaining the intensity of the aesthetic experience. As we indicated in our definition of art, the creation of art depends upon the artist's personal attempt to achieve what he feels to be significant. The experience of the finished product is also evaluated in terms of significance. It is with the aesthetic experience of the artist's product that we are primarily concerned. In order to understand it, we must first examine the sensory aspects of perception, even though we will find that the significance of art ultimately depends upon trans-sensory aspects of experience.

2. There is a universally held but inaccurate concept or model of the aesthetic experience. This model posits a single correct way of providing an art object; the simultaneous and intrinsic value attributes of that correct perception are, of course, also correct. This model is usually, but not necessarily, identical with a person's own experience. In other words, the concept postulates a single, objective truth about a work of art, and if we, as individuals, do not perceive it completely (as we usually feel we do) then it is still available to us. If we do have wrong perceptions, they may be corrected.

As we grow older we find that our experiences of, and opinions about, specific works of art change. According to the model, we have had incorrect experiences and are now having correct ones. But the feeling of correctness—as opposed, for example, to a student's possible acceptance of incorrectness because of his willingness to learn—does not guarantee correctness. Frequently, an experience that we feel certain is right is replaced somewhat later by another significantly different but equally correct experience of the same work of art. Looking back at our past aesthetic experiences, we often feel that they were incorrect and that we now perceive the truth, although the degree of certainty is no greater now than it was previously. At every moment the true, objective aesthetic work seems revealed to us, but these truths are not consistent through time nor, as nearly as we can determine, do they usually agree with others' perceptions of the same work. Even at the present moment, a single sense may contradict itself. Locke and Berkeley both referred to the experiment in which one hand is placed in hot water and the other hand in cold water for several minutes, and then both hands are put into water of moderate temperature: The same water feels cold to one hand and warm to the other—a clear demonstration of the relativity of perception and value.

The *feeling* of correctness in aesthetic judgment is self-contradictory and impossible to verify. Actually, the concept or model is false; the single correct way of perceiving a work of art, and the single correct set of value attributes coexistent in that experience, do not exist.

Just as a person who does not believe in free will still experiences life— unless he is psychotic—as if he had free will, an intellectual *belief* in the subjectivity of value does not prevent a person from *feeling* the truth of the incorrect model I have sketched. Although everyone feels that value is objective, a person may simultaneously believe in its subjectivity. This is not intended as merely a philosophical statement. Since an artist's beliefs obviously determine the character of the work he produces, I am attempting to discuss those questions which seem to have specific practical relevance to the expansion of art by the avant-garde. In other words, a belief among artists in the subjectivity of values would be functional *whether or not* it was philosophically correct. The rest of my discussion of aesthetics is presented in this same spirit: While attempting to establish an intellectual position that I believe is true, I am also endeavoring to document—by analogy, if you prefer to evade the philosophical issues—certain generative factors in modern art.

The objectification of perception—the feeling that the world is as it appears to be—has been called *phenomenal absolutism.* In *The Influence of Culture on Visual Perception,* Marshall H. Segall, Donald T. Campbell, and Melville J. Herskovits write:

> The normal observer naïvely assumes that the world is exactly as he sees it. He accepts the evidence of perception uncritically. He does not recognize that his visual perception is *mediated* by indirect inference systems. . . .
> Socially, one important aspect of phenomenal absolutism is the observer's assumption that all other observers perceive the situation as he does, and that if they respond differently it is because of some perverse willfulness rather than because they act on different perceptual content.[2]

Although I shall concentrate on the trans-sensory aspects of aesthetic experience, sensory perception should be mentioned first. The authors of *The Influence of Culture on Visual Perception*—an important presentation of basic concepts with an extensive bibliography on the psychological and cultural aspects of perception—believe that their studies demonstrate that human perception is culturally influenced. They found that people in different cultures were differentially susceptible to certain geometric illusions. This means that culture can change not merely the meaning and interpretation of what is seen but the actual perception itself. Although their work is not conclusive, and more investigation must be done, it is a provocative attempt to investigate an area where "pure" data are very difficult to obtain.

If any of the senses is studied through psychophysical measurement, individual differences in perception become apparent. If any continuum of objective physical stimuli is correlated with the perception-reactions to those stimuli, the variety of response is one of its most apparent aspects. Take, for example, the relationship between the change in the physical intensity of light entering the eye and the observed change in brightness. Obviously, some measurable change in brightness will not be perceived by any human being. Although quite marvelous, the human eye, even discounting "noise" in the nerve system, is not perfect. The amount of increase or decrease in intensity that is needed before a change is perceived will actually vary from person to person. How, then, can judgments of "correct" and "incorrect" response be made? All of us are "wrong" at one physical level, because we see no change in brightness when a change in intensity is actually occurring; a few people, whose eyes are the most sensitive to brightness of any in the human race, are "correct" when they perceive changes that no one else can, and everyone else is "incorrect"; and so forth. It is possible, of course, to calculate averages and set up norms, but this is not quite the same thing.

Or consider so-called color blindness. Some people think that it exists only in such dramatic forms as the inability to distinguish red from green. Red/green color blindness is the most common form and occurs in over five per cent of men and less than one per cent of women, but there is also an entirely different type of deficiency in the perception of color which affects men and women equally. Most simply, this *anomalous color vision* is a reduction in sensitivity to one or more of the three basic color systems (red, green, and blue) that are involved in perception. One result, apparently, is that people with color anomaly cannot distinguish as many or as subtle saturation changes within a particular hue, for example, as can people with normal color vision. It is important to note that it has been estimated that as much as twenty per cent of the population—one out of every five—is "color weak" in one way or another.

Since these weaknesses show up as variations in threshold-level discriminations, they are very difficult to determine without precision equipment. While the inability to distinguish red from green becomes apparent when merely trying to obey a traffic signal light, the question of whether an unsaturated blue-gray can be distinguished from a slightly more saturated blue-gray, for example, is not as available to everyday experience. Many people are color deficient without knowing it; it would be entirely possible to go through life without becoming aware that you had anomalous color vision.

In my senior year at college, I was doing an experimental thesis on "The depth effects of color," and I wanted to pretest each of the subjects in order to exclude any who did not have normal color vision. I found that in administering the test plates, in which numbers can be read in a field of colored dots if you have normal vision, I had to use the key to see if the answers were correct. Although I had absolutely no hint of it previously, I found at the age of twenty-two that I was color deficient. Except for the necessity of taking the test, I might never have known of this anomalous color vision.

In spite of these facts, it is somewhat startling to learn that even the most striking forms of color blindness were not discovered until the nineteenth century by a chemist, John Dalton, who found that he was unable to distinguish between certain chemicals that could be visually differentiated only on the basis of color. The point is that a color blind (or color deficient) person is not really blind; he sees something. We learn that the sky is blue, the clouds are white, the trees and grass are green, and so forth. But there are cues other than color for recognizing the sky, clouds, and trees, and if you can make color discriminations that I cannot, we still agree on terminology. I call the sky *blue* and the clouds *white*, and any difference in the quality of perception will not be indicated by difficulties in, or a breakdown of, communication. The industrial revolution and the rise of science brought with them widespread specific informational use of color and increased the possibility that deviations from the norm in color perception would be discovered, but still the subtleties of anomalous color vision are seldom manifest in everyday life.

The point is that even on the most basic level of aesthetic experience, that of the purely sensory, we may expect a great variety in perceptual response to the same work of art. The fact that almost all of this variation occurs within a relatively narrow and subtle range does not matter. Theoretically, no difference can be dismissed as insignificant, and a difference in perception must always be related to, or cause, a difference in aesthetic response. In addition, the total variation in any situation increases geometrically as more than one dimension of the experience is taken into account— as the parameters of brightness, color perception, visual acuity, astigmatism, and so forth are all considered as part of the purely sensory perception of a painting, for example. Whether or not we all see the same painting depends upon the standards that are used. Compared to Ted Williams, the famous baseball player—about whom one of his hunting companions is reported to have said, "He can tell what kind of ducks they are before we can see any ducks"—most of us demonstrate sensory deficiency.

If sensory receptors are physically unable to register and transmit particular objective stimuli, the universality of the experience breaks down at a very basic level. Another level at which the same thing can happen is that where the sensory information is "translated" from the neural code into experience. Two exactly identical neural messages may be experienced differently. With the addition of subjective meaning to the sensory input, the same encoding may have many possible manifestations as experience.

When a small dot of light is viewed from a distance in a completely dark room, it will appear to move even though it is actually stationary. The rate, direction, distance, and pattern of the perceived movement varies from person to person. This is known as the autokinetic effect, a phenomenon that has yet to be fully explained although many have tried. Experiments have shown that the reported perceptions of the autokinetic effect change when the judgments are made in a group rather than alone. The individuals in the group tend to see the movements in the same way as they are reported by others. Since there is nothing with which to compare the size of the light, its distance and movement, estimates or standards are more readily adopted or learned from others. Each group develops its own more or less common opinion about the movement of the light.

Interior and exterior validation are both irrelevant in this case. Since the movement of the light, which is ostensibly controlled by the experimenter, could actually be changing from observation to observation, a subject is not aware that his perception when viewing alone has later changed to conform with that of the other subjects. And since the light actually remains stationary, one judgment of movement cannot be considered more correct than another.

In the same way, the famous distorted rooms used in experiments by Adelbert Ames, Jr. show that the same objective stimulus can be seen in different ways by the same person and that perception is related to learning. When a person looks into the viewing window of one of the Ames rooms, he sees, for example, an apparently normal room with doors indicated on the side walls and two windows represented on the rear wall. But strange things happen in the room. A boy standing at the right seems much taller than a man standing at the left, although both are normally proportioned. The apparent size of inanimate things placed in the room is also distorted, and a chair, in this case, placed at the left looks much smaller than one placed at the right.

Actually it is the room that is distorted: In the example I have described, the rear wall, which appears to be perpendicular to the observer's line of sight, actually slopes away from right to left. The room is built in false perspective, so that the image on the viewer's retina is the same as that which would be created by a rectangular room. Our habit of interpreting this particular retinal configuration as being "a rectangular room" is so strong that it persists in spite of the size contradictions that occur. Because of the apparent shape of the room and their relationship to it, two people or things of equal size are seen at the same apparent distance even though one is actually much closer than the other; rather than appearing closer, the nearer figure seems much larger than the distant one. The illusion of linear perspective creating a diminution in size as the distance from the observer increases has become "real."

Ames's distorted-room experiments demonstrate, among other things, the point at which experience ceases to be merely sensory and takes on transsensory aspects. The *gestalt* or retinal configuration or pattern—in this case the false perspective lines of the room—may still be thought of as sensory material, but the meaning of the particular *gestalt* is shown to be dependent upon additional factors. It is these additional, trans-sensory elements that become of major significance in the perception of art. There seems to be no doubt that learning has much to do with them. Just as it was established by learning, the meaning or interpretation of the retinal configuration may be changed through learning. By touching the distorted room and its contents with a long pole or by bouncing a ball back and forth in it, the observer may teach himself to see the actual shape and the true relationships involved.

If there are grounds for questioning whether, on a purely sensory level, any two of us perceive the physical world in exactly identical ways, the assumption that there is one correct set of value attributes related to any particular work of art is more obviously unjustified. This is not the place to discuss in detail the character and development of values, but one interesting experiment, which Elliot Aronson and J. Merrill Carlsmith conducted with four- and five-year-old children, illustrates something of the manner in which values are created, formed, or introjected.

The experimenters asked their young subjects to rate a number of toys on their attractiveness. Then they selected one of the toys designated as very attractive by each child and told him he could not play with it. Half the children were threatened with mild punishment if they played with the toy, and half were told they would be punished severely. The experimenters left the room; none of the children played with the forbidden toys. When the children were again asked to rate the attractiveness of all the toys, a striking and significant thing happened: Those children who had been promised severe punishment still rated the forbidden toys as high as, or even higher than, the preliminary rating, while those who had been threatened with mild punishment found the forbidden toy much less attractive than they had previously.

There are many implications of this experiment, but the point I want to emphasize is that the new values that were created in half of the children— the low attractiveness of the chosen toys—were no less true or real than the previous high rating of the same toy. In each case the rating was an indication of how the child really felt about the toy. The fact that we can find a direct cause, in the experimenters' behavior, for the change in values does not invalidate the experience or cause the quality to change. The same is true of the values felt in art. One cause is no more valid or correct than another. All values are real.

(To oversimplify, the learning of new values took place in this case primarily with those children who, because of the mildness of the threat, could not successfully explain to themselves why they did not want to play with the forbidden toys. Those who were threatened with severe punishment were quite clear in their minds why they refrained from playing with the toys, and they retained their previous values, or frustration made the toys seem even more desirable. This is merely one of the more subtle aspects of value formation, and even though it is not difficult mentally to substitute "works of art" for "toys" and to contemplate the functioning of the mechanism in relation to art, the purpose of mentioning the experiment is not to explain specifically any particular example of aesthetic experience but to establish the basic fact that values are learned.)

In final contrast to traditional aesthetics that posits an identical sensory experience for every observer or listener is the wide variety of perceptual variations that actually result from the time factor involved in the appreciation of every art. A painting is not seen completely in one glance. The eye moves from point to point, from detail to larger view; it hesitates, changes speed, skips sections, and doubles back to make comparisons. There is no strict control or rule determining the length or characteristics of this process. Composition of various sorts is supposed to "guide the eye," but this, at best, only creates certain likely possibilities; it may be thought of as governing the *average* reaction to some extent, but it cannot eliminate the wide variation in individual responses.

The implication of traditional aesthetics is that a painting has an objective reality that can be studied until it is completely apprehended. Thus any two people who look at a painting until it is "all perceived" have identical and correct responses. But this is like saying that two columns of numbers are the same because their sum is the same; the aesthetic experience does not work by addition. Once the eye has followed a certain visual path over a painting at a certain rate, for example, this movement becomes a unique part of the total aesthetic experience, qualifying everything that comes after it. These variations in the total experience are subtle. Perhaps for practical purposes they may be ignored. But from a theoretical point of view, they are very important and must be recognized as another factor that causes a great variety in the aesthetic experience.

These perceptual differences are not eliminated from such forms as drama and music that use time in a more conscious and controlled manner. Each member of an audience perceives the work from a different distance and angle; each is free at any moment to focus his attention on particular details at the expense of the whole. Even in film, which comes as close as possible to presenting the same sensory data at each performance, the viewer may examine each image with the same kind of variation in visual focus and emphasis that exists in the perception of a painting.

Thus in this section I have touched on some of the perceptual, cognitive, and valuative aspects of the aesthetic experience in terms of their distribution and variation and in terms of their relationship to learning. By indicating the variation and equivalency of perceptions at every level of experience, I am emphasizing a relativistic concept of art in contrast to the traditional independent or objective one. By discussing learning, I am stressing the particular relationship of the total perception to things, events, and states that preceded it rather than to the sensory data of which it is also composed; the aesthetic experience is placed in the continuum of time rather than entirely in the perceptual present.

One category of objects we call "works of art," and, as R. L. Gregory wrote in *Eye and Brain:*

> The seeing of objects involves many sources of information beyond those meeting the eye when we look at an object. It generally involves knowledge of the object derived from previous experience, and this experience is not limited to vision but may include the other senses; touch, smell, hearing, and perhaps also temperature or pain. Objects are far more than patterns of stimulation: objects have pasts and futures; when we know its past or can guess its future, an object transcends experience and becomes an embodiment of knowledge and expectation. . . .[3]

In the next section, we will examine ways in which works of art "transcend" direct sensory experience to become embodiments of knowledge and expectation.

3. Another completely unsatisfactory concept put forward by traditional aesthetics is that the experience of art is hermetic, sealed off, as it were, from any connection with the rest of life. According to this view, art is perceived "for itself alone." Its appreciation employs a detachment and psychical distance unlike that involved in everyday existence. The following quotations, taken almost at random, illustrate the wide acceptance of this point: "But only the sensuous appearance of the aesthetic object . . . is attended to in aesthetic contemplation" (Theodor Lipps); We experience on object aesthetically "when we look at it . . . without relating it, intellectually or emotionally, to anything outside of itself" (Erwin Panofsky); "Every real work of art has a tendency to appear thus dissociated from its mundane environment" (Susanne Langer); "to appreciate a work of art we need bring with us nothing from life, no knowledge of its ideas and affairs, no familiarity with its emotions . . . " (Clive Bell).

I do not mean to deny that a hermetic and "pure" aesthetic experience is possible. That is, it seems to be possible. Most of us have had it many times. But if we carefully limit our attention and clear our minds in order to attend only to the sensuous appearance of the aesthetic object and do not relate it, intellectually or emotionally, to anything outside of itself, this is only an alteration in consciousness. The human mechanism is still functioning, and most of this functioning occurs on an unconscious level. In the unconscious, the person is far from hermetic. When we describe the broad context of the aesthetic experience in this section, it should be remembered that most of the aesthetic experience is produced at this unconscious level. In other words, being in a pure hermetic state of aesthetic contemplation does not mean that the unconscious is functioning hermetically. This would be impossible. Therefore the hermetic state has little meaning when considering the whole perceptual system, and does not, in fact, exist at the most crucial levels.

Anything may be looked at "aesthetically." The hermetic aesthetic consciousness can be adopted in order to experience any object or action. The chosen thing is then seen "for itself alone" with no reference to function or practicality. This demonstrates that the traditional hermetic experience derives as much from the perceiver as from the nature of the work of art. It is self-induced. It is emotionally "inflated" by personal manipulation of areas of attention and a habituated control of affect. It is determined by social traditions and learned by the individual, relying to a good extent on devices that are quite comparable to self-hypnosis, semi-trance states, autosuggestion, and various contemplative devices that limit consciousness. After all, the Eastern contemplative adept is apparently successful in erasing all but the fact of consciousness itself.

It is my position that the hermetic consciousness is not a necessary condition for experiencing art. Since it has been dominant in our culture for some time, many works have been, and are being, produced to be experienced in this way. There is no reason why these works should not be contemplated, at least part of the time, in that state for which they were conceived. But not all art is meant to be experienced in this way.

The fact that a pure state of so-called aesthetic appreciation can exist does not mean that it should be adopted for the experiencing of all art, nor does its existence, in itself, validate or justify the theories to which it is linked. The separation of the traditional aesthetic experience from everyday life makes it seem precious, escapist, and romantic. Its autocontrolled aspects make it seem arbitrary and overly self-indulgent.

Art, in a perceptual sense, is no different from non-art things and objects. It does not require a different perceptual state. It does not need to be looked at with a mental attitude or set unlike that involved in everyday life. It is not hermetic.

(I must emphasize that this does not mean that there is no difference between art and life. The mere fact that a thing is art makes it quite different from the other things we experience. But this is a mental distinction, not a perceptual one; it does not depend on a particular way of looking at the world. Exactly how the knowledge that a thing is art brings trans-sensory elements into existence that are not present in the experiencing of other objects will be discussed later in this section.)

In general, we may equate the hermetic aesthetic experience of "the thing for its own sake" with perception at a sensory level as was discussed in the last section. In this section, we will consider what can be called the *trans-sensory* aspects of the aesthetic experience. The "purity" of the traditional aesthetic experience is achieved by the repression or the rejection from consciousness of these elements. Only later, in reflection and cogitation, are they permitted into awareness as aspects of a different and nonaesthetic state. But it is important to understand that these factors come into play automatically on an unconscious level. The trans-sensory aspects of perception therefore function even in the traditional hermetic state. They operate whether we are aware of them or not. The elaboration and exploitation of these elements by consciousness gives the "open" or nonhermetic state an entirely different character, however. Thus the discussion of the trans-sensory elements of experience applies just as well to the traditionally defined aesthetic experience as it does to the more open one that I propose.

Especially since we learn how to see and hear, life is always the ground against which a work of art is experienced. Art is always perceived in terms of life. The hermetic attitude does not contradict this but merely prevents consciousness from "flowing back" into life, so to speak. The person feels "cut off" from real life, even though this is not actually the case. In reality, life exists as a contrast conception of art. The formal differences between art and life can be important aspects of experience, and they would not be known if the experience were truly hermetic. Conscious attention to this comparison and contrast of a work of art with all aspects of life naturally produces experience of a different quality from when the process is entirely unconscious. There is no reason, however, why only the latter should be considered "aesthetic."

Observable qualities—that is to say, the sensory aspect of a piece—may be modified in experience by trans-sensory informational elements. I have stated, as an aesthetic axiom not requiring proof, the fact that two sensory perceptions that differ in any respect will have different value attributes in an individual's experience. But the rule "Two objects that do not differ in any observable qualities cannot differ in aesthetic value," stated by Monroe C. Beardsley in his book *Aesthetics*, is not axiomatic. Information may change the character of an experience, making it quite different from another even though the sensory material is identical. The identity of the creator, for example, is often not an intrinsic sensory part of the work, and yet the knowledge can greatly influence the perception of the work; a rose by any other name might not smell as sweet.

As long ago as 1935, M. Sherif demonstrated experimentally that subjects tended to rank short prose passages, all actually written by the same person although ascribed to different authors, in accordance with their own previously given rating of the authors. In other words, a subject's previous appreciation of an author's work or his opinion of the author's position significantly affected his evaluation of the work.

(At the same time, Sherif also demonstrated that the prestige effect could be overcome statistically by "special effort." This effort is the same as that used in creating the hermetic aesthetic state. The psychic action in this state not only imposes another level of functioning on the perceptual one, but a misinterpretation of the effort may, when added to the basic unreality of the situation, be partly responsible for the heightened affect. At any rate, "correction" of experience is conscious and would not operate on unconscious elements.)

The influence of this same factor on perception is demonstrated by forgeries. For seven years *Christ and the Disciples at Emmaus* by Johannes Vermeer of Delft hung in the Boymans Museum in Rotterdam, admired as a great work of art by thousands of visitors. Abraham Bredius, one of the leading experts on Vermeer, called it *"the* masterpiece" of the artist. Then, in 1945, Hans van Meegeren admitted having forged it and other "masterpieces." The whole experience of these works changed. They no longer generated the intense aesthetic response that they had previously, although their observable qualities were unchanged. At least I prefer to consider the change in experience an aesthetic one. Traditional aesthetics would claim that *aesthetically* the experience remained the same, and the "nonaesthetic" aspects of experience were what was altered. This distinction is crucial, and I will return to the point later. For now I will only suggest that the "extirpation" or rejection of the artist's identity from the total experience is unnecessary, artificial, and extremely difficult.

Knowing an artist's name means, in part, that while we are perceiving his work, we are remembering, to some extent, whether conscious of it or not, all of his other works to which we have been exposed. We recognize a particular artist's style. We see the present work in terms of his past works. It is common to feel that such cumulative data make any particular artistic creation easier to understand and interpret: An artist's goal or purpose, for example, seems much easier to perceive by comparing works covering a span of time and implying directionality than it does from a single work. Additions from whatever level of memory and neural trace certainly make the experience "larger" and more complex. With the consideration of recognition and memory, we have entered into the crucial historical context of art. I am not referring now to the learning processes that were mentioned earlier. Learning, of course, is also historical but functions primarily as a structuring device, determining our perceptions and their meanings, among other things. The historical elements to which I want to draw attention now function as contrast conceptions: They are the bases for comparisons of various kinds made between the past and the present. Obviously, *a work of art may have meaning and significance not in terms of its sensory body alone but in comparisons to some other work or works.* (The two works that are thus compared could both be presented directly to experience—it is a simple matter to compare paintings hung next to each other in a museum, for example— but memory almost always provides one element, and the phenomenon may be considered as primarily a historical one.)

Let us say that a painter makes a reference to a work by another artist. He basically adopts the other painter's subject matter or style and makes changes or modifications. These changes or modifications become part of the aesthetic material of the work, but they can only be perceived if the other work is also seen or remembered: Two sets of data are needed to indicate a difference. Thus a "third quality" can be created by the comparison of two works of art. This comparison quality does not lie directly in the sensuous appearance of a single work itself, but it is the result of the comparison of that work with a second. These comparison qualities may exist in any dimension of the work: the subject matter, the forms and shapes in space and time, the ways of perceiving the world, and so forth.

Although the intended comparison of a work of art with only the other work is possible and gives the clearest model for the concept, the situation is hardly ever that explicit or limited. Most frequently, the contrast element against which a work is perceived is a particular style or even the total field of the art form itself.

Thus we have the concept of "the new" that is so fundamental to the avant-garde. Newness is a contrast conception. It exists only in the difference between things, and it is not visible in consciousness if, as directed by traditional aesthetics, a work is seen "for itself alone." This is not to suggest a value judgment: The new is not good merely because it is new, and the question of significance will be taken up in a later section. The new, however, can be an element in the total aesthetic experience. It and other trans-sensory comparison factors are intentionally employed by many artists and recognized by many people in their appreciation of the work. Allowances must be made for them in any realistic and accurate aesthetic theory.

Obviously, whether or not a particular element is perceived as new depends upon the individual. What is new to one person is not new to another. The same thing is true for other contrast elements. They depend for their perception upon the unique psychological field or ground against which they are seen. Thus they are different from person to person. Even two experiences of the same unchanging work by the same person may be quite different because the psychological context that creates these elements has changed. But the fact that contrast elements are not objectively fixed does not alter their importance. They are still elements of the aesthetic experience. As such they have the possibility of engendering positive or negative values, depending upon the taste of the perceiver.

It should not be inferred that contrast elements are created by the artist only as a result of conscious intent. The factors governing creativity are unconscious to a great extent, and there is no reason why an artist would have to believe in the principle of comparison factors before they could be found in his work. The same holds true for appreciation. Contemporary criticism stresses comparisons very heavily. It discusses, for example, the "dialectics" of modern painting and sculpture as works "comment on" each other. But the perception of contrast elements does not need to reach consciousness in order to register as part of the experience. There is no reason why newness or any of the other contrast factors could not be noted and evaluated without any conscious awareness of the factor.

In some respects, a contrast effect is like an afterimage. What is seen later depends upon what was looked at earlier: The contrast element in the total perception of the work of art or a moving red dot, for example, depends upon the work that formed the first half of the comparison or the green dot that caused the afterimage. In these terms, the process can be seen as historically unidirectional, moving from the past to the present. Newness depends upon the "subtraction" of all earlier work from the particular current work being perceived and this process is not reversible. The later is not "subtracted" from the earlier. Thus if the quality of newness or innovation exists, it continues to exist relative to its own place in history and cannot be taken away by later works. (Although the perceived significance of the innovation may, of course, change.) Newness may be measured at any point in the historical continuum and not just at the present moment, but such measurements are always made in the direction of later compared to earlier.

Actually, there is a contrast element that is measured in the opposite direction—against the current of time, so to speak. Similarities of later work to earlier work are perceived as what could be called *influence*. (I use the word to indicate a comparison quality and do not mean to imply that only perceptual similarities are necessary to establish actual influence. Other historical facts such as availability would be necessary in addition to priority in time sequence.) The influence of a work on other work is, interestingly enough, a quality that does not exist in a newly completed work, but which may accumulate as the work ages.

From this point of view it is nonsense to look at, say, Picasso's *Les Demoiselles d'Avignon,* painted in 1907, as if it had just been completed. Viewed hermetically, "outside of time," it only seems tentative, incomplete, and drably colored. In the context of time, the influence that this single painting has had on perception can create an intense feeling. All of its pure characteristics take on entirely different values in terms of historical aesthetics. This does not mean that the comparison qualities of influence need to be considered consciously. Cerebration is not necessary in order to perceive the influence of the past on the present.

Thus the date of a work's creation is another of the informational elements that, like knowledge of the author's identity, place the perception in its complete context. Whether the dating derives from figures carved into a piece of sculpture, from a printed card hanging next to the work in a museum, from published material, or from the resources of memory, it becomes an important catalyst and an intrinsic part of the aesthetic experience.

Among the other information about the work of art that can become part of the aesthetic experience is the history and data of a work's creation. I remember, for example, the girl who dismissed one of Jasper Johns's major works as "just old paint brushes stuck into a can." She had not looked carefully enough to see that the piece had actually been cast from a can filled with brushes and then painted to resemble the original. Even so, the fact that the particular material was bronze, important to the aesthetic appreciation of the piece, was unavailable to her visually—although in this case it could be found in the title: *Painted Bronze.*

In order to make his *Stoppages-Etalon,* Marcel Duchamp dropped three threads, each one meter in length, from a height of one meter and fastened them in position. The knowledge of his procedure is crucial to an appreciation of the work, but it cannot be obtained from the sensory study of the piece itself. In a like manner, information about methods, techniques, materials, and creative history of any work may be important, although they are not necessarily so.

Thus we can distinguish between traditional aesthetics and what could be called the *historical* or *situational* aesthetics suggested by the work of the avant-garde. Traditional aesthetics asks a particular hermetic attitude or state of mind that concentrates on the sensory perception of the work "for its own sake" and is different from that used in daily life. Historical aesthetics makes use of no special attitude or set, and art is viewed just as anything else in life. In this way, everything pertinent in any way to the work of art and the perception of it becomes part of the "aesthetic experience." The experience can therefore be seen as open rather than hermetic and as including factors that are considered "nonaesthetic" by traditional theory. The aesthetic experience can then be defined as any experience in which the attention is focused on a work of art.

But the simple awareness that the object of perception is a work of art gives the experience a particular character that is different from the experience of non-art objects. This is not a sensory distinction. If one imaginatively substitutes a non-art object or action for art, the experience will not be the same, if only because of the artificiality and pretense involved. Art is life, but life cannot be art. An object seen as a work of art is psychologically placed in a cultural-historical context that determines the characteristics of the experience. Traditional aesthetics asks that the perception of a work of art exist "outside of time," as it were. Situational or historical aesthetics sees the work in the context of time where the trans-sensory elements are of fundamental importance.

4. The concept of "art as communication" is another aspect of traditional aesthetics that has to be abandoned in the light of modern psychology and avant-garde art. This concept posited the artist as "sender" and the person experiencing the work as "receiver" of a "message" about life. The artist was "trying to say something." If difficulties occurred in transmission of the message, they were due to either the artist's inadequacies in expression or the receiver's imperfect reception or understanding. This is a very simplified model, but even the most sophisticated communication theory does not apply to all art. It may apply to some art, of course, and some artists certainly attempt to communicate, but it is now realized that the model we have described is an inaccurate one and that the attempt to communicate is unnecessary.

At least since psychoanalysis, it has been apparent that not all of the "message" in a work of art is intentional. We now know that there is also a "latent content," to use the term that Freud applied to the analysis of dreams, and that the unconscious, as well as consciousness, gives form to the work of art. The work may still be seen as a message sent from the complete psyche of the artist, but this is communication in which the sender himself does not know the message. Any creation of man is seen as expressive, whether or not it is a work of art. The model begins to break down.

If the concept of communication is retained with its nonrational ad-juncts, the psychoanalyst becomes the best possible and most efficient receiver, interpreting the unconscious elements of the work and "understanding" the complete message. But even psychoanalysts seem to read different messages in the same work. Their own discipline has pointed out subjective mechanisms such as projection that tend to register the message that the unconscious wants to register; just as "noise" is added to visual data by the optic nerve, the message is determined in part by the psychological characteristics of the human receiver.

The third place that our model of communication breaks down is in the message itself. A message is a symbolic construct: That which is present refers to that which is absent. All representational art is symbolic, in this sense, and can certainly be considered as communication. But abstract art may not be symbolic at all; it may merely be itself. A work of art may intend no external reference.

This, of course, does not eliminate the possibility of a "message" being received. Anything may be seen as a symbol. Any line, color, shape, or even a blank canvas, can be interpreted as having philosophical reference at some level. The Rorschach inkblots used in projective testing of personality have no intentional references; they are merely inkblots, but many different "messages" are "received" from them. Thus the "message" quality of an experience can be seen to depend in part upon the set or readiness of the receiver to perceive a message. If you look for a message in anything, you will see one. If art is believed to be communication, it will appear to be communication, even though the artist is not intending to create a symbol or send a message.

I do not mean to imply that symbolic interpretation of a work is necessarily wrong, even when it is understood that no reference of any sort was intended. We certainly cannot limit ourselves to the artist's intent. Any work, in a sense, becomes in part an open-ended metaphor: The work is *like* anything on any level of consciousness with which we want to compare it. A certain abstract painting, for example, may be compared to a particular event in history, to the emotions at a certain time of day, to social relationships, to the structure of the universe, or to life itself—to anything that the mind can conceive. If the comparison seems to be meaningful and important, it cannot be considered wrong or improper. At the same time, interpretation and the analogy of a work to something other than itself should not be considered as a necessity; the work may exist only on a perceptual level.

5. Art *seems* to be significant. One of the most salient characteristics of the aesthetic experience is the impression or feeling of significance. In the first section I distinguished between art and other nonfunctional man-made creations such as decorations and entertainments on the basis of an intention in art to achieve significance. But to feel the significance of something is not the same thing as being able to demonstrate that significance objectively. The intent to embody significance does not mean that it is achieved.

Significance cannot be argued on the basis of one person's experience. What is significant to one person is not significant to another, and the reasons that an individual feels that significance exists in a work are a psychological question. Experience is very complex, and there could be as many different reasons that significance was sensed in a particular work as there were people who indicated they perceived the quality. If a work of art does have objective significance, it is obvious that that significance does not necessarily correlate directly with individual experience.

The traditional attitude is that since values seem to be objective, they are objective. This objectivity of value has never been satisfactorily demonstrated. At the same time, traditional aesthetics states that the values of a work are unrelated to practical life and lie only in the experience itself. This is consistent with the hermetic view that art is separate from life: Its significances are of its own order and are not related to mundane existence. (Since one historical view of the spirit separates it rather rigorously from the things of this world, my own earlier identification of art with spiritual concerns might seem to follow this line of thought, but I was merely using the word as indicative of the apparent depth and personal quality of the aesthetic experience—as a synonym, in other words, for the most intense and private kind of perceived significance.) Although it cannot yet be proved, however, I believe that art does have a kind of objective significance based in culture.

Before going into the question of objective significance, certain false standards must be pointed out. Some people see anything that is well-done as "art." Thus they have the art of juggling, the art of blowing glass, the art of playing chess, and so forth. Our definition of art in the opening section excluded most of these possibilities. But there are those who would attribute significance to works of art, as included in our definition, on the basis of whether or not they are well-made or well-done. Craft, technique, and talent are sometimes mistaken for significance.

I still remember the young girl at the old Whitney Museum on Eighth Street who, on seeing a large painting by Franz Kline, called gleefully to the elderly woman who was accompanying her, "Oh, I could do that!" If she had really known the technical requirements of the work, I doubt whether she would have acted superior. But the little girl implied that Kline's painting was not significant because it was, or seemed, easy to do. The attitude is common.

Today many artists have their work manufactured commercially by artisans and fabricators, and the little girl could certainly emulate one of their works merely by telling the craftsman what she wanted or by making a simple sketch. Technically, any carpenter could do some modern sculpture. But there is no reason that an artist actually has to make the physical work himself as long as he determines its characteristics. The point is that the ease with which a work of art is made (or the apparent ease with which it is made) has nothing to do with the significance of the work.

Nor does technique make a work important. Admiration may certainly be involved. We tend to envy things we cannot do ourselves and to "do" them through empathy, getting a kind of excitement out of vicariously accomplishing the extremely difficult. But admirable qualities are not the same as significance.

To relate talent to significance rests upon the same kind of assumptions. Talent means the natural ability, as opposed to learned or acquired ability, to do a particular thing well. This does not mean that a person without very much talent cannot accomplish as much as a person with a great amount of talent. Many other factors are involved. And the definition of the particular talent obviously depends upon the specific characteristics of the thing that is done. Once a human activity is clearly delimited, the talent related to it may be perceived. We can speak of a talent for running, or dancing, or drawing, and so forth. But when it becomes a question of innovation, the known and previously established standard does not exist, and talent cannot be measured or considered a factor. A person may have little talent for dancing in the traditional sense but become a great dancer by changing the definition and limits of dance.

In general, talent, technique, and difficulty are easy to appraise. There tends to be greater agreement in this kind of judgment, and standards are more readily available from non-art sources, making opinions based on these dimensions of a work much safer from a social point of view. But attention paid to these factors may only distract attention from the characteristics that make the work art. Ultimately, significance only derives from what is created, not from the technical accomplishments of that creation.

If art does not exist merely "for its own sake" and the experience itself is not the only measure of its importance, then significance depends upon what is referred to as *the relationship of art to reality*. The meaning of the phrase depends entirely upon what is meant by "reality." Thus the questions or problems of the significance of art and of the relationship of art to life, are in general, relatively recent; perhaps they have become pressing only since the development of the avant-garde. In the Renaissance, for example, the significance of art was easily explained to everyone's satisfaction by its subject matter, and even music developed "subject matter" through its religious use and context. But meaning, reference, symbolism, and representation are not the only kinds of connections with reality. Abstract art, by definition, has no relationship to the recognizable sensory patterns that we perceive as the real things of the world, and yet it, too, is felt to be related to reality. It is merely a slightly broader and less literal meaning of the word *reality*.

Music has always been basically a nonreferential art. Over half a century ago—long before the current concern with the medium being the message— painting and sculpture became abstract. Now there is no art form that is representational throughout its entire spectrum. We are primarily concerned, therefore, with reality not as things and emotions but as principles and types. In other words, in discussing significance, we are primarily concerned with the significance of abstract or nonrepresentational art.

Art, by definition, does not have a practical purpose. It is not created to accomplish a particular physical result. On the other hand, it may certainly have psychological and sociological implications and consequences. A tool is used to achieve a certain desired change in the state or condition of things; art is not a tool. But changes also occur without the use of tools and without the intent to make a change. Learning, for example, may be accomplished through teachers and teaching machines, but these are certainly not the only ways to learn. Thus art, even though it does not have a practical use, may cause changes.

The particular changes with which I am concerned are changes in the consciousness of man. Certainly the consciousness of man has changed. Its range, scope, and content have vastly increased. Cross-cultural comparisons give us an analogy for history and make this obvious: The consciousness of so-called primitive people may not be any better or worse than that of "civilized" man, but it is entirely different. History has produced changes in consciousness.

The important changes are those more or less permanent ones in the state and organization of consciousness. Any previously unknown thing in the perceptual field changes consciousness, but only the content of consciousness. Some things, however, may be of such a nature as to cause a reorganization of consciousness itself, of its expectancies, its values, and its functioning. In other words, most of experience may be integrated into consciousness without changing the character or nature of consciousness itself; some types of experience, on the other hand, can cause a complete change in the structure and efficiency of consciousness itself.

The alteration of consciousness is dramatically illustrated during sicknesses and in the effect of certain drugs. A feverish person or one who is "high" sees the world in an entirely different way. These changes are usually only temporary, however, and we are concerned here with those basic changes that occur when consciousness is forced against the things of this world, so to speak, rather than withdrawn from them.

The things of this world and the character of consciousness are interrelated. A thing or an action can force a reorganization of consciousness; a particular state of consciousness is necessary before a certain thing can be created or a certain action performed. Each may affect the other. Flying at 30,000 feet from New York to San Francisco in a few hours and watching the country move by as if it were a huge map forcefully presents to consciousness aspects of time and space that could only have been imagined a century ago. The invention of the airplane, on the other hand, depended upon knowledge that could only have been accumulated in a scientific-technological society and on aspects of consciousness not present in all cultures. The experience of flight causes changes in consciousness; flight was only possible because of changes in consciousness. This is only one example from many possible ones.

There is no question that extensive changes in the consciousness of man have taken place in the past and that consciousness will continue to change. There have been, and there will continue to be, concomitant changes in attitudes, beliefs, morals, social structure, and every other aspect of life, including art. This does not prove the causal relationship of art to these changes, however. From the whole cultural history of man it might theoretically be possible to remove all of art without affecting the rest in any way. Art might only follow and reflect changes that are due to other causes. There is no way to prove this.

It would seem unlikely, however, that changes in consciousness are not due, in part, to art. Art is vitally interrelated with the rest of culture, and the proposition that it can originate changes should not be too difficult to accept. One way of phrasing the problem, at least in analogy, might be to ask whether one sense modality has any effect on another. There is the common concept of each sense being localized in its own precise area of the brain, and this could be compared to the view that perceptions of art only affect other perceptions of art and not perceptions of the "real world." The effect of one sense on another is far from understood, but the model of discrete brain areas is not accepted as accurate at the most refined level. In *Subcortical Mechanisms of Behavior*, Robert A. McCleary and Robert Y. Moore write that "It seems best not to regard any one level of the brain as having sole control of particular behavioral functions, functions not shared or influenced to some extent by certain structures at other levels. . . . The brain is so redundantly interlocked that it is difficult to know where a given subsystem begins or ends."[4] Thus we can believe that intersensory transfer takes place at some level. The way in which art changes the perception of life may not be understood, but it can be assumed that these changes take place.

Since changes in consciousness are psychological, they exist only in the individual. But when enough people develop similar states of consciousness, the change may be seen as cultural rather than personal. On a social-psychological level, an objectivity can be claimed for changes in consciousness. Thus we can establish an objective standard by which the significance of a work of art may be judged. A work of art can be seen as significant to the extent that it tends *to change basically the consciousness of man.*

As we have explained, if art is able to alter fundamentally the consciousness of man, it will indirectly produce changes in practical areas of life. This is not to suggest that a scientist looks at a painting and is so changed by the experience that he designs an experiment that he could not previously conceive. But, in time, it is *as if* this were true. Thus an artist may be seen as acting directly on the world.

But on an individual level, art seldom basically alters consciousness instantaneously. I am not referring to those passing states that frequently continue to grip us after we leave a gallery, theatre, or concert hall, so that we briefly perceive the world in terms of art, but, as indicated before, to fundamental changes in the character or nature of consciousness that are not necessarily noticed by the individual. Perhaps a few people have been so drastically affected by a unitary experience of a work of art that their basic relationship to the data of reality has been changed. But just as the familiar "Eureka" experience of creativity or cases of sudden religious conversion, such as St. Paul's, can actually be seen to have a long, if unconscious, genesis in time, a work of art generally takes more than a moment to effect an alteration in individual consciousness. In certain cases the organization and dynamics of conciousness may be such that they may be quickly and easily changed, but change is more apt to be an extended process involving adjustments to new data and the elimination of conflicts and contradictions.

On a cultural level, it is even more apparent that alteration of consciousness is not an instantaneous phenomenon. The impact of any single work on society is not merely the sum total or average of all individual changes in consciousness that it causes. A work may also influence other works, thereby effecting additional changes. Or any alterations it does produce may be the basis for non-art creations that in turn cause further changes.

Thus there is a cultural diaspora or diffusion involved in the functional relationship between art and the rest of the culture. In some cases, perhaps, little diffusion is necessary. The rate and duration of the assimilation are not constant. But in time, a work may become "translated" into other cultural modes of thought and perception. Art becomes philosophy; philosophy becomes political and scientific theory; politics and science change the mass entertainment industries, public utilities, and social structure.

At the same time, of course, changes at any of these other levels may also be forming consciousness in a way that will allow or predispose a previously impossible kind of art to be created. Social structure and philosophy are also becoming art.

This relationship between art and culture is elaborate and interwoven. Its processes are widespread and subtle. This means, for one thing, that the most apparent examples of the assimilation of art by society should not be taken as the only ones, as necessarily important, or as standards of measurement. One style of art, for example, is not more important than another merely because it is accepted more widely or has greater influence on popular culture. I am not suggesting a kind of public opinion poll in which those works that are the most popular or are taken up by design, fashion, entertainment fads, and so forth are declared the winners. In adopting art for its own mundane purposes, popular culture may take only those aspects of the art that have not required a basic change in consciousness. The most profound influences of art on life may be the least obvious.

Dispersion through the popular culture is one possible way for art to change consciousness, but it is not the best or only way. Art can also be disseminated, explained, and "translated" through the more specialized channels of higher education, theory, and philosophy, for example. Words may mirror a change in consciousness. Thought that is caused, provoked, based on, influenced, or made possible by an exposure to a work of art is one of the basic contacts of art with mundane reality and, ultimately, with significance.

One way to illustrate these relationships is to make an extended analogy between art and science. This does not mean that art and science can be equated in every respect. Obviously, there are fundamental differences. But certain important points about art may be illustrated by comparing it with science.

In the first place, both art and science are specialities. Neither is available at a very subtle level to a very large segment of the population. Everyone knows certain basic principles of chemistry or physics, of course, even if he has not had a specialized education and does not know the proper terminology. And anyone can look at a painting, listen to a piece of music, or attend a performance, and we can call the resulting experience an aesthetic one. But neither art nor science can be grasped to any extent without study and specialized involvement. The fine points of both may be experienced only by those with particular experience in the field.

In science this kind of specialization is taken for granted. We are not surprised when we cannot understand many of the words in a technical journal that has wide distribution within a particular field. A person who has not studied mathematics does not expect to understand an advanced formula. But many people think that art can be seen as well by the person with no specialized background as it can be the specialist. Art is deprecated as a coterie enterprise, while scientific collaborations are praised. It is frequently attacked as esoteric. Like the esoteric nature of science, it is necessary for art to exist on this level, however, in order to achieve significance. In our terms, entertainment, decoration, and beauty may be for the mass audience, but art is not. Like the scientist, the avant-garde artist is working for a very limited audience whose experience, understanding of historical developments and current concepts in the field, and interest make it possible for it to appreciate points that are unavailable to a general audience.

In science certain current and pressing problems are widely recognized. Many medical research people are trying to find a cure for cancer. Many others all over the world are perfecting heart transplants. Although it is possible that individual scientists may be working alone in entirely unique areas, there is a tendency in science for many people to be involved simultaneously on the same problem. The theory of natural selection was formulated independently at the same time by both Charles Darwin and Alfred Russell Wallace.

I believe that the same is true in art. Certain problems are widely felt. Even when isolated from each other's work, artists may develop in the same direction. At each moment in history certain possibilities exist and others have been closed off.

All scientists are not involved with adding to the total of man's knowledge. Some teach, promulgating the knowledge that already exists. Others work in areas such as quality control where scientific techniques are necessary. In the same way, not all artists are concerned with the new. Many are satisfied to work in accepted styles and manners. But in art as in science, it is the new that gives the field its significance. The scientific meaning of the word *experiment* does not fit artistic creation with any precision, but it accurately indicates the ambition of some artists to investigate new areas of experience.

The dispersion of art into the culture that was mentioned before may also be clarified by analogy with science. Scientific discoveries exist at a theoretical level that can be understood only by a relatively small number of specialists. In part, these discoveries suggest other theoretical research and remain, so to speak, within the area of science. But they are also simplified and explained so that a broader public can understand them. They may cause modifications in existing products or methods. Their practical implications may bring about the invention of many new tools and techniques that were previously impossible. A purely theoretical discovery may have a wide impact on culture even though it, in itself, is never perceived or understood by the general public. The "translation" of art into life occurs in an analogous manner.

From this point of view, abstract art is not "dehumanized," as many have said. It lacks humanity no more than scientific research does. Abstraction can be seen as a specialized language that has an abundance of intra-art contrast elements. It is perceived primarily in terms of other art in the manner discussed previously. This does not mean that representational art is not seen in the historical context. All art is abstract to a certain extent, and representation has its own aesthetic history. But representational art, by definition, allows certain direct comparisons with the world that can be made outside of the cultural-historical context of art. The terminology is, to this extent, available to a wider audience.

Scientific research can have two kinds of significance. It can be provocative and suggestive, even if incorrect, and thus lead to further investigations. Or it can be the basis for new developments in the practical world. As has been suggested, this is analogous to the significance of art. The power of certain works to alter consciousness may be severely limited by their particular context. They may only influence artists and not be seen as significant except by a limited number of people. Other works are able to influence culture in a more diffuse way and on a wider level, perhaps fundamentally altering the consciousness of man.

Thus the word *significance* has been used in two different ways: as a psychological concept and on the social-psychological level. On the social level, significance can have a kind of objectivity. Shakespeare and Picasso are great, whether or not I care for them. The reasons are as much a part of the work as any other element. The work cannot be separated from its historical context. Of course this is a limited kind of objectivity. The historical context is not absolutely fixed, and a degree of change is involved. On the other hand, it is not unstable.

The connection between the two kinds of significance, the subjective and the objective, lies in the method of validating the art experience. This whole concept is hypothetical. It is based on the feeling and assumption that art somehow is useful practically to the individual. As we have discussed before, this does not mean that it functions in the world as a tool to achieve certain ends. But art can be seen as a psychological tool. In this sense, it is used in order better to understand the nature of reality. This occurs on an integrative unconscious level. I do not mean that only we understand information about reality, but that we are able to understand more of its organization and basic structure. From this point of view, changes in individual consciousness allow more information to enter, but they are not necessarily caused by information as such.

If we better understand the nature of reality, we should be able to function better. I believe that this is true. As I see it, art enables us to live more "accurately" and, therefore, more successfully. But there is no way to prove this. We cannot, in the same way, objectively prove the accuracy of religious beliefs, although they engender similar feelings of truth and usefulness. In this sense, all art is religious. Or, in philosophical terms, it is metaphysical. The usefulness of truth and the danger of using false information also explains why "good" art is seen as being moral and "bad" art as immoral.

On the psychological level, each person validates or "checks out" the usefulness of art for himself. What is useful for one person is not necessarily useful for another. This is especially true because we function in culture. Much of the usefulness of art may be "only" social and cultural.

Thus the relationship between perceived significance on an individual level and our objective sociopsychological significance exists in two entirely different modes. One of these modes could be called the retrospective. With the perspective of time, the various interrelationships of art with the other aspects of culture become clear. Michelangelo is great in an objective sense. In all likelihood, greatness will also be perceived as a quality of his work. Among other particular negative psychological factors, there might be a reaction against his fame, but his work is more apt to be seen positively because of "reinforcements" from later cultural developments. In retrospect Michelangelo's art is justified and supported by its influence on ethical and philosophical as well as iconographic areas. Whether or not the observer knows Michelangelo's name or has studied art history is not the vital point. The influence of a work of art on culture tends to create and assure its own appreciation. It will "check out" in many different ways.

The second way in which significance can be experienced as an attribute of a work of art could be called the hypothetical mode. It involves estimates about the future rather than judgments about the past. A work that has just been created cannot be put into the same kind of historical context that an older work can. It may be related to art and non-art sources in the culture, but the impact of the work on culture and consciousness cannot be appraised objectively. The work, of course, will not yet have been able to create its own context of appreciation. But the future of the work may, in a sense, be estimated. The potential of a work to influence culture and change certain aspects of consciousness may become a hypothetical dimension of the aesthetic experience.

Changes in culture emphasize the difficulty and the pertinence of the historical mode. If the future is expected to be exactly like the past, all judgments become "retrospective" even when they are made about the future. On the other hand, a changing culture means that the character and nature of prevalent tendencies must be understood in order to make accurate estimates about the future. These tendencies, of course, derive from the past, but as the cultural rate of change increases, their origin and genesis tend to grow closer to the present moment. The history that is vital is very recent history.

This suggests that avant-garde art would not be recognizable as such if accelerating cultural change had not increased its visibility. Artists have always been concerned with the future. The hypothetical mode has always been pertinent. But there has not always been much difference between retrospective and hypothetical judgments. The concern for the directionality of art that defines the avant-garde becomes magnified by rapid cultural change.

Strangely enough, change seems to be understood by the youthful better than by the elderly. Perhaps it is because the older people tend to explain change in terms of the past, while the young, looking with naive need, see the unique character and qualities of the transition. At any rate, there is a close identification between the avant-garde and youthful attitudes of self-actualization and learning.

6. Thus we have a view of art that does not rely on a subjective aesthetic attitude or state. This view proposes that the way in which art is perceived is basically the same as the way in which the world is perceived, and that a change in one can bring about a change in the other. The various sense modalities are seen as unified at a deep level where there is an exchange between them. Therefore, even though consciousness precedes perception, certain perceptions are able to change the limits or basic character of consciousness itself. It is upon these changes that the significance of art depends.

Knowledge determines, in part, the nature of experience. Like a person whose eyes are not yet fully adapted to the light, we can see only what the specific conditions and content of our consciousness allow us to see. And since the consciousness of man changes, the work of art created now will not be experienced in the same way in the future anymore than we can experience the art of the past just as it was when it was first produced. From this point of view, all art is mental rather than physical. Of course this makes the aesthetic experience subjective and relativistic, but it would require an absolute god-like omniscience to be aware of all the factors that could contribute to the experience of any work and to make the manifold experiences of all men objective.

It was suggested, however, that history gives a kind of cultural objectivity to the significance of art. This same kind of objectivity cannot be obtained in the present, and the perception and evaluation of contemporary art must exist in a different, hypothetical, mode.

Since the perception of all aesthetic elements, including the new, varies from person to person, it is important to stress the aspect of specialization. The understanding of art by artists and by others who spend their lives involved with art has somewhat more importance, in these terms, than the average or usual reaction. Art, as we have been concerned with it here, can be more subtle and demanding than the so-called popular arts.

Because of their emphasis upon the sociopsychological context of perception, these views of art could be called *situational aesthetics*. Because of a simultaneous emphasis upon history and the influence of time, they could be called *historical aesthetics*. They were given impetus by a desire to explain the attitude of the avant-garde that "A work of art that is created today is not good because it is new, but it cannot be significant unless it is new."

If the aesthetic emphasis is primarily on the mental state engendered by certain creations of man, there are no physical or technical limitations on what can be art. There are no rules that theatre must use words, that paintings must be illusionistic or nonillusionistic, that music must be harmonic, and so forth. Anything that an artist presents as having experiential significance is considered art.

L. Moholy-Nagy

The Function of Art

Art is the most complex, vitalizing, and civilizing of human actions. Thus it is of biological necessity. Art sensitizes man to the best that is immanent in him through an intensified expression involving many layers of experience. Out of them art forms a unified manifestation, like dreams which are composed of the most diverse source material subconsciously crystallized. It tries to produce a balance of the social, intellectual, and emotional existence; a synthesis of attitudes and opinions, fears and hopes.

Art has two faces, the biological and the social, the one toward the individual and the other toward the group. By expressing fundamental validities and common problems, art can produce a feeling of coherence. This is its social function which leads to a cultural synthesis as well as to a continuation of human civilization.[1]

Today, lacking the patterning and refinement of emotional impulses through the arts, uncontrolled, inarticulate and brutally destructive ways of release have become commonplace. Unused energies, subconscious frustrations, create the psychopathic borderline cases of neurosis. Art as expression of the individual can be a remedy by sublimation of aggressive impulses. Art educates the receptive faculties and it revitalizes the creative abilities. In this way art is rehabilitation therapy through which confidence in one's creative power can be restored.

Reprinted from *Vision in Motion* (Theobald, 1946), by permission of Hattula Moholy-Nagy. Copyright © 1947 by Sibyl Moholy-Nagy, Chicago.

L. MOHOLY-NAGY

THE "PROFESSIONAL" ARTIST

The best representatives of the arts whether in music, poetry, sculpture, or painting, even in their single works, always express the spiritual state of the age. Today a painting or a sonata is a tightly woven fabric of which the historic warp may often disappear under the richly textured modern yarns of the weft. Nevertheless, the soundness of the weave is dependent on both. The contemporary artist organizes his work within this given historical and cultural framework, but he derives his subject matter from his social and spiritual interests. These are expressed in different periods with different means and themes, such as a still-life, a portrait, a landscape, or an abstraction, all possessing a sensory directness as well as freedom, order, and harmony which are among the organic qualities of art. On the other hand the intensity of the artist's work is dependent upon the uniqueness of his purpose and his ability of transference. Thus the professional artist's solutions are dependent upon the existing body of knowledge in addition to the socio-biological components. But if he wishes to stir his audience and appeal to his senses, he has to create powerful new relationships. He can do so either by developing tendencies or by opposing them. The gradual elimination of the still existing feudal residues, that is, obsolete economic theories, obsolete patterns of individual behavior, obsolete sexual and family relationships is not an automatic matter.

It is unimaginable that, along with the economists, philosophers and politicians who advance suggestions for social changes, the most intuitive and responsive people in a society, namely, the artists, have no say. Tyranny and dictatorship, manifestos and decrees will not recast the mentality of the people. The unconscious but direct influence of art represents a better means of persuasion for conditioning people to a new society either by its projective or satiric-destructive means.

The true artist is the grindstone of the senses; he sharpens eyes, mind, and feeling; he interprets ideas and concepts through his own media. In the midst of vast social controversies he cannot escape that task. He has to take sides and proclaim his stand; indeed the artist has a formative ideological function, otherwise his work would be only an exercise of skill in composition. Hitler was aware of this. He propagandized trash; he tried to destroy modern art, science, and philosophy as the greatest sources of opposition to his vicious system of oppression. He banned the contemporary, the "degenerate" art, as he called it from the galleries and museums, burned books, and forbade the teaching of Einstein's theories.

He sensed that the content of art is basically not different from the content of our other utterances. The only difference is that art is produced mainly by subconscious organization of the means implicit in the cultural and social setting of the period. To be sure, there are numerous opportunities for expression and research in all fields but among them only a few which are positively related and favored by the dynamic forces of the age. In intuitively choosing certain esthetic or technical problems, the most sensitive and advanced artist is a tool for the recording of the time-expressive contents. That is, form and structure denote definite spiritual trends. The work of the artist corresponds to the creative problems in other fields, complementing them in the structure of civilization of that particular period.

Art may press for the sociobiological solution of problems just as energetically as the social revolutionaries do through political action. The so-called "unpolitical" approach of art is a fallacy. Politics, freed from graft, party connotations, or more transitory tactics, is mankind's method of realizing ideas for the welfare of the community. Such a "weltanschauung" is transformed by the arts into emotional form, and becomes retroactive in the realm of the conscious existence. This suggests that not only the conscious but also the subconscious mind absorbs social ideas which are then expressed in the specific media of the arts.[2] Otherwise any problem could be successfully solved only through intellectual or verbal discourse. The difficulty lies in mass participation. The masses are filled with a petit bourgeois ideology, the masculine superman ideal promoted by papers and radios, books and films —by the unofficial education which the people have been taught to enjoy in spite of lip service to casual revolutionary political ideas. Once their sensitivity is killed, they are unable to receive the message of art whether contemporary or old.

The success theory of the profit economy pays a high premium to the anti-artist. Artists are considered effeminates who do not have the stamina to participate in competition. This is not only untrue, as are most clichés, but tragic since at present art is perhaps the only field where convention does not completely suppress sentiment and where the omnipotence of thought and the independence of emotion are kept relatively intact. To follow the divining rod of intuition and expressive desire may often act as a psychological life-saver especially in periods of hidden and open suppression of independent thought. The phrase that "the artist represents the consciousness and memory of his time" is a good characterization of his function. No society can exist without expressing its ideas, and no culture and no ethics can survive without participation of the artist who cannot be bribed.

Art represents the uncensored statement of its author; this is one of its most positive characteristics. No one but the painter, the author, the composer is the sole master of his performance. The simpler his medium and the less investment it involves, the easier it is to avoid possible censorship and to preserve the ways of genuinely free expression.

Through his sensitivity the artist becomes the seismograph of events and movements pertaining to the future. He interprets the yet hazy path of coming developments by grasping the dynamics of the present and by freeing himself from momentary motivations and transitory influences but without evaluating their trends. He is interested only in the recording and communicating of his vision. This is what materializes in his art. He cannot misuse such a situation. To be a "fulltime" worker, a "professional," involves a moral responsibility. This is why the secured existence of the uncompromising and incorruptible artist is so important to society. If he does not have adequate tools and materials, he cannot produce his best. His records cannot be fluid and direct if he cannot consecrate his life to constant work in his craft, if he has to fight for minimum subsistence.

The silly myth that the genius has to "suffer" is the sly excuse of a society which does not care for its productive members unless their work promises immediate technological or economic applications with calculable profit.

ART AND SCIENCE

The task of the professional artist is not only to vitalize people but also to continue and synthetize spiritual traits. For this, besides the unconscious elements, he must have conscious source material, sound scientific outlook though not necessarily a method. But most people educated in the liberal arts, and frightened by badly taught mathematics and physics, have an awed respect for science in any of its possible interpretations. Because of this fear, they are suspicious of an art which uses elements reminiscent of geometrical shapes, synthetic materials, and optical instruments.

In popular short-cut theories there is the problem of "chaotic nature" versus "organized machine"; sober science versus mystical religion; social planning against free enterprise. This is oversimplification. The eyes of the artist record cows and dynamos, trees and skyscrapers equally well. They represent visual raw material for him. And this is the real issue. The actual aim is sociobiological synthesis. This cannot be acheived without "laboratory experimentation," though this is another objection to contemporary art, voiced often by the layman. But without experimentation there can be no discoveries and without discoveries no regeneration. Although the "research work" of the artist is rarely as "systematic" as that of the scientist they both may deal with the whole of life, in terms of relationships, not of details. In fact, the artist today does so more consistently than the scientist, because with each of his works he faces the problem of the interrelated whole while only a few theoretical scientists are allowed this "luxury" of a total vision. The main difference between the problems of artist and those of scientist is the difference in the form of their materialization and grasp. Plastic art is expressed with means largely comprehensible by sensory experiences on a nonverbal level. Even if, as in old paintings, the creative impetus is screened by the logical presentation of a describable theme, it is not the landscape or still-life that results in art, but the creative act by which the subject matter is transmuted into visual form. On the other hand, a scientific discourse is stated in rational intellectual terms even if the impulse to it comes from subconscious regions of the intuition. On the basis of sentimental education, many still believe that the emotional depth of the artist will be endangered by the attempt to organize his elements consciously. But the artist ought not to be afraid of conscious traits in his work, as the conscious approach will be translated by him into terms affecting the senses. The conscious problems of research are on a rather modest scale anyhow, overshadowed by the intuitive forces and the subconscious mechanism of expression. In every art work there remains a great number of components which cannot be verbalized, only approached intuitively. Even product designs executed with a largely conscious approach generally answer more questions than their producers originally expected they could. The reason is that so far product designs have shown the most obvious integration of intuition and science, form and function. Their analysis can sometimes be helpful in giving more effective information; it may stimulate new techniques in the subconscious transubstantiation of such information. Analysis can eliminate also the repetition of overused elements and create an inner security for new solutions.

L. Moholy-Nagy

Space-Time Problems

Social conditions, the arts, sciences, the development of an industrial technology with prefabrication, new materials, and new processes are the determining factors to realize the new architectural development. From them the architect and planner will draw inspiration and factual knowledge, resulting in a changed conception of space. Every great period in human civilization organically creates its particular spatial conception. Though such space conceptions were utilized in the construction of shelter, they were also frameworks for the articulation of visual arts, play, dancing, lighting; in fact, for the mastery of life in every detail.

The history of articulated space, the special space conceptions of different periods, have been determined by the grasp of one, two, three or more dimensions.

The magnificence of the Egyptian temple could be comprehended by walking through a basically one-dimensional straight line, the sphinx alley, leading towards its facade.

Later the Greek architects of the Acropolis designed a two-dimensional approach to the temple so that the visitors had to move through the Propylaen, between the Erechteion and Parthenon, around the colonnades toward the main entrance.

The gothic cathedral also applied this concept most intriguingly to the

Reprinted from *Vision in Motion* (Theobald, 1946), by permission of Hattula Moholy-Nagy. Copyright © 1947 by Sibyl Moholy-Nagy, Chicago.

interior. The spectator was placed in the midst of the nave, vaults, balcony, and choir, and became the center of coordinated space cells of all directions.

The renaissance and the baroque brought man into closer contact with the inside and outside of the building. Apart from the "hanging gardens" of Semiramis and the Moorish-Spanish architecture, these were man's first attempts to integrate building and nature, not merely fit building into its surroundings. In our age of airplanes architecture is viewed not only frontally and from the sides, but also from above—vision in motion. The bird's-eye-view, and its opposites, the worm's and fish-eye-views, have become a daily experience. Architecture appears no longer static but, if we think of it in terms of airplanes and motor cars, architecture is linked with movement. The helicopter, for example, may change the entire aspect of town and regional planning so that a formal and structural congruence with the new elements, time and speed, will manifest itself.

Already the great spans of large airplane hangars require a new departure for space articulation since the columns, which former architecture used as a most effective means in modulating and articulating space, have been eliminated. But the problem of space articulation in contemporary architecture is a simple affair in comparison with the complex problems of planning for a new space comprehension caused by the infinite acceleration of speed.

RENDERING MOTION (SPACE-TIME) ON THE STATIC PLANE

Motion in space can be grasped if its reality is perceptible through the senses. Difficulties arise only if illusionist motion has to be perceived, as in the cubist paintings which rendered objects as if the spectator were moving around them.

These interpretations of vision in motion denote not only an artistic achievement but also an important practical step in visual perception as well as in the skill of rendering. The mass construction of war planes, for instance, called for complex working instructions. But the workers could not comprehend their tasks through references contained in the customary blueprints. Factories had to resort to new methods of visualization called *production illustration* mainly derived from the findings of contemporary painters, photographers, and motion picture men, all of whom tried to translate the space-time sequence of production into a visually perceivable language. In this way a speeding up of the work was accomplished. This process is only in its infancy. Photomontage, superimpositions, diagrams, explosion, phantom, x-ray, cut-away techniques, stroboscopic motion projections, and other combinations may enlarge its scope tremendously.

SPEED

Motion, accelerated to high speed, changes the appearance of the objects and makes it impossible to grasp their details. There is clearly recognizable difference between the visual experience of a pedestrian and a driver in viewing objects. The motor car driver or airplane pilot can bring distant and unrelated landmarks into spatial relationships unknown to the pedestrian. The difference is produced by the changed perception caused by the various speeds, vision in motion. To prove this Jean Carlu, the eminent French poster designer, made an experiment in 1937. He mounted two posters on two conveyor belts which moved at different speeds. The one poster, made by Toulouse-Lautrec around 1900, was moved at six to seven miles per hour (approximately the speed of a horse and buggy); the other, a contemporary poster, was moved at fifty miles per hour (the speed of an automobile). Both posters could be read easily. Then Carlu accelerated the speed of the Toulouse-Lautrec up to fifty miles per hour, and at this speed the poster could be seen only as a blur. The implications are obvious. The artist, architect, advertising and display man, must count with the quickly moving vehicles requiring a new orientation toward spatial organization and communication. A new viewpoint in the visual arts is a natural consequence of this age of speed which has to consider the moving eye. (And what an improvement it would be if the signmakers of streets and highways were also aware of this fact.)

Jean Labatu (Princeton University) had the task of preparing effective outdoor advertising for a factory site half a mile long, situated along a highway with heavy motor traffic. Studying the problem, he found that the required water displays, fountains, light, even the shape of the pool which had to mirror the buildings, had to be related to the speed, that is, the rapidly changing position of the spectator at the wheel. On the basis of calculations as to time and vista, he suggested a "time-facade." It consisted of continuous mobile light and water displays placed so that they could be perfectly seen in thirty to sixty seconds, the time it took a car to drive along the site at thirty to sixty miles per hour. Such an approach translates the static meaning of advertising into a kinetic process, "shooting at a moving target."

Photography, motion pictures, the speed studies of futurism and cubism handled such aspects intuitively, anticipating the vision in motion of a motorized world long before an actual need existed for a new visual education based upon scientific standards. Safe air travel, for instance, is greatly dependent upon the skill and visual alertness of pilot and navigator. Their vision in motion—especially at landing—the flashquick ability to identify small details within vast areas, has to be conditioned to the new validities of speed since even radar or other mechanical equipment can fail.

ANALYSIS OF SPEED

Speed itself can become the subject of a visual analysis. We know of innumerable photographic shots of arrested motion such as sport scenes, jumps, and dives. On the other hand we can observe slowly unfolding buds, moving clouds taken at intervals; similarly the effect of time exposures of moving objects on streets and merry-go-rounds. Experiencing speed that can be arrested, rendered, stretched and compressed, in short, articulated, we can state that we have possession of it, that we are approaching a new vocabulary of space-time.

Harold Edgerton (M.I.T.) found a new way to render speed in stroboscopic photography.[1] The relationship between the velocities of the dissected movements gave him the clue to improving the action of golfers, turbines, spinning wheels and various kinds of machinery. These pictures are juxtaposed details of frozen movements analyzable and in relationship to each other and the whole cycle of motion. They clearly show that space-time can not only be articulated but also employed as a means of expression. These speed photographs are of more recent date, but they are astonishingly similar to futuristic paintings. In fact, they are their exact repetitions: for example, *Dog on the Leash,* 1912; *Speed,* 1913, both by Balla; *Nude Descending a Staircase,* 1912, by Marcel Duchamp. They all show the same juxtaposition of frozen movement.

The problem of futurism is similar to that of cubism. The difference is that cubism takes to motion as a means of better grasp of the object in space; futurism is interested in motion for the sake of motion. Although both used superimpositions, most of the futurist paintings seem merely a new naturalism beside the spatial sophistication of cubism.

Around 1910 the futurists had begun to emphasize movements, saying, "The world's splendor has been enriched by a new beauty—the beauty of speed. . . . " "We shall sing," they continued, "of the man at the steering wheel. . . . Who can still believe in the opacity of bodies since our sharpened and multiplied sensitiveness has penetrated the obscure manifestations of the medium? Why should we forget in our creation the double power of our sight, capable of giving results analogous to those of the x-rays?" Umberto Boccioni in *Power of the Street*, 1912, projected such a double power of sight and such a fusion of the manifold elements of a street, into one simultaneous, expressive representation. Pablo Picasso did the same in the mural of the bombing of Guernica, the Basque city. The painting is a monument of human torment and a powerful symbol of the agony of the heroic Spanish loyalists. Visiting him in 1937, before the painting was placed in the Spanish Pavilion at the Paris World's Fair, he said that he had attempted to render *"the inside and outside* of a room simultaneously."

Among the Guernica studies which Picasso made there are a number of drawings that record not only the space-time visualization of the successive changes of physical motion, but also the psychological space-time, the emotional metamorphosis caused by horror in the doomed creatures.

In the old arts, horror was usually rendered through the distortion of the facial muscles, distortion of the open mouth, by enlarged and protruding eyeballs. Picasso intensified this approach by moving and distorting the usually immovable and undistortable elements of the body, such as the eyes, ears, and nose. In *Guernica* he shifted the eyes away from their normal position; he turned the ears upside down. In the studies for the mural he transformed the eye into a cup and the lower eyelid into a saucer from which tears poured. He exposed the tongue of a screaming, horror-stricken victim as a flame, at other times as a dagger to signify despair. In one of these studies he showed a dozen variations of a face, changing the profile of a young mother under the impact of unspeakable suffering—into the distorted, crumbled features of an old woman. This was done through interweaving the features of a panicky, quickly aging, hideous creature, each expression growing out of the other without breaking the oneness. The same etching, if looked at upside down, solved the enigma by displaying the deteriorated, piggish visage of Hitler, the cause of the bestial destruction. The old technique of the trashy "double image" postcards was used here with unusual subtlety to make the psychological space-time as transparent as an x-ray photograph.

TRANSPARENCY AND LIGHT

The passion for transparencies is one of the most spectacular features of our time. In x-ray photos, structure becomes transparency and transparency manifests structure. The x-ray pictures, to which the futurist has consistently referred, are among the outstanding space-time renderings on the static plane. They give simultaneously the inside and outside, the view of an opaque solid, its outline, but also its inner structure. They have to be studied to reveal their meaning; but once the student has learned their language, he will find them indispensable. In my pictures I have tried to follow this line of space-time articulation by painting on waterclear, transparent plastics, introducing direct light effects, mobile reflections and shadows, indicating a trend away from the static pigmentation of surfaces toward a kinetic "light painting." The problem is only how to control these colored "light paintings" with the same precision as the painter of yesterday controlled the effects of his pigments.

PHOTOGRAPHIC PRACTICE

Different space and time levels usually appear in photographic rendering as superimpositions. The reflections and transparent mirrorings of the passing traffic in the windows of motor cars or shops are one example. Mirroring means in this sense the changing aspects of vision, the sharpened identification of inside and outside penetrations. In such renderings there is a blending of independent elements or events into a coherent whole. Superimpositions of photographs and distortion by reflection, as frequently seen in motion pictures, can be applied as a new visual language to represent dreams, acting as a space-time symbol, even synonym.

Photomontage has a similar connotation. The final effect is a synopsis of actions, composed of originally unrelated space and time elements juxtaposed and fused into a unity.

A cameraless picture (photogram) can also be understood as vision in motion since it is a diagram of the motion of life, creating the space-time continuum which literally is the photogram.[2]

* * * * *

We are heading toward a kinetic, time-spatial existence; toward an awareness of the forces plus their relationships which define all life and of which we had no previous knowledge and for which we have as yet no exact terminology. The affirmation of all these space-time forces involves a reorientation of all our faculties.

Space-time stands for many things: relativity of motion and its measurement, integration, simultaneous grasp of the inside and outside, revelation of the structure instead of the facade. It also stands for a new vision concerning materials, energies, tensions, and their social implications.

This conception is still unpredictable in its consequences for the improvement of the affairs of mankind though the artist as well as the designer already experiment with it on a new level of consciousness. The designer has to think in terms of integrated processes of materials and production, sales, distribution, financing, and advertising; the contemporary artist consciously or intuitively tries to express the substance of his specialized field as the result of forces in space and time and to integrate it with the social reality. He prepares a new and creative vision for the masses, and with it a new orientation for a healthier life plan. But in order to benefit society, the artist's work must penetrate everyone's daily existence.

Marshall McLuhan

The Relation of Environment to Anti-Environment

Under the heading that "What exists is likely to be misallocated" Peter Drucker in *Managing for Results* discusses the structure of social situations. "Business enterprise is not a phenomenon of nature but one of society. In a social situation, however, events are not distributed according to the normal distribution of a natural universe (that is, they are not distributed according to the bell-shaped Gaussian curve). In a social situation a very small number of events *at one extreme*—the first 10 percent to 20 percent at most—account for 90 percent of all results; whereas the great majority of events accounts for 10 percent or so of the results." What Drucker is presenting here is the environment as it presents itself for human attention and action. He is confronting the phenomenon of the imperceptibility of the environment as such. It is this factor that Edward T. Hall also tackles in *The Silent Language*. The ground rules, the pervasive structure, the overall pattern eludes perception except insofar as there is an anti-environment or a counter-situation constructed to provide a means of direct attention. Paradoxically, the 10 percent of the typical situation that Drucker designates as the area of effective cause and as the area of opportunity, this small factor is the environment. The 90 percent area is the area of problems generated by the active power of the 10 percent environment. For the environment is an active process pervading and impinging upon all the components of the situation. It is easy to illustrate this.

Any new technology, any extension or amplification of human faculties

Reprinted from *Windsor University Review* (1966), by permission of the author.

when given material embodiment, tends to create a new environment. This is as true of clothing as of speech, or script, or wheel. This process is more easily observed in our own time when several new environments have been created. To take only the latest one, TV, we find a handful of engineers and technicians in the 10 percent area, as it were, creating a set of radical changes in the **90 percent of daily life. The new TV environment is an electric circuit that takes as its content the earlier environment, the photograph and the movie in particular. It is in the interplay between the old and the new environments that there is generated an innumerable series of problems and confusions. They extend all the way from how to allocate the time of children and adults to the problem of pay-TV and TV in the classroom. The new medium of TV as an environment creates new occupations. As an environment, it is imperceptible except in terms of its content. That is, all that is seen or noticed is the old environment, the movie. But even the effects of TV on the movie go unnoticed, and the effects of the TV environment in altering the entire character of human sensibility and sensory ratios is completely ignored.**

The content of any system or organization naturally consists of the preceding system or organization, and in that degree acts as a control on the new environment. It is useful to notice all of the arts and sciences as acting in the role of anti-environments that enable us to perceive the environment. In a business civilization we have long considered liberal study as providing necessary means of orientation and perception. When the arts and sciences themselves become environments under conditions of electric circuitry, conventional liberal studies, whether in the arts or sciences, will no longer serve as an anti-environment. When we live in a museum without walls, or have music as a structural part of our sensory environment, new strategies of attention and perception have to be created. When the highest scientific knowledge creates the environment of the atom bomb, new controls for the scientific environment have to be discovered, if only in the interest of survival.

The structural examples of the relation of environment to anti-environment need to be multiplied as a means of understanding the principles of perception and activity involved. The Balinese say: "We have no art—we do everything as well as possible." This is not an ironic but a merely factual remark. In a preliterate society art serves as a means of merging the individual and the environment, not as a means of training perception upon the environment. Archaic or primitive art looks to us like a magical control built into the environment. Thus to put the artifacts from such a culture into a museum or anti-environment is an act of nullification rather than of revelation. Today what is called *Pop Art* is the use of some object in our own daily environment as if it were anti-environmental. Pop Art serves to remind us, however, that we have fashioned for ourselves a world of artifacts and images that are intended not to train perception or awareness but to insist that we merge with them as the primitive man merges with his environment. The world of modern advertising is a magical environment constructed to produce effects for the total economy but not designed to increase human awareness. We have designed schools as anti-environments to develop the perception and judgment of the printed word. There are no means of training provided to develop similar perception and judgment of any of the new environments created by electric circuitry. This is not accidental. From the **development of phonetic script until the invention of the electric telegraph** human technology had tended strongly towards the furtherance of detachment and objectivity, detribalization and individuality. Electric circuitry has quite the contrary effect. It involves in depth. It merges the individual and the mass environment. To create an anti-environment for such electric technology would seem to require a technological extension of consciousness itself. The awareness and opposition of the individual are in these circumstances as irrelevant as they are futile.

The structural features of environment and anti-environment appear in the age-old clash between professionalism and amateurism, whether in sport or in studies. Professional sport is environmental and amateur sport is anti-environmental. Professional sport fosters the merging of the individual in the mass and in the patterns of the total environment. Amateur sport seeks rather the development of critical awareness of the individual and, most of all, critical awareness of the ground rules of the society as such. The same contrast exists for studies. The professional tends to specialize and to merge his being uncritically in the mass. The ground rules provided by the mass response of his colleagues serve as a pervasive environment of which he is uncritical and unaware.

The party system of government affords a familiar image of the relations of environment and anti-environment. The government as environment needs the opposition as anti-environment in order to be aware of itself. The role of the opposition would seem to be that of the arts and sciences in creating perception. As the government environment becomes more cohesively involved in a world of instant information, opposition would seem to become increasingly necessary but also intolerable. Opposition begins to assume the rancorous and hostile character of a Dew Line, or a Distant Early Warning System. It is important, however, to consider the role of the arts and sciences as Early Warning Systems in the social environment. The models of perception provided in the arts and sciences alike can serve as indispensable means of orientation to future problems well before they become troublesome.

The legend of Humpty-Dumpty would seem to suggest a parallel to the 10 to 90 percent distribution of causes and effects. The impact that resulted in his fall brought into play a massive response from the social bureaucracy. But all the king's horses and all the king's men could not put Humpty-Dumpty back together again. They could not recreate the old environment, they could only create a new one. Our typical response to a disrupting new technology is to recreate the old environment instead of heeding the new opportunities of the new environment. Failure to notice the new opportunities is also failure to understand the new powers. This means that we fail to develop the necessary controls or anti-environments for the new environment. This failure leaves us in the role of automata merely.

W. T. Easterbrook has done extensive exploration of the relations of bureaucracy and enterprise, discovering that as soon as one becomes the environment, the other becomes an anti-environment. They seem to bicycle along through history alternating their roles with all the dash and vigor of tweedle-dum and tweedle-dee. In the eighteenth century when realism became a new method in literature, what happened was that the external environment was put in the place of anti-environment. The ordinary world was given the role of art object by Daniel Defoe and others. The environment began to be used as a perceptual probe. It became self-conscious. It became an "anxious object" instead of being an unperceived and pervasive pattern. Environment used as probe or art object is satirical because it draws attention to itself. The romantic poets extended this technique to external nature transforming nature into an art object. Beginning with Baudelaire and Rimbaud and continuing in Hopkins and Eliot and James Joyce, the poets turned their attention to language as a probe. Long used as an environment, language became an instrument of exploration and research. It became an environment. It became Pop Art.

The artist as a maker of anti-environments permits us to perceive that much is newly environmental and therefore most active in transforming situations. This would seem to be why the artist has, in many circles in the past century, been called the enemy, the criminal. It helps to explain why news has a natural bias toward crime and bad news. It is this kind of news that enables us to perceive our world. The detective since Poe's Dupin has tended to be a probe, an artist of the big town, an artist-enemy, as it were. Conventionally, society is always one phase back, is never environmental. Paradoxically, it is the antecedent environment that is always being upgraded for our attention. The new environment always uses the old environment as its material.

In the Spring 1965 issue of the *Varsity Grad* Glenn Gould discusses the effects of recorded music on performance and composition. One of his main points is that as recorded music creates a new environment the audience in effect becomes participant both in performance and in composition. This is a reversal or chiasmus of form that occurs in any situation where an environment is pushed up into high intensity or high definition by technological change. A reversal of characteristics occurs as in the case with bureaucracy and enterprise. An environment is naturally of low intensity or low definition. That is why it escapes observation. Anything that raises the environment to high intensity, whether it be a storm in nature or violent change resulting from a new technology, such high intensity turns the environment into an object of attention. When an environment becomes an object of attention it assumes the character of an anti-environment or an art object. When the social environment is stirred up to exceptional intensity by technological change and becomes a focus of much attention, we apply the terms *war* and *revolution*. All the components of *war* are present in any environment whatever. The recognition of war depends upon their being stepped up to high definition.

Under electric conditions of instant information movement both the concept and the reality of war become manifest in many of the situations of daily life. We have long been accustomed to war as that which goes on between publics or nations. Publics and nations were the creation of print technology. With electric circuitry the publics and nations became the content of the new technology: "The mass audience is not a public as environment but a public as content of a new electric environment." And whereas "the public" as an environment created by print technology consisted of separate individuals with varying points of view, the mass audience consists of the same individuals involved in depth in one another and involved in the creative process of the art or educational situation that is presented to them. Art and education were presented to the *public* as consumer packages for their instruction and edification. The new mass audience is involved immediately in art and education as participants and co-creators rather than as consumers. Art and education become new forms of experience, new environments, rather than new anti-environments. Pre-electric art and education were anti-environments in the sense that they were the content of various environments. Under electric conditions the content tends however towards becoming environmental itself. This was the paradox that Malraux found in *The Museum Without Walls*, and that Glenn Gould finds in recorded music. Music in the concert hall had been an anti-environment. The same music when recorded is *music without halls,* as it were.

Another paradoxical aspect of this change is that when music becomes environmental by electric means, it becomes more and more the concern of the private individual. By the same token and complementary to the same paradox the pre-electric music of the concert hall (the music when there was a public instead of a mass audience) was a corporate ritual for the group rather than the individual. This paradox extends to all electrical technology whatever. The same means which permit, for example, a universal and centralized thermostat do in effect encourage a private thermostat for individual manipulation. The age of the mass audience is thus far more individualistic than the preceding age of the *public*. It is this paradoxical dynamic that confuses every issue about "conformity" today and "separatism" and "integration." Profoundly contradictory actions and directions prevail in all of these situations. This is not surprising in an age of circuitry succeeding the age of the wheel. The feedback loop plays all sorts of tricks to confound the single plane and one-way direction of thought and action as they had been constituted in the pre-electric age of the machine.

Applying the above to the Negro question, one could say that the agrarian South has long tended to regard the Negro as environmental. As such, the Negro is a challenge, a threat, a burden. The very phrase *white supremacy* quite as much as the phrase *white trash* registers this environmental attitude. The environment is the enemy that must be subdued. To the rural man the conquest of Nature is an unceasing challenge. It is the Southerner who contributed the cowboy to the frontier. The Virginian, the archetypal cowboy as it were, confronts the environment as a hostile, natural force. To man on the frontier, other men are environmental and hostile. By contrast, to the townsmen, men appear not as environmental, but as content of the urban environment.

Parallel to the Negro question is the French Canada problem. The English Canadians have been the environment of French Canada since the railway and Confederation. However, since the telegraph and radio and television, French Canada and English Canada alike have become the content of this new technology. Electric technology is totally environmental for all human communities today. Hence the great confusion arising from the transformation environments into anti-environments, as it were. All the earlier groupings that had constituted separate environments before electricity have now become anti-environments or the content of the new technology. As such, the old unconscious environments tend to become increasingly centres of acute awareness. The content of any new environment is just as unperceived as the old one had been initially. As a merely automatic sequence, the succession of environments and of the dramatics thereto appertaining, tend to be rather tiresome, if only because the audience is very prone to participate in the dramatics with an enthusiasm proportioned to its unawareness. In the electric age all former environments whatever become anti-environments. As such the old environments are transformed into areas of self-awareness and self-assertion, guaranteeing a very lively interplay of forces.

Eric Havelock in his book *Preface to Plato* has clarified the stages by which the written word served to detribalize the Greek world. After the tribal encyclopedia of oral and memorized wisdom, writing enabled man to organize knowledge by categories and classifications; what Plato called the *ideas*. With the origin of classified data, or visual organization of knowledge, there came also representation in the arts. Representation is itself a form of matching or classifying, unknown to preliterate or native artists. Today we return to nonobjective art, nonrepresentational art, because in the electric age we are leaving the world of visual organization of experience.

The visual sense, alone of our senses, creates the forms of space and time that are uniform, continuous and connected. Euclidean space is the prerogative of visual and literate man. With the advent of electric circuitry and the instant movement of information, Euclidean space recedes and the non-Euclidean geometries emerge. Lewis Carroll, the Oxford mathematician, was perfectly aware of this change in our world when he took Alice through the looking glass into the world where each object creates its own space and conditions. To the visual or Euclidean man, objects do not create time and space. They are merely fitted into time and space. The idea of the world as an environment that is more or less fixed, is very much the product of literacy and visual assumptions. In his book *The Philosophical Impact of Modern Physics* Milic Capek explains some of the strange confusions in the scientific mind that result from the encounter of the old non-Euclidean spaces of pre-literate man with the Euclidean and Newtonian spaces of literate man. The scientists of our time are just as confused as the philosophers, or the teachers, and it is for the reason that Whitehead assigned; they still have the illusion that the new developments are to be fitted into the old space or environment.

One of the most obvious areas of change in the arts of our time has not only been the dropping of representation, but the dropping of the story line. In poetry, in the novel, in the movie, narrative continuity has yielded to thematic variation. Such variation in place of story line or melodic line has always been the norm in native societies. It is now becoming the norm in our own society and for the same reason, namely that we are becoming a non-visual society.

In the age of circuitry, or feedback, fragmentation and specialism tend to yield to integral forms of organization. Humpty-Dumpty tends to go back together again. The bureaucratic efforts of all the king's horses and all the king's men were naturally calculated to keep Humpty-Dumpty from ever getting together again. The Neolithic age, the age of the planter after the age of the hunter, was an age of specialism and division of labor. It has reached a somewhat startling terminus with the advent of electric circuitry. Circuitry is a profoundly decentralizing process. Paradoxically, it was the wheel and mechanical innovation that created centralism. The circuit reverses the characteristics of the wheel, just as xerography reverses the characteristics of the printing press. Before printing, the scribe, the author, and the reader tended to merge. With printing, author and publisher became highly specialized and centralized forms of action. With xerography, author, and publisher, and reader tend to merge once more. Whereas the printed book had been the first mass-produced product, creating uniform prices and markets, xerography tends to restore the custom-made book. Writing and publishing tend to become services of a corporate and inclusive kind. The printed word created the Public. The Public consists of separate individuals, each with his own point of view. Electric circuitry does not create a Public. It creates the Mass. The Mass does not consist of separate individuals, but of individuals profoundly involved in one another. This involvement is a function, not of numbers, but of speed. The daily newspaper is an interesting example of this fact. The items in the daily press are totally discontinuous and totally unconnected. The only unifying feature of the press is the date line. Through that date line the reader must go, as Alice went, "through the looking glass." If it is not today's date line, he cannot get in. Once he goes through the date line, he is involved in a world of items for which he, the reader, must write a story line. He makes the news, as the reader of a detective story makes the plot.

Just as the printed press created the Public as a new environment, so does each new technology or extension of our physical powers tend to create new environments. In the age of information, it is information itself that becomes environmental. The satellites and antennae projected from our planet, for example, have transformed the planet from being an environment into being a probe. This is a transformation that the artists of the past century have been explaining to us in their endless experimental models. Modern art, whether in painting, or poetry, or music, began as a probe and not as a package. The symbolists literally broke up the old packages and put them into our hands as probes. And whereas the package belongs to a consumer age, the probe belongs to an age of experimenters.

One of the peculiarities of art is to serve as an anti-environment, a probe that makes the environment visible. It is a form of symbolic, or parabolic, action. *Parable* means literally "to throw against," just as *symbol* means "to throw together." As we equip the planet with satellites and antennae, we tend to create new environments of which the planet is itself the content. It is peculiar to environments that they are complex processes that transform their content into archetypal forms. As the planet becomes the content of a new information environment, it also tends to become a work of art. Where railway and machine created a new environment for agrarian man, the old agrarian world became an art form. Nature became a work of art. The romantic movement was born. When the electric circuit went around the mechanical environments, the machine itself became a work of art. Abstract art was born.

As information becomes our environment, it becomes mandatory to program the environment itself as a work of art. The parallel to this appears in Jacques Ellul's *Propaganda* where he sees propaganda, not as an ideology or content of any medium, but as the operation of all the media at once. The mother tongue is propaganda because it exercises an effect on all the senses at once. It shapes our entire outlook and our ways of feeling. Like any other environment, its operation is imperceptible. When an environment is new, we perceive the old one for the first time. What we see on the late show is not TV, but old movies. When the emperor appeared in his new clothes, his courtiers did not see his nudity, they saw his old clothes. Only the small child and the artist have that immediacy of approach that permits perception of the environmental. The artist provides us with anti-environments that enable us to see the environment. Such anti-environmental means of perception must constantly be renewed in order to be efficacious. That basic aspect of the human condition by which we are rendered incapable of perceiving the environment is one to which psychologists have not even referred. In an age of accelerated change, the need to perceive the environment becomes urgent. Acceleration also makes such perception of the environment more possible. Was it not Bertrand Russell who said that if the bath water got only half a degree warmer every hour, we would never know when to scream? New environments reset our sensory thresholds. These, in turn, alter our outlook and expectations.

The need of our time is for the means of measuring sensory thresholds and of discovering exactly what changes occur in these thresholds as a result of the advent of any particular technology. With such knowledge in hand it would be possible to program a reasonable and orderly future for any human community. Such knowledge would be the equivalent of a thermostatic control for room temperatures. It would seem only reasonable to extend such controls to all the sensory thresholds of our being. We have no reason to be grateful to those who juggle the thresholds in the name of haphazard innovation.

Marcel Duchamp

Apropos of "Readymades"

IN 1913 I HAD THE HAPPY IDEA TO FASTEN A BICYCLE WHEEL TO A KITCHEN STOOL AND WATCH IT TURN.

A FEW MONTHS LATER I BOUGHT A CHEAP REPRODUCTION OF A WINTER EVENING LANDSCAPE, WHICH I CALLED *PHARMACY* AFTER ADDING TWO SMALL DOTS, ONE RED AND ONE YELLOW, IN THE HORIZON.

IN NEW YORK IN 1915 I BOUGHT AT A HARDWARE STORE A SNOW SHOVEL ON WHICH I WROTE "IN ADVANCE OF THE BROKEN ARM."

IT WAS AROUND THAT TIME THAT THE WORD *READYMADE* CAME TO MIND TO DESIGNATE THIS FORM OF MANIFESTATION.

A POINT WHICH I WANT VERY MUCH TO ESTABLISH IS THAT THE CHOICE OF THESE "READYMADES" WAS NEVER DICTATED BY ESTHETIC DELECTATION.

THIS CHOICE WAS BASED ON A REACTION OF VISUAL INDIFFERENCE WITH AT THE SAME TIME A TOTAL ABSENCE OF GOOD OR BAD TASTE . . . IN FACT A COMPLETE ANESTHESIA.

ONE IMPORTANT CHARACTERISTIC WAS THE SHORT SENTENCE WHICH I OCCASIONALLY INSCRIBED ON THE "READYMADE."

Talk delivered by Duchamp at the Museum of Modern Art, New York, October 19, 1961. Reprinted from *Art and Artists,* I/4 (July, 1966), by permission of the publisher.

93

MARCEL DUCHAMP

THAT SENTENCE INSTEAD OF DESCRIBING THE OBJECT LIKE A TITLE WAS MEANT TO CARRY THE MIND OF THE SPECTATOR TOWARDS OTHER REGIONS MORE VERBAL.

SOMETIMES I WOULD ADD A GRAPHIC DETAIL OF PRESENTATION WHICH IN ORDER TO SATISFY MY CRAVING FOR ALLITERATIONS, WOULD BE CALLED "READYMADE AIDED."

AT ANOTHER TIME WANTING TO EXPOSE THE BASIC ANTINOMY BETWEEN ART AND READYMADES I IMAGINED A "RECIPROCAL READYMADE": USE A REMBRANDT AS AN IRONING BOARD!

I REALIZED VERY SOON THE DANGER OF REPEATING INDISCRIMINATELY THIS FORM OF EXPRESSION AND DECIDED TO LIMIT THE PRODUCTION OF "READYMADES" TO A SMALL NUMBER YEARLY. I WAS AWARE AT THAT TIME, THAT FOR THE SPECTATOR EVEN MORE THAN FOR THE ARTIST, ART IS A HABIT-FORMING DRUG AND I WANTED TO PROTECT MY "READY-MADES" AGAINST SUCH CONTAMINATION.

ANOTHER ASPECT OF THE "READYMADE" IS ITS LACK OF UNIQUENESS . . . THE REPLICA OF A "READYMADE" DELIVERING THE SAME MESSAGE; IN FACT NEARLY EVERY ONE OF THE "READYMADES" EXISTING TODAY IS NOT AN ORIGINAL IN THE CONVENTIONAL SENSE.

A FINAL REMARK TO THIS EGOMANIAC'S DISCOURSE:

SINCE THE TUBES OF PAINT USED BY THE ARTIST ARE MANUFACTURED AND READY MADE PRODUCTS WE MUST CONCLUDE THAT ALL THE PAINTINGS IN THE WORLD ARE "READY-MADES AIDED" AND ALSO WORKS OF ASSEMBLAGE.

Morse Peckham

Art and Disorder

I

It is an honor and a privilege to have the opportunity to address the members of this division of the American Psychological Association and to submit my notions about art to their judgment. I daresay I am not far wrong if I think that, in spite of divergences of opinion, we are all in agreement that traditional philosophical aesthetics is hopelessly bankrupt. I feel quite sure that a good many of us have felt the frustration and bafflement of attempting to derive operational propositions from that aesthetics and to set up experiments based upon such propositions. Indeed, aesthetics seems to provide no directions even for the simple observation of human behavior when it can be categorized as artistic behavior. Nor, to make matters worse, can it provide any rules for determining when a human being is, or is not, engaged in artistic activity.

Happily, we are not alone. In recent years a number of philosophers have subjected traditional aesthetics to the most penetrating analysis and have arrived at uniformly negative results. Briefly, the denial of any validity to traditional aesthetics reduces itself to the denial of the basic assumption of all aesthetics: all works of art have something in common. Or, more precisely, the word *art* refers to a category all members of which have in common at least one attribute. If this is not the case, then it follows that traditional aesthetics collapses. And not only aesthetics. The theoretical and practical criticism of any of the arts of which I have any knowledge is full of sentences of the form: "Poetry is x"; "music is y"; "painting is z"; and so on. The fact that thousands of such sentences have been uttered by critics, that any num-

Delivered at the annual meeting of the American Psychological Association, September, 1966. First published in *Literature and Psychology*, XVI (Spring, 1966). Reprinted by permission from *The Triumph of Romanticism* (University of South Carolina Press, 1970). Copyright © 1966 by Leonard F. Manheim and Morton Kaplan. Copyright © 1970 by University of South Carolina Press.

ber of times critics of poetry have said, "At last we know what poetry really is," seems to discourage no one. They go right on making such statements, and the fact that no such statements have ever been widely or more than temporarily accepted never seems to suggest to them that there might be something radically wrong.

Nevertheless, in spite of the happy clearing of the air which is the result of the revelation of the logically unsound assumptions of aesthetics and criticism, a new and severe difficulty now appears. If "art" is not a valid category, then, strictly speaking, there is nothing to talk about. The category "art" collapses into the category "artifact." Or, if we shift ground to artistic behavior, whether of artist or perceiver, it collapses into all behavior. To talk about art at all involves the assumption that art can be distinguished from whatever is not art; but if all works of art have nothing in common, then it is impossible to make that distinction. To be sure, for psychologists, or even for critics and aestheticians, what the highest cultural level currently calls *art* is good enough. The psychologist has merely to say that he is investigating what his culture calls *art*. For him the term need not convey anything more. He still has a field of investigation. But when he wants to move outside of that particular culture, into, let us say, the cultural level in which comics and jokes and blue movies may or may not be art, he is in trouble. And he is in worse trouble when he wishes to move into societies other than his own, societies in which the term *art* does not exist. After all, in the current sense, it has existed in our culture for only a few hundred years. Paleolithic man had paintings, but are they art? Or rather, they are certainly art to us, if we want to call them art, but were they art to a people of whom we can reasonably be sure that they had no category "art"?

Nor is it satisfactory to talk about "artistic behavior." In some ways it helps a great deal to do so. It helps so much that I should like to assert at once that I myself am not interested in art but in artistic behavior. To me a work of art is the deposit or consequence of artistic behavior. But even this shift of reference leaves us worse off than before. The artifactual definition of art, even though only a matter of cultural convention, permits us to investigate whatever surviving from the past is currently called art, but we can scarcely investigate the artistic behavior of the Middle Ages, or even of yesterday. Clearly, if the term *art* is going to be of any use at all, we must find some way of distinguishing works of art from other surviving artifacts.

II

I cannot here give my argument in full, which is developed in my recently published book *Man's Rage for Chaos: Biology, Behavior, and the Arts* (1965). I can only offer my solution to this difficulty and explain what I mean by it. To begin with, not only do I assert that the only proper object of investigation is artistic behavior, but also that such behavior is most usefully considered as a social role, patterned, learned, culturally transmitted, governed by rules, and elicited by the semiotic stimuli of a particular class of situation. A work of art, then, is any artifact in the presence of which an individual plays a particular social role. Furthermore, a work of art is what the perceiver observes in what has been culturally established as an artistic perceiver's space. Thus Andy Warhol's piles of Brillo boxes are works of art because they are exhibited in an art gallery; the situation defines them as works of art, by eliciting in the observer the art perceiver's role. An assertion that such works are not works of art by an observer actually in such a culturally defined artistic space is itself an admission that they are art. That is, it has occurred to such a perceiver that they are. That he should deny what the situation tells him is so is of no importance. The denial of the high-status term *art* to a work we dislike is too common to be taken seriously. The point is that the question should arise. And that it should arise is itself an answer to the question.

Extending the role metaphor for human behavior, I go on to assert that a work of art may be defined as an occasion for a human being to perform the art-perceiving role in the artistic situation, that is, on the artistic stage. An artist is merely one whose social role it is to produce such occasions. As the recent rash of happenings has vividly demonstrated, the artist can produce anything so long as he can persuade his audience to play their art-perceiving roles. It is also obvious that some members of the audience will and some will not. As to why this should be so, I will return. In any case, with this definition of the artist we can dismiss him from further consideration. Clearly, he has to learn the perceiver's role before he can play the artist's role. But what kind of occasion he produces, his famed creativity, is no different from any other kind of cultural innovation. Artistic creativity presents no special problem, other than the problem as to why some people want to be artists. But that problem does not differ from the problem of why some people want to be policemen, or psychologists, or English teachers. All the tremendous amount of verbiage about the special problem of artistic creativity is, from this point of view, barking into an empty cave. It tells us something about the high status of the artist in our culture, but that is about all.

But we may go further than this, and proceed to what I call my final definition of a work of art. It is any perceptual field which an individual uses as an occasion for performing the role of art perceiver. A piece of driftwood placed upon a mantel becomes a work of art, because in our culture the mantelpiece has been conventionalized as an artistic space. But to the man who placed it there, it was a work of art as soon as, having found it on the beach, he perceived it as a work of art. Thus the Chinese placed interesting rocks in their gardens not in order to make them works of art but because they were works of art as soon as they decided that they were. The advantage of this position lies, for example, in its explanation of the confusion in traditional aesthetics between art and nature. A landscape is a work of art as soon as the individual decides to perform the art perceiver's role when he is looking at it. If he does not so decide, then it is not a work of art. And this accounts for the constant arguments in criticism as to whether a particular work should be accepted into the canon. For some people there may be something about it that makes it impossible for them to play the art perceiver's role.

On the basis of these definitions, it is possible, I think, to solve the conundrum of how we are to know whether or not a particular work was produced to be the occasion for the art perceiver's role, whether or not it functioned as a work of art in its particular culture. Any object, then, or perceptual field, from any culture, may be properly categorized as having been the occasion for artistic perception if a chronologically arranged sequence of such objects shows both functional identity and nonfunctional stylistic dynamism. I do not think I shall here arouse much antagonism if I assert that all behavior is styled, though in some critical and aesthetic circles such a statement would probably arouse intense disagreement. By *style* I mean this: all behavior is patterned, and patterns are stabilized and culturally transmitted because they are biological adaptations, or functional. But a behavioral pattern is, after all, a construct based upon innumerable unique percepts. It is apparent, then, that a functional pattern continues to be functional even though each individual exhibits unique variations of that pattern. That is, every pattern is styled. But even style is a construct, because in fact every recurrence of the individual's uniquely stylized performance of the pattern exhibits a novel configuration. Further, all behavioral patterning drifts. Not only is there the physiological limitation of the individual, but patterns must be transmitted by a semiotic or communication process, and any such transmission invariably involves loss both of content and of structure. Normally, an individual develops his unique style of performing a pattern and adheres pretty closely to it, although the limitations of memory and the exigencies of particular situations are responsible for a certain drift. After all, one of our tests for determining that an individual is disturbed is that his style, his way of performing cultural patterns, begins to disintegrate.

However, when we examine the behavior of artists, the producers of occasions for artistic perception, we find a striking difference. We find something more than drift; we find a dynamism. Let me give a couple of examples. The American axe handle is famous for the elegance and beauty of its curves as well as for its superior efficiency. The European axe handle is still a straight shaft. The reason is easy to find. Europe had few trees and a lot of people; America had a lot of trees and very few people. It was, therefore, adaptational to increase the man-hour productivity of the American tree-cutter by designing a more efficient axe handle. But the point is that once the new axe handle had been established, it remained unchanged. Its stylistic dynamism was functional.

The teakettle has had a different history. It took a long time to develop, but apparently by the end of the nineteenth century it had achieved functional perfection. The last change of importance was to make it of aluminum. Yet I daresay that among my readers there are a number of people young enough never to have seen the old-fashioned gooseneck teakettle. For along in the late 1930s the manufacturers of teakettles began to subject the teakettle to "design." The result is that it is now impossible to buy in any department store and almost any neighborhood store anything but a teakettle which is a handsome enough piece of sculpture but is also a functional disaster. You burn your fingers on the handle, and when you pour, the steam scalds your hand. The teakettle, like almost everything else in the modern kitchen, has become a work of art. Its sad fate is a salutary reminder that art can be a terrible nuisance. The teakettle, then, has exhibited in the past thirty years nonfunctional stylistic dynamism. As a tool it has become dysfunctional, though this is not to deny that artistic behavior has an adaptational function, but merely to assert that the tool function of an object, whether a teakettle or a religious painting, and its artistic function can be, and probably always are, incompatible. Lest my point should have been lost, let me repeat that any object, or perceptual field, from any culture may, then, be properly categorized as having been the occasion for artistic perception if a chronologically arranged sequence of such objects shows both functional identity and nonfunctional stylistic dynamism.

But it is possible to go further than this. It appears that we may categorize as a work of art any artifact or any perceptual field, if it can be placed in a sequence of similar objects or fields which shows a greater rate of dynamism than other such sequences from the same culture. If, moreover, we find a series of sequences ranging from a low rate of dynamism to a high rate, we may say that in that culture the last sequence was the occasion from the most intense and devoted artistic perception. The higher the rate of stylistic dynamism and the more frequent the stylistic revolutions, the higher the cultural level for which the art is being produced. Properly applied, this principle is a way of determining the cultural level for which a particular sequence was made; further, as an artistic style descends from the higher cultural level to the lower, its rate of stylistic dynamism slows down, and vice versa.

It appears, then, that art is, after all, a valid category, and that for the category art there is a defining attribute. But that attribute can never be located in a unique work of art, or a unique instance of artistic behavior, whether artist's or perceiver's, but only in a sequence of functionally identical artifacts or behavioral patterns. The commercial amphora of the ancient Mediterranean world remained virtually unchanged for centuries, but the amphorae used for banquets and other ceremonial occasions show all kinds of changes in both profile and decoration. The defining attribute of art, then, can only be located in functionally identical sequences of artifacts or behavioral patterns, and it is nonfunctional stylistic dynamism.

III

I think it may be said that the central interest of all human beings is to create a predictable world. This may be an explanation of why it is that behavioral patterns are transmitted with as much exactness as possible and why it is that unpredicted behavior in ourselves or others should be taken as a sign of behavioral crisis and should often bring about crisis in the observers of such behavior. It would certainly seem to be an explanation of why innovation is usually resisted. Or perhaps it is not an explanation but merely a tautological restatement. Certainly, it may be said with some confidence that the unpredictable person is precisely the socially useless person, and that the goal of social training is to produce predictability. Of an individual whose behavior is unpredictable we say that he is disoriented. From this point of view the behavior of artist and perceiver is extremely atypical. The artist's role requires him to create occasions in which the perceiver's predictions will be frustrated, and the perceiver's role requires him to look for them. Hence the erection of artistic innovation into a special problem is no more than a response to this extremely peculiar condition. On the other hand, it is of course not true at all that innovation is to be found only in artistic behavior, nor do I wish to imply that it is or that it is not uniquely found there, only that artistic innovation in the perspective of tool function is nonfunctional or even dysfunctional. Nevertheless, an investigation of the innovating situation, when it conforms to the demands of social roles, shows a striking parallelism with the artistic situation. When we examine the circumstances in which such innovation takes place, such as the situation of the scientist, the scholar, or the great corporation president, it is obvious that it is characterized by psychic insulation. The laboratory, the study, the presidential office, even the design of university campuses, localities in which innovation is at least *supposed* to take place, are all marked by insulation from sensory stimulation which is not immediately pertinent to the problem at hand. Now it is obvious that the artistic perceiver is also psychically insulated; and the more the work **of art to be perceived is characterized by nonfunctional stylistic dynamism** the greater the insulation. Popular music can be successfully experienced in situations in which considerable extraneous stimulation is present. Yet when jazz moved to a higher cultural level in the 1940s and was characterized by a higher rate of such dynamism, people stopped dancing and started listening. The nightclub devoted to progressive jazz suddenly became a concert hall.

Innovation involves, of course, problem-searching, problem exposure, and problem-solving. I do not suggest that artistic perception is a matter of problem-solving, though artistic creation is. Rather, what problem-solving and the behavior of the art perceiver have in common is psychic insulation that permits disorientation, a discontinuity of perceptual experience. Henceforth, instead of nonfunctional stylistic dynamism I shall use the term *discontinuity*, and the theory I am about to propose I call a general theory of the discontinuity of artistic perception.

It is obvious, therefore, that what is needed here is a theory of perception; and the theory I have adopted is the one frequently referred to, at least a few years ago, as the New Look in perception theory. It goes by various names, and has been arrived at by various schools of psychologists on quite different routes. *Directive state theory, expectancy* or *expectation theory, transactionalism, Tote theory,* and *perceptual model theory* are the terms most frequently encountered. The essence of this position has been well stated by George Miller: "The organism struggles to reduce the mismatch between its own criteria and perceived reality." In this proposition the two elements I would emphasize are "criteria" and "perceived reality." The heart of the matter is that in any perceptual situation the criteria are not derived from perceived reality. Or, to use the terminology I prefer, the orientation that the organism applies to a given situation exists a priori to the perceptual phenomena of that situation. Now that orientation is best considered, I believe, as a system of categorization that the individual applies because he has responded to conventionalized clues in the situation. That is, an orientation does not prepare an individual to deal with a particular situation but only with a category of situations. The orientation may also be identified as an expectational set. For *mismatch* I substitute the term *cognitive disparity*. The extraordinary thing about perception, therefore, is that cognitive disparity may be reduced by, to use a currently popular term, *feedback*. The orientation, or set, is capable of being corrected. However, two other qualifications need to be introduced at this point.

First is that before cognitive disparity can emerge and feedback take place, the individual must sense that something is wrong, that somehow or other his orientation is not successfully organizing the perceptual data. This experience I call *cognitive tension*. Thus in the perceptual situation we have the following sequence: orientation, or expectancy, cognitive tension, cognitive disparity, problem location, problem-solving, feedback, corrected orientation. But all kinds of things can go wrong. The problem may be wrongly located; the solution may be incorrect; the feedback may be incomplete; and the orientation may be even less well adapted to that category of situation than it was at the beginning.

But something even more important may happen. The statement from Miller comes from a passage in his *Psychology: The Science of Mental Life*, which certainly leaves the reader with the impression that return to homeostasis is achieved by carrying through the entire procedure from application of criteria to reduction of mismatch and, presumably, correction of criteria. But to my mind he has left out an element of great importance. In this sequence it seems to me obvious that the critical stage is the stage of cognitive tension. The organism must endure cognitive tension until it has located a problem, and it must endure the tension of problem exposure until it has solved the problem. But the critical stage is the first stage: enduring cognitive tension.

Now although Miller is, of course, perfectly correct when he says that the organism struggles to reduce the mismatch, it must also be added that it doesn't struggle very hard. Miller gives us too much credit. Homeostasis is not achieved by going through the whole cycle. It is ordinarily achieved by resolving the tension before disparity and problem location have emerged. The great human motto is, "Millions for the orientation but not one cent for the reality." The defense of the orientation and not the tribute to reality is what we prize above all else. As I have suggested above, only in conditions of psychic insulation is there a tendency for the entire cycle to be carried out, and certainly the history of culture, and even the history of scientific investigation, indicates that cognitive short-circuiting can and usually does occur at any stage in the cycle. Thomas S. Kuhn, in his study of the history of scientific research, has shown how even the scientist, whose role requires him to seek out problems and whose situation provides him with a high degree of psychic insulation, nevertheless commonly ignores perceptual data which his orientation—Kuhn uses the word *paradigm*—cannot organize. In short, the organism prefers homeostasis to any awareness of mismatch, or cognitive tension. There are two ways which it can use to dissolve that tension without going on to problem exposure. One is simply to suppress the awareness of data that violate expectancy; the other is to find new grounds for justifying the orientation. One might even say, sanctifying the orientation.

Perception, then, selects, simplifies, reduces, and organizes. That such behavior is adaptational, or biologically functional, is obvious. But on the other hand, the very character of perception, which enables us successfully to find our way about in the world, is the element in our behavior that disqualifies us for successful adaptation. The reason is that the perceptual model must eliminate data that are essential to successful situational adaptation. The hunter concentrating on spearing a charging lion ignores the tickling of the poisonous spider; the man with a fear of all authority figures misses the data which if properly observed would have shown him how to defeat the authority, when it was to his interest to do so. The very aspect of our behavior that qualifies us to deal with the environment disqualifies us. Functional perception is dysfunctional as well. I was interested to read in the conclusion to Berelson and Steiner's *Human Behavior* a statement of precisely this point. But these authors, quite understandably, considering the limitations of their fascinating task, do not go on to draw what seems to me an inevitable conclusion. Given this condition, there must be some form of human activity that is devoted to the practice or rehearsal of the endurance of cognitive tension; and this rehearsal must occur in situations in which nothing is at stake, in which the appearance or nonappearance of a genuine problem is a matter of indifference. That activity is, I believe, artistic behavior, and works of art are produced to provide occasions for the rehearsal for the endurance of cognitive tension; they train us to stand our ground when we encounter disorienting situations.

If such a position can be sustained, we will have an adaptational or biologically functional explanation for art; and we will be able to understand the expenditure of enormous, inconceivable resources of energy, intelligence, innovation, and economic wealth upon creating, exhibiting, and contemplating works of art. For my part, I think it astounding that a couple of thousand human beings should sit in silence and darkness while a hundred more make peculiar noises on odd instruments. The explanation I have suggested is the only way I can understand such strange behavior, and I should add that the only way I can ultimately think about human behavior is in terms of biologi-

bute is that it always offers the second kind, but only for the observer who has cal adaptation of the organism to the environment. It is, if you wish, my metaphysic.

IV

My next task is to offer ground for the acceptance of this proposition by analyzing a few works of art and explaining the terminology and justification of my mode of analysis, but before I can do that, a couple of digressions or qualifications are desirable.

The obviously weak point in my argument is this. Only too easily can it be asked, "Are not such terms as *orientation, expectancy, set, directive state, perceptual criteria, perceptual model,* and so on—are these words not hypostatizations? Are not you and the psychologists you depend on victims of the fallacy of misplaced concreteness? Has anyone ever seen an orientation? If not, what evidence is there that there are such things? Furthermore, are not these merely substitutes, intervening variables, for mentalism? Are they not merely means of smuggling into a behavioristic framework substitutes for the naughty and forbidden word *mind?*" The only answer to such questions is, "Well, unfortunately, yes." It helps, of course, to say that there is no claim that these terms refer to phenomenally existent entities, but that rather they are constructs. The question still remains, "On what empirical grounds are such constructs erected?"

Now the perceptual theorists I have depended on insist almost to a man that such explanations of perception invalidate behaviorism, or at least neobehaviorist S→ R theory. To be sure, of late neobehaviorism has been getting some terribly hard knocks. Attack has particularly come from something called phenomenology, and it is of interest to note that phenomenology, as found in Heidegger and, particularly, in Sartre is a remarkable parallel to those theories I shall lump under the general name of expectancy theory, just as that theory shows remarkable similarities to recent philosophy of science and also of certain new developments in philosophical ethics, or value theory. But profound as the phenomenological philosophers may be, nobody would call them elegant, or even very clear. My reading in current attacks on behaviorism, in spite of my original feeling that expectancy theory irreparably damaged it, has led me to reconsider the matter, to attempt to meet these embarrassing questions; and here, unqualified as I am to deal with such matters, I am very much on my own. I have encountered no efforts to meet these questions, and only one to reconcile expectancy theory and behaviorism. In short, current attacks on behaviorism, though consonant with my own directive state, have made me much more sympathetic with behaviorism, though aware of its limitations. It is wise to remember George Miller's caution: "No one can now foresee what benefits or dangers may some day come from these fumbling efforts with caged animals and nonsense syllables—but we had better be prepared for success."

The irresistible advantage and appeal of all forms of behaviorism is that the behaviorist insists that all conclusions be based on, and only on, phenomenally observable behavior. "What is the organism doing?" the behaviorist asks, and that is the rock on which he builds his house. It is a very firm rock, though we have yet to see very much in the way of a house. By eliminating the word *mind* from his vocabulary, the behaviorist hoped to get away from talking about the unobservable, but in doing so he denied himself the opportunity to talk about a whole class of observables. Consequently, nearly twenty years ago it was felt necessary to introduce our old and now somewhat limp and bloodless friend, the intervening variable. But this self-denial was, I believe, quite necessary, and was based upon a logical error, which in turn was based upon a misconception of language and all signs. We are instructed from childhood that a noun is a name for a thing. Even the great Wittgenstein, to whom I must refer as a matter of ritual, asserted that "Objects can only be named. Signs are their representatives." A sign, then, names an object. If no object can be located, then the sign or name is invalid. If mind cannot be located, then we should stop using the term *mind*.

But, for reasons I cannot go into here, I believe that the notion that a word, or any sign, verbal or nonverbal, refers to an object is entirely in error. A sign refers not to an object but to a category of perceptual or phenomenal configurations. Such a category has a range of configurations and a set of attributes, that is, denotation and connotation. But a word does not denote an object; it denotes a range or community of configurations. And I would go even further and assert that a categorial stability is almost impossible, that in any situation in which a word is used the range and attributes of its category differ from its use in all other situations, even though very slightly.

The proper question to ask, then, is, What is the range and what are the attributes of this word in this situation? In the very loose situation of psychological investigation, "mind" has a perfectly valid function; it refers to interpretational variability, the observable phenomenon that individuals act differently in the same situation and that the same individual acts differently in various instances of the same category of situation. That is, the way an individual interprets a situation varies independently from the variability of the situation itself. In turn, my use of the term *interpretation* depends upon a general theory of semiosis, according to which all configurations are, to the perceiving organism, signs. Such sign functions are conventionally established, even if the convention is held by only one individual. Numerous experiments have shown that if a configuration is encountered which is not conventionally interpretable, which has no semantic function, which cannot be categorized by some existent categorial system, the perceiver cannot tolerate such a degree of cognitive tension and forthwith makes sense out of it, makes it meaningful, by assigning it to the range of an existent category, even when such assignment is wildly inappropriate. It seems to me that Professor Ralph Stogdill's proposal that expectation theory and behaviorism can be reconciled is well founded. There is no such thing as "mind," just as there is no such thing as "tree," and no such entity as Morse Peckham. But when we use the word *mind* we are, after all, talking about observable phenomena, phenomena that the behaviorist can theoretically handle and, I should say, is already beginning to handle with some success.

Perhaps this digression was unnecessary and irrelevant, but I always like to display my assumptions quite openly. At least it permits me to say, I believe, this. When an individual uses the term *orientation* or *directive state*, and so on, he is in fact predicting that the particular organism he is examining will behave in a particular way whenever it finds itself in a particular situation. Thus, even when the psychoanalyst talks about an unconscious fear of the father in language that I find hopelessly unacceptable, he is nevertheless predicting that his patient will tend to categorize authority figures in any situation in such a way that they have to him the same attributes of the feared and hated father, and that he will behave accordingly. The psychoanalyst may fancy he is talking about the unconscious mind; he is really making predictions, and many that he makes are highly reliable.

My second digression is less of one. It is the question of the semantic function of works of art, or content, as it is traditionally referred to. In recent decades a considerable fuss has been made about the abandonment of the distinction between form and content, or the demonstration that they are both one. So far as I am concerned the result merely serves to deprive both terms of what little referential value they formerly had. I propose frankly to reinstate the distinction, with a difference, analyzing the problem from the point of view of a roughhewn but I believe adequate general theory of signs. In my book I go into this problem at some length. Here I can but give briefly my conclusions.

Since I believe all experienced perceptual configurations are signs, it is no great trick for me to assert that works of art also are sign structures, if they consist of words, or sign packages, if they do not. The function of signs, including verbal signs, I believe to be, in the last analysis, behavioral control.

Two classes of signs may be distinguished, natural and artificial. Artificial signs may further be broken down into arbitrary signs, of which words are the most prominent instance; configurational signs, of which traditional European painting is an example; and what, for want of better words, I call nonsituational or primary signs. These are the signs of music; of color, depth, verticality, horizontality, and so on in painting; in architecture, verticality, horizontality, shadow, plasticity, screen opening, and so forth; and in poetry the various kinds of phonic overdetermination. Merely to give an instance of what I am talking about, but not to suggest that anyone at this point accept my position uncritically, I find the sense of demand signified in poetry by alliteration and assonance, in music by upward pitch motion, in painting by verticality, and in architecture by verticality and solidity. The only point I wish to make here is that I can discover no kind of semantic function in art which is not to be found also outside of art, and, for primary signs, also in the natural world.

Thus, departing sharply from the most common kind of contemporary poetic theory, I believe that nothing can be said in a work of art that cannot be said outside of art. There is nothing that a poet or any artist says by virtue of the fact that he is an artist. What he says is in response to extra-artistic cultural demands. The culture may demand that the poet devote himself to a particular kind of subject matter, but his role as artist in itself, as distinguished from other socially established roles, provides no unique rules or directions in this matter; nor does his medium make it possible for him to say something which nonartists cannot say. The semantic or conventional aspect of art may be conveniently regarded in terms of the tool metaphor, in the sense that a Madonna is a religious tool, or an abstract painting is a tool for separating from situations signs of the sense of demand and acceptance, adequacy and inadequacy, fixity and flexibility, expression and inhibition, and so on. What stylistic dynamism the semantic aspect of art exhibits, therefore, is a matter of functional dynamism, not of nonfunctional dynamism or discontinuity.

V

One of the most common criteria for excellence in art is that it serves as a stimulus for intense emotion. Now there are only two ways emotion can be elicited; by presenting a sign configuration to which the perceiver is conditioned to respond emotionally, or by disorienting him, by violating his expectations, by offering the occasion for a discontinuity of perceptual experience. A work of art may or may not offer the first kind of emotional elicitation, just as any sign stucture or package may or may not. Art's distinguishing attri-

been properly trained by his culture to bring the appropriate expectational set to that particular work. There are two sources of this training, normal experience and special experience. Of the second kind music is the most obvious example. One must be trained to expect certain musical processes before one can experience their violation. Nevertheless, the individual, because of the tendency to simplify and organize perception, can, if sufficiently sensitive and intelligent, build up a weighted average of exposure to a particular musical or other artistic style without special training. But the ordinary mode in our culture is special training for the high arts. As for normal experience, let me give two examples.

I shall begin with fiction, because it was a long time before I could understand how to apply my theory to this kind of art. A fiction begins by presenting a problem, usually in the form of something that doesn't make sense, or something that is not readily comprehensible. For most of us here the purest kind of fiction available is the detective story. Now in normal behavior, when a problem is encountered, the individual either suppresses awareness of it or devotes his energy to solving it. But fiction makes both impossible. On the contrary, it postpones the solution of the problem and prevents its suppression. And what we call well-made fiction introduces a number of problems related to the major problems. Fiction is endurable only because nothing is at stake, because it is made up, invented, because it is a lie. Consider the mild and amused contempt we have for the reader whose tolerance of cognitive tension is so low that he must peek at the back of the book to find out how the story comes out, how the problem is solved.

Another example of the violation of normal expectations is to be found in the language of poetry in English, and in a good many other languages as well. English poetry is characterized by badly made sentences; the poet is constantly messing up the syntax. In teaching poetry even at the college level it is necessary constantly to require the students to straighten it out. Their tendency is to do what is normal in any disorienting situation, to seize upon the recognizable feature and ignore the rest of the syntactical and semantic information. But this is true at much higher levels. I have seen graduate students helpless before Browning's *Sordello,* which, to be sure, is the most syntactically disordered poem in English before the twentieth century. Professional students of poetry have been arguing for decades over the syntax of Hopkins' "The Windhover."

But poetry also requires special training, or lengthy experience, so that the correct set of rhythmic and junctural expectations be acquired. Current theory, though it has been questioned, asserts that there are four levels of stress in English. Poetic convention recognizes two kinds of syllables, accented and unaccented, or, more properly, stressed and nonstressed, or, sometimes, weak and strong. Now rhythm, if it means anything, refers to the regular recurrence in time or space of identical or interchangeable perceptual configurations. Rhythm, by this definition, is the one thing that English poetry does not have. Or rather, it has it in patches, and the higher the cultural level for which the poem was written, the less frequent the patches of regularity. But when we see a poem our expectation is for rhythm, that is, for the recurrence every second syllable or every third syllable of a stress. These are the only two possible rhythms in English poetry. In recent years the metaphor "counterpoint" has been used to describe this phenomenon, but it is a very bad metaphor. In music counterpoint refers to the simultaneous presentation of two or more melodic configurations; but in poetry we expect a regular or rhythmic stress configuration and we are offered a violation of that expectation. Hence we experience a constant disorientation, the poet offering only enough patches of rhythmic regularity to reinforce our expectation.

This principle also explains the line, which is a typographical device to indicate the recurrence of juncture, or pause, or hiatus in the phonic stream. In English blank verse, a fairly long juncture is required at the end of every tenth syllable. The violation of that expectation, when it has been reinforced for a number of lines, is one of the most powerful effects in poetry; it is usually called the *run-on line*. The poet also has another means of discontinuity, though less powerful, in the internal juncture, or caesura, which is prescribed to occur after the fifth syllable, but which we can move back or forth, multiply, or eliminate. When Shakespeare's plays are examined in the more or less reliable chronological order objectively established, a striking phenomenon leaps to the attention. The order of the plays corresponds to the increasing frequency of violated line and junctural expectations. All kinds of explanations have been offered for this, but on the theory presented here, it is obvious that a highly gifted poet writing for twenty years in the same verse form unavoidably increases the frequency of this kind of discontinuity. This Shakespearean phenomenon is an instance of what I call *external discontinuity*, and it is to be found in the work of every artist of the higher cultural levels I have examined.

Whenever I encounter in aesthetics or criticism the word *form*, my mind goes blank. But from the point of view presented here, it is possible to locate a semantic function for this almost meaningless term. In artistic perception *form* refers to the expectancy; form is not a character of the work, which is irregular and indeed in any normal use of the term, formless, but of the perceptual a priori. Form, then, is a mode of perception; and art violates form. Hence I call this aspect of the work of art *the formal aspect*, as opposed to the *conventional* or *semantic aspect*. External discontinuity, as we have seen, refers to the violation of the expectations a particular series of works has built up. But the individual work also exhibits, as I have pointed out, discontinuity which can be experienced independently from the series. The kind I have examined is implicit discontinuity. It is the violation of any perceptual form implied by the perceiver's recognition of a perceptual field which, in his culture, is an art situation, or by his application of those rules to any perceptual field not hitherto, in his culture, so conventionalized. This is why the Chinese connoisseur can see a naturally formed rock as a work of art, and also why a contemporary sculptor can so perceive a mashed automobile.

A second kind is internal discontinuity, which is the violation of a perceptual form established in that particular work of art. It, too, can be experienced in the perception of fields not hitherto defined as works of art. Let me give a few examples. In poetry, the seventeenth-century Pindaric ode proceeds by presenting a rhyme scheme often enough to build up expectation for its continuation, and then violates it. Another device is to present a pattern of lines of varying length, to repeat the first couple of lines of that pattern, and then to violate. Ordinarily, internal discontinuity depends upon the establishment of a pattern within a work, but in the Pindaric ode the poet can depend upon the practiced reader to expect a familiar stanzaic line pattern upon the presentation of only the first part of it. What we have here is an instance of implied discontinuity which is then used for internal discontinuity before the implication is made explicit.

The final kind of discontinuity I identify is modal discontinuity. It is the violation of those perceptual forms which are the sources of implicit and internal discontinuity in a given work of art. It is also the violation of an expectancy that a particular mode of sign structure or package already established in a work should be continued in that work. That is, it is the violation in the latter case of a functional style for nonfunctional purposes. The shift from a comic mode to a serious or tragic mode in the Shakespearean tragedy is an obvious instance. Another is the introduction of songs into a spoken play. The first kind of modal discontinuity is less common in nondramatic poetry. An instance may be found in Spenser's "Epithalamion," in which twenty-three long stanzas of either eighteen or nineteen lines are followed by a stanza of only seven. This also shows the second kind of modal discontinuity, a shift in verbal functional style. But the most common kind of modal discontinuity is syntactical discontinuity, from patches of rhythmic regularity to patches of rhythmic violation, and from junctural explicitness to junctural violation.

To clarify what I am talking about I shall turn to music, compared with which poetry is comparatively poverty-stricken. Or rather, since poetry can depend upon the violation of syntactical expectancies, which are reinforced millions of times in the experiences of any individual, poets have not found it necessary to develop other possibilities. Music, however, is the art that requires the greatest amount of special training for both the artist and the perceiver. Consequently, of all the arts it is perhaps richest in discontinuity. There is still another reason why this should be so. The problem of the poet, the painter, and the architect is to adjust the degree of formal discontinuity he wishes to the semantic aspect. This is by no means easy. From this point of view a study of European images of the Madonna is extraordinarily instructive. The iconographic, or semantic, regulations were fairly stringent, and the ingenuity displayed by painters in creating continuous external discontinuity and interesting internal, implicit, and modal discontinuities is very great. Music, on the other hand, for the most part has only to present primary signs. Up to the nineteenth century, these were under considerable situational control, but even so the possibilities for musical discontinuity are so great that the composer can say the same thing over and over without boring us. Indeed, compared with poetry and painting and even architecture, music cannot say very much. Its semantic aspect is limited, but its formal aspect is extraordinarily rich, at least in our culture.

The simplest kind of musical internal discontinuity is the theme and variations. Imitation, it has been said, is the breath of life in music; but of course, as might be expected, it is not imitation at all, but the violation of a unique pattern or melody. The principle of musical development, then, is internal discontinuity. Melody itself depends upon implicit discontinuity. That is, diatonic music, the kind that is most familiar to all of us, still, creates melody by violating scale and triad expectations. For instance, the concerti grossi of Vivaldi almost invariably in the fast first and third movements present melodies that violate triadic expectations, while the slow second movements violate scale expectations. If C is given and followed by D, the expectancy for E is very great. If E is followed by F, the expectation for G is even greater; but if instead of G the melodic line offers A-sharp, which is not even in the scale of C major, the violation comes as a real shock. All melodies are created in this manner. Or rather melodies are melodies because they imply a scale or a triad but do not make the scale or triad explicit. The typical sequence of movements in the Vivaldi concerto grosso is an example of both kinds of modal discontinuity; the first accounts for the shift from triadic implication to scale implication and back again; the second for the shift from fast tempo to slow tempo and back again, for to my mind the continuum from slow to fast tempo is a sign of the sense of the continuum from energy conservation to high energy release.

At this point I should like to offer an instance of what I believe to be the explanatory powers of my proposal. One of the most common phenomena in the history of music is the assertion that a new musical style has no melodies. A nineteenth-century example is *Tristan and Isolde*, of which numerous original perceivers asserted that it was utterly unmelodic. To us that is an almost inconceivable statement. Another instance is Schönberg's *Pierrot Lunaire,* which for years to me was just one damned note after another. But suddenly one day I heard the most delicious melodies. What accounts for this? *Tristan* offers a degree of chromaticism hitherto unparalleled in Western music, as well as a frequency of large and unusual melodic leaps. In other words, the triadic and scale expectations are so frequently and intensively violated that the expectancies themselves disappear. *Pierrot Lunaire* is quite a different case. *Tristan* should be listened to with diatonic expectancies, but Schönberg, beginning with *Pierrot*, is properly listened to with the expectancies of the chromatic, not the diatonic, scale. Melody requires the perceiver to make a new form as he listens. But if the requirements are too great, many a perceiver cannot do so, let alone experience its subsequent violations. My own experience with Schönberg's twelve-tone music moved from total disorientation, to the perception of individual notes, to the perception of melody and the acceptance of the harmonies, to the realization, which came after the event, that the appropriate perceptual form was the chromatic scale. My judgment moved correspondingly from irritation to boredom to toleration to emotion to, now, the experience of finding this twelve-tone music ravishingly beautiful and as easy to listen to as Vivaldi— and a lot more interesting. Clearly, acceptance of a really striking external discontinuity depends upon the personality, both experience in the appropriate artistic series and toleration of cognitive tension. It is only too evident that most people can tolerate so little cognitive tension that they can never accept a radically new artistic style. But at the highest cultural levels there is considerable support, for there innovation in all areas of human behavior is highly valued.

I shall now turn briefly to painting. To begin with, painting is like fiction and the syntactical aspect of poetry: the formal expectations are developed in normal experience, rather than by special training. In recent years, it has been discovered that all over the world children start making the same visual signs more or less in the same order; the smear, the line, the cross, the x, the square, the circle, the triangle, and finally the free or biomorphic closed form. The development of iconicity follows the ability to create complex signs with an increasing configurational isomorphism to perceptual configurations. These packages of signs have been called children's art, and to a sophisticated observer they are, of course, art if he wishes to categorize them as art. But they do not function as art for the children. Rather, the emergence of these signs in children's behavior is the emergence of configurational sign behavior, and is parallel to the emergence of verbal, or arbitrary, sign behavior. These signs, up to the biomorphic free shape, are the implicit forms of perception before paintings. Children also make three-dimensional signs out of mud, sticks, stones, and, in our culture, blocks, and these are the implicit forms for sculpture and architecture.

VI

There remain two further problems and my theory is complete, though most sketchily presented. Here again, I can scarcely defend in detail my solutions to either of them, but I do wish to present them to you as indications that I have tried to create a complete theory.

First I should like to offer a more thorough and formal definition of external discontinuity. The term refers to the discontinuous relation between a work of art and its predecessors in the same category. An example would be Tchaikovsky's Sixth Symphony with the slow movement at the end. The explanation for external discontinuity lies in the fact that when particular devices for achieving implicit, internal, and modal discontinuity have been used for any period of time the perceiver comes to anticipate them, or predict them; the artist's role, therefore, requires him to innovate new devices. This predictability explains why it is that art has a stylistic history, and why, at least for individual observers, works of art wear out.

What predictability does *not* explain is why the historical dimension of art is also characterized by stylistic continuity, why we can recognize, say, Baroque, or Rococo, or modern styles, and why the boundaries of these stylistic fields can be approximately determined, or why stylistic historians working in entirely different kinds of art so often tend to agree that the stylistic boundaries of different arts occur at about the same time. For example, in music, architecture, painting, poetry, and the novel, universally recognized modern styles all appeared between 1905 and 1912, although the artists responsible were quite unknown to each other. It is an extraordinary instance of cultural convergence. Such convergences are the only empirical evidence that the formal aspects of the arts are somehow related to each other. Certainly there is no other evidence, for the various discontinuities in each are entirely dependent upon rules manipulating quite disparate media and work by violating quite different perceptual forms.

The answer I propose comes from examining not works of art, but rather the behavior of artists. I cannot present my evidence here, but only my conclusion. When an artist makes a decision that results in external discontinuity, what controls that decision? To what values is he responding? It cannot be the formal medium, which he can manipulate any way he pleases, nor can it be the values of the semantic aspect, which vary quite independently. The artist's decisions, then, are not controlled by anything uniquely characteristic of art. The values that determine what he does must, then, be extra-artistic. They must come from somewhere else in the culture, and they must have continuous control over several generations of artists.

From about 1720 or 1730 to about 1800 external discontinuity in all the high arts moved steadily toward a reduction of implicit, external, and modal discontinuity. What could have caused this? This was the period of the Enlightenment, and the Enlightenment ideal was the perfect adaptation of organism to environment. Everything, whether in thought or politics or economics, was aimed toward problem-solving and tension reduction. Consequently, for reasons I have already presented, the preference for problem-solving over problem exposure and for tension reduction over endurance of cognitive tension meant that a great many problems were too hastily resolved, to put it very mildly. It was the great era of facile pseudo-solutions. It was also the era in which sentimentality, that great technique of tension reduction, was identified and made into a cult.

With such values regnant at the higher cultural levels, it is apparent that the decisions of artists influenced by such values must lead to a steady reduction of internal, modal, and implicit discontinuity. On the basis of my examination of this period, of the seventeenth-century or Baroque styles, and of the nineteenth- and twentieth-century Romantic styles, including the modern styles, I conclude, therefore, that stylistic continuity is the consequence of the fact that the decisions of artists about discontinuity are responses to the regnant values of their cultural milieu.

This proposition also accounts for the common chronological boundaries of the historical styles. When there is a major shift in regnant cultural values, there will be corresponding redirection of the formal aspects of the arts. And this also is how the arts are related. Attempts in the manner of Spengler or Wylie Sypher to relate them on the assumption that a style is a symbol of a set of values or a metaphysic are bound to fail, and in fact have never been widely accepted. The reason is that a discontinuity is not a configuration but the violation of an expected configuration and therefore cannot be a conventionalized sign. Discontinuities have no semantic function, except to the stylistic historian. The arts are related because the accumulation of external discontinuity in each art moves in the same direction as in all the other arts.

To conclude, the role of the artist demands that he offer violations of formal expectancies, that he offer occasions for the rehearsal of the endurance of cognitive tension. And the role of the perceiver demands that he search for such occasions and that he respond to them to the best of his ability. Artistic behavior, then, is not a pretty ornament to life but a terrible necessity that keeps man alive, aware, capable of perceiving that he is neither adequate nor inadequate to the demands of his environment but a perilous mixture of the two, capable of evading the sentimentalities of comedy and of tragedy. Art is the ingredient in human behavior that enables man to innovate, because it trains him to endure the cognitive tension which is the necessary preliminary to problem perception and genuine and meaningful innovation. To me, only such a psychological and biological explanation of artistic behavior can serve to make comprehensible the outpouring of energy, devotion, treasure, and creativity at the feet of the terrible idol of art. Of all man's burdens, art is one of the most unendurable, and one of the most necessary. Deprived of it, he could not continue to be man.

George Brecht

Chance-Imagery

Art is not the most precious manifestation of life. Art has not the celestial and universal value that people like to attribute to it. Life is far more interesting.

—Tristan Tzara[1]

The purpose of this article is to encourage insight regarding chance-imagery, especially certain less intuitively obvious formal aspects. Every statement of opinion is as wrong in one sense as it is right in some other, for every distinction is an artificial one, an arbitrary subdivision of what is actually a unified whole. This is one of the reasons that words about art are so infinitely inferior to the art itself. Art unites us with the whole; words only permit us to handle a unified reality by maneuvering arbitrarily excised chunks.

With this apology for juggling words at all, let us indicate how we intend to approach an infinitely broad and complex subject, chance and its relation to the arts. (*Arts* here is taken in a broadly historical, but actually no longer appropriate, sense.)

First, a working definition (*Chance*).

Some background (*Dada and Surrealism*).

A focal point in development (*Jackson Pollock*).

Randomness.

Coda.

CHANCE

The word *chance* (with a Latin root relating to the falling of dice) can conveniently be taken to mean that the cause, or system of causes, responsible for a given effect is unknown or unlooked-for or, at least, that we are unable to completely specify it. Of course, in the real world, causes are also effects, and effects causes. The fall of a die, for example, is the effect of an infinite number of (largely unknown) causes (among which we can imagine resilience of the die, hardness of the table, angle of contact to be included), and this effect, in turn, may be the cause of my winning a certain amount of money.

It is sometimes possible to specify only the universe of possible characteristics that a chance event may have. For example, a toss of a normal die will be expected to give a number from one to six. Any particular face will be expected to turn up in about one-sixth of a great many throws. But the outcome of any one toss remains unknown until the throw has been made. It is often useful to keep in mind this "universe of possible results," even when that universe is hypothetical, for this clarifies for us the nature of our chance event as a selection from a limited universe. We should note here that events are defined as due to chance in a relative way. There is no absolute chance or random event, for chance and randomness are aspects of the way in which we structure our universe. These are elementary considerations with many ramifications, but I hope they will serve as a conceptual baseline for the discussion to follow, which should clarify the nature of chance. We shall later discuss the random event, as a special type of bias-free chance event.

In connection with art, and the affective image, we shall indicate two aspects of chance, one where the origin of images is unknown because it lies in deeper-than-conscious levels of the mind, and the second where images derive from mechanical processes not under the artist's control. Both of these processes have in common a lack of conscious design.

DADA AND SURREALISM

In the sense that there is a certain lack of conscious control in everything we do, the use of chance in art could be traced (academically) to the cave drawings of prehistoric man; but the first explicit use of chance in painting seems to have come shortly before World War I. If we admit automatism as chance, then the improvisations of Kandinsky (1911), painted "rather subconsciously in a state of strong inner tension," would take precedence

GEORGE BRECHT

over the first *papiers colles* of Picasso (1912), in which were incorporated for-
tuitous scraps of newspaper and cardboard.

(The question of the chance nature of automatism might be endlessly debated. It seems to me that the answer lies in the distinction between our seeking immediate causes or ultimate causes or automatic actions. It takes little
reflection to see that ultimate causes might readily and reasonably be ascribed to chance, but psychoanalytic theory has taught us to expect "conscious ignorance and unconscious knowledge of the motivation of psychic
accidentalness,"[2] and it does not always take very deep or lengthy probing to
reveal immediate causes for the psychically accidental. At any rate, it is
practical to consider chance as being defined by *consciously* unknown causes,
and by this definition, at least, automatism is a chance process.)

Since we are restricting ourselves to the generation of chance-images,
and not to their appreciation, we shall indicate only the place of the unconscious (including the subconscious, or fore-conscious) as a source of significant images. The importance of chance to the unconscious has manifold
facets, not only in modern psychology, but also (and particularly) in Oriental
thought (such as that manifested in the *I-Ching* or in Zen).

The Dadaists considered the unconscious to be a source of images free
from the biases engrained in us by parents, social customs and all the other
artificial restrictions on intellectual freedom:

> We are now in a position to formulate the problem of art, more accurately
> the problem of expression, as it appeared to the writers of and Literature
> group (Aragon, Breton, Soupault): only the unconscious does not lie, it alone is
> worth bringing to light. All deliberate and conscious efforts, composition, logic
> are futile. The celebrated French lucidity is nothing but a cheap lantern. At
> best the "poet" can prepare traps (as a physician might do in treating a pa-
> tient), with which to catch the unconscious by surprise and to prevent it from
> cheating. . . . — Marcel Raymond[3]

> The unconscious is inexhaustible and uncontrollable. Its force surpasses us. It
> is as mysterious as the last particle of a brain cell. Even if we knew it, we could
> not reconstruct it. — Tristan Tzara[1]

As far as affective form is concerned, chance is an aspect of the universe
made significant by unconscious interactions, but it is not the only aspect.
When the largely iconoclastic displays of Dada were superseded by the more
systematic researches of the Surrealists, Breton, for one, in the *First Surrealist Manifesto* (1924), made this general interest in the unconscious explicit:

During the course of Surrealist development, outside all forms of idealism, outside the opiates of religion, the marvelous comes to light within *reality*. It comes to light in dreams, obsessions, preoccupations, in sleep, fear, love, chance; in hallucinations, pretended disorders, follies, ghostly apparitions, escape mechanisms and evasions; in fancies, idle wanderings, poetry, the supernatural and the unusual; in empiricism, in *super-reality*.[4]

(This statement, written in 1924, followed *The Interpretation of Dreams* by twenty-four years, and *Psychopathology of Everyday Life* by twenty.)

It is useful practically to include automatism in a consideration of chance in art, and it is only our viewpoint which makes it a chance process but there is actually no reason why the others of Breton's categories could not also be included. We exclude them arbitrarily from this discussion only to preserve a certain tightness in our consideration of the methodological resources of the contemporary research "artist," which we will take up further on. Automatism is also an aspect of chance in the sense that we accept its product as something which it really is not. In all of Breton's manifestations of the marvelous (a handy summary) we read into phenomena characteristics which they do not possess in an absolute way. Duchamp called this *irony* ("a playful way of accepting something"), and the concept is a critical one in understanding the vector through Dada, Pollock, the present-day chance-imagists, and the future. The idea will appear again in the section on Pollock, and shows up particularly as a method I've called the *irrelevant process* (also discussed later).

We are more interested, though, in the mechanically chance process, and here Duchamp did the pioneer work. In 1913 he undertook what seems to be the first explicit use of chance for the creation of an affective image, in the *3 stoppages étalon*. He made these images by holding a thread one meter long, "straight and horizontal," one meter above a blank canvas. After letting it fall onto the canvas, it was fixed with a trickle of varnish into the chance convolution in which it fell. This process was repeated to give three such canvases.

Duchamp seems to consider three phenomena basic to his exploitation of chance: wind, gravity, and aim. (This discussion is based largely on an article about Duchamp by Harriet and Sidney Janis; see reference 5.) The *3 stoppages étalon* illustrate gravity; wind was used to create the cloud formations for *La Mariée mise à nu par ses célibataires, même* (1915-1923): "Air currents blowing a piece of mesh gauze against a screen, imprinted a limpid rectangle upon it. The experiment repeated three times gave three chance images, variations on the square. . . . The third device in allowing shapes to create themselves and thus void the responsibility of the hand, is termed by

Duchamp *adresse,* that is, skill in aiming. Nine marks were made upon the glass by the impact of shots of matches dipped in paint, from a toy cannon. . . . Aiming nine shots at a given point, these formed a polygram as a result of variation in the aim-control and accompanying conditions. He then converted the flat polygram or floor plan into an elevation plan. Here the nine points became the locations for the nine malic forms in perspective." [5]

Duchamp's theories on the use of chance seem highly developed, but not exhaustive. Other Dadaists, especially Arp, Ernst, and Tzara, later developed other important applications of chance:

> Arp composed collages by picking up chance scraps of paper, shuffling them, and gluing them down just as they fell (example: the "Squares arranged according to the laws of chance," a collage of 1916).

> Ernst developed the "decalcomania of chance" wherein, for example, ink was spread between two sheets of paper, which were then pulled apart (example: "Decalcomania, 1936" by Oscar Dominguez).

> Tzara composed poems by drawing words from a hat. ("To make a dadaist poem/Take a newspaper./Take a pair of scissors./Choose an article as long as you are planning to make your poem./Cut out the article./Then cut out each of the words that make up this article and put them in a bag./Shake it gently./Then take out the scraps conscientiously./The poem will be like you./And here you are a writer, infinitely original and endowed with a sensibility that is charming though beyond the understanding of the vulgar." [6]

> *Frottage* was a "semi-automatic process for obtaining patterns or designs by rubbing canvas or paper that has been placed over a rough surface such as planking, embossing, a brick wall, etc. (example: Ernst, "The Horde," ca. 1927). This is an example of a technique for which we shall later have a more general term—the *irrelevant process.*[7]

> A very interesting technique of the Surrealists, which permitted the cause of an event to be lost, so to speak, in multiplicity, was that of the *cadavre exquis,* wherein several persons each made part of a picture, folding the paper to cover his addition, before passing the drawing to the next participant. (An example is the "Figure," 1926-27, by Yves Tanguy, Joan Miro, Max Morise, and Man Ray, illus. in ref. 4 p. 251.)

The ability of the unconscious to reconcile opposites is nowhere so evident as in Dada, for within a periphery of nonsense the ridiculous and the profound were made to evince each other: "Dada wished to destroy the reasonable frauds of men and recover the natural, unreasonable order. Dada wished to replace the logical nonsense of the men of today with an illogical nonsense. That is why we beat the Dadaist bass drum with all our might and trumpeted the praises of unreason. . . . Dada like nature is without meaning. Dada is for infinite meaning and finite means." (Gabrielle Buffet-Picabia, 1949.[8]) Within such a (frameless) framework, chance played a major part, as testified by Arp himself [9]: "Chance opened up perceptions to me, immediate spiritual insights. Intuition led me to revere the law of chance as the highest and deepest of laws, the law that rises from the fundament. An insignificant word might become a deadly thunderbolt. One little sound might destroy the earth. One little sound might create a new universe." The almost incredibly incisive mind of Tristan Tzara, as early as 1922, even recognized the relationship of all this to Oriental philosophy (in one of the most convincing of Dada documents, the "Lecture on Dada"): "Dada is not at all modern. It is more in the nature of a return to an almost Buddhist religion of indifference."[10] Such aspects of reality as Oriental thought—scientific thought—Dada—chance become somewhat clearer in such a light. Perhaps chance is the most allusive of the phenomena studied by the Dadaists and Surrealists because it is capable of being most widely generalized. We shall see.

The Second World War helped to disperse the European Dadaists and Surrealists, and many of the most original artists—Breton, Ernst, Tanguy, Masson—regrouped in New York, particularly around two New York galleries, the Julien Levy Gallery and Peggy Guggenheim's Art of This Century.

JACKSON POLLOCK

Jackson Pollock's first show was held at Peggy Guggenheim's gallery in 1943. Here he was able to associate with the proponents of that "sacred disorder" which was later to become the key to his own original style. "To them Pollock owed his radical new sense of freedom, and he spoke more than once of his dept to their unpremeditated and automatic methods. By elevating the appeal to chance and accident into a first principle of creation, the Surrealists had circumvented the more rigid formalisms of modern art."[11] It is not difficult to find their influence in Pollock's paintings of the war years (for example, *Guardians of the Secret*, 1943). Pollock acheived a profound, sustained and irrational synthesis of all the principles that had preceded him in Dada, and in a way consistent with his contemporary world. His paintings seem much less manifestations of one of a group of techniques for releasing the unconscious (as the Dada experiments seemed), than they do of a single, integrated use of chance as a means of unlocking the deepest possible grasp of nature in its broadest sense.

Not to get lost in conjecture, let us briefly give evidence for two points, first that Pollock's calligraphy was truly automatic and second that there is a considerable element of chance in the ultimate arrangement of pigment in the chance-paintings of roughly 1947-1951.

First, part of a statement by Pollock,[12] made in 1947:

> When I am *in* my painting, I'm not aware of what I'm doing. It is only after a sort of "get acquainted" period that I see what I have been about.[13]

Again, from an earlier statement:

> ... The fact that good European moderns are now here is very important, for they bring with them an understanding of the problems of modern painting. I am particularly impressed with their concept of the source of art being the unconscious. This idea interests me more than these specific painters do. . . .

Aside from the lack of conscious control of paint application in these paintings, there are technical reasons for looking at this complex of interdependent forms as predominantly chance events. For one thing, the infinite number of variables involved in determining the flow of fluid paint from a source not in contact with the canvas cannot possibly be simultaneously taken into account with sufficient omniscience that the exact configuration of the paint when it hits the canvas can be predicted. Some of these variables, for example, are the paint viscosity, density, rate of flow at any instant; and direction, speed and configuration of the applicator, to say nothing of nonuniformity in the paint. Even if we deny automatism, and claim omniscience for an unconscious molded by a long learning period, it is obvious that in some of Pollock's paintings of this period (in *One, 1950*, for example) differently colored streams of paint have flowed into each other after application, resulting in a commingling completely out of the artist's hands. Never before Pollock were chance processes used with such primacy, consistency and integrity, as valuable sources of affective imagery.

Paintings get to be what they are physically through an interaction of method and material, and they have their effect in an interaction between painting and observer. As far as the observer is concerned, Pollock has demonstrated that the ability of humans to appreciate complex chance-images is almost unlimited. Here I would like to introduce the general term *chance-imagery* to apply to our formation of images resulting from chance, wherever these occur in nature. (The word *imagery* is intentionally ambiguous enough, I think, to apply either to the physical act of creating an image out of real materials, or to the formation of an image in the mind, say by abstraction from a more complex system.) One reason for doing this is to place the painter's, musician's, poet's, dancer's chance images in the same conceptual category as natural chance-images (the configuration of meadow grasses, the arrangement of stones on a brook bottom), and to get away from the idea that an artist makes something "special" and beyond the world of ordinary things. An Alpine peak or an iris petal can move us at times with all the subtle power of a *Night Watch* or one of the profound themes of Opus 131. There is no a priori reason why moving images should originate only with artists.

This leaves *art* to mean something *constructed*, from a starting point of preconceived notions, with the corollary that as art approaches chance-imagery, the artist enters a oneness with all of nature. This idea has in essence been well expressed by Suzuki:

> There is something divine in being spontaneous and not being hampered by human conventionalities and their artificial hypocrisies. There is something direct and fresh in this lack of restraint by anything human, which suggests a divine freedom and creativity. Nature never deliberates; it acts directly out of its own heart, whatever this may mean. In this respect Nature is divine. Its "irrationality" transcends human doubts or ambiguities, and in our submitting to it or rather accepting it, we transcend ourselves.[14]

> Our inner life is complete when it merges into Nature and becomes one with it.[15]

When an artist achieves this essential oneness with all of nature, everything he creates illuminates nature, as well as himself.

Reason has cut man off from nature.   —Hans Arp[16]

* * * * *

RANDOMNESS

Chance images are characterized by a lack of conscious design. When these images are "hand-made," and conscious thought is evaded, so that the images have their source in deeper-than-conscious areas of the mind, we will prefer the Surrealists' term *automatic* to the word *random*, though *random*, in the way it is used in everyday speech, might seem appropriate (as meaning, for example, "without definite aim, direction, rule, or method," [20]). We will prefer this usage in order to restrict *random* to a technical meaning which it has more commonly in statistics, where it applies to special techniques for eliminating bias in sampling. The term *strict randomness* is useful for ensuring that the word *random* is understood in this technical sense, but, in general, we shall merely say *random*, and it should always be understood here that the technical meaning is implied. Chance is sometimes used in painting in such a way that the images are neither clearly automatic nor random, and here we can only refer to chance-images or chance-processes.

It remains to indicate, then, what this technical meaning comprises, recognizing that, in general, the reason for the importance of randomness for purposes of scientific inference will be the same as the reason for its importance in the arts, that is, the elimination of bias. It is not intuitively obvious that strict randomness is difficult to achieve; therefore let us indicate the general presence of bias where human choice or ordinary mechanical systems are involved. This will give us an intuitive insight into approaches capable of eliminating bias, and will lead finally to a working definition of randomness itself.

Concerning a general bias in human choice, Kendall and Smith [21] have made the following interesting statement:

> It is becoming increasingly evident that sampling left to the discretion of a human individual is not random, although he may be completely unconscious of the existence of bias, or indeed actively endeavoring to avoid it. House-to-house sampling, the sampling of crop yields, even ticket-drawing have all been found to give results widely divergent from expectation.

Yule and Kendall [22] have given an example of human bias that was detected in the course of agricultural experiments carried out in England. The heights of wheat plants were to be measured at two stages in their growth. Of the sets of eight plants sampled for measurement at each of the two stages, two were selected "at random" by eye, and the other six were selected by strictly random methods. Analysis of the measurements showed clearly that, in the samples selected by eye, there was a clear bias toward selecting taller shoots in May, before the ears of wheat had formed, while in June, after further maturation, another bias toward selecting plants of more like average height, and avoiding the extremely tall or short plants, was evidenced.

I have attempted some one-hand typing of series of random digits, and found not only a bias toward a greater frequency of higher digits (regardless of the hand used for the typing), but also peculiar patterns in the series; digits being followed unusually often by certain other digits, for example. (For an interesting discussion of chance numbers, and further references on this subject, see section twelve of Freud's *Psychopathology of Everyday Life* in *The Basic Writings of Sigmund Freud*.)

One might expect to avoid human bias by using mechanical systems, but experience has shown that it is now easy to find simple unbiased mechanical systems. Perfectly balanced coins and roulette wheels, like perfectly cubical and homogeneous dice, seem to occur rarely in nature, if at all. Weldon [23] for example, threw twelve dice 4,096 times. For unbiased dice the probability of a four, five, or six is ½, so that he should have obtained one of these faces 24,576 times. These three faces actually occurred 25,145 times, which is a statistically significant bias. Even an electronic analog of a roulette wheel, built by the Rand Corporation for the generation of random digits, after careful engineering and re-engineering to eliminate bias, was found again to have statistically significant biases, after running continuously for a month, in spite of the fact that tests showed the electronic equipment itself to be in good order.[24]

How can bias be avoided? First, it can be reduced by resorting to compound chance events. And, formally it can be eliminated by the use of random numbers.

By making the chance-event a compound of two or more independent events, elements in the compound event can be made more nearly independent of each other, and thus biases can be avoided. For example, in the Surrealist *cadavre exquis*, it was made impossible for any one person to foresee the overall result of combining the independently contributed parts of the drawing, so that bias in the relationship of elements in the compound chance-event (drawing) was avoided. John Cage has also used this technique in his *Music for Four Pianos,* wherein four pianists play independently of each other, the resulting rhythmic and melodic pattern being thus freed of personal bias. In fact, this technique has been used, in a much-refined way, to generate a table of strictly random numbers (those published by the Interstate Commerce Commission[25]). Independent columns of digits from waybills received by the commission deriving from numerical data such as shipment weight, revenue, car serial number, and so forth, were used as a basic set from which the final set was derived.

Tables of random numbers provide a convenient and reliable means of avoiding bias in selection; convenient because they allow random selection of anything that can be numbered, reliable because they can be verified to be statistically random. Tests for randomness in random number tables are described in references 21 and 26.

Randomness, then, implies an independence of each individual choice from every other choice, plus an aggregate impartiality toward the characteristic being sampled. In tables of random digits, for example, a state of randomness implies both that the occurrence of any particular digit at a particular point in the table is independent of the occurrence of all the other digits, and that the proportional occurrence of that digit in the long run is arbitrarily close to some preestablished value. Practically speaking, this means that in a table such as the Rand table, the digit five in a certain place is just as likely to be followed by a six, seven, eight or nine as it is to be followed by a zero, one, two, three, or four, and also that in the table as a whole, the proportion of digits five should be reasonably close to one tenth.

* * * * *

CODA

Chance in the arts provides a means for escaping the biases engrained in our personality by our culture and personal past history, that is, it is a means of attaining greater generality. The result is a method of approach with wide application. The methods of chance and randomness can be applied to the selection and arrangement of sounds by the composer, to movement and pace by the dancer, to three-dimensional form by the sculptor, to surface form and color by the painter, to linguistic elements by the poet. Science tells us that the universe is what we conceive it to be, and chance enables us to determine what we conceive it to be (for the conception is only partly conscious). The receptacle of forms available to the artist thus becomes open-ended, and eventually embraces all of nature, for the recognition of significant form becomes limited only by the observer's self. It must be obvious too that the infinite range of application of these methods is compounded when the matter of materials is also considered, and this is a subject we have only incidentally touched on here. One hopes that so-called avant-garde painters will some day look beyond the classical oil medium with the same open-minded receptivity that, say, Pierre Schaeffer did in his field, in 1948. ("Quand on s'entête contre toute logique, c'est qu'on attend quelque chose d'un hasard, que cette logique n'aurait pas su prévoir. Mon mérite est d'avoir apercu. entre cent expériences, celle, apparement aussi décevant que les autres, qui creait l'évasion. Encore fallait-il avoir l'audace de généraliser.")[28]

I doubt that an increase in our ability to recognize significance in the chance-images that nature presents all about us will mean an end of the personal activities that we have been calling art. The artist will probably continue to make significant images, both because some such images rarely occur in nature, and because of a personal release that comes about from such activity:

> The painter makes paintings in the urgent need to discharge his own emotions and visions. —Pablo Picasso[29]

> Pictures are vehicles of passion, of all kinds and orders, not pretty luxuries like sports cars. In our society, the capacity to give and to receive passion is limited.

For this reason, the act of painting is a deep human necessity, not the production of a hand-made commodity. —Robert Motherwell[30]

But it seems to me that we fall short of the infinite expansion of the human spirit for which we are searching, when we recognize only images that are artifacts. We are capable of more than that.

AN AFTER-NOTE

In 1957, when this article was written, I had only recently met John Cage and had not yet seen clearly that the most important implications of chance lay in his work rather than in Pollock's. Nor could I have foreseen the resolution of the distinction between choice and chance which was to occur in my own work.

We are eight years farther on the spiral, and I prefer work to re-work. "Chance-Imagery" is presented in the form in which it was originally written.

November, 1965

Carl D. Clark and Loris Essary

Semi-constructs of the Secrétaire du Registre

And, so, we sit around passing the time and confusi
on grows . . . . an incredible sense of what is the pu
rpose if you know what I mean. What Tzara might have c
alled a feeling of oildrums and peonies. Amid this dol
or, what is art? The seas seem calm. Deception. A feel
ing of perhaps this is a

sign of   growing   A person said to us: "How c
old; pe   rhaps a   an you hope to convert peopl
n indic (grace)   ation o   e if they don't understand w
f not a   dmittin   hat you're doing?" Another a
g something that should   sked if we were getting mone
be said, of not properly   y from the highway departmen
administering slaps to s   t. On the whole, the second
ome people's psychic fac   question is less insulting t
es.   han the first.

How hard it is when everything encourages us to sle
ep, though we may look about us with cautious, clingin
g eye, to wake and yet look about

                    us as in a d   The reversal of mea
In a certain sense, ream, with e   ning that accompani
everything is ever yes that no   es the apocalypse i
ywhere at all time longer know   s one that reaches
s.   their functi   into all aspects of
   -Alfred North   on and whose   our social and indi
      Whitehead   gaze is turn   vidual lives, and r
                    ed inward.   eaches back into ou
It would be incredi   -Artaud   r history, the hist
bly inconvenie   ory of Western thou
nt to have an   ght. Its implication is that the "good
unambiguous la   life" is one of the most vicious man h
nguage, and, t   as produced . . . . our mania for clea
herefore, merc   nliness, sanity, decorum, and moderati
ifully, we hav   on only serves to heighten our dirt, m
e not got one.   adness, barbarism, and excess.
   -Bertrand   -John Vernon
      Russell

Reprinted from *Interstate*, no. 2 (1974), by permission of the authors. Copyright © 1974 Interstate Magazine.

No man lives in external truth among salts and acids, but in the warm phantasmagoric chamber of his brain, with the painted windows and the storied walls.
                    —William James

A work is "eternal" not because it imposes a single meaning on different men, but because it suggests the different meanings to a single man, speaking the same symbol in all ages: the work disposes. Every reader who is prepared to resist being intimidated by the letter knows this; does he not sense that he is coming into contact with what lies beyond the text, as though the primary language of the work gave rise to other words in him, teaching him a new tongue? That is what we call dreaming.

The borders of my language are the borders of my world.
                —Wittgenstein

                    —Barthes

A. A violent order is disorder; and
B. A great disorder is an order. These
Two things are one.
          —Wallace Stevens

Rest and quiet? Leave them to the dead where they belong.
          —Heraclitus

Questioner: Surely you believe in a beginning, middle and an end?
Godard: Oh, yes. But not necessarily in that order.

There are 3.2 billion seconds in a century.

The Mind, that Ocean where each Kind
Does straight its own resemblance find;
Yet it creates, transcending these,
Far other World, and other Seas;
Annihilating all that's made
To a green Thought in a green Shade.
          —Marvell

And time remains around us like pools of color.
          —Yves Bonnefoy

There are 3.2 billion people on the earth.

It is the computer's and image-maker's turn to take chaos by the scruff of the neck and make sense out of it. Already computer scientists admit that random events conspire towards particular patterns.

Man passes through forests of symbols which watch him with familiar eyes.
          —Baudelaire

          —Mark Slade

Let us move on to the clock without hands.

CARL D. CLARK AND LORIS ESSARY

I was born down and country I wrestled with reality f
music was my up.   or forty years, and
Then when I mad   I am happy to state
e my way up to   FORM   that I finally won
the top, I foun   FOLLOWS   out over it.
d that everyone   FUNCTION.   -Elwood P. Dowd
was trying to g   -Louis
et down.   Sullivan   A style sets up
    -Roger   an horizon of e
        Miller   In LANGUAGE OF CHA   xperience.
                  NGE, Mark Slade se   -E. H.
                  ts up two systems   Gombrich
                  that exist in the
world: the mechanical and the organic:

the mechanical: the organic:
    certainty,   probability,
    static,   dynamic,
    permanent,   wha   changing,
    content, .   t i   process,
matching wheels,   s h   electronic circuits
boundaries fixed,   ere,   boundaries open,
primary causes,   is   primary effects,
    nouns,   els   verbs,
        geometric,   ewh   topological,
    components,   ere.   patterns,
piecemeal data,   configurations,
    single field,   wha   total field,
point of view,   t i   points of view,
    rational,   s n   non-rational,
    deductive,   ot   inductive,
    behaviour,   her   experience,
subject-object divided, e,   subject-object fused
    science,   is   magic,
    landscape.   now   inscape.
                         her
                         e.

Obscurity is   Vishavasara Tantra   Risking repetit
creative if   ition, what is
it is such a bright and pure   necessary is for art t
illumination that our fellow   o not only pass the co
men are blinded by it.   nsciousness of Euclid,
        -Tzara   Newton and Locke, but
                               for it to pass the poi
This century has been haunt   nt of Einsteinian cons
ed by the spectre of the pos   ciousness at which art
sibility that Bacon actually   has been stuck for fif
did write Shakespeare.   ty years.

        Without dimension, where length,
            breadth, and highth,
        And time and place are lost; where
            eldest night
        And chaos, ancestors of nature,
            hold
        Eternal anarchie . . . .
                -Milton

The first problem then for literature, if it is to have a part to play in this present space age, is to begin to accept new forms and new ideas. This does not mean denying the stream of literary history that has gone before it, but building upon that very stream. Science does not deny Newton even though it is today beyond Einstein . . . . Thus, in art, the sentence must be destroyed because it never existed.... Only words exist. And words engender thought.
     –Arlene Zekowski

The absolute object slightly turned is a metaphor of the object.
    –Stevens

The pen is mightier than the sword/But no match for a gun.
    –The Beach Boys

My goal is to teach you to pass from something that is disguised nonsense to something that is patent nonsense.
    –Wittgenstein

  Il s'agit de cet objet . . . .
    –Bonnefoy

If you're listening to this song,
You may think the chords are going
    wrong;

Fragments
are
the
only
forms
I
trust.
  –Barthelme

But they're not:
He just wrote them like that
*   *   *   *   *   *   *
Cause it's only a northern song.
    –The Beatles

Just like everything else.
And on
and on
and on . . . .

Kenneth Burke

On Form

These observations are offered in connection with the exceptionally interesting article, "The End of the Renaissance," by Leonard B. Meyer, in the
Summer, 1963, issue of *The Hudson Review*. The piece is brilliantly effective
in building up a contrast between what the author calls traditional "teleological" music and certain contemporary "anti-teleological," "unkinetic," or
"static" trends. Thus, it is primarily concerned with these new methods in
music, and with the theory on which they are based. Also, in the course of
making his point, Dr. Meyer says many things that help me reinforce and
qualify some speculations on literary form as developed in my book, *Counter-
Statement* (particularly the essays, "Psychology and Form" and "Lexicon
Rhetoricae"). And I dare hope that some readers may be interested in
considering the subject a bit further, fortunately in the spirit of discussion
rather than of controversy.

First, as for the theory in its simplicity, let me quote a paragraph from a
talk I gave when restating my definition two years ago at the Midwest
Theatre Conference, Summer 1961 (a greatly condensed version of the talk
appeared in the *University of Chicago Magazine,* October, 1961):

> The theory to which I subscribed when first thinking of form in classical drama
> involved a definition of form as the arousing and fulfilling of expectations in the
> audience. That is, form in literature is an arousing and fulfilling of desires: one
> part of a work leads the reader to anticipate another part and to be gratified by
> the sequence. This notion of fulfilling of desires can also be treated as a ful-

Reprinted from the *Hudson Review,* by permission of the author and the publisher.

filling of expectations because one or the other of those terms will bring out one or another aspect of that problem.

The shift between "desire" and "expectation" involves a difference of emphasis. In a tragedy, for instance, the destruction of the hero may be "logically" indicated, regardless of our sympathies. Here the term *expectation* would fit best. The principle of "poetic justice" (with the triumph of good and the vanquishing of evil) would be the clearest instance of developments for which the term *desire* would be a better fit. But in any classically constructed work, the two principles will cooperate. And even when our beloved or admired hero goes to his inevitable doom, the work is "formally correct" only insofar as, in a profounder sense, we are brought to *will* his sacrifice. (Sadistic and masochistic trends in poetry readily lead to a departure from such tests.)

In my "Lexicon Rhetoricae" the general principle of such "fulfillment" was, as they would say now, "broken down" into subdivisions, which will be considered later.[1] At present the important consideration is the fact that the concept of "fulfillment" can itself be found to reveal a quite different set of implications. Thus whereas, for a long time, I had worked with the distinction between "self-expression" and "communication" (and with schemes whereby the two variously correct or reenforce each other), I gradually came to realize that some such third term as "consummation" was needed, for the discussion of formal principles. If anyone is interested, the subject is explicitly discussed in the last two pages of my article on Richard Blackmur, "The Criticism of Criticism," in the Autumn 1955 issue of *Accent*. (The matter is also discussed, from a more general point of view, in an article, "Motion, Action, Words," that appeared in the December 1960 issue of *Teachers College Record*).

The point, briefly, is this: In my studies of terminology, I came to see how inexorably certain directions of thought (with corresponding conclusions or "fulfillments") are implicit in the nature of the terms we use when confronting a given problem, or situation. (Simplest example: The difference between Darwinian and Fundamentalist statements about human motives.) A terminology is a kind of photographic "screen" which will "let through" some perceptions and "filter out" others. I began to suspect that this fact about the nature of "terministic screens" is the sheerly technical or "logological" counterpart of the theological formula, "believe that you may understand" (*crede ut intelligas*). Technically, the choice of a terminology in terms of which to state one's proposition is equivalent to the "act of faith" (*credere*) through which one can arrive at understanding (*intelligere*). And the *tracking down of the implications in a terminology* (as with physicists making bombs or biologists breeding pedigreed bugs for possible use in bacteriological war) is not just an example of either "self-expression" or "communication," but of "consummation." Thus, in the talk I gave at Chicago, I tried to analyze Ionesco's play, *Victims of Duty,* as a "consummatory" way of developing the implications of the title (naturally, within the limits of the author's insights).

For Dr. Meyer's succinct preparatory statement about the principle of expectation as operative in classical musical form, see the paragraph beginning at the bottom of p. 172 [of *Hudson Review*]. But as regards the main burden of his article (his concern with the "anti-teleological" element in "random, or indeterminate music"), I submit that much of the theory and corresponding practices discussed in the article would clearly fall under the head of what I would treat in terms of "consummation," or "tracking down the implications of a terminology." For, just as the principle of consummation in literature may lead a writer to kinds of discovery not directly attributable to either self-expression or communication as motive, so the efficiently end-of-the-line "anti-teleological" kind of music is presented by its theorists in terms that reject both self-expression and communication as musical aims. Also, in detailing so graphically the tie-up between the rationale for such music and the methods for producing it, Dr. Meyer shows us an almost perfect instance of "consummation" (at least such consummatory thoroughness as may be exemplified by the tracking down of implications in specialized scientific terminologies).

But though Dr. Meyer's article clearly indicates how the principle of *consummation* may lead to the flouting of *communication* (and its kinds of "meaningfulness") as an artist's proclaimed criterion of workmanship, the fact remains that, insofar as a work does arouse an audience's interest, it can do so only by embodying some principles of appeal. That is, to the extent that the product engages our attention it necessarily confronts tests of communication.

A person who talks to us excitedly in a language we do not understand will at the least "communicate" to us his state of excitement—and similarly, the "random and indeterminate" inventions of contemporary musical gadgetry must if nothing else engage us by the evidence of their inventiveness, however much the planning and results may differ from the "teleological" inventiveness of a Bach fugue.

A poem might conceivably be composed by sheer accident (for instance, by picking up pied type and arranging the letters in arbitrary order with one's eyes shut). Yet regardless of its *random origins,* when we turn our attention to the record of these accidents we are automatically or inevitably involved in the *laws* of their appeal. For when an art object engages our attention, by the sheer nature of the case we are involved in at least as much of a *communicative* relationship as prevails between a pitchman and a prospective customer. Whether or not a work is *designed* to "entertain," it can claim our suffrage or our sufferance only insofar as, by hook or crook, it *does* "entertain" in some way or other.

We might sum up the point thus: A theory of form as sheerly *aleatory* would not suffice for a discussion of a work's *reception* when read or performed, even if the work did arise by *wholly* aleatory processes (considerations which, so far at least, do not seem to have been met). Regardless of what a work was designed to do, and regardless of how that design (or paradoxical lack of design) came into being, if ever the work is presented to an audience it must be treated *as though* designed to hold the attention of an audience. For such a principle is implicit in the very nature of attention, which can't be attentive without, by the same token, implying that the object of attention is in some respect there to be attended to.

Maybe I keep saying this over and over again because it's like trying to disprove the metaphysical doctrine of solipsism, which is impervious to contradiction, even though if *I* tell *you* solipsistically that the world is all in *my* mind, *you* know that it is not, and if *you* tell *me* solipsistically that the world is all in *your* mind, *I* know that it is not. Obviously, such "refutation" must begin by positing the reality of an audience *outside* the realm of the solipsist's powers of creation (in brief a *social* situation which is precisely what solipsism rules out).

Fortunately, the theory of aleatory music *does* concede the existence of an audience, since we are told what kind of attention such an audience is expected to cultivate for the appreciation of each sound, in and for itself, without regard for its relation to other sounds in the same sequence. But the injunction to ignore the relatedness of sounds in a sequence (even while the inventor spends so much time gambling to set up a sequence however fluctuant), suggests to me somewhat those courtroom situations where a lawyer schemes to bring some point before a jury, even though he knows in advance that the judge will instruct the jury to disregard it. Show me two "unrelated" things, one after the other—and willy-nilly, you have built up for me a relationship between them, no matter how much I am told to disregard it.

So, in accordance with the proposition that no critic is required to accept without question any artists' formulation of the principles said by them or their spokesmen to be embodied in their art; and in accordance with the related proposition that criticism's efforts to translate any kind of *poetry* into terms of its corresponding *poetics* should not cease until all elements seem adequately accounted for, I'd still maintain that, no matter how "random and indeterminate" may be the (almost *pedantically* planned) conditions under which such works arise, the nature of their *origins* cannot adequately account for any claim they may make upon our attention. Ergo, so far as criticism is concerned, the search for the rules of their appeal (if any) must continue.

At this point, a whole new set of avowals presents itself for consideration. And whereas I began by rejoicing at the opportunity to enlist Dr. Meyer's excellent essay in my cause (as regards the laws of appeal embodied in classical art), I now want to introduce these other considerations.

Happily, they are not in basic conflict with his distinction between the "teleological" and "anti-teleological" (the teleological anti-teleology of planned planlessness), which is primarily concerned with certain musicians' rationale and methods of *production*. For I am shifting the emphasis to considerations of *reception*, which I contend necessarily involves *some kind of communicative* test, insofar as it involves *any* presentation of the works before an audience. In brief, unless the inventors of this music are willing to produce it and perform it without ever letting it be witnessed by an audience, questions of communication necessarily figure. Otherwise, there is no point to the musicians' *exhibiting* the results of their *partially* random inventions. To exhibit is necessarily to solicit attention, however coy or gruff or self-indulgent or self-protective may be one's ways of setting up the situation.

I say *partially* random because (as per earlier remarks on the *crede, ut intelligas* principle) many decisive departures from sheer randomness were already inherent in whatever particular kind of "random situation" the experimenter set up for a given aleatory enterprise. Even a pack of cards shuffled and dealt at random is by the nature of the case of selection of *one particular nomenclature* in terms of which the randomness is to be experienced. And since any art is a species of symbolic action, each art is necessarily "de-termined" by the particular nature of the terms through which it acts. The question thus gets down to this: Despite the obvious physicality of sound, is the *act* of musical production reducible to sheer *motion?* And even if the act of musical *production* is so reducible, is the act of *audience participation* similarly reducible to terms of sheer motion? Or is it not inevitable that, just as the musician *acts* by selecting the particular kind of situation in terms of which he will let random *motions* take their course, so an audience *acts* by consenting to let its attention follow in these particular grooves. The appreciation of a sound qua sound is an appreciation of an *essence* for its own sake. And as Santayana's philosophy makes clear, nothing could be more thoroughly in the realm of "Spirit." (That is, nothing could be more thoroughly in the realm of *symbolic action*.)

Have I hung on too long? It was hard to resist! For I feel that the very thoroughness of this supposed "break" with past criteria helps all the more to point up the justification for those criteria. Obviously, however, if any criteria of classical "teleological" form are to be applied with regard to forms that arise with combinations like those due to a throw of dice, the principles must at least be applied with a difference.

The following considerations, then, seem particularly relevant to Dr. Meyer's article:

(1) Apparently "anti-teleological" form quite thoroughly dispenses with what I'd call *syllogistic* progression (works deliberately so constructed that they lead in an arrowlike directedness towards a culmination and resolution).

(2) But for that very reason, much of such music should accommodate itself exceptionally well to what I'd call *minor* or *incidental* forms, brief episodes often so sharply demarcated that they can be appreciated one by one, like epigrams. (However, I have already indicated why such a stress upon a sequence of such details in themselves cannot wholly avoid a sense of *relatedness* among successive steps in the sequence.)

(3) The works might be found to possess a high degree of what I'd call *conventional* form (or *categorical expectancy*), once you get over the tendency to think of new conventions purely in terms of their "break" with past conventions. Conventional form is no less conventional simply because it happens to embody new conventions which set up correspondingly new kinds of expectation. Indeed, the "experimental" aspect of much modern work (at least partly an esthetic reflection of the scientific attitude towards the methods of the laboratory) awakens in us a kind of expectation that can make us categorically receptive to novelty, even to the extent where we would resent too great similarity to the kinds of expectation associated with sheerly traditional art-forms.

(3-a) In particular, at this point, could we not introduce our principle of "negative" expectation (a later concept, not discussed in the "Lexicon Rhetoricae")? When a few moments of avant-garde music are played, you may experience none of the keenly "teleological" anticipation that you find, say, in a phrase by Mozart, where the announcement of an antecedent prepares you for its completion in a "logically" related consequent. But in almost no time, you sense what kind of sound *not* to expect. Indeed, the new conventions quickly set up a whole set of *categorical* expectations that, however tentative, almost *tyrannically* rule out kinds of sound we had learned to expect in connection with past norms of conventional form.

(3-b) Perhaps the notion of "negative" expectation is but a slightly different slant on what I originally called *qualitative* progression: a turn which is not directly expected, but which, when it arrives, is received as the kind of surprise, or contrast, or ellipsis (or "leap") that somehow "fits" the situation (thereby indicating that the conditions for this turn were implicitly, or "naturally," present).

(4) And most important of all, there is repetitive form, perhaps the most compelling of all expectations, the requirement that, in some strategic respect, *the same general kind of procedure* will be maintained throughout a given work. Just as Kant says that the human mind can't avoid thinking in terms of substance, so I'd contend that, insofar as a work is identifiable at all, it must to that extent possess a measure of substance (some kind of "unity," however loose) that would fall under the heading of repetitive form, and that thus gratifies our expectations by going on being the kind of thing we tend to expect, however great the surprises and variations encountered en route.

In sum, then: If to these various kinds of expectancy and the principle of consummation, we add the fragmentation and perversion or sophistication (extension and over-simplification) of classical formal principles, might even "random and indeterminate" music be analyzed as less of a break with traditional poetic principles than it might otherwise appear to be? Indeed, if you'll admit such a chart of continuous terms as I indicate on p. 145 of *Permanence and Change* (Hermes Edition) could we not treat even an audience's interest in new sounds for their own sake as involving but the variation of a quite "classical" response, the appeal of "wonder"?

I say as much, not through any basic resistance to any experiments now being undertaken by contemporary artists in any field, but owing to my investment in a theory of "symbolic action." And though I find much to sympathize with in aesthetic cults of sheer motion, I take it that any such cults are necessarily "Isms," hence in the realm of *action*. Accordingly, since classical models of poetic theory take for granted a Dramatistic view of man, I hold it most likely that principles of poetics based on the analysis of classical models will be found applicable to all modes of symbolic action (such as I take all artistic styles to be), once we approach new work, not by asking that it abide by classical models, but by asking wherein it *modifies* classical models. Hence we resist only at the point where, in any manifesto, we are assured that some recent kind of symbolic action is really as much of a break with traditional poetic principles as it might otherwise seem to be. Such claims are likely to be more worthy of study as advertising or as revelations of artists' psychology than as poetics.

George Kubler

Style and the Representation of Historical Time

Humans surely are not unique in their capacity for identifying different events as being recurrent. Other animals also project their organic needs under the same guise of identity among successive stimuli.

G. A. Brecher showed in 1932 that the snails read space into succession.[1] As an art historian, I am overly familiar with the notion of style, which is another way of imposing space upon time and of denying duration under the illusion that successive events are similar events. To spatialize time is a faculty shared both by snails and by historians.

I.

This paper has three parts. The first one is about resemblances between the writing of history and the painting of pictures. The second part concerns the nature of duration as historians perceive it. The third part considers whether the idea of style is suitable to studies of duration.

The writing of history resembles the painting of pictures, as Thucydides remarked in the *Moralia.* It depends upon many schemes and conventions of representation. These may tentatively be grouped as a) conventions in the *selection* of what to represent from the immense complexity of any portion of duration, and b) conventions as to the mode of *figuration* among these selections.

Reprinted from the *Annals of the New York Academy of Sciences* CXXXVIII/2 (1967), by permission of the author and the publisher.

a) *Selection.* 1. Unique cases and general cases form a gradient at whose extremes the possibility of history vanishes. The historian selects a median position on the gradient, in order to resolve the antithesis between a microstructure where no two actions are alike, and a macrostructure where all actions are alike. The position selected depends upon the historian's desire to represent activity as having purpose.

Everything about a work of art is contrived to force us to perceive it as a unique object occupying one place and having unusually integral properties of material, technique, form and significance. Our habit of meeting it in a museum or on a stage or in a concert hall, where it bids for our attention with the illusion that it is a single point in space, time, and feeling, further masks the historical reality of every work of art. That reality is totally different from the illusion of uniqueness.

Historically, every work of art is a fragment of some larger unit, and every work of art is a bundle of components of different ages, intricately related to many other works of art, both old and new, by a network of incoming and outgoing influences. These larger units, these bundles of components, and these interrelations across time and space, constitute the study of historical style which is also called stylistic analysis.

2. Narrative and statistical presentations are antithetical. They require the historian to decide upon his unit of study, for example, biographical or categorical, and upon an approach, either qualitative (the great man) or quantitative. Both are possible in the same work.

Some kinds of historical representation are less viable than others: the chronicler today tells us much less in the long run than the economic historian or the statistician. There is accordingly a hierarchy of the modes of historical representation in respect to generalizing power. But there is also an inverse hierarchy by immediacy and authenticity in which the chronicler who witnessed the events, is our primary source, and the statistician is very far from the events he describes. Whom shall we believe? Of course we believe them both, for different qualities of experience, yet equally.

3. Events may be treated synchronously or diachronously, that is, as events at rest in a cross section of relationships or as events in duration, under unceasing change in motion and flow. In synchronous treatment, events are either densely or sparsely arrayed. In the diachronous view, events are rapid or slow. Dense array and rapid happenings are not equivalent (neither are sparse and slow).

Synchronous treatments tend towards the definition of structures; diachronous ones towards the distinction of separate evolutions. Synchronism is synthetic: diachronism is analytic.

4. Having no intrinsic segmentation of its own, time divides only for organisms experiencing sequences of actions. The historian is at liberty to stress either the regularity of artificial periods (centuries, decades) or the irregularity of actual durations.

In either case, he is exploring a psychological phenomenon called *transduction*. Here, repetitive stimulations, as by works of art of the same class, induce a *spatialization*, or illusion of coherent surface, which some of us call style.

The phenomenon has been studied in snails: when the belly is repeatedly prodded, the snail begins to crawl, that is, he transforms periodic stimulation into a perceptual object by a process called the transduction of simultaneity into duration.[1]

b) *Figuration* is as complex as everything that the painter does after deciding what he is going to paint.

For the historian it is the beginning of the last lap. Usually the prior matter of selection requires from him a nearly total commitment of his available time and energy.

How to frame the question is so much of his work (as with the true painter), that the presentation becomes merely a matter of how to pay the bills, as it were, for the existing contracts.

5. At any past moment, what was then present may be regarded as consisting mainly of latent possibilities. Equally truthful, it may be regarded as consisting mainly of explicit actualities. The historian is free to find his own conventional resolution between these extremes.

In the first case, where possibility is stressed, the historian is concerned with futurities, with emergent values, and his work is forward-looking, imposing the past upon that which is to come. In the second case, (the explicit actuality) the factual stock is inventoried and the past is brought into alignment with the inventory. Here the historian's work looks to the rear, imposing the present order upon the valuation of the past.

6. Distinct possibilities of figuration are available according to whether the historian prefers relations of "cause and effect," or relations of "conditions and events."

The causal search is one that imposes an excessively simple pattern of explanation upon events. Since every event, however minute, may be infinitely complex, the causal interpretation always betrays the haste of practical urgency. More flexible and expressive is the statement of conditions for any event. The conditional search is necessarily tentative, and it frays into many strands of doubt. Pictorially the difference between cause and condition resembles the difference between Picasso and Velazquez, between abstraction and illusion.

7. Historians have to decide the relation of figure to ground in their representations of duration. A historical personage, for instance, stands to the conditions limiting his actions much as a visible design drawn upon the page stands to its background. Sometimes the ground has greater visibility than the figure, and vice versa, depending upon the historian's preference or position.

Figure and ground are like recurrent events and sequences of events. In *The Shape of Time* (1962) I tried to replace the *cyclical* notion of recurrence by a *sequential* idea. The unit of happening is a serial episode: a chain of events with beginning, middle, and end. The scale can be any scale.

The aforementioned conventions surely do not exhaust the possible or eventual range of the historian's devices for portraying duration. Like poets and painters, he too is engaged in a constant search for mimetic schemes of representation, and in testing their relatedness to the events being discussed. These however, usually can be known only via historical means and presentations. In the dialectical progression he therefore tests his representations more on other representations rather than on events proper, since all past events are no longer available to observation save as artifacts or contingent traces of the activity under study, which we can know only in documents, chronicles, and histories.

My purpose here in stressing the conventionality of everything the historian writes is to mark clearly the categorical difference between any duration, and the histories or portrayals that may be written about it. A duration and its history differ as greatly as what we see differs from a painting of that sight. By this token history is like sight.

Nor should it be forgotten that a written history becomes a part of duration in much the same way as a painting becomes part of what we see, and even of *how* we see it. Thus the writing of history has many modes. They all affect the nature of our perception of duration. Every portrayal affects the identity of what is portrayed, as much as the subject conditions its portrayals.

The subject of history is time. If we grant that time has no specially privileged divisions, the situation resembles the natural world we perceive with the sensory manifold. Time can be structured only as variously as the varieties of historical perception at our disposal.

II

Painting is about the world of vision, and history is about duration. Therefore, having paid respect to the parallel of history and painting, we should look at the nature of duration. This I consider as sequence among actions of the same class. Five axioms about such actions are proposed as relevant to the nature of duration.

I. Similar actions by the same agent cannot occupy the same time. If they do, the recipient is different and the action also.

II. No one agent can perform the same action more than once without ageing.

III. Actions can be only similar but not identical, being different as to agent, or as to time, or as to location.

IV. Actions repeated undergo change.

V. The agent changes with each repeated action.

Duration thus consists of distinct actions which resist classification, because each action differs from every other action in the microstructure of happening as to time, place, and event. Yet the large-scale classing of actions is continually needed for activity to seem to have purpose.

I. Often one discovers that he is apparently doing several different things at the same time such as playing organ chords with ten fingers and both feet, or reading aloud by a sick friend's bedside, while thinking about what to say to the family, as well as rising to close the door on a draft, and re-arranging the furniture. Yet none of these actions is continuous: each has interstices for intrusive actions, even reading aloud, which is far more dis-continuous than we realize, consisting of bits of action separated by intervals like doorways for other actions.

II. No one agent can perform an action more than once without ageing.

The question arises: is there such an agent as a single agent? Each individual admittedly houses several identities or role-players. Is the agent an individual or does his individuality reside in a part he plays? Is he a cluster of attitudes seen through time, or a single facet caught in action and engage-ment? The question revolves for all practical needs when we compare the many-faceted person, which is each of us, to a revolving cog-wheel, present-ing only one facet in each instant, unless the engaging sprocket jams the action by some unexpected motion of its own.

The single identity of any agent depends, in short, upon the position and motion of the person perceiving his identity. The singleness is assured by the shorter durations, and by instantaneous exposure to a reliable and constant perceptor.

III. Actions can only be similar, but not identical, being different as to agent, or as to time, or as to location.

To suppose identical actions by the same agent, we must admit the idea. that time is reversible, which is contrary to experience. For actions to be identical, they must recur exactly as to agent and place and time. Hence recurrence would be like reversal in time.

IV. Actions repeated undergo change.

Since place and agent differ for successive actions, however similar they seem, the actions themselves are necessarily different. The one quality of time never noted is its absolute power to erode and erase identities between actions. These identities are created only by the abstracting mind, engaged in making time tangible by arresting it.

V. The agent changes with each repeated action.

The proof is seen in certain autobiographies rewritten after a lapse, as in the case of Igor Stravinsky, whose two lives appeared years apart, as well as in biographies rewritten by the same biographer, like Bertram Wolfe's two lives of Diego Rivera, written years apart. The "same" stories are told twice, but they are different stories, weighted and valued differently by different narrators.

III

The notion of style has long been the art historian's principal mode of classing works of art. By style he selects and shapes the history of art. We therefore need to correlate, if we can, style and duration.

Uncritical usage in the history of art permits the word *style* to be used in different and mutually exclusive ways. On the one hand, style is cited as a configuration of qualities shared by many objects spread throughout a long span of time, as though the shared configuration were immutable in composition and intensity.[2]

On the other hand, style preferably means all the systemic changes we observe in the history of a cluster of traits or forms, much as the word *weather* stands for constantly changing relationships of temperature, pressure, humidity. The anthropologist, A. L. Kroeber, described style as a strand in culture, which is best studied as to content, structure, and flow, with development as its most characteristic trait.[3]

James Ackerman, the art historian, likewise specified style as a relational concept, under the operational view that the concept of style "is a means of establishing relationships among individual works of art,"[4] like the concepts of society and culture, which are also based on relationships.

If we proceed on the assumptions that style is both relational and developmental, we need to test the connection between relatedness and change. Several propositions, seven at least, can easily be advanced, together with their counter-propositions.

1. Styles, being historical configurations, are neither perpetual nor in random change. Being in change, however, their identity is in doubt at every instant.

2. Elements dispersed evenly throughout all historical time cannot mark style. Yet style presupposes such stable configurations within limited durations.

3. Style is identifiable only among time-bound elements. Yet if the components are in differential change, as they always are, the relation among them is a changing one.

4. Presupposing a style presupposes that it has a beginning and an end, although the components may have begun earlier, and might end later than the style itself.

5. Each kind of human action has its styles: no actions or products escape style. Yet the preceding observations suggest that such configurations are more instantaneous than extended in duration.

6. We participate in going styles, and we observe past style. But the operations of esthetic choice are unpredictable: a past style may at any instant be revived.

7. Different styles can coexist, like languages in one speaker. Such coexistence itself can be more various than style.

I conclude that it is probably impossible to portray the content of any duration, without invoking the idea of style, if only as a classificatory convenience. Yet when style is mentioned the problem arises as to which one among many entities or components is regarded as having style. Even an isolated, single object, such as the Parthenon, or a human body, belongs to several different developmental systems. Each of these—the blood, the skin, the kidney—displays differing systematic ages. The rose window, for example, at Chartres Cathedral, has a systematic age unlike that of the ogival vaults, and the two pieces, vault and rose, should therefore be ascribed to different styles, which the usual classification as "Gothic" lumps together.

Thus a major contradiction arises from the use of the term *style*. The idea of style is best adapted to static situations, in cross-cut or synchronous section. It is an idea unsuited to duration, which is dynamic, because of the changing nature of every class in duration.

The necessary solution of this difficulty with style is to restrict the use of the word to discussions removed from duration. When flow and change are ignored, and when development is disregarded, style remains useful as a taxonomic convenience. But wherever the passage of time is under consideration, with its shifting identities and continuous transformations, the taxonomic notion, represented by the term *style,* becomes irrelevant. Thus style and the flow of happening are antinomies. Style pertains to a timeless sphere; and flow concerns change.

I conclude that the idea of style is best adapted to the description of synchronous situations involving groups of related events. But style is a notion unsuitable to diachronous durations, because of the composite nature of every imaginable class as a bundle of durations, each having widely different systematic ages.

In short, the idea of style is better suited to extension than to duration. When we are dealing with large durations, words describing time work better than extensional words like *style*.

Nelson Goodman

Art and Authenticity

> *... the most tantalizing question of all: If a fake is so expert that even after the most thorough and trustworthy examination its authenticity is still open to doubt, is it or is it not as satisfactory a work of art as if it were unequivocally genuine?*

—Aline B. Saarinen

New York Time Book Review, 30 July 1961, p. 14

1. THE PERFECT FAKE

Forgeries of works of art present a nasty practical problem to the collector, the curator, and the art historian, who must often expend taxing amounts of time and energy in determining whether or not particular objects are genuine. But the theoretical problem raised is even more acute. The hardheaded question why there is any aesthetic difference between a deceptive forgery and an original work challenges a basic premise on which the very functions of collector, museum, and art historian depend. A philosopher of art caught without an answer to this question is at least as badly off as a curator of paintings caught taking a Van Meegeren for a Vermeer.

The question is most strikingly illustrated by the case of a given work and a forgery or copy or reproduction of it. Suppose we have before us, on the left, Rembrandt's original painting *Lucretia* and, on the right, a superlative imitation of it. We know from a fully documented history that the painting on the left is the original; and we know from X-ray photographs and microscopic examination and chemical analysis that the painting on the right is a recent fake. Although there are many differences between the two—for example, in authorship, age, physical and chemical characteristics, and market value—we cannot see any difference between them; and if they are moved while we sleep, we cannot then tell which is which by merely looking at them. Now we are pressed with the question whether there can be any aesthetic difference between the two pictures; and the questioner's tone often intimates that the answer is plainly *no*, that the only differences here are aesthetically irrelevant.

We must begin by inquiring whether the distinction between what can and what cannot be seen in the pictures by "merely looking at them" is entirely clear. We are looking at the pictures, but presumably not "merely looking" at them, when we examine them under a microscope or fluoroscope. Does merely looking, then, mean looking without the use of any instrument? This seems a little unfair to the man who needs glasses to tell a painting from a hippopotamus. But if glasses are permitted at all, how strong may they be and can we consistently exclude the magnifying glass and the microscope? Again, if incandescent light is permitted, can violet-ray light be ruled out? And even with incandescent light, must it be of medium intensity and from a normal angle, or is a strong raking light permitted? All these cases might be covered by saying that "merely looking" is looking at the pictures without any use of instruments other than those customarily used in looking at things in general. This will cause trouble when we turn, say, to certain miniature illuminations or Assyrian cylinder seals that we can hardly distinguish from the crudest copies without using a strong glass. Furthermore, even in our case of the two pictures, subtle differences of drawing or painting discoverable only with a magnifying glass may still, quite obviously, be aesthetic differences between the pictures. If a powerful microscope is used instead, this is no longer the case; but just how much magnification is permitted? To specify what is meant by merely looking at the pictures is thus far from easy; but for the sake of argument,[1] let us suppose that all these difficulties have been resolved and the notion of "merely looking" made clear enough.

Then we must ask who is assumed to be doing the looking. Our questioner does not, I take it, mean to suggest that there is no aesthetic difference between two pictures if at least one person, say a cross-eyed wrestler, can see no difference. The more pertinent question is whether there can be any aesthetic difference if nobody, not even the most skilled expert, can ever tell the pictures apart by merely looking at them. *But notice now that no one can ever ascertain by merely looking at the pictures that no one ever has been or will be able to tell them apart by merely looking at them.* In other words, the question in its present form concedes that no one can ascertain by merely looking at the pictures that there is no aesthetic difference between them. This seems repugnant to our questioner's whole motivation. For if merely looking can never establish that two pictures are aesthetically the same, something that is beyond the reach of any given looking is admitted as constituting an aesthetic difference. And in that case, the reason for not admitting documents and the results of scientific tests becomes very obscure.

The real issue may be more accurately formulated as the question whether there is any aesthetic difference between the two pictures *for me* (or for x) if I (or x) cannot tell them apart by merely looking at them. But this is not quite right either. For I can never ascertain merely by looking at the pictures that even I shall never be able to see any difference between them. And to concede that something beyond any given looking at the pictures by me may constitute an aesthetic difference between them for me is, again, quite at odds with the tacit conviction or suspicion that activates the questioner.

Thus the critical question amounts finally to this: Is there any aesthetic difference between the two pictures for x at *t*, where *t* is a suitable period of time, if *x* cannot tell them apart by merely looking at them at *t*? Or in other words, can anything that *x* does not discern by merely looking at the pictures at *t* constitute an aesthetic difference between them for *x* at *t*?

2. THE ANSWER

In setting out to answer this question, we must bear clearly in mind that what one can distinguish at any given moment by merely looking depends not only upon native visual acuity but upon practice and training.[2] Americans look pretty much alike to a Chinese who has never looked at many of them. Twins may be indistinguishable to all but their closest relatives and acquaintances. Moreover, only through looking at them when someone has named them for us can we learn to tell Joe from Jim upon merely looking at them. Looking at people or things attentively, with the knowledge of certain presently invisible respects in which they differ, increases our ability to discriminate between them—and between other things or other people—upon merely looking at them. Thus pictures that look just alike to the newsboy come to look quite unlike to him by the time he has become a museum director.

Although I see no difference now between the two pictures in question, I may learn to see a difference between them. I cannot determine now by merely looking at them, or in any other way, that I *shall* be able to learn. But the information that they are very different, that the one is the original and the other the forgery, argues against any inference to the conclusion that I *shall not* be able to learn. And the fact that I may later be able to perceive a distinction between the pictures that I cannot perceive now makes the

149

actual differences between them aesthetically important to me now.

Furthermore, to look at the pictures now with the knowledge that the left one is the original and the other the forgery may help develop the ability to tell which is which later by merely looking at them. Thus, with information not derived from the present or any past looking at the pictures, the present looking may have quite different bearing upon future lookings from what it would otherwise have. The way the pictures in fact differ constitutes an aesthetic difference between them for me now, because my knowledge of the way they differ bears upon the role of the present looking in training my perceptions to discriminate between these pictures, and between others.

But that is not all. My knowledge of the difference between the two pictures, just because it affects the relationship of the present to future lookings, informs the very character of my present looking. This knowledge instructs me to look at the two pictures differently now, even if what I see is the same. Beyond testifying that I may learn to see a difference, it also indicates to some extent the kind of scrutiny to be applied now, the comparisons and contrasts to be made in imagination, and the relevant associations to be brought to bear. It thereby guides the selection, from my past experience, of items and aspects for use in my present looking. Thus not only later but right now, the unperceived difference between the two pictures is a consideration pertinent to my visual experience with them.

In short, although I cannot tell the pictures apart merely by looking at them now, the fact that the left-hand one is the original and the right-hand one a forgery constitutes an aesthetic difference between them for me now because knowledge of this fact (1) stands as evidence that there may be a difference between them that I can learn to perceive, (2) assigns the present looking a role as training toward such a perceptual discrimination, and (3) makes consequent demands that modify and differentiate my present experience in looking at the two pictures.[3]

Nothing depends here upon my ever actually perceiving or being able to perceive a difference between the two pictures. What informs the nature and use of my present visual experience is not the fact or the assurance that such a perceptual discrimination is within my reach, but evidence that it may be; and such evidence is provided by the known factual differences between the pictures. Thus the pictures differ aesthetically for me now even if no one will ever be able to tell them apart by merely looking at them.

But suppose it could be *proved* that no one ever will be able to see any difference? This is about as reasonable as asking whether, if it can be proved that the market value and yield of a given U.S. bond and one of a certain nearly bankrupt company will always be the same, there is any financial difference between the two bonds. For what sort of proof could be given? One might suppose that if nobody—not even the most skilled expert—has ever been able to see any difference between the pictures, then the conclusion that I shall never be able to is quite safe; but, as in the case of the Van Meegeren forgeries[4] (of which, more later), distinctions not visible to the expert up to a given time may later become manifest even to the observant layman. Or one might think of some delicate scanning device that compares the color of two pictures at every point and registers the slightest discrepancy. What, though, is meant here by "at every point"? At no mathematical point, of course, is there any color at all; and even some physical particles are too small to have color. The scanning device must thus cover at each instant a region big enough to have color but at least as small as any perceptible region. Just how to manage this is puzzling since *perceptible* in the present context means "discernible by merely looking," and thus the line between perceptible and nonperceptible regions seems to depend on the arbitrary line between a magnifying glass and a microscope. If some such line is drawn, we can never be sure that the delicacy of our instruments is superior to the maximal attainable acuity of unaided perception. Indeed, some experimental psychologists are inclined to conclude that every measurable difference in light can sometimes be detected by the naked eye.[5] And there is a further difficulty. Our scanning device will examine color—that is, reflected light. Since reflected light depends partly upon incident light, illumination of every quality, of every intensity, and from every direction must be tried. And for each case, especially since the paintings do not have a plane surface, a complete scanning must be made from every angle. But of course we cannot cover every variation, or even determine a single absolute correspondence, in even one respect. Thus the search for a proof that I shall never be able to see any difference between the two pictures is futile for more than technological reasons.

Yet suppose we are nevertheless pressed with the question whether, if proof *were* given, there would then be any aesthetic difference for me between the pictures. And suppose we answer this farfetched question in the negative. This will still give our questioner no comfort. For the net result would be that if no difference between the pictures can in fact be perceived, then the existence of an aesthetic difference between them will rest entirely upon what is or is not proved by means other than merely looking at them. This hardly supports the contention that there can be no aesthetic difference without a perceptual difference.

Returning from the realm of the ultra-hypothetical, we may be faced with the protest that the vast aesthetic difference thought to obtain between the Rembrandt and the forgery cannot be accounted for in terms of the search for, or even the discovery of, perceptual differences so slight that they can be made out, if at all, only after much experience and long practice. This objection can be dismissed at once; for minute perceptual differences can bear enormous weight. The clues that tell me whether I have caught the eye of someone across the room are almost indiscernible. The actual differences in sound that distinguish a fine from a mediocre performance can be picked out only by the well-trained ear. Extremely subtle changes can alter the whole design, feeling, or expression of a painting. Indeed, the slightest perceptual differences sometimes matter the most aesthetically; gross physical damage to a fresco may be less consequential than slight but smug retouching.

All I have attempted to show, of course, is that the two pictures can differ aesthetically, not that the original is better than the forgery. In our example, the original probably is much the better picture, since Rembrandt paintings are in general much better than copies by unknown painters. But a copy of a Lastman by Rembrandt may well be better than the original. We are not called upon here to make such particular comparative judgments or to formulate canons of aesthetic evaluation. We have fully met the demands of our problem by showing that the fact that we cannot tell our two pictures apart merely by looking at them does not imply that they are aesthetically the same—and thus does not force us to conclude that the forgery is as good as the original.

The example we have been using throughout illustrates a special case of a more general question concerning the aesthetic significance of authenticity. Quite aside from the occurrence of forged duplication, does it matter whether an original work is the product of one or another artist or school or period? Suppose that I can easily tell two pictures apart but cannot tell who painted either except by using some device like X-ray photography. Does the fact that the picture is or is not by Rembrandt make any aesthetic difference? What is involved here is the discrimination not of one picture from another but of the class of Rembrandt paintings from the class of other paintings. My chance of learning to make this discrimination correctly—of discovering projectible characteristics that differentiate Rembrandts in general from non-Rembrandts—depends heavily upon the set of examples available as a basis. Thus the fact that the given picture belongs to the one class or the other is important for me to know in learning how to tell Rembrandt paintings from others. In other words, my present (or future) inability to determine the authorship of the given picture without use of scientific apparatus does not imply that the authorship makes no aesthetic difference to me; for knowledge of the authorship, no matter how obtained, can contribute materially toward developing my ability to determine without such apparatus whether or not any picture, including this one on another occasion, is by Rembrandt. Moreover, where information is such as to be important to me when I have it, it is important to me to have, and thus important to me whether I have it or not.

Incidentally, one rather striking puzzle is readily solved in these terms. When Van Meegeren sold his pictures as Vermeers, he deceived most of the best-qualified experts; and only by his confession was the fraud revealed.[6] Nowadays even the fairly knowing layman is astonished that any competent judge could have taken a Van Meegeren for a Vermeer, so obvious are the differences. What has happened? The general level of aesthetic sensibility has hardly risen so fast that the layman of today sees more acutely than the expert of twenty years ago. Rather, the better information now at hand makes the discrimination easier. Presented with a single unfamiliar picture at a time, the expert had to decide whether it was enough like known Vermeers to be by the same artist. And every time a Van Meegeren was added to the corpus of pictures accepted as Vermeers, the criteria for acceptance were modified thereby; and the mistaking of further Van Meegerens for Vermeers became inevitable. Now, however, not only have the Van Meegerens been subtracted from the precedent-class for Vermeer, but also a precedent-class for Van Meegeren has been established. With these two precedent-classes before us, the characteristic differences become so conspicuous that telling other Van Meegerens from Vermeers offers little difficulty. Yesterday's expert might well have avoided his errors if he had had a few known Van Meegerens handy for comparison. And today's layman who so cleverly spots a Van Meegeren may well be caught taking some quite inferior school-piece for a Vermeer.

In answering the questions raised above, I have not attempted the formidable task of defining *aesthetic* in general,[7] but have simply argued that since the exercise, training, and development of our power of discriminating among works of art are plainly aesthetic activities, the aesthetic properties of a picture include not only those found by looking at it but also those that determine how it is to be looked at. This rather obvious fact would hardly have needed underlining but for the prevalence of the time-honored Tingle-Immersion theory,[8] which tells us that the proper behavior on encountering a work of art is to strip ourselves of all the vestments of knowledge and experience (since they might blunt the immediacy of our enjoyment), then submerge ourselves completely and gauge the aesthetic potency of the work by the intensity and duration of the resulting tingle. The theory is absurd on the face of it and useless for dealing with any of the important problems of aesthetics; but it has become part of the fabric of our common nonsense.

3. THE UNFAKABLE

A second problem concerning authenticity is raised by the rather curious fact that in music, unlike painting, there is no such thing as a forgery of a known work. There are, indeed, compositions falsely purporting to be by Haydn as there are paintings falsely purporting to be by Rembrandt; but of the London Symphony, unlike the *Lucretia*, there can be no forgeries. Haydn's manuscript is no more genuine an instance of the score than is a printed copy off the press this morning, and last night's performance no less genuine than the premiere. Copies of the score may vary in accuracy, but all accurate copies, even if forgeries of Haydn's manuscript, are equally genuine instances of the score. Performances may vary in correctness and quality and even in "authenticity" of a more esoteric kind; but all correct performances are equally genuine instances of the work.[9] In contrast, even the most exact copies of the Rembrandt painting are simply imitations or forgeries, not new instances, of the work. Why this difference between the two arts?

Let us speak of a work of art as *autographic* if and only if the distinction between original and forgery of it is significant; or better, if and only if even the most exact duplication of it does not thereby count as genuine.[10] If a work of art is autographic, we may also call that art autographic. Thus painting is autographic, music nonautographic, or *allographic*. These terms are introduced purely for convenience; nothing is implied concerning the relative individuality of expression demanded by or attainable in these arts. Now the problem before us is to account for the fact that some arts but not others are autographic.

One notable difference between painting and music is that the composer's work is done when he has written the score, even though the performances are the end-products, while the painter has to finish the picture. No matter how many studies or revisions are made in either case, painting is in this sense a one-stage and music a two-stage art. Is an art autographic, then, if and only if it is one-stage? Counterexamples come readily to mind. In the first place, literature is not autographic though it is one-stage. There is no such thing as a forgery of Gray's *Elegy*. Any accurate copy of the text of a poem or novel is as much the original work as any other. Yet what the writer produces is ultimate; the text is not merely a means to oral readings as a score is a means to performances in music. An unrecited poem is not so forlorn as an unsung song; and most literary works are never read aloud at all. We might try to make literature into a two-stage art by considering the silent readings to be the end-products, or the instances of a work; but then the lookings at a picture and the listenings to a performance would qualify equally as end-products or instances, so that painting as well as literature would be two-stage and music three-stage. In the second place, printmaking is two-stage and yet autographic. The etcher, for example, makes a plate from which impressions are then taken on paper. These prints are the end-products; and although they may differ appreciably from one another, all are instances of the original work. But even the most exact copy produced otherwise than by printing from that plate counts not as an original but as an imitation or forgery.

So far, our results are negative: not all one-stage arts are autographic and not all autographic arts are one-stage. Furthermore, the example of printmaking refutes the unwary assumption that in every autographic art a particular work exists only as a unique object. The line between an autographic and an allographic art does not coincide with that between a singular and a multiple art. About the only positive conclusion we can draw here is that the autographic arts are those that are singular in the earliest stage; etching is singular in its first stage—the plate is unique—and painting in its only stage. But this hardly helps; for the problem of explaining why some arts are singular is much like the problem of explaining why they are autographic.

4. THE REASON

Why, then, can I no more make a forgery of Haydn's symphony or of Gray's poem than I can make an original of Rembrandt's painting or of his etching *Tobit Blind*? Let us suppose that there are various handwritten copies and many editions of a given literary work. Differences between them in style and size of script or type, in color of ink, in kind of paper, in number and layout of pages, in condition, do not matter. All that matters is what may be called *sameness of spelling*: exact correspondence as sequences of letters, spaces, and punctuation marks. Any sequence—even a forgery of the author's manuscript or of a given edition—that so corresponds to a correct copy is itself correct, and nothing is more the original work than is such a correct copy. And since whatever is not an original of the work must fail to meet such an explicit standard of correctness, there can be no deceptive imitation, no forgery, of that work. To verify the spelling or to spell correctly is all that is required to identify an instance of the work or to produce a new instance. In effect, the fact that a literary work is in a definite notation consisting of certain signs or characters that are to be combined by concatenation, provides the means for distinguishing the properties constitutive of the work from all contingent properties—that is, for fixing the required features and the limits of permissible variation in each. Merely by determining that the copy before us is spelled correctly we can determine that it meets all requirements for the work in question. In painting, on the contrary, with no such alphabet of characters, none of the pictorial properties—none of the properties the picture has as such—is distinguished as constitutive; no such feature can be dismissed as contingent, and no deviation as insignificant. The only way of ascertaining that the *Lucretia* before us is genuine is thus to establish the historical fact that it is the actual object made by Rembrandt. Accordingly, physical identification of the product of the artist's hand, and consequently the conception of forgery of a particular work, assume a significance in painting that they do not have in literature.[11]

What has been said of literary texts obviously applies also to musical scores. The alphabet is different; and the characters in a score, rather than being strung one after the other as in a text, are disposed in a more complex array. Nevertheless, we have a limited set of characters and of positions for them; and correct spelling, in only a slightly expanded sense, is still the sole requirement for a genuine instance of a work. Any false copy is wrongly spelled—has somewhere in place of the right character either another character or an illegible mark that is not a character of the notation in question at all.

But what of performances of music? Music is not autographic in this second stage, either, yet a performance by no means consists of characters from an alphabet. Rather, the constitutive properties demanded of a performance of the symphony are those *prescribed in* the score; and performances that comply with the score may differ appreciably in such musical features as tempo, timbre, phrasing, and expressiveness. To determine compliance requires, indeed, something more than merely knowing the alphabet; it requires the ability to correlate appropriate sounds with the visible signs in the score—to recognize, so to speak, correct pronounciation though without necessarily understanding what is pronounced. The competence required to identify or produce sounds called for by a score increases with the complexity of the composition, but there is nevertheless a theoretically decisive test for compliance; and a performance, whatever its interpretative fidelity and independent merit, has or has not all the constitutive properties of a given work, and is or is not strictly a performance of that work, according as it does or does not pass this test. No historical information concerning the production of the performance can affect the result. Hence deception as to the facts of production is irrelevant, and the notion of a performance that is a forgery of the work is quite empty.

Yet there are forgeries of performances as there are of manuscripts and editions. What makes a performance an instance of a given work is not the same as what makes a performance a premiere, or makes it a performance by a certain musician or upon a Stradivarius violin. Whether a performance has these latter properties is a matter of historical fact; and a performance falsely purporting to have any such property counts as a forgery, not of the musical composition but of a given performance or class of performances.

The comparison between printmaking and music is especially telling. We have already noted that etching, for example, is like music in having two stages and in being multiple in its second stage; but that whereas music is autographic in neither stage, printmaking is autographic in both. Now the situation with respect to the etched plate is clearly the same as with respect to a painting: assurance of genuineness can come only from identification of the actual object produced by the artist. But since the several prints from this plate are all genuine instances of the work, however much they differ in color and amount of ink, quality of impression, kind of paper, and so on, one might expect here a full parallel between prints and musical performances. Yet there can be prints that are forgeries of the *Tobit Blind* but not performances that are forgeries of the London Symphony. The difference is that in the absence of a notation, not only is there no test of correctness of spelling for a plate but there is no test of compliance with a plate for a print. Comparison of a print with a plate, as of two plates, is no more conclusive than is comparison of two pictures. Minute discrepancies may always go unnoticed; and there is no basis for ruling out any of them as inessential. The only way of ascertaining whether a print is genuine is by finding out whether it was taken from a certain plate.[12] A print falsely purporting to have been so produced is in the full sense a forgery of the work.

Here, as earlier, we must be careful not to confuse genuineness with aesthetic merit. That the distinction between original and forgery is aesthetically important does not, we have seen, imply that the original is superior to the forgery. An original painting may be less rewarding than an inspired copy; a damaged original may have lost most of its former merit; an impression from a badly worn plate may be aesthetically much further removed from an early impression than is a good photographic reproduction. Likewise, an incorrect performance, though therefore not strictly an instance of a given quartet at all, may nevertheless—either because the changes improve what the composer wrote or because of sensitive interpretation—be better than a correct performance.[13] Again, several correct performances of about equal merit may exhibit very different specific aesthetic qualities—power, delicacy, tautness, stodginess, incoherence. Thus even where the constitutive properties of a work are clearly distinguished by means of a notation, they cannot be identified with the aesthetic properties.

Among other arts, sculpture is autographic; cast sculpture is comparable to printmaking while carved sculpture is comparable to painting. Architecture and the drama, on the other hand, are more nearly comparable to music. Any building that conforms to the plans and specifications, any performance of the text of a play in accordance with the stage directions, is as original an instance of the work as any other. But architecture seems to differ from music in that testing for compliance of a building with the specifications requires not that these be pronounced, or transcribed into sound, but that their application be understood. This is true also for the stage directions, as contrasted with the dialogue, of a play. Does this make architecture and the drama less purely allographic arts? Again, an architect's plans seem a good deal like a painter's sketches; and painting is an autographic art. On what grounds can we say that in the one case but not the other a veritable notation is involved? Such questions cannot be answered until we have carried through some rather painstaking analysis.

Since an art seems to be allographic just insofar as it is amenable to notation, the case of the dance is especially interesting. Here we have an art without a traditional notation; and an art where the ways, and even the possibility, of developing an adequate notation are still matters of controversy. Is the search for a notation reasonable in the case of the dance but not in the case of painting? Or, more generally, Why is the use of notation appropriate in some arts but not in others? Very briefly and roughly, the answer may be somewhat as follows. Initially, perhaps, all arts are autographic. Where the works are transitory, as in singing and reciting, or require many persons for their production, as in architecture and symphonic music, a notation may be devised in order to transcend the limitations of time and the individual. This involves establishing a distinction between the constitutive and the contingent properties of a work (and in the case of literature, texts have even supplanted oral performances as the primary aesthetic objects). Of course, the notation does not dictate the distinction arbitrarily, but must follow generally—even though it may amend—lines antecedently drawn by the informal classification of performances into works and by practical decisions as to what is prescribed and what is optional. Amenability to notation depends upon a precedent practice that develops only if works of the art in question are commonly either ephemeral or not producible by one person. The dance, like the drama and symphonic and choral music, qualifies on both scores, while painting qualifies on neither.

The general answer to our somewhat slippery second problem of authenticity can be summarized in a few words. A forgery of a work of art is an object falsely purporting to have the history of production requisite for the (or an) original of the work. Where there is a theoretically decisive test for determining that an object has all the constitutive properties of the work in question without determining how or by whom the object was produced, there is no requisite history of production and hence no forgery of any given work. Such a test is provided by a suitable notational system with an articulate set of characters and of relative positions for them. For texts, scores, and perhaps plans, the test is correctness of spelling in this notation; for buildings and performances, the test is compliance with what is correctly spelled. Authority for a notation must be found in an antecedent classification of objects or events into works that cuts across, or admits of a legitimate projection that cuts across, classification by history of production; but definitive identification of works, fully freed from history of production, is achieved only when a notation is established. The allographic art consolidates its emancipation not by proclamation but by notation.

5. A TASK

The two problems of authenticity I have been discussing are rather special and peripheral questions of aesthetics. Answers to them do not amount to an aesthetic theory or even the beginning of one. But failure to answer them can well be the end of one; and their exploration points the way to more basic problems and principles in the general theory of symbols.

Many matters touched upon here need much more careful study. So far, I have only vaguely described, rather than defined, the relations of compliance and sameness of spelling. I have not examined the features that distinguish notations or notational languages from other languages and from nonlanguages. And I have not discussed the subtle differences between a score, a script, and a sketch. What is wanted now is a fundamental and thoroughgoing inquiry in the nature and function of notation in the arts.

Jack Burnham

Systems Esthetics

A polarity is presently developing between the finite, unique work of high art, that is, painting or sculpture, and conceptions that can loosely be termed *unobjects,* these being either environments or artifacts that resist prevailing critical analysis. This includes works by some primary sculptors (though some may reject the charge of creating environments), some gallery kinetic and luminous art, some outdoor works, happenings, and mixed media presentations. Looming below the surface of this dichotomy is a sense of radical evolution that seems to run counter to the waning revolution of abstract and nonobjective art. The evolution embraces a series of absolutely logical and incremental changes, wholly devoid of the fevered iconoclasm that accompanied the heroic period from 1907 to 1925. As yet the evolving esthetic has no critical vocabulary so necessary for its defense, nor for that matter a name or explicit cause.

In a way this situation might be likened to the "morphological development" of a prime scientific concept—as described by Thomas Kuhn in *The Structure of Scientific Revolutions* (1962). Kuhn sees science at any given period dominated by a single "major paradigm"; that is, a scientific conception of the natural order so pervasive and intellectually powerful that it dominates all ensuing scientific discovery. Inconsistent facts arising through experimentation are invariably labeled as bogus or trivial—until the emergence of a new and more encompassing general theory. Transition between major paradigms may best express the state of present art. Reasons for it lie in the nature of current technological shifts.

The economist, J. K. Galbraith, has rightly insisted that until recently the needs of the modern industrial state were never served by complete expression of the esthetic impulse. Power and expansion were its primary aims.

Special attention should be paid to Galbraith's observation. As an arbiter of impending socio-technical changes his position is pivotal. For the Left he represents America's most articulate apologist for Monopoly Capitalism; for the Right he is the socialist *éminence grise* of the Democratic Party. In *The New Industrial State* (1967) he challenges both Marxist orthodoxies and American mythologies premised upon laissez-faire capitalism. For them he substitutes an incipient technocracy shaped by the evolving technostructure. Such a drift away from ideology has been anticipated for at least fifty years. Already in California think-tanks and in the central planning committees of each soviet, futurologists are concentrating on the role of the technocracy, that is, its decision-making autonomy, how it handles the central storage of information, and the techniques used for smoothly implementing social change. In the automated state power resides less in the control of the traditional symbols of wealth than in information.

In the emergent "superscientific culture" long-range decision-making and its implementation become more difficult and more necessary. Judgment demands precise socio-technical models. Earlier the industrial state evolved by filling consumer needs on a piecemeal basis. The kind of product design that once produced "better living" precipitates vast crises in human ecology in the 1960s. A striking parallel exists between the "new" car of the automobile stylist and the syndrome of formalist invention in art, where "discoveries" are made through visual manipulation. Increasingly "products"—either in art or life—become irrelevant and a different set of needs arise: these revolve around such concerns as maintaining the biological livability of the earth, producing more accurate models of social interaction, understanding the growing symbiosis in man-machine relationships, establishing priorities for the usage and conservation of natural resources, and defining alternate patterns of education, productivity, and leisure. In the past our technologically-conceived artifacts structured living patterns. We are now in transition from an *object-oriented* to a *systems-oriented* culture. Here change emanates, not from *things*, but from the *way things are done*.

The priorities of the present age revolve around the problems of organization. A systems viewpoint is focused on the creation of stable, on-going relationships between organic and nonorganic systems, be these neighborhoods, industrial complexes, farms, transportation systems, information centers, recreation centers, or any of the other matrices of human activity. All living situations must be treated in the context of a systems hierarchy of values. Intuitively many artists have already grasped these relatively recent distinctions, and if their "environments" are on the unsophisticated side, this will change with time and experience.

The major tool for professionally defining these concerns is systems analysis. This is best known through its usage by the Pentagon and has more to do with the expense and complexity of modern warfare, than with any innate relation between the two. Systems analysts are not cold-blooded logicians; the best have an ever-expanding grasp of human needs and limitations. One of the pioneers of systems applications, E. S. Quade, has stated that "Systems analysis, particularly the type required for military decisions, is still largely a form of art. Art can be taught in part, but not by the means of fixed rules. . . . " [1] Thus "The Further Dimensions" [2] elaborated upon by Galbraith in his book are esthetic criteria. Where for some these become the means for tidying up a derelict technology, for Galbraith esthetic decision-making becomes an integral part of any future technocracy. As yet few governments fully appreciate that the alternative is biological self-destruction.

Situated between aggressive electronic media and two hundred years of industrial vandalism, the long held idea that a tiny output of art objects could somehow "beautify" or even significantly modify the environment was naive. A parallel illusion existed in that artistic influence prevails by a psychic osmosis given off by such objects. Accordingly lip service to public beauty remains the province of well-guarded museums. Through the early stages of industrialism it remained possible for decorative media, including painting and sculpture, to embody the esthetic impulse; but as technology progresses this impulse must identify itself with the means of research and production. Obviously nothing could be less true for the present situation. In a society thus estranged only the didactic function of art continues to have meaning. The artist operates as a quasipolitical *provocateur*, though in no concrete sense is he an ideologist or a moralist. *L'art pour l'art* and a century's resistance to the vulgarities of moral uplift have insured that.

The specific function of modern didactic art has been to show that art does not reside in material entities, but in relations between people and between people and the components of their environment. This accounts for the radicality of Duchamp and his enduring influence. It throws light on Picasso's lesser position as a seminal force. As with all succeeding formalist art, cubism followed the tradition of circumscribing art value wholly within finite objects.

In an advanced technological culture the most important artist best succeeds by liquidating his position as artist vis-à-vis society. Artistic nihilism established itself through this condition. At the outset the artist refused to participate in idealism through craft. "Craft-fetishism,"[3] as termed by the critic Christopher Caudwell, remains the basis of modern formalism. Instead the significant artist strives to reduce the technical and psychical distance between his artistic output and the productive means of society. Duchamp, Warhol, and Robert Morris are similarly directed in this respect. Gradually this strategy transforms artistic and technological decision-making into a single activity—at least it presents that alternative in inescapable terms. Scientists and technicians are not converted into "artists," rather the artist becomes a symptom of the schism between art and technics. Progressively the need to make ultrasensitive judgments as to the uses of technology and scientific information becomes "art" in the most literal sense.

As yet the implication that art contains survival value is nearly as suspect as attaching any moral significance to it. Though with the demise of literary content, the theory that art is a form of psychic preparedness has gained articulate supporters.

> Art, as an adaptive mechanism, is reinforcement of the ability to be aware of the disparity between behavioral pattern and the demands consequent upon the interaction with the environment. Art is rehearsal for those real situations in which it is vital for our survival to endure cognitive tension, to refuse the comforts of validation by affective congruence when such validation is inappropriate because too vital interests are at stake....[4]

The post-formalist sensibility naturally responds to stimuli both within and outside the proposed art format. To this extent some of it does begin to resemble "theater," as imputed by Michael Fried. More likely though, the label of *theatricality* is a red herring disguising the real nature of the shift in priorities. In respect to Mr. Fried's argument,[5] the theater was never a purist medium, but a conglomerate of arts. In itself this never prevented the theater from achieving "high art." For clearer reading, rather than maintaining Mr. Fried's adjectives, *theatrical* or *literalist* art, or the phrase used until now in this essay, *post-formalist esthetic*, the term *systems esthetic* seems to encompass the present situation more fully.

The systems approach goes beyond a concern with staged environments and happenings; it deals in a revolutionary fashion with the larger problem of boundary concepts. In systems perspective there are no contrived confines such as the theater proscenium or picture frame. Conceptual focus rather than material limits define the system. Thus any situation, either in or outside the context of art, may be designed and judged as a system. Inasmuch as a system may contain people, ideas, messages, atmospheric conditions, power sources, and so on, a system is, to quote the systems biologist, Ludwig von Bertalanffy, a "complex of components in interaction,"[6] comprised of material, energy, and information in various degrees of organization. In evaluating systems the artist is a perspectivist considering goals, boundaries, structure, input, output, and related activity inside and outside the system. Where the object almost always has a fixed shape and boundaries, the consistency of a system may be altered in time and space, its behavior determined both by external conditions and its mechanisms of control.

In his book, *The New Vision,* Moholy-Nagy described fabricating a set of enamel on metal paintings. These were executed by telephoning precise instructions to a manufacturer. An elaboration of this was projected recently by the director of the Museum of Contemporary Art in Chicago, Jan van der Marck, in a tentative exhibition, "Art by Telephone." In this instance the recorded conversation between artist and manufacturer was to *become part of the displayed work of art.* For systems, information, in whatever form conveyed, becomes a viable esthetic consideration.

Fifteen years ago Victor Vasarely suggested mass art as a legitimate function of industrial society. For angry critics there existed the fear of undermining art's fetish aura, of shattering the mystique of craft and private creation. If some forays have been made into serially produced art, these remain on the periphery of the industrial system. Yet the entire phenomenon of reproducing an art object *ad infinitum* is absurd; rather than making quality available to a large number of people, it signals the end of concrete objects embodying visual metaphor. Such demythification is the Kantian Imperative applied esthetically. On the other hand, a system esthetic *is* literal in that all phases of the life cycle of a system are relevant. There is no end product that is primarily visual, nor does such an esthetic rely on a "visual" syntax. It resists functioning as an applied esthetic, but is revealed in the principles underlying the progressive reorganization of the natural environment.

Various postures implicit in formalist art were consistently attacked in the later writings of Ad Reinhardt. His black paintings were hardly rhetorical devices (nor were his writings) masking Zen obscurities; rather they were the means of discarding formalist mannerism and all the latent illusionism connected with post-realistic art. His own contribution he described as:

The one work for the fine artist, the one painting, is the painting of the one-sized canvas. . . . The single theme, one formal device, one color-monochrome, one linear division in each direction, one symmetry, one texture, one free-hand brushing, one rhythm, one working everything into dissolution and one indivisibility, each painting into one overall uniformity and nonirregularity.[7]

Even before the emergence of the anti-formalist "specific object" there appeared an oblique type of criticism, resisting emotive and literary associations. Pioneered between 1962 and 1965 in the writings of Donald Judd, it resembles what a computer programmer would call an entity's *list structure*, or all the enumerated properties needed to *physically* rebuild an object. Earlier the phenomenologist, Maurice Merleau-Ponty, asserted the impossibility of *conceptually* reconstructing an object from such a procedure. Modified to include a number of perceptual insights not included in a "list structure," such a technique has been used to real advantage by the anti-novelist, Alain Robbe-Grillet. A web of sensorial descriptions is spun around the central images of a plot. The point is not to internalize scrutiny in the Freudian sense, but to infer the essence of a situation through detailed examination of surface effects. Similar attitudes were adopted by Judd for the purpose of critical examination. More than simply an art object's list structure, Judd included phenomenal qualities which would have never shown up in a fabricator's plans, but which proved necessary for the "seeing" of the object. This cleared the air of much criticism centered around meaning and private intention.

It would be misleading to interpret Judd's concept of "specific objects" as the embodiment of a systems esthetic. Rather object art has become a stage towards further rationalization of the esthetic process in general—both by reducing the iconic content of art objects and by Judd's candidness about their conceptual origins. However, even in 1965 he gave indications of looking beyond these finite limits.

A few of the more general aspects may persist, such as the work's being like an object or even being specific, but other characteristics are bound to develop. Since its range is wide, three-dimensional work will probably divide into a number of forms. At any rate, it will be larger than painting and much larger than sculpture, which, compared to painting, is fairly particular. . . . Because the nature of three dimension isn't set, given beforehand, something credible can be made, almost anything.[8]

In the 1966 "68th American Show" at the Chicago Art Institute, the sculptor, Robert Morris, was represented by two large, L-shaped forms which were shown the previous year in New York. Morris sent plans of the pieces to the carpenters at the Chicago museum where they were assembled for less than the cost of shipping the originals from New York. In the context of a systems esthetic, possession of a privately fabricated work is no longer important. Accurate information takes priority over history and geographical location.

Morris was the first essayist to precisely describe the relation between sculpture style and the progressively more sophisticated use of industry by artists. He has lately focused upon material-forming techniques and the arrangement of these results so that they no longer form specific objects but remain uncomposed. In such handling of materials the idea of *process* takes precedence over end results: "Disengagement with preconceived enduring forms and orders of things is a positive assertion."[9] Such loose assemblies of materials encompass concerns that resemble the cycles of industrial processing. Here the traditional priority of end results over technique breaks down; in a systems context both may share equal importance, remaining essential parts of the esthetic.

Already Morris has proposed systems that move beyond the confines of the minimal object. One work proposed to the City of New York last fall was later included in Willoughby Sharp's "Air Art" show in a YMHA gallery in Philadelphia. In its first state Morris's piece involved capturing steam from the pipes in the city streets, projecting this from nozzles on a platform. In Philadelphia such a system took its energy from the steam-bath room. Since 1966 Morris's interests have included designs for low relief earth sculptures consisting of abutments, hedges, and sodded mounds, visible from the air and not unlike Indian burial mounds. "Transporting" one of these would be a matter of cutting and filling earth and resodding. Morris is presently at work on one such project and unlike past sculptural concerns, it involves precise information from surveyors, landscape gardeners, civil engineering contractors, and geologists. In the older context, such as Isamu Noguchi's sunken garden at Yale University's Rare Book Library, sculpture defined the environment; with Morris's approach the environment defines what is sculptural.

More radical for the gallery are the constructions of Carl Andre. His assemblies of modular, unattached forms stand out from the works of artists who have comprised unit assembly with the totality of fixed objects. The mundane origins of Andre's units are not "hidden" within the art work as in the technique of collage. Andre's floor reliefs are architectural modifications —though they are not subliminal since they visually disengage from their surroundings. One of Andre's subtler shows took place in New York last year. The viewer was encouraged to walk stocking-footed across three areas, each 12 by 12 feet and composed by 144 one-foot-square metal plates. One was not only invited to see each of these "rugs" as a grid arrangement in various metals, but each metal grid's thermal conductivity was registered through the soles of the feet. Sight analysis diminishes in importance for some of the best new work; the other senses and especially kinesthesis makes "viewing" a more integrated experience.

The scope of a systems esthetic presumes that problems cannot be solved by a single technical solution, but must be attacked on a multileveled, interdisciplinary basis. Consequently some of the more aware sculptors no longer think like sculptors, but they assume a span of problems more natural to architects, urban planners, civil engineers, electronic technicians, and cultural anthropologists. This is not as pretentious as some critics have insisted. It is a legitimate extension of McLuhan's remark about Pop Art when he said that it was an announcement that the entire environment was ready to become a work of art.

As a direct descendant of the "found object," Robert Smithson's identifying mammoth engineering projects as works of art ("Site-Selections")[10] makes eminent sense. Refocusing the esthetic away from the preciousness of the work of art is in the present age no less than a survival mechanism. If Smithson's "Site-Selections" are didactic exercises, they show a desperate need for environmental sensibility on a larger than room scale. Sigfried Giedion pointed to specific engineering feats as *objets d'art* thirty years ago. Smithson has transcended this by putting engineering works into their natural settings and treating the whole as a time-bound web of man-nature interactions.

Methodologically Les Levine is possibly the most consistent exponent of a systems esthetic. His environments of vacuum-formed, modular plastic units are never static; by means of experiencing ambulation through them, they consistently alter their own degree of space-surface penetrability. Levine's *Clean Machine* has no ideal vantage points, no "pieces" to recognize, as are implicit in formalist art. One is *processed* as in driving through the Holland Tunnel. Certainly this echoes Michael Fried's reference to Tony Smith's night time drive along the uncompleted New Jersey Turnpike.[11] Yet if this is theater, as Fried insists, it is not the stage concerned with focused-upon events. That has more to do with the boundary definitions that have traditionally circumscribed classical and post-classical art. In a recent environment by Levine rows of live electric wires emitted small shocks to passersby. Here behavior is controlled in an esthetic situation with no primary reference to visual circumstances. As Levine insists, "What I am after here is physical reaction, not visual concern." [12]

This brings to mind some of the original intentions of the "Group de Recherches d'Art Visuel" in the early 1960s. The Paris-based group had sought to engage viewers kinesthetically, triggering involuntary responses through ambient-propelled "surprises." Levine's emphasis on visual disengagement is much more assured and iconoclastic; unlike the labyrinths of the GRAV, his possesses no individual work of art deflecting attention from the environment as a concerted experience.

Questions have been raised concerning the implicit anti-art position connected with Levine's *disposable* and *infinite* series. These hardly qualify as anti-art as John Perreault has pointed out. Besides emphasizing that the context of art is fluid, they are a *reductio ad absurdum* of the entire market mechanism that controls art through the fiction of "high art." They do not deny art, they deny scarcity as a legitimate correlative of art.

The components of systems—whether these are artistic or functional—have no higher meaning or value. Systems components derive their value solely through their assigned context. Therefore it would be impossible to regard a fragment of an art system as a work of art in itself—as say, one might treasure a fragment of one of the Parthenon friezes. This became evident in December 1967 when Dan Flavin designed six walls with the same alternate pattern of "rose" and "gold" eight-foot fluorescent lamps. This "Broad Bright Gaudy Vulgar System," as Flavin called it, was installed in the new Museum of Contemporary Art in Chicago. The catalog accompanying the exhibition scrupulously resolves some of the important esthetic implications for modular systems.

> The components of a particular exhibition upon its termination are replaced in another situation. Perhaps put into non-art as part of a different whole in a different future. Individual units possess no intrinsic significance beyond their concrete utility. It is difficult either to project into them extraneous qualities, a spurious insight, or for them to be appropriated for fulfillment or personal inner needs. The lights are untransformed. There are no symbolic transcendental redeeming or monetary added values present. [13]

Flavin's work has progressed in the past six years from light sources mounted on flat reliefs, to compositions in fluorescent fixtures mounted directly on walls and floors, and recently to totalities such as his Chicago "walk-in" environment. While the majority of other light artists have continued to fabricate "light sculpture"—as if *sculpture* were the primary concern—Flavin has pioneered articulated illumination systems for given spaces.

By the fact that most systems move or are in some way dynamic, kinetic art should be one of the more radical alternatives to the prevailing formalist esthetic. Yet this has hardly been the case. The best publicized kinetic sculpture is mainly a modification of static formalist sculpture composition. In most instances these have only the added bonus of motion, as in the case of Tinguely, Calder, Bury, and Rickey. Only Duchamp's kinetic output managed to reach beyond formalism. Rather than visual appearance there is an entirely different concern which makes kinetic art unique. This is the peripheral perception of sound and movement in space filled with activity. All too often gallery kinetic art has trivialized the more graspable aspect of motion: this is motion internalized and experienced kinesthetically.

There are a few important exceptions to the above. These include Otto Piene's early "Light Ballets" (1958-1962), the early (1956) water hammocks and informal on-going environments of Japan's *Gutai* group, some works by Len Lye, Bob Breer's first show of "Floats" (1965), Robert Whitman's laser show of "Dark" (1967), and most recently, Boyd Mefferd's "Strobe-Light Floor" (1968).

Formalist art embodies the idea of deterministic relations between a composition's visible elements. But since the early 1960s Hans Haacke has depended upon the invisible components of systems. In a systems context, invisibility, or invisible parts, share equal importance with things seen. Thus air, water, steam, and ice have become major elements in his work. On both coasts this has precipitated interest in "invisible art" among a number of young artists. Some of the best of Haacke's efforts are shown outside the gallery. These include his *Rain Tree*, a tree dripping patterns of water; *Sky Line,* a nylon line kept aloft by hundreds of helium-filled white balloons; a weather balloon balanced over a jet of air; and a large-scale nylon tent with air pockets designed to remain in balance one foot off the ground.

Haacke's systems have a limited life as an art experience, though some are quite durable. He insists that the need for empathy does not make his work function as with older art. Systems exist as on-going independent entities away from the viewer. In the systems hierarchy of control, *interaction* and *autonomy* become desirable values. In this respect Haacke's *Photo-Electric Viewer Programmed Coordinate System* is probably one of the most elegant, responsive environments made to date *by an artist* (certainly more sophisticated ones have been conceived for scientific and technical purposes). Boundary situations are central to his thinking.

A "sculpture" that physically reacts to its environment is no longer to be regarded as an object. The range of outside factors affecting it, as well as its own radius of action, reach beyond the space it materially occupies. It thus merges with the environment in a relationship that is better understood as a "system" of interdependent processes. These processes evolve without the viewer's empathy. He becomes a witness. A system is not imagined, it is real.[14]

Tangential to this systems approach is Allan Kaprow's very unique concept of the Happening. In the past ten years Kaprow has moved the Happening from a rather self-conscious and stagy event to a strict and elegant procedure. The Happening now has a sense of internal logic which was lacking before. It seems to arise naturally from those same considerations that have crystallized the systems approach to environmental situations. As described by their chief inventor, the Happenings establish an indivisibility between themselves and everyday affairs; they consciously avoid materials and procedures identified with art; they allow for geographical expansiveness and mobility; they include experience and duration as part of their esthetic format; and they emphasize practical activities as the most meangingful mode of procedure.[15] . . . As structured events the Happenings are usually reversible. Alterations in the environment may be "erased" after the Happening, or as a part of the Happening's conclusion. While they may involve large areas of space, the format of the Happening is kept relatively simple, with the emphasis on establishing a participatory esthetic.

The emergence of a "post-formalist esthetic" may seem to some to embody a kind of absolute philosophy, something which, through the nature of its concerns cannot be transcended. Yet it is more likely that a "systems esthetic" will become the dominant approach to a maze of socio-technical conditions rooted only in the present. New circumstances will with time generate other major paradigms for the arts.

For some readers these pages will echo feelings of the past. It may be remembered that in the fall of 1920 an ideological schism ruptured two factions of the Moscow Constructivists. The radical Marxists, led by Vladimir Tatlin, proclaimed their rejection of art's false idealisms. Establishing themselves as "Productivists," one of their slogans became: "Down with guarding the traditions of art. Long live the constructivist technician."[16] As a group dedicated to historical materialism and the scientific ethos, most of its members were quickly subsumed by the technological needs of Soviet Russia. As artists they ceased to exist. While the Productivist program might have had some basis as a utilitarian esthetic, it was crushed amid the Stalinist anti-intellectualism that followed.

The reasons are almost self-apparent. Industrially underdeveloped, food and heavy industry remained the prime needs of the Soviet Union for the next forty years. Conditions and structural interdependencies that naturally develop in an advanced industrial state were then only latent. In retrospect it is doubtful if any group of artists had either the knowledge or political strength to meaningfully affect Soviet industrial policies. What emerged was another vein of formalist innovation based on scientific idealism; this manifested itself in the West under the leadership of the Constructivist emigres, Gabo and Pevsner.

But for our time the emerging major paradigm in art is neither an *ism* nor a collection of styles. Rather than a novel way of rearranging surfaces and spaces, it is fundamentally concerned with the implementation of the art impulse in an advanced technological society. As a culture producer, man has traditionally claimed the title, *Homo Faber: man the maker* (of tools and images). With continued advances in the industrial revolution, he assumes a new and more critical function. As *Homo Arbiter Formae* his prime role becomes that of man the maker of *esthetic decisions*. These decisions— whether they are made concertedly or not—control the quality of all future life on the earth. Moreover these are value judgments dictating the direction of technological endeavor. Quite plainly such a vision extends beyond political realities of the present. This cannot remain the case for long.

Arnold Berleant

Aesthetics and Contemporary Arts

Different Features of Objects Under Industrial Production

Pre-Industrial	Industrial
intricacy	simplicity
expensiveness	economy
uniqueness	uniformity
rarity	quantity
irregularity	precision
human error, fallibility	flawlessness
intuition	calculation
age	newness
permanence	change, improvement
treasuring	expendability
art and utility sharply distinguished	functionalism, art object "working"
representation, realism	geometric forms, abstractions

Fundamental Social Changes

Pre-Industrial	Industrial
aristocratic	democratic
demographic isolation	population masses
local, regional culture	mass culture (audiences, communication, production)
individual production of goods by single craftsmen	group production in quantity by specialized labor
hierarchical, tribal social model	mechanical, electronic social model

New Materials and Objects in Art

The scientific model, scientific concepts and laws
the machine
materials from technology, machine products
standardized objects (repeated patterns)
electronic mechanisms and instruments
ordinary materials
ordinary objects

New Perceptual Activities

extended range of perception
greater inclusiveness of objects
inclusion of other sensory receptors—tactile, kinesthetic
rejection of aesthetic prohibitions, e.g., erotic
elimination of distinctions between
object and perceiver, spectator
creator and object
creator and perceiver
performer, artist, and perceiver
integration of art with life
chance
prosaic events
commonplace objects
dethroning of art, inclusion of primitive, grotesque brutal, dreamlike
functionalism, art as skill, technology
social commentary

Reprinted from the *Journal of Aesthetics & Art Criticism* (Winter, 1970), by permission of the author.

New Forms and Movements in Art

theater of cruelty
theater of the absurd

Happenings

photography

film
environments

functional architecture

kinetic sculpture

objets trouvées

assemblages

new movements in painting
impressionism
abstract expressionism
futurism
cubism
dada
surrealism
pop art
op art
minimal art

modern dance

aleatoric music

serial music

electronic music

The New Aesthetic

Negative Features

1. Denial of importance of unity, harmony. These contribute to the isolation of the art object.
2. Rejection of the ideal (i.e., beauty) as the end of art.
3. Denial of distance and of the contemplative attitude.
4. Denial of disinterestedness.
    a. Denial of separation of art object from life.
    b. Denial of the uniqueness of art, of institutional arrangements that perpetuate this, i.e., museums.

Positive Features

1. continuity between life and art.
    a. Process, movement
    b. Functionalism
2. Perceptual integration of elements in the aesthetic situation.
3. Artistic creation as a cooperative enterprise.

Basic Concept: THE AESTHETIC FIELD

1. A more inclusive "general theory of aesthetics."
2. Integration of
    a. artist
    b. object
    c. perceiver
    d. performer
3. Functional relation between
    a. creator-perceiver-performer
    b. object working
    c. aesthetic experience as a functional activity
4. Inclusiveness
    a. materials
    b. events
5. Diffusion
    a. greater continuity between aesthetic and non-aesthetic
    b. closer connection of art with society, as commentary, satire, criticism

José A. Argüelles

Art as Internal Technology: The Return of the Shaman— The Descent of the Goddess

In the psychedelic experience we are confronted with the abolition of history. But the abolition of history is the recovery of the sacred dimension, "for all history," as Mircea Eliade wrote in the foreword to his book on shamanism, "is in some measure a fall of the sacred, a limitation and a diminution."[1] Certainly the life of every culture is a "history," a departure from the sacred primary experience, but only to the extent that the *reliving* of the primary experience is not an important life-goal. In technological civilization the spontaneous possibility of living again a fuller revelation of the sacred has been so thoroughly diminished that it is viewed as a crime and a direct threat to the very existence of society. Why is this so? As an ideology history is oriented toward the future. Any experience that transcends this ideology is therefore regarded as archaic or regressive. *Archaic* is generally thought to mean antiquated or outdated, in keeping with the historical point of view, but its root is a verb meaning *to begin*. In a sense what is archaic may not be backward at all, but a beginning. From the historical point of view what is important is the utopian end and not the beginning; thus historical consciousness wishes to abolish the archaic experience by whatever means, for it does not believe in the possibility of a new beginning. From the sacred point of view, however, it is history that is "outdated," or actually "overdated."

The very meaning of religion, which art once served as a handmaiden, is

Reprinted by special arrangement with Shambhala Publications, Inc., Berkeley, CA, from *The Transformative Vision*, by José A. Argüelles. Copyright © 1975 by José A. Argüelles.

to bind back into one, to relate to the beginning, to the origin of all things. True religion implies a reversal of the historical process. An authentic religious revival, as foreseen by Huxley, is a return to the "beginning," to the primordial state of unity. This "beginning" is omnipresent as the on-going self-renewal of the cosmos in all its aspects. When Timothy Leary was traveling about the country exhorting people to create their own religion, he was calling for a reversal of history by returning to this "beginning"—beginning with the individual. The typical person immersed in the kind of revelations brought on by psychedelics must confront something far vaster than his own memory could encompass. It makes no difference whether the contents of this vast realm are explained as the evolutionary spectrum encapsulated within the genetic configuration of the particular individual or as the primary encounter with the supernatural embodiments of the archetypes. The significant fact is the realization of an immensity that no words can describe, and that impoverishes the grand illusions of the individual ego. There may well be as a result of such an experience the desire, the need, the urge to participate more fully in a religious life, even to the point of creating one's own religion. If this is the choice, then one faces a staggering decision: Where does one begin, and how?

Since one is at a "beginning," an affinity with archaic material is felt very naturally. In the collapse of history, which is the "end," the archaic, the "beginning," is all that remains, Ouroboros once again. Whereas history is built on temporal ephemera, the contents of the archaic are embedded in the self-renewing cosmic experience that transcends time. It is curious how history and the myth of progress distort our perceptions, so that we think of alchemy, shamanism, and yoga, for instance, as things of the distant past, while in fact all of the mystical techniques that were relegated to the past in the European cultural continuum have continued to exist side by side with history. The endurance of the archaic is all the more astonishing, given the merciless willingness of technological civilization to uproot, desecrate, and where necessary, even to commit genocide in order that the progressive forces of history could prevail. But as the inner psychic house of history begins to collapse, suddenly appearing through the debris are the glints and glimmers of an eternal magic. The walls and features of the outer house of history remain more or less intact, but as the inner house is slowly reconstructed, the outer walls lose their supports. The structure built according to the precepts of the remaining archaic material calls for a totally different design and points of stress. The blueprint of the archaic is not ancient, but an eternal beginning, making itself available whenever the barriers of history and materiality have exhausted themselves.

JOSÉ A. ARGÜELLES

The archaic presents a curious counterpoint to technology. While technology is an instrument of externality, the archaic begins with a consideration of the internal structure of things, which is universal and all-encompassing. Archaic techniques constitute an internal technology. Academic art and culture could persist in the West as long as they adhered to an essentially external and linear logic. The most exquisite examples of modern Western art are no doubt the musical compositions of eighteenth-century masters like Bach and Mozart; in their work the linear, external logic of the post-Renaissance mind is perfectly wedded to a sensual form and spiritual structures demanding that kind of rigorous technical support. By comparison, baroque and neoclassical visual art is barren and pretentious, dependent as it is on the historical anecdote for meaning. Freed of any such anecdotal necessity— for Mozart and Bach the opera or mass was not prerequisite but integral to musical form—music could use the linear, external technique perfectly to convey very diffuse and abstract feelings and states of consciousness. But this perfection could be sustained only for a brief historical moment. With the crushing triumph of late eighteenth-century technology, the *techniques* by which inner meaning could be developed—namely alchemy and a vital harmonic Pythagorean tradition of mystical mathematics—disappeared. Thereafter, Western artists were to be deprived of an internal technology. Though it was to be rediscovered haphazardly and incompletely from time to time by visionaries like Blake, Goethe, Seurat, and Kandinsky, more common was the spectacle of a Picasso on the one hand, improvising on the external logic of Western art, or a Pollock on the other, flirting with the inner realm yet lacking the discipline and the knowledge to master it. Only the late work of Kandinsky and Klee, among the self-conscious artists of modernism, approaches the true precincts of the archaic, the former painting images in a manner reminiscent of Australian x-ray painting or of the *huichol* yarn-painting of Mexico, the latter creating pictographs and hieroglyphs stammering toward the articulation of a new world.

What separates the art of most modern Western visionaries from the kind of integral achievement that characterizes the archaic, however, is an intense inner discipline—the development of an internal technology. From the archaic point of view, internal technology—discipline of the psychic energies—precedes and underlies the fabrication of any artifact. Whereas the knowledge underlying the development of historical culture is intellectual and literate, that of the archaic disciplines derives from a living oral tradition. *Tradition* literally means to give over, or to hand down, not in books but literally by word of mouth and symbols. From the historical, scientific point of view, tradition has been interpreted as precluding *direct* experience, and it is therefore considered a deterrent to progress. This view is not altogether correct, since archaic traditions emphasized the necessity of direct experience or revelation to confirm their teachings. What the historical position actually favors is human endeavor for its own sake. The ideology of modern history, which is progress at all costs, is directly opposed to tradition, which is rooted in the cosmic sense of being, a sense in which even progress is an egotistic illusion. To cultivate the cosmic sense of being precedes in importance any expression of it, and for this reason, the archaic endures beyond the historical, since its real essence is continuity in change. Defined this way, *tradition* is the transmission of an inner quality of being rather than an external expression of it. From the traditional point of view, even history is a sacred deviation; it is the trump card of the Fool.

What the lingering presence of the archaic suggests is not an allegiance to a specific set of goals, values, or techniques, but the necessary development and refinement of consciousness, beginning with the individual. In other words, the individual's first responsibility is to his own conscious development. Because the ideology of history favors the collective values of competition, patriotism, and the work ethic, values that keep the individual in bondage to external goals, the individual must be extremely vigilant in order to preserve his humanity. But history itself being a deviation, a trick the collective ego plays on itself, the yogi and the shaman meditating on the outskirts of civilization bide their time waiting for the refugees.

Though he eagerly sought the shaman, Artaud lacked the patience and the discipline necessary to find him; eventually he went insane. Faring somewhat better, Ginsberg tracking through the jungles of South America or wandering through India was able to transform *Howl* into the mantric chanting of the Vedas—the wisdom of the seers. Trying to avoid practicing Pavlovian psychology within the walls of academe, Leary had the discipline necessary to make some sense of Mind-at-Large as it oozed and manifested through him. In creating his own religion, the League for Spiritual Discovery, Leary resorted to archaic tradition for discipline and support. Appropriately enough, the purest analogue that Leary, Alpert, and Metzner could find for the *psychedelic experience* was *The Tibetan Book of the Dead*—a manual archaic in the fullest sense of the word. Because it embodies an ancient wisdom of death, *The Tibetan Book of the Dead* is also a wisdom of the beginning that is eternally now. The implication was that psychedelics, when properly used, are a vital instrument of rebirth into the sacred dimension. In *Psychedelic Prayers,* Leary rephrased the *Tao Teh Ching*, one of the most *archaic* manuals of the way, in terms of his own genetic vision. Like Jung's notion of archetypes, Leary's notion of the cosmic vision is placed within the genetic structure of the individual; therefore what is most archaic is within us, genetically encoded in the psychophysical structure of the organism. The wisdom of our contemporary ancients, the shamans and the yogis, is an organic wisdom intrinsic to our own nature. The perennial philosophy, the means of gaining that wisdom, is no different than the development of our own consciousness, for which purpose the force of history is both a repressive burden and a challenge.

The initial use of drugs to reacquaint Faustian man with the reality of this wisdom acts as a stick of dynamite to break up the logjam of materialistic confusion and error. But used continually without an appropriate ritual prescription, psychedelics can only be a poison. More important is the development of the discipline—the internal technology—that an understanding of the inner realm demands.

We are in a unique evolutionary position, and when I speak of tradition and the necessity of developing an internal technology, I am by no means advocating the thoughtless or wholesale embrace of the traditions of another culture. Yet to begin at the beginning, to begin again, is to embark on an archaic path. Though the shamans and the yogis of the existing archaic traditions may offer the post-Faustian refugee essential help, the point is not to become them but to become ourselves. The vision of what we are to become is already within us, awaiting the proper discipline through which it might be appropriately expressed.

An initial seed-glimpse of the "archaic future" is provided by the outpouring of mandalas sparked by the psychedelic revolution. The mandala is the most archaic symbol; its spontaneous projection is an indication that the deeper levels have been sounded. Being the most archaic symbol, the mandala is also the best symbol of the primordial state of unity. Like the previous "early warning" mandalas of Jung, the mandalas of the 1960s and '70s are unique; embodying the archaic form-principle of the centered wheel or sphere, they derive from no particular past culture but from a realization of the immediate evolutionary condition of consciousness. This is evident, for example, in the mandalas of Paul Laffoley, whose work focuses on the universality of the "visionary point," the eternal point at which "time moving forward meets time moving backward." For Laffoley this is the point that "precedes the world's mystical experience, the Omega point."[2] The reference to the visionary philosophy of Pierre Teilhard de Chardin is clear. The visionary point artistically symbolized by the spontaneous return of the archaic form of the mandala is really a sign that the new beginning, the Great Return, has taken root, not in just a few individuals as it did after the First World War, but in the collective consciousness of mankind. Correspondingly, and in opposition to orthodox Darwinian theory, Teilhard de Chardin declared: "No proof exists that man has come to the end of his potentialities, that he has reached his highest point. On the contrary, everything suggests that at the present time we are entering a peculiarly critical phase of super-humanization."[3] This critical visionary moment can achieve its end only by the simultaneous transcendence of the physicalist mentality that has been modern history's mainstay and the unleashing of what Buckminster Fuller describes as humanity's unique capacity for the metaphysical. The landing of humans on the moon in 1969 had its psychic correspondence in the greater realization of our intrinsic weightlessness. It is astonishing to think that all of our institutions, our technological power and military might, are simply the embodiments of values that have no weight. These embodiments drag us down, much as the moon "drags" around the earth.

In physical terms civilization has reached a point of maximum entropy, the unparalleled grossness of what the visionary media artist Willard Van de Bogart calls *industrial anarchy.* In a paper entitled "Entropic Art" Van de Bogart wrote, "That area of thought on this planet that has been the alternate symbol system, separate and apart from 'Industrial Anarchism,' is art." As an inherent symbolic system art has traditionally been the

> ... unconscious overseer of man's activities. ... Initially art was glorious with a high degree of spirituality. ... But then the unexpected ... the machine culture and industrial consciousness. No longer the aristocracy . . . revolt was in the wind ... and equality for all became the people's revolution. However, the gap in the symbol system transfer was neglected. Further and further the symbols receded until today we have artists cutting up their bodies in protest to the inhumanity that is in operation within the social system. . . .
>
> The art symbol system of man is now revealing in a synergistic way the hierarchy of the earth plan's entropic system of Industrial Anarchy. These art symbols are coming about so that man can restructure his system to the point that evolutionary synergy will in fact be made possible by thinking of art as a utopian mechanism that serves as a safety valve to prevent the human species' extinction.[4]

Van de Bogart is representative of those artists who, having seen through the barrenness of the philosophy behind technology, are using the most advanced techniques of electronic media to penetrate the blind wall of technocracy. As Van de Bogart has explained, "Media projections are the only real possibilities for noncultural constructs for the evolution of man's mind."[5] Exemplifying this trend of thought in his recent book, Gene Youngblood described Jordan Belson's masterwork, the 1964 film *Re-Entry,* as follows:

> Simultaneously a film on the theme of mystic reincarnation and actual spacecraft reentry into the earth's atmosphere. . . .*Re-Entry* is chiefly informed by two specific sources: John Glenn's first space trip, and the philosophical concept of the *Bardo,* as set forth in the . . . so-called *Tibetan Book of the Dead.* . . . With imagery of the highest eloquence, Belson aligns the three stages of the Bardo with the three stages of space flight: leaving the earth's atmosphere (death—[Chikhai Bardo]), moving through deep space (Karmic illusions—[Chonyid Bardo]), and reentry into the earth's atmosphere (rebirth—[Sidpa Bardo]).[6]

A similar idea was developed in the popular movie *2001*. In yet another film, *Lapis* (1963-66) by James Whitney, the computer was used to develop exquisite mandalas that are synchronized with Indian ragas, powerfully recreating the experience of primal cosmic awareness.

Consciously or unconsciously, willfully or not, even the most technically sophisticated artists have arrived at the precincts of the *archaic*. Through the artist, the scientist and the shaman begin to merge into one. But it should be kept in mind that the primary function of the archetypal figures of the shaman and the yogi is not to create art or science, but to heal, to make whole, to maintain a balance between psyche and techne. This is achieved through an understanding of the laws governing the creation and maintenance of the world. The inner is always drawn to the outer and vice versa; the microcosmic contains the macrocosmic just as easily as the macrocosmic contains the microcosmic. In the beginning is the end, and in the end is the beginning.

The transubstantiation of materiality through art produces spiritual power. In the Catholic ritual transubstantiation makes the bread and wine the actual body and blood of Christ, without changing the presence of bread and wine. This is brought about not by overt action but by the action of psyche in conformity with certain laws governing the processes of internal growth and relationship. But the belief system known as materialism totally ignores the laws of internal necessity, by which transubstantiation, for instance, is made possible. Ignoring the laws of internal necessity, materialism has no real place for art, the means by which all matter may be regenerated as spirit. The primitive peoples of the world have indeed been able to speak to rocks and listen to voices issuing from mountain-tops simply because for them art is the transubstantiation of materiality. Because Western civilization has lost this art, which is the essence of art, both the physical body and the intuitive psychic faculties have been neglected in favor of a disembodied and exalted intellectualism whose chief fruit has been the gargantuan planetary system of runaway technology. Instead of a harmoniously integrated and thorough psychophysical training, the civilized human is educated to use and rely on the intellect alone, while dealing with a world of inert but exploitable matter, of which nobody is a part.

This materialistic world view came fully into being during the latter part of the eighteenth century. The music of Bach and Mozart, of which I spoke earlier, succeeds only because it achieves a subtle balance between the internal psychic structures derived from late Medieval culture and the outer linear forms of the mechanistic Renaissance world view. With the triumph of technology and intellectual materialism, the delicate psychophysical balance was destroyed. In the nineteenth century the composer Franz Liszt, overcome by a bodily passion he could not understand, gave up music to search for God. God-mad, Van Gogh committed suicide because his intuitive mind and his physical body had no way of relating to each other. What we have been calling art for the last few centuries has largely emanated from the misunderstandings between the body and the mind that have taken place in the free-fire zone of the psyche. What Huxley said of Freud—that he was not materialistic enough since in paying attention only to the mouth and the anus he ignored the rest of the body as well as the psyche—is true of modern civilization as a whole. Because materialism is a psychological condition, the technological methods of dealing with such problems as pollution, crime, terrorism, poverty, disease, and madness only worsen them. The only solution possible is a radical one, that is, a solution that goes to the roots. And the roots of human behavior are not material but psychological.

Despite the brilliant technological ingenuity of our materialistic civilization, the general level of human consciousness has scarcely ever been more debased, degraded, depressed, and desperate. Blind to anything but the grossest forms and subjected to a tyrannical dualism that assigns a separate reality to the creative act, the individual is divorced from creativity. The problem is compounded by the fact that a primary value is assigned to the *artifact* or the event as the quantifiable proof that creation has occurred. Since the educational process discourages the widespread attainment of the psychomotor abilities required by the practical or craft skills, in favor of the more socially and economically prestigious attainment of intellectual, mechanical, or clerical skills, relatively few members of society seem to have artistic abilities. This state of affairs seems to validate the assumption that creativity is a special and distinct human attribute.

Once he is attuned to the psychological and spiritual nature of the world crisis, the internal technologist must first seek to transcend the ceaseless intellectual thinking principle upon which material progress depends. Because the practice of seeing through thought is fundamental to all experience of a cosmic nature, the mandala and other primary geometrical forms have persisted throughout human culture. Transcending the grip of intellectualization, rationalization, or conceptualization, one will almost certainly experience the mandalic nature of the primordial. Second, in whatever form the sacred is experienced there must be a complete identification of self with the object of experience. At its most primary level, art is not a thing done but a dissolution of the ego; nor is anything "created." Whereas the materialistic view is that creation is an addition to reality, from the point of view of internal technology, creation is actually a dissolution of duality and a merging into a unitive state, producing a transformation of reality—the transubstantiation of which I previously spoke. What technological civilization refers to as the archaic work of art may well be the residue of an active realization of nonduality.

In the art of Tantra, both of India and Tibet, we have perhaps the purest example of an archaic nondualizing tradition that has survived quite intact. The rediscovery of Tantra art by the technological world and its subsequent popularity are further signs that the circle is completing itself. In Tantra, as in certain American Indian rituals, art is not a specialized profession or a particular style but a path to greater self-realization open to anyone willing to cast aside the mind-forged manacles of man. Of course, to choose this path requires the reversal of all logical and historical processes. The extent to which individuals are capable of undergoing this initial transformation is the extent to which a new world view is being brought forth.

The power of Tantra and the ritualistic art of the American Indians derives from a religious impulse profoundly wedded to an intuitive and systematic knowledge of the laws governing the creation and perpetuation of the world. This religious impulse is utterly lacking in the art of technological modernism, which has finally exhausted and broken itself in the chaos of intellectual conceptualization. Yet in the charnel ground where concept art disintegrates, a new consciousness more appropriate to the temple than to the studio or gallery has slowly emerged. This deeply conscious change in attitude, type, and quality of artistic activity, which has appeared largely unannounced, is as significant as any change that has occurred since the Renaissance. However the various efforts in the realm of the developing consciousness may find expression—whether in the lifestyle of a commune or the practice of art in a certain medium—they do not constitute a movement but a *mutation*. A movement is a calculated reaction to a preceding event operating within a strict causal framework; but a mutation is a function of evolutionary necessity without parallel or precedent.

We are now witnessing the final reversal of Renaissance values. Naturally this could not have come about without the formative base of European culture. But to follow the prevailing standard is to widen the ever more apparent abyss separating the psychic from the physical. If one encounters this dilemma head-on, a transfiguration occurs, accompanied by a unitive experience that engenders a resolve to leap over the abyss. The resolve may be associated with a thirst for gnosis—a more fundamental knowledge, a knowledge that may become an integral part of oneself. At this point a revitalized human expression becomes possible.

If art is no longer specialized, then it becomes a means of relating to the whole; that is, it becomes an activity that responds to and helps direct environmental impulses rather than an art (or a technology) that is imposed on the environment. This is why knowledge of the laws of the creation and perpetuation of the world is a prerequisite for the practice of art. The most direct source for knowledge of this nature is one's own organism. But to gain knowledge from this source requires psychophysical techniques that make direct and immediate use of the biopsychic system centered in our bodies, which are the ultimate environment and ground of experience.

Through archaic techniques such as *hatha yoga* and *tai chi chuan*, for instance, psyche and body may be revitalized and their union experientially reaffirmed. Psychophysical exercises, consciously undertaken, enable the organism to reassert its autoregulatory and self-expressive capacity, which has been greatly diminished by the artifical dependencies that technological civilization instills in the individual. In fact, the confusion resulting from "industrial anarchy" is so profound that only through exposure to a seemingly *opposite* system of behavior can the stifling ego-consciousness fostered by present ways of life be adequately confronted and transformed. Thus the archaic systems and their various gurus and teachers are an essential part of the present "end" phase of neotechnic civilization. At one point Don Juan told Carlos Castaneda that the system of magical thought into which he was attempting to initiate him existed only so that, juxtaposed to his old, Cartesian mental set, it would enable Carlos to see the absurdity of both—and all—human conceptual systems and thereby arrive at a realization of the truth.

Slowly and often painfully uncovering an authentically open and destructured vision of the world, the internal technologist appears in his or her role as a *healer, one who makes whole*. Psychophysically healed, his negative, materialistic tendencies transformed, and initiated into a knowledge of the laws governing the creation, perpetuation, and destruction of the world, the internal technologist exemplifies the integration of archaic wisdom with a full realization of man's present evolutionary situation. Beyond merely pointing out the present stagnation in the human condition, the responsibility of the artist of renewed awareness is personally to bring about a new harmony beginning with his own organism. In other words, the internal technologist has the potential of becoming a *center* by coordinating his own organism's physical, emotional, and mental functions. Since the human species itself is potentially a network of centers, and hence an organism whose rhythmic and harmonious order depends on the rhythm and harmony of its individual centers, the artist as internal technologist has a definite role to play in human survival. Moreover, to add a further dimension, the earth itself depends on the superior coordination of the human race for its ultimate fulfillment. But there will be no absolute realization by all the members of the planetary hierarchy until there is a real coordination of individual centers. Charles Henry expressed the double-blind imperative of this situation:

> The development of the individual is impossible without the development of the species as the development of the species is impossible without the development of the individual. . . .The result of this important consequence is that individuality tends to be collective, and that collectivity tends to be individual. The realization of this double end would be the age of absolute harmony; the complexity of the rhythm which sweeps the species along is the same in consequence for the individual.[7]

What makes the internal technologist a "center" is the interior wedding of the feminine right hemisphere and the masculine left hemisphere: the result is synergistic, and not at all like adding two and two and getting only four. Whatever the internal technologist does is art, for art in these terms is an integration of the open way (psyche, the female) and the way of power (techne, the male). The open way is the descent of the goddess, the yin, *shakti, dakini,* mother-muse who symbolizes inspiration, submission, intuition, wisdom as innate appreciation. The way of power is that with which we usually identify art or technique. It is male; it is yang, disintegrated, it is the artist or the technocrat; integrated, it is the yogi or the shaman; it symbolizes the qualities of expiration, ability, implementation; its wisdom is skill in means. For the revitalized artist of whatever sex, the intrinsically feminine psyche no longer is the disembodied muse of the romantic poet but is incorporated once again as the vitally functioning intuitive structure of being. Correspondingly, woman is no longer the "lesser faith," *fides minor,* hence feminine, but the goddess, the matrix, the openness of nature through which spirit finds the vessel appropriate to its expression. Man and woman are no longer master and slave, nor are they at war with each other, but they realize in and through their uniqueness the fullness of the universe. They are representatives on earth of the primary cosmic principle; both must live in harmony with each other, or else they jeopardize the precarious balance of the cosmos.

Reflecting the integration brought about by an activated internal technology, the expressive language of the new vision is necessarily symbolic and androgynous. Symbols may be described as compressed information, and as Van de Bogart has written, "Compression of information is the next step toward global sanity."[8] Because the language of the new vision is symbolic, it is capable of conveying immediately through simple forms a multiplicity of meaning; because it is androgynous, it evokes the marriage of heaven and hell, the physical and the psychic, man and woman, the archaic and the evolving, the terrestrial and the celestial, the sacred and the profane. What is coming into being is a language of renewed archetypal significance based on a profoundly religious orientation. In being religious—bound back into one —this orientation implies a transvaluation of everything commonly understood as either art or technology.

The problem of art cannot be solved apart from the problem of life; rather than speak of art in the context of what is coming to birth, it may be wiser to speak of an art-whole, a mystic space in which the pattern of human behavior is so radically altered that the very concept "art" no longer has any validity. Purged of the separatist notions of art and technology, we may approach a mode of behavior in which the expressive function of the human organism is so indissolubly wedded to an intuitive knowledge of the laws governing the creation and maintenance of the world that our least response is pregnant with a vitality and a meaning of which mechanized existence has long since deprived us. Where once alienated, literally educated masses sought an escapist refreshment in the entertaining spas of the theater, the museum, or the television tube, we may envision participatory ceremonies that are therapeutic, consciousness-enhancing, and synesthetically involving.

Our journey began with the transformation of mythic experience into the schizophrenic, splintered-world of art, and of the artistic experience into history itself; now through the transformative mind of the visionary artist, we find that history diminishes in the swelling tide of a new myth based on the reunited antipodes of the human mind. The return of the shaman, the descent of the goddess, usher us once again into another beginning.

Dick Higgins

Intermedia

Much of the best work being produced today seems to fall between media. This is no accident. The concept of the separation between media arose in the Renaissance. The idea that a painting is made of paint on canvas or that a sculpture should not be painted seems characteristic of the kind of social thought—categorizing and dividing society into nobility with its various sub-divisions, untitled gentry, artisans, serfs and landless workers—which we call the feudal conception of the Great Chain of Being. This essentially mechanistic approach continued to be relevant throughout the first two industrial revolutions, just concluded, and into the present era of automation, which constitutes, in fact, a third industrial revolution.

However, the social problems that characterize our time, as opposed to the political ones, no longer allow a compartmentalized approach. We are approaching the dawn of a classless society, to which separation into rigid categories is absolutely irrelevant. This shift does not relate more to East than West or vice versa. Castro works in the cane fields. New York's Mayor Lindsay walks to work during the subway strike. The millionaries eat their lunches at Horn and Hardart's. This sort of populism is a growing tendency rather than a shrinking one.

We sense this in viewing art which seems to belong unnecessarily rigidly to one or another form. We view paintings. What are they, after all? Expensive, handmade objects, intended to ornament the walls of the rich or, through their (or their government's) munificence, to be shared with the large numbers of people and give them a sense of grandeur. But they do not allow any sense of dialogue.

Pop art? How could it play a part in the art of the future? It is bland. It is pure. It uses elements of common life without comment, and so, by accepting the misery of this life and its aridity so mutely, it condones them. Pop and Op are both dead, however, because they confine themselves, through the media which they employ, to the older functions of art, of decorating and suggesting grandeur, whatever their detailed content or their artists' intentions. None of the ingenious theories of the Mr. Ivan Geldoway combine can prevent them from being colossally boring and irrelevant. Milord runs his Mad Avenue gallery, in which he displays his pretty wares. He is protected by a handful of rude footmen who seem to feel that this is the way Life will always be. At his beck and call is Sir Fretful Callous, a moderately well-informed high priest, who apparently despises the Flame he is supposed to tend and therefore prefers anything that titillates him. However, Milord needs his services, since he, poor thing, hasn't the time or the energy to contribute more than his name and perhaps his dollars; getting information and finding out what's going on are simply toooooo exhausting. So, well protected and advised, he goes blissfully through the streets in proper Louis XIV style.

This scene is not just characteristic of the painting world as an institution, however. It is absolutely natural to (and inevitable in) the concept of the pure medium, the painting or precious object of any kind. That is the way such objects are marketed since that is the world to which they belong and to which they relate. The sense of "I am the state," however, will shortly be replaced by "After me the deluge," and, in fact, if the High Art world were better informed, it would realize that the deluge has already begun.

Who knows when it began? There is no reason for us to go into history in any detail. Part of the reason that Duchamp's objects are fascinating while Picasso's voice is fading is that the Duchamp pieces are truly between media, between sculpture and something else, while a Picasso is readily classifiable as a painted ornament. Similarly, by invading the land between collage and photography, the German John Heartfield produced what are probably the greatest graphics of our century, surely the most powerful political art that has been done to date.

The ready-made or found object, in a sense an intermedium since it was not intended to conform to the pure media, usually suggests this, and therefore suggests a location in the field between the general area of art media and those of life media. However, at this time, the locations of this sort are relatively unexplored, as compared with media between the arts. I cannot, for example, name work that has consciously been placed in the intermedium between painting and shoes. The closest thing would seem to be the sculpture of Claes Oldenburg, which falls between sculpture and hamburgers or Eskimo Pies, yet it is not the sources of these images themselves. An Oldenburg Eskimo Pie may look something like an Eskimo Pie, yet it is neither edible nor cold. There is still a great deal to be done in this direction in the way of opening up aesthetically rewarding possibilities.

In the middle 1950s many painters began to realize the fundamental irrelevance of Abstract Expressionism, which was the dominant mode at the time. Such painters as Allan Kaprow and Robert Rauschenberg in the United States and Wolf Vostell in Germany turned to collage or, in the latter's case, dé-collage in the sense of making work by adding or removing, replacing and substituting or altering components of a visual work. They began to include increasingly incongruous objects in their work. Rauschenberg called his constructions *combines* and went so far as to place a stuffed goat—spattered with paint and with a rubber tire around its neck—onto one. Kaprow, more philosophical and restless, meditated on the relationship of the spectator and the work. He put mirrors into his things so the spectator could feel included in them. That wasn't physical enough, so he made enveloping collages which surrounded the spectator. These he called *environments*. Finally, in the spring of 1958, he began to include live people as part of the collage, and this he called a *happening*.

The proscenium theater is the outgrowth of seventeenth century ideals of social order. Yet there is remarkably little structural difference between the dramas of D'Avenant and those of Edward Albee, certainly nothing comparable to the difference in pump construction or means of mass transportation. It would seem that the technological and social implications of the first two industrial revolutions have been evaded completely. The drama is still mechanistically divided: there are performers, production people, a separate audience and an explicit script. Once started, like Frankenstein's monster, the course of affairs is unalterable, perhaps damned by its inability to reflect its surroundings. With our populistic mentality today, it is difficult to attach importance—other than what we have been taught to attach—to this traditional theater. Nor do minor innovations do more than provide dinner conversation: this theater is round instead of square, in that one the stage revolves, here the play is relatively senseless and whimsical (Pinter is, after all, our modern J. M. Barrie—unless the honor belongs more properly to Beckett). Every year fewer attend the professional Broadway theaters. The shows get sillier and sillier, showing the producers' estimate of our mentality (or is it their own that is revealed?). Even the best of the traditional theater is no longer found on Broadway but at the Judson Memorial Church, some miles away. Yet our theater schools grind out thousands on thousands of performing and production personnel, for whom jobs will simply not exist in twenty years. Can we blame the unions? Or rents and real estate taxes? Of course not. The subsidized productions, sponsored at such museums as New York's Lincoln Center, are not building up a new audience so much as re-cultivating an old one, since the medium of such drama seems weird and arti-ficial in our new social milieu. We need more portability and flexibility, and this the traditional theater cannot provide. It was made for Versailles and for the sedentary Milords, not for motorized life-demons who travel six hundred miles a week. Versailles no longer speaks very loudly to us, since we think at eighty-five miles an hour.

In the other direction, starting from the idea of theater itself, others such as myself declared war on the script as a set of sequential events. Impro-visation was no help; performers merely acted in imitation of a script. So I began to work as if time and sequence could be utterly suspended, not by ignoring them (which would simply be illogical) but by systematically re-placing them as structural elements with change. Lack of change would cause my pieces to stop. In 1958 I wrote a piece, *Stacked Deck*, in which any event can take place at any time, as long as its cue appears. The cues are pro-duced by colored lights. Since the colored lights could be used wherever they were put, and audience reactions were also cuing situations, the performance-audience separation was removed and a happening situation was established, though less visually oriented in its use of its environment and imagery. At the same time, Al Hansen moved into the area from graphic notation experi-ments, and Nam June Paik and Benjamin Patterson (both in Germany at the time) moved in from varieties of music in which specifically musical events were frequently replaced by nonmusical actions.

Thus the Happening developed as an intermedium, an uncharted land that lies between collage, music, and the theater. It is not governed by rules; each work determines its own medium and form according to its needs. The concept itself is better understood by what it is not, rather than what it is. Approaching it, we are pioneers again, and shall continue to be so as long as there's plenty of elbow room and no neighbors around for a few miles. Of course, a concept like this is very disturbing to those whose mentality is compartmentalized. *Time, Life* and the High Priests have been announcing the death of Happenings, regularly since the movement gained momentum in the late fifties, but this says more about the accuracy of their information than about the liveliness of the movement.

We have noted the intermedia in the theater and in the visual arts, the Happening, and certain varieties of physical constructions. For reasons of space we cannot take up here the intermedia between other areas. However, I would like to suggest that the use of intermedia is more or less universal throughout the fine arts, since continuity rather than categorization is the hallmark of our new mentality. There are parallels to the Happening in music, for example, in the work of such composers as Philip Corner and John Cage, who explore the intermedia between music and philosophy, or Joe Jones, whose self-playing musical instruments fall into the intermedium between music and sculpture. The constructed music of Emmet Williams and Robert Filliou certainly constitute an intermedium between poetry and sculpture. Is it possible to speak of the use of intermedia as a huge and inclusive movement of which dada, futurism, and surrealism are early phases preceding the huge ground-swell that is taking place now? Or is it more reasonable to regard the use of intermedia an irreversible historical innovation, more comparable to the development of instrumental music than, for example, to the development of romanticism?

Harold Rosenberg

Criticism and Its Premises

The first requirement of art criticism is that it shall be relevant to the art under consideration; how correct are its evaluations of specific art objects is of lesser importance. The accuracy of a critic's judgments cannot be determined by his contemporaries, in any case. But the inflection given by art criticism to the general thinking about art affects not only the responses of appreciators of art but the creative attitudes of artists as well. When this thinking is trivial or beside the point, painting and sculpture become the speciality of feature writers, decorators, dealers, and speculators in masterpieces.

In order to be relevant, art criticism today must maintain a continuing sensitivity to major characteristics peculiar to the modern epoch that affect the situation of art, including the outlook, rituals, and objectives of those who create it. A mind blind to the radical material, social and intellectual innovations of the twentieth century, and the influence of these innovations upon contemporary modes of creation can only respond to significant modern works with confusion and/or bitterness. For such a mind, criticism has one purpose: to provide a defensive barrier against new work and new ideas by applying "values" presumably drawn from the great achievements of the past. Criticism so oriented leads neither to intelligent perusal of individual works nor to genuine debate concerning the cultural losses and gains of modernism. It merely drops a curtain of polemics between the critic and the

Reprinted, abridged, from *Art on the Edge* (Macmillan, 1975), by permission of the author.

artist and contributors to the estrangement of the public from all art, past as well as present, since only through apprehending, by means of present-day creations, how art is created, can the creations of other periods be genuinely appreciated.

The following are propositions which in my opinion ought to be more or less explicitly recognized by contemporary critical thinking as creating new problems for art and for art criticism.

Proposition 1: That creation of art in the twentieth century is an activity within the politico-cultural drama of a world in the process of remaking itself.

Modern art is saturated with issues and ideologies that reflect the technological, political, social, and cultural revolutions of the past one hundred years. Regardless of the degree to which the individual artist is conscious of these issues, he in fact responds to them in choosing among aesthetic and technical alternatives. By choosing a certain mode of handling line, form, and color, he will have affiliated himself with an aesthetic grounded on the obligation of art to communicate judgments of the artist's environment, while a different choice will have identified him with the concept that for art reality is that which comes into being through the act of painting. *Thus, choices having to do with method in art become in practice attitudes regarding the future of man.* Hence, art in our time cannot escape having a political content and moral implications. Criticism that is unaware of this is fatally poverty stricken.

In the changed relation between art and history, the automatism involved in the application of craft skills has been replaced by acts of the mind occurring *at the very beginning of the making of a work.* Whether these acts be acts of the artist or of the teacher, their effect is to remove art from the realm of habit, manual dexterity, and traditional taste into that of philosophy. In the new situation, art emerges from theory. We shall return to this subject—the new dependence of art upon ideas—in Proposition 3.

The consciousness of standing in the midst of developing events lends urgency to the painter's meditations on possible courses to follow. In the past a single tradition, rather than a selection among possible futures, determined stylistic affiliation. Modern art tends toward separate concentrations of energy and conflicts of will rather than toward homogeneity of style and meaning. The historical consciousness also pervades the art museum, the art gallery, and the private collection in the form of attempts to forecast which trends and personalities in art will survive. Art today shares in the general awareness that tomorrow is being shaped by a relentless weeding out of short-lived impulses. On its profounder levels, modern art is acutely aware of itself as a participant in the contest to affect the future, as one of the powers engaged in giving form to the unknown.

Proposition 2: That the politico-cultural drama has in our century assumed global dimensions and that the artist now works in an environment unbounded by time and place.

Under the unrelaxing pressure of political, social, and intellectual development since World War I, local, regional, and national traditions have been steadily dissolving and are being absorbed into worldwide systems. The individual artist, whether in Tokyo, New York, or São Paulo, is confronted by the activity of art everywhere, without the mediation of an inherited outlook or style. He is confronted too, by the constant unveiling, through anthropological and archaeological research, of the totality of human thought, belief, and accomplishment.

The almost simultaneous transmission of works and styles throughout the world by means of film and print has brought into being a universal pictorial vocabulary. This communication, however, is restricted to surface approximations. Lacking the scale and texture of the originals, to say nothing of their physical and cultural settings, the reproductions fall short of conveying the experience that gave rise to the artworks themselves. Art in the global interchange tends to appear as consisting of various categories of decoration. The constantly augmented mass of art studied in the form of emotionally vacant images facilitates the rise of new academicism based on abstractions drawn from art history. Contemporary art, especially, is dealt with as if it consisted of designs the emotional and social content of which may be ignored. Also, the description and classification of art as artifacts contributes to the formation of a worldwide bureaucracy with scholarly pretensions concerning the goals of creation.

Thus the internationalization of art becomes a factor contributing to the estrangement of art from the artist. The sum of works of all times and places stands against him as an entity with objectives and values of its own. In turn, since becoming aware of the organized body of artworks as the obstacle to his own aesthetic self-affirmation, the artist is pushed toward anti-intellectualism and willful dismissal of the art of the past.

Proposition 3: That with the weakening of traditional attitudes, assumptions, techniques, and subjects, styles now originate in abstract ideas and idea-based art movements.

Aesthetic programs have replaced regional masterpieces as authority and as inspiration. "Every modern activity," said Paul Valéry, "is dominated and governed by *myths* in the form of *ideologies*" (his italics). The roots of contemporary creation lie not in observations of nature nor in earlier works of art but in theoretical interpretations of these. The new relation of art and ideas has imposed upon art the necessity for a self-consciousness that has rendered skillful copying obsolete. The theoretical content of modern art imposes new demands upon criticism, primarily for clear differentiation between what may be analyzed in a painting or sculpture and what must be left to the intuition of the spectator as unique and inaccessible to language.

Proposition 4: That with change established as the norm of present-day life, the capacity for innovation and for recasting old art into new forms has become a primary virtue in art.

The centrality of art in our civilization depends upon its role as the testing ground of the conditions and possibilities of creation. Imitation of the art of earlier centuries, as that done by Picasso or Modigliani, is carried on not in order to perpetuate ancient values but to demonstrate that new aesthetic orders now prevail. In our era, art that ceases to seek the new becomes at once intellectually insignificant, a species of homecraft. The nature of originality is open to debate—in fact, needs desperately to be debated. But no disagreement exists regarding the value of the new in art. On the other hand, the dedication of art to novelty complicates the problem of values and exposes art to sensationalism and the influence of fashion and publicity.

Proposition 5: That the break between the present and the past makes the future opaque and plunges art into a permanent state of uncertainty.

"No one can say what will be dead or alive tomorrow in literature, philosophy, aesthetics: no one yet knows what ideas and modes of expression will be inscribed on the casualty list, what novelties will be proclaimed."—Valéry.

That condition in which the future cannot be depended upon to resemble the past constitutes a state of crisis. Or, if one prefers, a state of permanent expectancy. Under such circumstances art takes as its point of departure the effort *to arrive at or create values* rather than to accommodate itself to existing criteria.

Criticism, too, must seek its values through particular instances—works, artists, art movements—rather than through the application of rules formulated by criticism in advance of the works. The modern mind is tempted to end its suspense by affirming systems of value, including aesthetic systems. Thus, in totalitarian countries the future course of events is charted and the duty is imposed upon art to serve in realizing that future. Means that promise to make art most effective as propaganda—for example, the idealization of facial expressions and bodily postures—are translated into aesthetic values. The result has been the ruin of art by political dictation. Comparable results have followed attempts in the West to reduce the risks of the unknown through calculating the future direction of art. The following observation of Valéry might be adopted as a critical axiom: "Since, henceforth, we must deal with the *new* of the irreducible type, our future is endowed with *essential unpredictability.*"

Proposition 6: That vast shiftings of population, both geographically (through migrations, exiles, displacements) and vertically (through revolutions, mass education, equalization of opportunity), have destroyed the stabilized social character of individuals and brought the problem of identity, personal and collective, into prominence as a theme of contemporary cultural forms.

Art movements in the twentieth century have tended to swing back and forth between extremes of individual self-searching (surrealism, abstract expressionism), self-identification with groups (regionalism, social realism), and technological objectivity (Bauhaus, optical art). The rhythms of self-affirmation and self-negation arising from the dialectics of identity stimulate the formation of new modes of art through opposition, overlapping, and merger, as in the rise of pop art as a depersonalized counterstatement to action painting. Impulses toward and away from identity should be recognized by criticism as providing an essential content of modern art, figurative as well as abstract.

Proposition 7: That ours is an epoch of excavations—archaeological, psychoanalytical, philological—which keep emptying into contemporary culture the tombs of all the ages of man.

Absorbing the flood of past art, art in our time continually reconstitutes itself as a theater of revivals. Styles of earlier periods, far and near, from the funerary carvings of the Aztecs to the realism of Courbet, are reawakened as experiences and as slogans by contemporary painting and sculpture.

Modern art is at one with radical politics and with psychotherapy in its fascination with the abyss of lost forms and powers. Like other significant modes of present-day action and research, its explorations periodically lead it to the verge of changing into something else. Thus modern art often crosses over into non-art and adopts anti-art attitudes. Besides augmenting consciousness, this negative strain acts as a lightning rod to divert from society and individuals more perilous temptations to self-surrender—totalitarian politics, drugs, mysticism. The reawakening of forms seems to have a profound function in a culture of change.

Part Two

Clement Greenberg

Modernist Painting

Modernism includes more than just art and literature. By now it includes almost the whole of what is truly alive in our culture. It happens, also, to be very much of a historical novelty. Western civilization is not the first to turn around and question its own foundations, but it is the civilization that has gone furthest in doing so. I identify Modernism with the intensification, almost the exacerbation of this self-critical tendency that began with the philosopher Kant. Because he was the first to criticize the means itself of criticism, I conceive of Kant as the first real Modernist.

The essence of Modernism lies, as I see it, in the use of the characteristic methods of a discipline to criticize the discipline itself—not in order to subvert it, but to entrench it more firmly in its area of competence. Kant used logic to establish the limits of logic, and while he withdrew much from its old jurisdiction, logic was left in all the more secure possession of what remained to it.

The self-criticism of Modernism grows out of but is not the same thing as the criticism of the Enlightenment. The Enlightenment criticized from the outside, the way criticism in its more accepted sense does; Modernism criticizes from the inside, through the procedures themselves of that which is being criticized. It seems natural that this new kind of criticism should have appeared first in philosophy, which is critical by definition, but as the nineteenth century wore on it made itself felt in many other fields. A more rational justification had begun to be demanded of every formal social activity, and "Kantian" self-criticism was called on eventually to meet and interpret this demand in areas that lay far from philosophy.

We know what has happened to an activity like religion that has not been able to avail itself of "Kantian" immanent criticism in order to justify itself. At first glance the arts might seem to have been in a situation like religion's. Having been denied by the Enlightenment all tasks they could take seriously, they looked as though they were going to be assimilated to entertainment pure and simple, and entertainment itself looked as though it were going to be assimilated, like religion, to therapy. The arts could save themselves from this leveling down only by demonstrating that the kind of experience they provided was valuable in its own right and not to be obtained from any other kind of activity.

Each art, it turned out, had to effect this demonstration on its own account. What had to be exhibited and made explicit was that which was unique and irreducible not only in art in general, but also in each particular art. Each art had to determine, through the operations peculiar to itself, the effects peculiar and exclusive to itself. By doing this each art would, to be sure, narrow its area of competence, but at the same time it would make its possession of this area all the more secure.

It quickly emerged that the unique and proper area of competence of each art coincided with all that was unique to the nature of its medium. The task of self-criticism became to eliminate from the effects of each art any and every effect that might conceivably be borrowed from or by the medium of any other art. Thereby each art would be rendered "pure," and in its "purity" find the guarantee of its standards of quality as well as of its independence. "Purity" meant self-definition, and the enterprise of self-criticism in the arts became one of self-definition with a vengeance.

Realistic, illusionist art had dissembled the medium, using art to conceal art. Modernism used art to call attention to art. The limitations that constitute the medium of painting—the flat surface, the shape of the support, the properties of pigment—were treated by the Old Masters as negative factors that could be acknowledged only implicitly or indirectly. Modernist painting has come to regard these same limitations as positive factors that are to be acknowledged openly. Manet's paintings became the first Modernist ones by virtue of the frankness with which they declared the surfaces on which they were painted. The Impressionists, in Manet's wake, abjured underpainting and glazing, to leave the eye under no doubt as to the fact that the colors used were made of real paint that came from pots or tubes. Cézanne sacrificed verisimilitude, or correctness, in order to fit drawing and design more explicitly to the rectangular shape of the canvas.

It was the stressing, however, of the ineluctable flatness of the support that remained most fundamental in the processes by which pictorial art criticized and defined itself under Modernism. Flatness alone was unique and exclusive to that art. The inclosing shape of the support was a limiting condition, or norm, that was shared with the art of the theater; color was a norm or means shared with sculpture as well as the theater. Flatness, two-dimensionality, was the only condition painting shared with no other art, and so Modernist painting oriented itself to flatness as it did to nothing else.

The Old Masters had sensed that it was necessary to preserve what is called the integrity of the picture plane: that is, to signify the enduring presence of flatness under the most vivid illusion of three-dimensional space. The apparent contradiction involved—the dialectical tension, to use a fashionable but apt phrase—was essential to the success of their art, as it is indeed to the success of all pictorial art. The Modernists have neither avoided nor resolved this contradiction; rather, they have reversed its terms. One is made aware of the flatness of their pictures before, instead of after, being made aware of what the flatness contains. Whereas one tends to see what is *in* an Old Master before seeing it as a picture, one sees a Modernist painting as a picture first. This is, of course, the best way of seeing any kind of picture, Old Master or Modernist, but Modernism imposes it as the only and necessary way, and Modernism's success in doing so is a success of self-criticism.

It is not in principle that Modernist painting in its latest phase has abandoned the representation of recognizable objects. What it has abandoned in principle is the representation of the kind of space that recognizable, three-dimensional objects can inhabit. Abstractness, or the nonfigurative, has in itself still not proved to be an altogether necessary moment in the self-criticism of pictorial art, even though artists as eminent as Kandinsky and Mondrian have thought so. Representation, or illustration, as such does not abate the uniqueness of pictorial art; what does do so are the associations of the things represented. All recognizable entities (including pictures themselves) exist in three-dimensional space, and the barest suggestion of a recognizable entity suffices to call up associations of that kind of space. The fragmentary silhouette of a human figure, or of a teacup, will do so, and by doing so alienate pictorial space from the two-dimensionality which is the guarantee of painting's independence as an art. Three-dimensionality is the province of sculpture, and for the sake of its own autonomy painting has had above all to divest itself of everything it might share with sculpture. And it is in the course of its effort to do this, and not so much—I repeat—to exclude the representational or the "literary," that painting has made itself abstract.

At the same time Modernist painting demonstrates precisely in its resistance to the sculptural, that it continues tradition and the themes of tradition, despite all appearances to the contrary. For the resistance to the sculptural begins long before the advent of Modernism. Western painting, insofar as it strives for realistic illusion, owes an enormous debt to sculpture, which taught it in the beginning how to shade and model towards an illusion of relief, and even how to dispose that illusion in a complementary illusion of deep space. Yet some of the greatest feats of Western painting came as part of the effort it has made in the last four centuries to suppress and dispel the sculptural. Starting in Venice in the sixteenth century and continuing in Spain, Belgium, and Holland in the seventeenth, that effort was carried on at first in the name of color. When David, in the eighteenth century, sought to revive sculptural painting, it was in part to save pictorial art from the decorative flattening-out that the emphasis on color seemed to induce. Nevertheless, the strength of David's own best pictures (which are predominantly portraits) often lies as much in their color as in anything else. And Ingres, his pupil, though subordinating color far more consistently, executed pictures that were among the flattest, least sculptural done in the West by a sophisticated artist since the fourteenth century. Thus by the middle of the nineteenth century all ambitious tendencies in painting were converging (beneath their differences) in an anti-sculptural direction.

Modernism, in continuing this direction, made it more conscious of itself. With Manet and the Impressionists, the question ceased to be defined as one of color versus drawing, and became instead a question of purely optical experience as against optical experience modified or revised by tactile associations. It was in the name of the purely and literally optical, not in that of color, that the Impressionists set themselves to undermining shading and modeling and everything else that seemed to connote the sculptural. And in a way like that in which David had reacted against Fragonard in the name of the sculptural, Cézanne, and the Cubists after him, reacted against Impressionism. But once again, just as David's and Ingres' reaction had culminated in a kind of painting even less sculptural than before, so the Cubist counter-revolution eventuated in a kind of painting flatter than anything Western art had seen since before Cimabue—so flat indeed that it could hardly contain recognizable images.

In the meantime the other cardinal norms of the art of painting were undergoing an equally searching inquiry, though the results may not have been equally conspicuous. It would take me more space than is at my disposal to tell how the norm of the picture's inclosing shape or frame was loosened, then tightened, then loosened once again, and then isolated and tightened once more by successive generations of Modernist painters; or how the norms of finish, of paint texture, and of value and color contrast, were tested and re-tested. Risks have been taken with all these, not only for the sake of new expression, but also in order to exhibit them more clearly as norms. By being exhibited and made explicit they are tested for their indispensability. This testing is by no means finished, and the fact that it becomes more searching as it proceeds accounts for the radical simplifications, as well as radical complications, in which the very latest abstract art abounds.

Neither the simplifications nor the complications are matters of license. On the contrary, the more closely and essentially the norms of a discipline become defined the less apt they are to permit liberties (*liberation* has become a much abused word in connection with avant-garde and Modernist art). The essential norms or conventions of painting are also the limiting conditions with which a marked-up surface must comply in order to be experienced as a picture. Modernism has found that these limiting conditions can be pushed back indefinitely before a picture stops being a picture and turns into an arbitrary object; but it has also found that the further back these limits are pushed the more explicitly they have to be observed. The intersecting black lines and colored rectangles of a Mondrian may seem hardly enough to make a picture out of, yet by echoing the picture's inclosing shape so self-evidently they impose that shape as a regulating norm with a new force and a new completeness. Far from incurring the danger of arbitrariness in the absence of a model in nature, Mondrian's art proves, with the passing of time, almost too disciplined, too convention-bound in certain respects; once we have gotten used to its utter abstractness we realize that it is more traditional in its color, as well as in its subservience to the frame, than the last paintings of Monet are.

It is understood, I hope, that in plotting the rationale of Moderist art I have had to simplify and exaggerate. The flatness towards which Modernist painting orients itself can never be an utter flatness. The heightened sensitivity of the picture plane may no longer permit sculptural illusion, or *trompe-l'oeil*, but it does and must permit optical illusion. The first mark made on a surface destroys its virtual flatness, and the configurations of a Mondrian still suggest a kind of illusion of a kind of third dimension. Only now it is a strictly pictorial, strictly optical third dimension. Where the Old Masters created an illusion of space into which one could imagine oneself walking, the illusion created by a Modernist is one into which one can only look, can travel through only with the eye.

One begins to realize that the Neo-Impressionists were not altogether misguided when they flirted with science. Kantian self-criticism finds its perfect expression in science rather than in philosophy, and when this kind of self-criticism was applied in art the latter was brought closer in spirit to scientific method than ever before—closer than in the early Renaissance. That visual art should confine itself exclusively to what is given in visual experience, and make no reference to anything given in other orders of experience, is a notion whose only justification lies, notionally, in scientific consistency. Scientific method alone asks that a situation be resolved in exactly the same kind of terms as that in which it is presented—a problem in physiology is solved in terms of physiology, not in those of psychology; to be solved in terms of psychology, it has to be presented in, or translated into, these terms first. Analogously, Modernist painting asks that a literary theme be translated into strictly optical, two-dimensional terms before becoming the subject of pictorial art—which means its being translated in such a way that it entirely loses its literary character. Actually, such consistency promises nothing in the way of esthetic quality or esthetic results, and the fact that the best art of the past seventy or eighty years increasingly approaches such consistency does not change this; now as before, the only consistency that counts in art is esthetic consistency, which shows itself only in results and never in methods or means. From the point of view of art itself its convergence of spirit with science happens to be a mere accident, and neither art nor science gives or assures the other of anything more than it ever did. What their convergence does show, however, is the degree to which Modernist art belongs to the same historical and cultural tendency as modern science.

It should also be understood that the self-criticism of Modernist art has never been carried on in any but a spontaneous and subliminal way. It has been altogether a question of practice, immanent to practice and never a topic of theory. Much has been heard about programs in connection with Modernist art, but there has really been far less of the programmatic in Modernist art than in Renaissance or Academic art. With a few untypical exceptions, the masters of Modernism have betrayed no more of an appetite for fixed ideas about art than Corot did. Certain inclinations and emphases, certain refusals and abstinences seem to become necessary simply because the way to stronger, more expressive art seems to lie through them. The immediate aims of Modernist artists remain individual before anything else, and the truth and success of their work is individual before it is anything else. To the extent that it succeeds as art Modernist art partakes in no way of the character of a demonstration. It has needed the accumulation over decades of a good deal of individual achievement to reveal the self-critical tendency of

Modernist painting. No one artist was, or is yet, consciously aware of this tendency, nor could any artist work successfully in conscious awareness of it. To this extent—which is by far the largest—art gets carried on under Modernism in the same way as before.

And I cannot insist enough that Modernism has never meant anything like a break with the past. It may mean a devolution, an unraveling of anterior tradition, but it also means its continuation. Modernist art develops out of the past without gap or break, and wherever it ends up it will never stop being intelligible in terms of the continuity of art. The making of pictures has been governed, since pictures first began to be made, by all the norms I have mentioned. The Paleolithic painter or engraver could disregard the norm of the frame and treat the surface in both a literally and a virtually sculptural way because he made images rather than pictures, and worked on a support whose limits could be disregarded because (except in the case of small objects like a bone or horn) nature gave them to the artist in an unmanageable way. But the making of pictures, as against images in the flat, means the deliberate choice and creation of limits. This deliberateness is what Modernism harps on: that is, spells out the fact that the limiting conditions of art have to be made altogether human limits.

I repeat that Modernist art does not offer theoretical demonstrations. It could be said, rather, that it converts all theoretical possibilities into empirical ones, and in doing so tests, inadvertently, all theories about art for their relevance to the actual practice and experience of art. Modernism is subversive in this respect alone. Ever so many factors thought to be essential to the making and experiencing of art have been shown not to be so by the fact that Modernist art has been able to dispense with them and yet continue to provide the experience of art in all its essentials. That this "demonstration" has left most of our old *value* judgments intact only makes it the more conclusive. Modernism may have had something to do with the revival of the reputations of Uccello, Piero, El Greco, Georges de la Tour, and even Vermeer, and it certainly confirmed if it did not start other revivals like that of Giotto; but Modernism has not lowered thereby the standing of Leonardo, Raphael, Titian, Rubens, Rembrandt or Watteau. What Modernism has made clear is that, though the past did appreciate masters like these justly, it often gave wrong or irrelevant reasons for doing so.

Still, in some ways this situation has hardly changed. Art criticism lags behind Modernist as it lagged behind pre-Modernist art. Most of the things that get written about contemporary art belong to journalism rather than criticism properly speaking. It belongs to journalism—and to the millennial complex from which so many journalists suffer in our day—that each new phase of Modernism should be hailed as the start of a whole new epoch of art making a decisive break with all the customs and conventions of the past. Each time, a kind of art is expected that will be unlike previous kinds of art, and so "liberated" from norms of practice or taste, that everbody, regardless of how informed or uninformed, will be able to have his say about it. And each time, this expectation is disappointed, as the phase of Modernism in question takes its place, finally, in the intelligible continuity of taste and tradition, and as it becomes clear that the same demands as before are made on artist and spectator.

Nothing could be further from the authentic art of our times than the idea of a rupture of continuity. Art is, among many other things, continuity. Without the past of art, and without the need and compulsion to maintain past standards of excellence, such a thing as Modernist art would be impossible.

POSTSCRIPT

The above appeared first in 1960 as a pamphlet in a series published by the Voice of America. It had been broadcast over that agency's radio in the spring of the same year. With some minor verbal changes it was reprinted in the spring 1963 number of *Art & Literature* in Paris, and then in Gregory Battcock's anthology *The New Art* (1966), where its date of publication in *Art & Literature* was erroneously given as 1965. . . .

I want to take this chance to correct another error, one of interpretation and not of fact. Many readers, though by no means all, seem to have taken the "rationale" of Modernist art outlined here as representing a position adopted by the writer himself: that is, that what he describes he also advocates. This may be a fault of the writing or the rhetoric. Nevertheless, a close reading of what he writes will find nothing at all to indicate that he subscribes to, believes in, the things that he adumbrates. (The quotation marks around *pure* and *purity* should have been enough to show that.) The writer is trying to account in part for how most of the very best art of the last hundred-odd years came about, but he's not implying that that's how it *had* to come about, much less that that's how the best art still has to come about. "Pure" art was a useful illusion, but this doesn't make it any the less an illusion. Nor does the possibility of its continuing usefulness make it any the less an illusion.

There have been some further constructions of what I wrote that go over into preposterousness: That I regard flatness and the inclosing of flatness not just as the limiting conditions of pictorial art, but as criteria of esthetic quality in pictorial art; that the further a work advances the self-definition of an art, the better that work is bound to be. The philosopher or art historian who can envision me—or anyone at all—arriving at esthetic judgments in this way reads shockingly more into himself or herself than into my article.

Clement Greenberg

Necessity of "Formalism"

There is the common notion of Modernism as something hectic, heated. Thus Irving Howe lists among the "formal or literary attributes of modernism" the fact that "Perversity—Which Is to Say: Surprise, Excitement, Shock,Terror, Affront—Becomes a Dominant Motif" (Introduction to a collection of essays by various hands called *The Idea of the Modern* [New York, 1967]). A related notion is that Modernism can be understood as an extreme version of Romanticism. But a long look at Modernism doesn't bear out either notion as a covering one.

Modernism is as specific a historical phenomenon as Romanticism was, but it doesn't represent nearly so specific an attitude, position, or outlook. Modernism may continue certain aspects of Romanticism, but it also reacts against Romanticism in general—just as in reviving certain aspects of Classicism it reacts against Classicism in general. In the context of what is signified by terms like "Romanticism" and "Classicism" when they are used *unhistorically*, Modernism as a whole distinguishes itself by its inclusiveness, its openness, and also its indeterminateness. It embraces the conventional polarities of literary and art history; or rather it abandons them (and in doing so exposes their limited usefulness). Modernism defines itself in the long run not as a "movement," much less a program, but rather as a kind of bias or tropism: towards esthetic value, esthetic value as such and as an ultimate. The specificity of Modernism lies in its being so heightened a tropism in this regard.

Reprinted from *New Literary History*, III/1 (Autumn, 1971), by permission of the author and the publisher. Copyright © 1971 by Clement Greenberg.

This more conscious, this almost exacerbated concern with esthetic value emerges in the mid-nineteenth century in response to an emergency. The emergency is perceived in a growing relaxation of esthetic standards at the top of Western society, and in the threat this offers to the serious practice of art and literature. The Modernist response to this emergency becomes effective because it takes place in actual production rather than in discourse; in fact, it is more conscious in the practice of art than it is in discourse or criticism. This response begins to make a break with many well-tried conventions and habits, ostensibly a radical break. But for the most part it remains only ostensibly a break and only ostensibly radical. Actually, it's a "dialectical" turn that works to maintain or restore continuity, a most essential continuity, continuity with the highest esthetic standards of the past. It's not particular past styles, manners, or modes that are to be maintained or restored, but standards, levels of quality. And these levels are to be preserved in the same way in which they were achieved in the first place: by constant renewal and innovation.

The emergency has proved to be a lasting one, and Modernism a lasting response to it. And so far it has been a more or less successful response. The higher standards of the past have been maintained in production, which does not have to mean that the best of the past has been matched in quality in a point-for-point way; it suffices that the best of Modernist production attains a similar qualitative level.

The Modernist preoccupation with esthetic value or quality as an ultimate is not new in itself. What makes it new is its explicitness, its self-consciousness, and its intensity. This self-consciousness and intensity (together with the nineteenth century's increasing rationality in fitting means to ends) could not but lead to a much closer and larger concern with the nature of the medium in each art, and hence with "technique." This was also a questioning concern and because it got acted on in practice by artists, poets, novelists, and composers, not by pedants, it could not but become an "artisanal" concern too (which does not mean the same thing as a "mechanical" concern—or at least the best of Modernism has shown that it does not mean the same thing). And it's this, the artisanal concern and emphasis of Modernism that has proved to be its covering emphasis, its enduring and also its saving one—the one that again and again brings Modernism back to itself.

Its artisanal emphasis is what more than anything else makes for the hard-headed, sober, "cold" side of Modernism. It's also part of what makes it react against Romanticism. An eventual tendency of Romanticism was to take medium and artisanry too much for granted and to consider them as more or less transparent or routine. I won't say that this was a decisive factor in the deterioration of standards, but it was a symptom of that deterioration. It was not just the soft-headedness of Romanticism popularized and in decline that provoked the hard-headed reaction of the first Modernists; it was also a certain unprofessionalism.

I don't for a moment contend that Modernism is exclusively an affair of hard-headedness and artisanal sobriety. I started out by saying that it distinguishes itself by its openness and inclusiveness of temper and attitude. And I set out to correct, not demolish, what I feel is too one-sided a view. Yet this view almost invites demolition when it comes to Modernist painting and sculpture (and maybe to Modernist music too). For these exhibit Modernism as almost crucially a concern in the *first* place with medium and exploratory technique, and a very workman-like concern. Manet and the Impressionists were paragons of hard-headed professionalism; so was Cézanne in his way, and so were Seurat and Bonnard and Vuillard; so were the Fauves—if ever there was a cool practitioner, it was Matisse. Cubism was overwhelmingly artisanal in its emphasis. And this emphasis remains a dominant one, under all the journalistic rhetoric, in Abstract Expressionism and *art informel.* Of course, Apollonian temperaments may produce Dionysian works, and Dionysian temperaments Apollonian works. Nor does artisanal hard-headedness exclude passion; it may even invite and provoke it. And of course, there were notable Modernist artists like Gauguin and Van Gogh and Soutine who were anything but soberly artisanal in outlook; but even they occupied themselves with questions of "technique" to an extent and with a consciousness that were uniquely Modernist.

Artisanal concerns force themselves more evidently on a painter or sculptor than on a writer, and it would be hard to make my point about the artisanal, the "formalist" emphasis of Modernism nearly so plausible in the case of literature. For reasons not to be gone into here, the medium of words demands to be taken more for granted than any other in which art is practiced. This holds even in verse, which may help explain why what is Modernist and what is not cannot be discriminated as easily in the poetry of the last hundred years as in the painting. . . .

It remains that Modernism in art, if not in literature, has stood or fallen so far by its "formalism." Not that Modernist art is coterminous with "formalism." And not that "formalism" hasn't lent itself to a lot of empty, bad art. But so far every attack on the "formalist" aspect of Modernist painting and sculpture has worked out as an attack on Modernism itself because every such attack developed into an attack at the same time on superior artistic standards. The recent past of Modernist art demonstrates this ever so clearly. Duchamp's and Dada's was the first outright assault on "formalism." That came from within the avant-garde, or what was nominally the avant-garde, and it stated itself immediately in a lowering of aspirations. The evidence is there in the only place where artistic evidence can be *there*: in the actual productions of Duchamp and most of the Dadaists. The same evidence continues to be there in the neo-Dadaism of the last ten years, in its works, in the inferior quality of these works. From which it has to be concluded that if Modernism remains a necessary condition of the best art of our time, as it has been of the best art of the hundred years previous, then "formalism," apparently, remains a necessary condition too, which is the sole and sufficient justification of either Modernism or "formalism."

And if "formalism" derives from the hard-headed, "cold" side of Modernism, then this must be its essential, defining side, at least in the case of painting and sculpture. That's the way it looks right now—and looks more than ever right now. The question is whether it will keep on looking that way in the future: that is, whether Modernism will continue to stand or fall by its "cold" side and by its "formalism." Modernism has been a failing thing in literature these past twenty years and more; it's not yet a failing thing in painting or sculpture, but I can imagine its turning into that in another decade (even in sculpture, which seems to have a brighter future before it than painting does). If so, this may come about in the same way that it has come about, as it seems to me, in literature: through the porousness of Modernism's "hot" side, the enthusiastic and hectic side, which is the one that middlebrows have found it easier all along to infiltrate.

There have, of course, to be deeper, larger factors in all this than the ambiguous difference between Modernism's "hot" and "cold" sides. If Modernism's "hot" side has become a liability in these past years, this is a symptom, not a cause; the cause, or causes, have to be sought outside Modernism and outside art or literature.

POSTSCRIPT

Art is, art gets experienced, for its own sake, which is what Modernism recognized in identifying esthetic value as an ultimate value. But this doesn't mean that art or the esthetic is a *supreme* value or end of life. The neglect of this distinction by the original art-for-art's-sakers—most of whom were not Modernists anyhow—compromised a valid perception.

POST-POSTSCRIPT

My harping on the artisanal and "formalist" emphasis of Modernism opens the way to all kinds of misunderstanding, as I know from tiresome experience. Quality, esthetic value originates in inspiration, vision, "content," not in "form." This is an unsatisfactory way of putting it, but for the time being there seems to be no better one available. Yet "form" not only opens the way to inspiration; it can also act as means to it; and technical preoccupations, when searching enough and compelled enough, can generate or discover "content." When a work of art or literature succeeds, when it moves us enough, it does so *ipso facto* by the "content" that it conveys; yet that "content" cannot be separated from its "form"—no more in Dante's than Mallarmé's case, no more in Goya's than in Mondrian's, no more in Verdi's than in Schoenberg's. It embarasses me to have to repeat this, but I feel I can count here on the illiteracy of enough of my readers in the matter of what can and what can't be legitimately put in words about works of art.

Jackson Pollock

My Painting

My painting does not come from the easel. I hardly ever stretch my canvas before painting. I prefer to tack the unstretched canvas to the hard wall or the floor. I need the resistance of a hard surface. On the floor I am more at ease. I feel nearer, more a part of the painting, since this way I can walk around it, work from the four sides and literally be *in* the painting. This is akin to the method of the Indian sand painters of the West.

I continue to get further away from the usual painter's tools such as easel, palette, brushes, etc. I prefer sticks, trowels, knives, and dripping fluid paint or a heavy impasto with sand, broken glass, and other foreign matter added.

When I am *in* my painting, I'm not aware of what I am doing. It is only after a sort of "get acquainted" period that I see what I have been about. I have no fears about making changes, destroying the image, etc., because the painting has a life of its own. I try to let it come through. It is only when I lose contact with the painting that the result is a mess. Otherwise there is pure harmony, an easy give and take, and the painting comes out well.

Reprinted from *Possibilities*, No. 1 (Winter, 1947-48), by permission of George Wittenborn, Inc.

Ad Reinhardt

"Art-as-Art"

The one thing to say about art is that it is one thing. Art is art-as-art and everything else is everything else. Art-as-art is nothing but art. Art is not what is not art.

The one object of fifty years of abstract art is to present art-as-art and as nothing else, to make it into the one thing it is only, separating and defining it more and more, making it purer and emptier, more absolute and more exclusive—nonobjective, nonrepresentational, nonfigurative, nonimagist, nonexpressionist, nonsubjective. The only and one way to say what abstract art or art-as-art is, is to say what it is not.

The one subject of a hundred years of modern art is that awareness of art of itself, of art preoccupied with its own process and means, with its own identity and distinction, art concerned with its own unique statement, art conscious of its own evolution and history and destiny, toward its own freedom, its own dignity, its own essence, its own reason, its own morality, and its own conscience. Art needs no justification with "realism" or "naturalism," "regionalism" or "nationalism," "individualism" or "socialism" or "mysticism," or with any other ideas.

The one content of three centuries of European or Asiatic art and the one matter of three millennia of Eastern or Western art, is the same "one significance" that runs through all the timeless art of the world. Without an

Reprinted from *Art International* (Lugano, December, 1962), by permission of the publisher.

art-as-art continuity and art-for-art's-sake conviction and unchanging art spirit and abstract point of view, art would be inaccessible and the "one thing" completely secret.

The one idea of art as "fine," "high," "noble," "liberal," "ideal" of the seventeenth century is to separate fine and intellectual art from manual art and craft. The one intention of the word *aesthetics* of the eighteenth century is to isolate the art experience from other things. The one declaration of all the main movements in art of the nineteenth century is of the "independence" of art. The one question, the one principle, the one crisis in art of the twentieth century centers in the uncompromising "purity" of art, and in the consciousness that art comes from art only, not from anything else.

The one meaning in art-as-art, past or present, is art meaning. When an art object is separated from its original time and place and use and is moved into the art museum, it gets emptied and purified of all its meaning except one. A religious object that becomes a work of art in an art museum loses all its religious meanings. No one in his right mind goes to an art museum to worship anything but art, or to learn about anything else.

The one place for art-as-art is the museum of fine art. The reason for the museum of fine art is the preservation of ancient and modern art that cannot be made again and that does not have to be done again. A museum of fine art should exclude everything but fine art, and be separate from museums of ethnology, geology, archaeology, history, decorative arts, industrial arts, military arts, and museums of other things. A museum is a treasure house and tomb, not a counting-house or amusement center. A museum that becomes an art curator's personal monument or an art-collector-sanctifying establishment or an art history manufacturing plant or an artists' market block is a disgrace. Any disturbance of a true museum's soundlessness, timelessness, airlessness, and lifelessness is a disrespect.

The one purpose of the art academy university is the education and "correction of the artist" -as-artist, not the "enlightenment of the public" or the popularization of art. The art college should be a cloister-ivyhall-ivory-tower-community of artists, an artists' union and congress and club, not a success school or service station or rest home or house of artists' ill-fame. The notion that art or an art museum or art university "enriches life" or "fosters a love of life" or "promotes understanding and love among men" is as mindless as anything in art can be. Anyone who speaks of using art to further any local, municipal, national, or international relations is out of his mind.

The one thing to say about art and life is that art is art and life is life, that art is not life and that life is not art. A "slice-of-life" art is no better or worse than a "slice-of-art" life. Fine art is not a "means of making a living" or a "way of living a life," and an artist who dedicates his life to his art or his art to his life burdens his art with his life and his life with his art. Art that is a matter of life and death is neither fine nor free.

The one assault on fine art is the ceaseless attempt to subserve it as a means to some other end or value. The one fight in art is not between art and non-art, but between true and false art, between pure art and action-assemblage art, between abstract and surrealist-expressionist anti-art, between free art and servile art. Abstract art has its own integrity, not someone else's "integration" with something else. Any combining, mixing, adding, diluting, exploiting, vulgarizing, or popularizing abstract art deprives art of its essence and depraves the artist's artistic consciousness. Art is free, but it is not a free-for-all.

The one struggle in art is the struggle of artists against artists, of artist against artist, of the artist-as-artist within and against the artist-as-man, -animal, or -vegetable. Artists who claim their artwork comes from nature, life, reality, earth or heaven, as "mirrors of the soul" or "reflections of conditions" or "instruments of the universe," who cook up "new images of man"—figures and "nature-in-abstraction"—pictures, are subjectively and objectively rascals or rustics. The art of "figuring" or "picturing" is not a fine art. An artist who is lobbying as a "creature of circumstances" or logrolling as a "victim of fate" is not a fine master artist. No one ever forces an artist to be pure.

The one art that is abstract and pure enough to have the one problem and possibility, in our time and timelessness, of the "one single grand original problem" is pure abstract painting. Abstract painting is not just another school or movement or style but the first truly unmannered and untrammeled and unentangled, styleless, universal painting. No other art or painting is detached or empty or immaterial enough.

The one history of painting progresses from the painting of a variety of ideas with a variety of subjects and objects, to one idea with a variety of subjects and objects, to one subject with a variety of objects, to one object with a variety of subjects, then to one object with one subject, to one object with no subject and no subject and no variety at all. There is nothing less significant in art, nothing more exhausting and immediately exhausted, than "endless variety."

The one evolution of art forms unfolds in one straight logical line of negative actions and reactions, in one predestined, eternally recurrent stylistic cycle, in the same all-over pattern, in all times and places, taking different times in different places, always beginning with an "early" archaic schematization, achieving a climax with a "classic" formulation, and decaying with "late" endless variety of illusionisms and expressionisms. When late stages wash away all lines of demarcation, framework, and fabric, with "anything can be art," "anybody can be an artist," "that's life," "why fight it," "anything goes," and "it makes no difference whether art is abstract or representational," the artists' world is a mannerist and primitivist art trade and suicide-vaudeville, venal, genial, contemptible, trifling.

The one way in art comes from art working and the more an artist works the more there is to do. Artists come from artists, art forms come from art forms, painting comes from painting. The one direction in fine or abstract art today is in the painting of the same one form over and over again. The one intensity and the one perfection come only from long and lonely routine preparation and attention and repetition. The one originality exists only where all artists work in the same tradition and master the same convention. The one freedom is realized only through the strictest art discipline and through the most similar studio ritual. Only a standardized, prescribed, and proscribed form can be imageless, only a stereotyped image can be formless, only a formularized art can be formulaless. A painter who does not know what or how or where to paint is not a fine artist.

The one work for a fine artist, the one painting, is the painting of the one-size canvas—the single scheme, one formal device, one color-monochrome, one linear division in each direction, one symmetry, one texture, one free-hand brushing, one rhythm, one working everything into one dissolution and one indivisibility, each painting into one over-all uniformity and non-irregularity. No lines or imaginings, no shapes or composings or representings, no visions or sensations or impulses, no symbols or signs or impastos, no decoratings or colorings or picturings, no pleasures or pains, no accidents or ready-mades, no things, no ideas, no relations, no attributes, no qualities—nothing that is not of the essence. Everything into irreducibility, unreproducibility, imperceptibility. Nothing "usable," "manipulatable," "salable," "dealable," "collectible," "graspable." No art as a commodity or a jobbery. Art is not the spiritual side of business.

The one standard in art is oneness and fineness, rightness and purity, abstractness and evanescence. The one thing to say about art is its breathlessness, lifelessness, deathlessness, contentlessness, formlessness, spacelessness, and timelessness. This is always the end of art.

Will Insley

The General Public Is Just as Disinterested in Advanced Art as Ever

Sensibility: engineered/ scientific/ geometric/ calculated/ measured/ removed/ acuteness of perception.

Avant-garde: construction/ object/ thing/ diagram/ reduced/ minimal/ basic/ furthest extension of sensibility/ formal visual construction.

Painting becomes the diagrammed object.

Definite abandoning of historical rectilinear context of painting as contained illusion, and an extension into actual surrounding space, to motivate and be motivated in turn.

The painting has become, at its farthest limit, a fragment of flat visual material.

As the problem has been clarified and reduced, the possibilities also diminish. The problem of particular color seems to be less and less important. Color becomes only a material coating giving a visual extension through intensity and light reflection to the base material object. What really counts is the object itself.

The reduction of the painting to a flat silhouette carries this tendency to its extreme.

Reprinted from *Art in America* (January-February, 1967), by permission of the author and the publisher.

WILL INSLEY

The ultimate values of sensitivity in the proportion of elements and the relation of closed and open space are exposed to the most stringent test. Only relationships of the most basic nature can withstand continual observation when all the emotional and seductive icing of the historical cake are removed.

The painting is a flat visual object, a systematic relationship of measured elements calculated to project a visual force beyond the material thing.

Sculpture and painting are visual engineering with no function other than visual existence.

Sculpture extends out more and more to contain rather than occupy space, and finally through a vast increase in scale to become monumental nonfunctional architectural environment.

There is a greater use of manufactured materials, steel, plastic, glass, as opposed to the natural materials of stone and wood.

Sculpture approaches the mass produced object.

The division between painting and sculpture tends to disappear as each assumes characteristics of the other.

The nature of the avant-garde is to explore the extreme limits and the previously neglected areas between traditional categories.

The painting becomes a wall.

The wall bends and becomes an environment.

The limits meet.

Sensibility has changed since the fifties.

Methods of work and thought are more direct and specific.

The variable choices of personal emotion and chance give way to a desire for logic and order.

The blob is replaced by the square.

To call this an academy, a context of established pattern and rule, is premature.

The range of method and material is too broad.

The trend of thought seems to be more one of how to get through and beyond the limitations of style.

What is considered yesterday's avant-garde? Abstract imp., pop, op?

Certainly none of these could be considered the rule basis of current thought.

Yesterday's avant-garde becomes not today's academy, but today's side issue.

At this late date the only rule from abstract imp. would seem to be the danger of too much freedom.

Pop op came (and went?) so quickly, much valuable ground is still left undigested. Many pop op artists are still at the beginning of investigations,

218

momentarily hindered by the stigma of last year's label.

The artist's condition has changed.

The acceleration of fashionable attention tends to limit the aperture of public view at any one time.

A reputation can be made and forgotten within a few seasons.

Behind all this, the genuinely creative artist just keeps on working.

The exhibiting and hiring of advanced artists by college and university art schools probably does as much as anything to lend academic status to the avant-garde in the eyes of the student.

However, the diversity of means and ends should soon be apparent.

Ultimately, the student is faced with possibilities beyond rules.

The general public is just as disinterested in advanced art as ever.

Joe Doe in Any Town would rather buy a Cadillac and thus his neighbors' approval and envy.

The limited public is paying more attention.

But then, art is getting more attention through the various media.

Among the limited, art is a social ornament, a badge of how in they are.

How many of them feel they really need it is something I honestly don't know.

There are a few individuals who need and want it. There always have been.

I guess that's enough for a start.

Linda Nochlin

Realism Now

Ever since Maurice Denis proclaimed in 1890 that a painting was essentially a flat surface covered with colors assembled in a certain order before it was a battlehorse, a nude woman, or an anecdote, realism has fought a losing battle for inclusion within the ranks of avant-garde art. Despite a few minor skirmishes—the Neue Sachlichkeit in Germany, the work of Balthus in France, some American attempts of noteworthy if provincial intensity—realism, in the sense of creating an accurate, detailed, and recognizable simulacrum of visual experience, has been relegated to the limbo of philistinism: the propaganda machines of Soviet party hacks or the sentimental platitudes of *Saturday Evening Post* covers. In the great forward march of modernism, that gradual stripping from visual art of all extravisual meaning, whether literary or symbolic, to paraphrase Barbara Rose, that rejection from painting of all that is nonpictorial, that reduction of art to its literal qualities—in painting, to the flatness and shape of the canvas itself—it would seem that realism is indeed aside from the point, *retardataire,* or, at the very least, sentimentally revisionist. Wistful attempts at "getting the human figure back into painting," such as The Museum of Modern Art's "New Images of Man" exhibition of 1959, supported by a heavy dose of popularized existentialism, only seemed to underline the point: despite a hortatory introduction by theologian Paul Tillich and a commendable effort to equate smeared contours with

Reprinted from *Realism Now* (Vassar College Art Gallery, 1968), by permission of the author. Copyright © 1968 by Linda Nochlin.

modern angst or calculated grotesquerie with contemporary alienation, the "new images" turned out for the most part to be not very different from the old expressionism, and modernism marched on its reductive course with Barnett Newman, Ad Reinhardt, Morris Louis, Jules Olitski, and Frank Stella in the vanguard.

To this view of modernism as a teleological progression toward more and more purely optical values in painting, the emergence of pop as a major force in the early sixties seemed to offer the first undeniable challenge. Yet, after the initial shock of confronting recognizable motifs drawn from contemporary life on the canvas had worn off, pop scale, coolness of tone and pictorial handling, its emphasis on surface and brilliant color, its flatness of form and emotion, and its use of ready-made imagery rather than direct perception made it assimilable to the modernist aesthetic position. Indeed, many of the qualities of pop have been correctly, if at times grudgingly, equated with those of cool or hard-edge abstraction.

How, then, do the new realists fit into the contemporary art scene? Or, one might ask, is it possible for a realist to be new at all in the second half of the twentieth century? The answer to this second question is, as the exhibition reveals, an unqualified yes. If pop drove the opening wedge into the entrenched view of modernism as a necessary and continuous progression starting with Paul Cézanne and ending with Stella (a progression that requires a bit of internal juggling to maintain its consistency, in order to disassociate the pure abstraction of Kasimir Malevich, who had worked uncomfortably close to the beginning of this unfolding of the reductive spirit, from that of Newman or Reinhardt, who were situated with greater chronological convenience near its end term), then the new realism has exploded the modernist myth entirely. Despite the patronizing attempts of some critics to consign the new realism to the peripheries of the contemporary art world—for example, Philip Leider's assertion that the work of Philip Pearlstein, Lennart Anderson, Jack Beal, and Alex Katz is "irrelevant to our fears and hopes for the best modern art" or at most "a respectable minor art," or Hilton Kramer's dismissal of a recent Alex Katz show as "the pictorial equivalent of *vers de société*," it has become increasingly clear during the course of the last two years that the new realism, far from being an aberration or a throwback in contemporary art, is a major innovating impulse. Its precise quality of novelty, it would seem to me, lies more in its connection with photography, with new directions in that most contemporary of all media, the film, or even with the advanced novel, than in its relation to traditional realist painting.

Yet if one rejects the narrow, abstractionist aesthetic teleology as the

LINDA NOCHLIN

proper framework for viewing the new realism, one must by no means ignore the central role played by recent abstract painting itself in the formulation of the new realist style. The largeness of scale, the constant awareness of the fieldlike flatness of the pictorial surface, the concern with measurement, space, and interval, the cool, urban tone, with its affirmation of the picture qua picture as a literal fact, the rejection of expressive brushwork, or, if it exists, the tendency toward bracketing its evocative implications through irony or over-emphasis—all of these elements bring the work of the new realists closer to the spirit of contemporary abstraction and serve to disassociate it irrevocably from the meretricious mini-platitudes of a self-styled "old" realist like Andrew Wyeth. The ladies of the suburban art-study clubs, who in recent years have dutifully gulped down large doses of Stella and Andy Warhol while secretly yearning for Something Nice they can Recognize, are not getting the answer to their prayers in Pearlstein's nudes or Gabriel Laderman's landscapes.

It is no mere coincidence that many of the new realists came to their present position after an earlier involvement with abstract art, and their concern with what might be considered purely formal problems remains constant. For Alex Katz, working on the tense borderline between the generalizing conventions of ready-made imagery and the concrete subtleties of immediate perception, the compositional problems presented by expanded scale—overlapping of volumes, cropping, the whole idea of gesture, "how things move to each other across a surface"—are major preoccupations. Philip Pearlstein, a former abstract expressionist, resolutely denies any evocative or expressive intention in his nudes or portraits, asserts that he is interested only in the problems of painting, and, like Flaubert in the nineteenth century, who dreamed of writing a novel about nothing at all, conceives of his enterprise as "the perfection of nothingness." Yvonne Jacquette tells us that the *James Bond Car Painting* is "part of a series concerning the space between objects"; Sidney Tillim seems primarily concerned with the interrelation of volumes within a compressed pictorial space; and the expressed aim of Neil Welliver, a former student of Josef Albers, Burgoyne Diller, and Conrad Marca-Relli, is "to make a 'natural' painting as fluid as a de Kooning." What is therefore the distinguishing feature of the new realism is not some phony superimposition of humanist values onto old formulas, but rather the assertion of the visual perception of things in the world as the necessary basis of the structure of the pictorial field itself; indeed, not since the impressionists, has there been a group so concerned with the problems of vision and their solution in terms of pictorial notation and construction. In making this assertion, they are at once reintroducing an element that, from the Renais-

222

sance to the twentieth century, had always been considered an irreducible property of the purely pictorial itself—that is, the recording of perceptual data—and at the same time, pointing out the incredibly changed nature of perception itself in the second half of the twentieth century. Whether this perception is direct, or mediated by the mechanical apparatus of the camera, as it is for so many of our artists, is irrelevant to the major issue. The very fact that Pearlstein, who never uses photographs but always works from the live model, was "accused" of relying upon them at a recent panel discussion is a good case in point. Instead of using photographs, Pearlstein has, as far as possible, transformed himself into a camera, and has assimilated many of the characteristics normally associated with photography, such as arbitrary cropping, the close-up, and radical disjunction of scale, to his painting style.

The act of perception is itself total, conditioned both in its mode and in its content by time, place, and concrete situation. While it may be willfully objective—and realists have traditionally tried to divest themselves of personal and cultural impedimenta—it cannot occur in a vacuum; it is this that makes the new realism so new and so completely of our time. Courbet's nudes could never have looked like Pearlstein's or Beal's or Leslie's. How could they, since they were painted before the invention of the close-up, the flood lamp, or phenomenology? Laderman's West Side Highway landscape could never have been painted by Pissarro, even though both were scrupulously recording visual facts, not merely because the West Side Highway did not exist when and where Pissarro was painting, but because Picturamic Postcard Vues and concepts like *alienation* and *distancing* were unavailable as well. Nor could John Button actually have *seen* his girl on the beach in that particular way if Mark Rothko had never painted or Andy Warhol had not made *My Hustler*. Richard Estes' New York seems light-years away from that of John Sloan or the ash-can school. Would the stringently controlled reflections in *Cocoanut Custard,* based on the objective recording of the camera lens, have come out that way if there had not been a Mondrian or hard-edge abstraction? Or has New York itself become harder-edged in the last fifty or sixty years? For Sloan, as for Manet, reflection immediately implied diffusion and blurring of the image on the canvas. (Think of the shimmering, hazy mirror mirage in the background of the *Bar at the Folies-Bergère.*) For Estes, who relies on the photograph "as a sketch to be used" rather than as "a goal to be reached," the photographic enlargement of reflections is too fuzzy. "Perhaps the more you show the way things look the less you show how they are or how we think they are," he muses, concerned with conveying the noncoincidence of tactile and visual reality.

Even in what might be considered a relatively neutral realm of subject matter, the still life, the impress of the immediate present makes itself felt. It is not merely the choice of subject that is contemporary—although the James Bond car, the New York drainpipe, the triple-decker hospital bed are particularly of the moment, and the interest of these painters in the theme of garbage or wastepaper may perhaps be related to a similar concentration on refuse, astutely pointed out by Siegfried Kracauer, in the medium of the film—but the choice of vantage point, of cropping, and the deliberate removal of compositional focus. Although the oblique view, the cutoff, and asymmetrical composition were exploited by the impressionists to convey a sense of the fleeting, the momentary, and the immediate, these devices were rarely used by them for the still life, which would seem by its very nature to resist such temporal definition. Nor is there anything very fleeting or momentary suggested by the firm, unbroken contours and deadpan, descriptive surfaces of the canvases of Jacquette, Tillim, or Nesbitt. Their closeup vantage point, radical cropping, and randomness of distribution are related to the dispassionate intimacy of the television screen and that rejection of a priori order and a posteriori significance associated with Alain Robbe-Grillet and the new novel as well as with the French new wave cinema. Indeed, Robbe-Grillet's call to arms: "Let it be first of all by their presence that objects and gestures establish themselves, and let this presence continue to prevail over whatever explanatory theory may try to enclose them in a system of references. . . . Gestures and objects will be there before being something; and they will still be there afterwards, hard, unalterable, eternally present, mocking their own 'meaning'"—this credo could serve as the leitmotif of the new realist outlook as a whole. William Bailey's *Eggs* "establishes" itself in this way, as does Don Nice's *Turnip*, which asserts its unique vegetable nonsignificance through sheer scale and scrupulous notation of detail. Jerrold Lanes's observation that Bailey's *Eggs* is reminiscent of *pittura metafisica* "but with no sense of volume or spatial interval" is very much to the point. It is precisely by refusing to impose the artifices of volume or interval upon his eggs that Bailey removes them from the realm of the "metaphysical," that is, from any context other than that of their sheer visual presence.

The world of the familiar, the ordinary, the experienced, and the commonplace has traditionally been the realm of realism ever since the time of Courbet and Flaubert and down to that of contemporary film, and with it have come the more or less standard accusations of willful ugliness, of lack of coherence or discrimination, of overemphasis on petty or distracting detail, and concomitant coldness or lack of emotion or expressiveness. *"Mme. Bovary,"* wrote one critic at the time of the novel's appearance in 1857, "represents obstinacy in description . . . . All the details seem to have been counted one by one, giving the same importance to each . . . . There is no emotion or feeling in it." Courbet was accused of painting objects just as one might encounter them, without any compositional linkage, and of reducing art to the indiscriminate reproduction of the first subject to come along. "He makes his stones as important as his stone breakers," complained one outraged critic of the eponymous painting. And, as is the case with the nineteenth-century realists, one feels with their twentieth-century counterparts that the ordinariness of the artistic statement, or even its ugliness, is precisely the result of trying to get at how things actually are in a specific time and place, rather than how they might be or should be. It is significant that these painters so often narrow down the boundaries of contemporaneity still further to their own immediate social circle, friends or family, to the space of their own studio or apartment or neighborhood, or, following the lead of the film, turn to the image of synecdoche, the substitution of the part for the whole, and zoom in for a close-up of an even more restricted fragment of these already circumscribed realms until, at the ultimate limit of reductive intimacy, they focus upon such nonsignificant background areas as underneath the kitchen sink or simply the floorboards of the apartment as a sufficient visual motif for their canvases. As in the case of similar techniques in the cinema, new or enlarged modes of presentation force us to come to terms with previously ignored aspects of the most ordinary experiences of our daily life.

This insistence upon a specific context, texture, and density as essential simply to *being* at a concrete historical moment is central to the impact a nineteenth-century realist work like Courbet's magnificent *Portrait of P. J. Proudhon* of 1865, where the philosopher, Courbet's close friend and mentor, is represented sitting on the back steps of his house, his smock sleeve clumsily rolled up to reveal the wrinkled sweater beneath, books and papers scattered around him, his two children rendered in their own world of self-absorbed concentration at his feet, the absent Mme. Proudhon indicated by the workbasket and mending on a nearby chair. All these details are related in terms of metonymy (the linking of elements by contiguity), which Roman Jakobson has asserted as the fundamental imagery of realist art, as opposed to the predominance of metaphor in romantic and symbolist works. One is, for example, drawn to examine Proudhon's shoes, not because they are particularly handsome or particularly affecting—certainly, they have none of the pathos or metaphysical implication of van Gogh's various pairs of empty boots—but simply because they are there as a separately rendered but relevant factor in the total situation of Proudhon in his garden. It is precisely the shoes' concrete literalness and, hence, their contiguous relationship to all the other concrete elements constituting the painting, which is their significance and their *only* significance in Courbet's portrait. It is exactly this sort of accuracy of "meaningless" detail that is essential to realism, for this is what nails its productions down so firmly to a specific time and a specific place and anchors realist works in a concrete rather than an ideal or a poetic reality. One notices the presence of explicitly delineated shoes in several of the new realists' paintings: in Pearlstein's portrait of his daughters, in Sidney Goodman's *Self-Portrait in Studio,* and in Welliver's *Red Slips,* where they have furnished the title of the canvas itself. The pictorial definition of these shoes is indeed so explicit that one could apply a more precise label to them—Keds, Mary Janes, Pediforms—just as one could refer to the Scotch tape on the table in Nesbitt's *Joseph Raffael's Studio,* the Hoover in Robert Bechtle's *Hoover Man,* the Kleenex in Jacquette's *James Bond Car Painting,* or the Exercycle in Goodman's *Dialogue;* these brand names are the identifying loci of our time and our world. One is reminded of a dramatic moment in one of Herb Gold's short stories where a character puts Hellman's—specifically Hellman's—mayonnaise on his artichoke, or, once more, of the film, where such brand-name explicitness is an essential quality of the medium.

Not only in the functioning of details, but in the more general area of tone and attitude, the contemporaneity of the new realists is akin to that of today's avant-garde cinema. Visual directness and emotional distancing are inherent to the aesthetic structure of both. Painters and filmmakers avoid involvement with narrative theme or symbolic content, and resolutely exclude any possibility of interpretation that would involve translating the visual "given" into terms other than its own, or reducing it to a mere transparent surface for an all-important "something more" lurking beneath. In both the new realism and the avant-garde cinema, the literalness of the imagery makes the art object dense and opaque; anything that would tend to pierce through the presented surface and give rise to narrative meaning or psychological implication is immediately put between parentheses and thereby assimilated to the opaque, continuous surface that constitutes the totality of the aesthetic statement. For example, the cloying or merely ingratiating associations usually evoked by the conjunction of large dogs and small children is consistently bracketed where it appears in new realist canvases: in the work of Alex Katz, the sentimental theme is severed from conventional response by exaggeration of scale, psychologically unmotivated cutting, and a posterlike deadening of the surfaces; in that of Neil Welliver, by an ironically brushy treatment, partly like congealed fifties expressionism, partly like an overblown picture postcard. In the case of Philip Pearlstein's young daughters, the artist's deadly unvenomous account of how it is with these girls—their solemn, gigantic presences completely detached from such irrelevant contexts as prettiness or paternal affection by means of cast shadow and strict contour—makes them as remote from trivial intimacy as a pair of Buddhas. In Jack Beal's paintings, the naked female body (another conventional nexus for subjective response), or its various fragmented parts, are simply one set of visual elements among others in the total pictorial pattern. As is so often the case in the visual world of the screen, the human being is here reduced to an object among objects, a mere subordinate portion of what film historian Siegfried Kracauer has defined as basic cinematic reality: those "ever-changing patterns of physical existence whose flow may include human manifestations but need not climax in them." Even when the brushwork seems "hot" and impulsive, as is the case of Paul Georges' *The Return of the Muse* or Jane Freilicher's *Field through a Window,* we are kept away from direct contact with the nude in the first painting by the self-consciously rueful presence of the artist himself within the canvas, and from a direct approach to the landscape in the second by the enclosing window frame, just as in the medium of the film we might be distanced from the subject by the sudden intrusive appearance of the director, or the introduction of the physical presence of the camera itself into the screen image.

The notion, central to the purist critique of representational art, that the very existence of subject necessarily implies narrative or symbolic significance, a position already called into question by modernist filmmakers like Warhol or Jean-Luc Godard, is contradicted with equal forcefulness by the new realist painters. What is the inner meaning of Warhol's eight-hour film of the Empire State Building? What is the deeper significance of a six-foot turnip? Both questions are equally irrelevant since filmmakers and painters demand that our responses be restricted to the cinematic or pictorial statements themselves rather than to the subjects of these statements. Pearlstein and Leslie, for example, are not painting ugly people or deliberately asserting a pessimistic view of human nature in general or feminine appearance in particular. They are simply painting their subjects as they actually see them, probing the appearance of naked human flesh under very strong front illumination from a very close vantage point. The painted images created in this way may war violently with our conventional notions of how a naked woman or a human face should look, and yet this by no means implies that the artists are working under the compulsion of viciousness or grotesquerie; the judgment of ugliness arises from the spectator's response to the pictorial situation, not that of the deliberately dispassionate artist to his subject; for some observers, the mere revelation of new aspects of a familiar situation may be profoundly disquieting, although such a reaction may be quite irrelevant to the intentions of the artist himself. In the final analysis, it seems clear that misinterpretations—and overreactions—arise from an inveterate tendency to reduce form to a kind of handy, disposable container for content, rather than considering form and content as modalities of a single, indivisible entity. The new realists would, on the contrary, stand by Godard's proposition: "Style is just the outside of content and content the inside of style, like the outside and the inside of the human body—both go together, they can't be separated," and its corollary, phrased with customary succinctness by William Carlos Williams: "No ideas but in things."

Lucy R. Lippard

10 Structurists in 20 Paragraphs

1

The works shown here are sculptures, or *primary structures* (a term I originally coined for use in a highly restrictive sense, but which was later adopted far more inclusively). The term *minimal* by which this idiom is journalistically designated, means little, and what meaning it has is rather insulting, as it implies esthetic attrition. These artists are not less esthetically ambitious or esthetically successful than anyone else; certainly their work is not literally smaller. On the contrary, they are approaching the concept of art on the most basic and therefore most difficult level. They are trying to focus on the essentials or the necessary in art; they have rejected aspects of sculpture that had become traditionally expected, sensing, perhaps, that the words *traitor* and *tradition* have the same Latin root. A traditionalist can be seen as one who has surrendered to his ancestors and betrayed his contemporaries. According to the painter Frank Stella, whose work around 1960 was most important to many of these sculptors: "It's just that you can't go back. It's not a question of destroying anything. If something's used up, something's done, something's over with, what's the point of getting involved with it?" Don Judd puts it more bluntly: "I consider the Bauhaus too long ago to think about it, and I never thought about it much."

Reprinted from the exhibition catalog, *Minimal Art* (Haags Gemeentemuseum, 1968), by permission of the author.

LUCY R. LIPPARD

2

There is more advanced sculpture than painting in America today. One reason is that sculpture, or in some cases a three-dimensional anti-sculpture, or structure, has provided an escape for those who feel the limitations of a pictorial idiom and an illusionary surface are too great to be overcome, who share Judd's conviction that "the main thing wrong with painting is that it is a rectangular plane placed flat against the wall. A rectangle is a shape itself; it is obviously the whole shape; it determines and limits the arrangements of whatever is on or inside of it." Painters do not agree. Jo Baer, whose work is always grouped with the sculptors shown here, has written: "Painters discarded the teleology of distance and pictorial depth when they discarded ground altogether, and paintings became objects altogether. This happened some time before they were inflated into wall objects, up-to-ceiling objects, and down-to-floor objects."

3

Most of these artists began as painters and moved into three-dimensions directly, bypassing sculptural training and tradition. They do not usually pay previous sculpture—American or European—the compliment of reaction; it is ignored. Most of this work is deliberately anti-sculptural in that it rejects the process of ordering parts, balancing or relating areas or forms. Most of these artists eschew the play of part against part aiming at a new spatial complexity by the single form—the space around, above, below, or within that form. They are opposed to fragmentation that stresses individual shapes and offer two alternatives among them: a radically self-contained form or an increasingly open and dematerialized form. Carl Andre requires "things in their elements, not in their relations."

4

When an absolutely symmetrical, repetitive, single, or serial scheme is employed, no one part is given precedence over another. The work becomes a whole rather than several different forms on a surface. It becomes nonrelational, and is thus an heir to Jackson Pollock's (or Claude Monet's) allover paintings. The historical precedents for a primary art are mostly found in the 1920s and 1930s. The Russian constructivists or suprematists, De Stijl, the Bauhaus, even certain dadaists, envisioned a tabula rasa as the way to change art's course, and used geometric frameworks in which to make these changes. But the modular and conceptual schemes so favored by the primary decade of American painting, the work of Barnett Newman, Ad Reinhardt and Mark Rothko and, later, of Frank Stella and Kenneth Noland. The youngest exhibitors here have more direct roots in the achievement of Judd, Morris, Andre, and LeWitt.

5

The steadfast denials of anything but the recent past, and the rejection of European influence, are not to be dismissed simply as chauvinism. They have to do with a conviction that the new and the difficult are the only goals worth attempting, that ideas as well as styles can be exhausted. An integral element of advanced art in America is a disaffection with "easy art" that unites the most stylistically various artists who have come into prominence since 1945. The most obvious manifestation of this disaffection is the Oedipal ritual of action and reaction inherited from art history. The ruling genre, the most seen and thus most imitable style, becomes "easy" and must be renounced for a more advanced, difficult art. Baudelaire's "I have a horror of being easily understood" has been echoed by artists widely ranging in style. *Beauty, prettiness,* and *subtlety* have become suspect words in their suggestion of a facile hedonism.

6

Hilton Kramer has located David Smith's contribution to American art (and not incidentally to the primary structure; for he is the sole sculptor to have any effect on its evolution) in Smith's submission of "the rhetoric of the School of Paris to the vernacular of the American machine shop." Like many artists in America and in Europe, the sculptors in this exhibition admire the technological advances of the commercial and engineering world. They find in modern industrial techniques an admirable disassociation from sentimentality, from the pretty, the petty, the decadent "sensitivity" and "good taste" of much informal abstraction. But their construction is workmanlike and unobtrusive rather than detailed or overpolished. Technology is only a tool; they have no desire to imitate it, and they steadfastly try to avoid the pitfalls of dazzling new materials that tend to overshadow all other qualities in the work. Purged by pop art, no longer veiled in myth or sociological baggage, the machine and the materials of modern technology can finally be taken for granted. Perhaps the most outstanding effect industrial society has had on primary art is the wholly absorbed principle of mass production and the principle of interchangeable parts which lies at the heart of American industrialism.

7

Moholy-Nagy's famous gesture of ordering a group of paintings by telephone from a sign painter has now become a matter of fact. Tony Smith ordered one of his first works the same way. Most of the structurists have their pieces made by professional industrial fabricators, men who have at their disposal the skills and equipment for making that particular form or surface, equipment no artist could possibly afford; in most cases it is difficult enough to afford the materials themselves. The fabrication process is a practical rather than an esthetic solution, and should not be overestimated as a factor in the artmaking process itself. While emphasis on the artist's mind rather than the artist's hand can be seen as a rejection of the expressionist 1950s, it does not rule out the expressive element.

Ronald Bladen, for example, does not consider himself in any way associated with those generally known as "minimal artists" because he employs a greater simplicity or reduction in order to achieve more drama. Tony Smith also views art as something vast and mysterious, whereas Judd, LeWitt, or Smithson look with great disfavor on anything that is not strictly factual or conceptual.

8

Primary structures may look alike at times, such as when several artists work with a cube or a free-standing box shape. But the motivations and attitudes behind these superficially similar works differ enormously. Robert Morris and Don Judd, for instance, have been mentioned in the same breath ever since they were the first to show aloof, single shapes. Morris is a cerebral and intellectual gymnast in the Duchampian tradition; in this group, the metaphysical complexity of his concepts is equaled (not paralleled) only by Carl Andre. Compared to Morris's ideational approach, Judd's is factual. In his own writings he stresses singlemindedness, physicality, wholeness, and direct confrontational experience. Morris says, "Unitary forms do not reduce relationships. They order them." Judd considers the primary structure "a vehicle for the fusion of distinct parts into an indivisible whole, for the incorporation of order and disorder, or the replacement of a rational structurists have mainly emerged from the innovations made in the last

geometric art with an alogical one."

9

Smith and Bladen are older than the others. Both had underground reputations before their work was seen, relatively late. Both consider themselves sculptors rathen than anti-sculptors, both retain the "romantic" values of a previous art superimposed on an understatement and structural clarity furthered by single or modular forms. Neither makes fully resolved models; they work intuitively on the basis of an idea. "My view is let's make it and see what the hell it is," says Smith. Bladen is concerned with "that area of excitement belonging to natural phenomena such as a gigantic wave poised before it makes its fall, or man-made phenomena such as the high bridge spanning two distant points." Smith's view of nature is removed to the structural or organic plane rather than being based on visible phenomena. Seen in particular, his and Bladen's work is as different as Judd's and Morris's. Where Bladen enjoys the drama of precarious stance, of immense forms tipped out of their expected axes, Smith demands stability: "I don't want to be involved in muscle, in feats of engineering. I don't want the facades to be deductible. I want my work inscrutable throughout; if you can see how it's made then it loses its mystery." And Morris, in turn, opposes Smith, asserting shapes that can be censored logically and immediately by the viewer, that create strong single gestalt sensations. Grosvenor, whose background in naval engineering has perhaps been overemphasized, seeks a dynamic effect like Bladen, but in a more extended form. He thinks of his work not as sculpture, but as "ideas which operate in the space between floor and ceiling."

10

A distinction could be made between structures that occupy space (Judd, Morris, Smithson), those that conquer space aggressively (Bladen, Smith, Grosvenor), those that deny or disperse it (Andre, Flavin) or those that incorporate it (LeWitt, and Smith's recent piece, *Smoke*). Obviously none of the generalizations in this text apply to all of the exhibitors, and almost none apply to Michael Steiner, whose polychromed relational sculptures have only the most tenuous connection with those of his colleagues, even within the uncategorized context of this exhibition.

11

Several of these artists hold that the idea is paramount and almost entirely eschew any preoccupation with physical scale, volume, mass, presence or expressiveness. For them, the making of the object is merely a traditional, expected step unnecessary to the esthetic. Andre and Smithson would probably agree with LeWitt that "the idea is the machine that makes the work." His aim is "not to instruct the viewer, but to give him information. Whether the viewer understands this information is incidental to the artist . . . he would follow his predetermined premise to its conclusion avoiding subjectivity. Chance, taste or unconsciously remembered forms would play no part in the outcome. The serial artist does not attempt to produce a beautiful or mysterious object but functions merely as a clerk cataloguing the results of his premise." As more and more sculpture is designed in the studio but executed elsewhere, the object becomes merely an end product. A number of still younger artists than those represented here are losing interest in any of the physical aspects of the work of art. Such a trend is provoking a profound dematerialization of art, especially of art as object. If it continues to prevail it may result in the object's becoming wholly obsolete.

12

Highly conceptual art supercedes the "formalism" found in the paintings of Noland and Stella or the sculpture of David Smith and Anthony Caro. Like the black paintings of Ad Reinhardt, it is anti-formal, for it has neutralized composition, color, and history. Dan Flavin, whose fluorescent light systems reiterate the lines of his interior spaces at the same time as they destroy their physicality, sees his work synonomizing "its past, present and future states without incurring a loss of relevance . . . I believe that art is shedding its vaunted mystery for a common sense of keenly realized decoration . . . we are pressing downward toward no art—a mutual sense of psychologically indifferent decoration—a neutral pleasure of seeing known to everyone."

13

The formless forms or neutral units used by these men (bricks, grids, square plaques, tetrahedra, progressions) do not draw attention to themselves as form so much as they add up to a whole form that is a shape rather than an image. The modules are the real materials, the building blocks. Often there is a scientific or mathematical basis or metaphor underlying their arrangement, but it tends to be very simple. None of this work, with the exception of Smithson's, can be seen as an illustration of scientific ideas. Crystallography, with its systematic clarity of dimension and allowance for disorder within the network of physical interactions, has offered fertile ground; its systems are variously applied. Judd was one of the first to cite its relationship to the new art, but his work bears no resemblance to Tony Smith's. Smith, who sees all science as science fiction ("I read it like romance and can't believe it") uses a space lattice because of its infinite flexibility. A similar grid is also used by LeWitt as a vehicle for a totally finite, self-completing scheme.

14

The determined stasis, inertia and "deadness" of some of these works relates them to the history and aims of the monument. The public aspect of this art has been much discussed recently. In his article, "Entropy and the New Monuments," Smithson adopted a literary application of the Second Law of Thermodynamics to the visual arts and related an energy drain to a timeless science-fictional art predicted by primary structures. Monumental analogues can be found not only in the future but in the past. A deliberately static primitivism is asserting itself in the midst of a simultaneously active "electric" world. Several artists have cited the pyramids, obelisks, ziggurats, and mounds of ancient cultures as more interesting than any twentieth century prototypes. Their interest is experiential and not nostalgic: "Grid patterns show up in Magdelanian cave painting. Context, intention, and organization focus the differences. The similarity of specific forms is irrelevant" (Morris).

15

The presence of industrial monuments such as gas or oil drums, water tanks, windowless buildings, concrete pillboxes, airports, highways, parking lots, and housing projects have inspired a certain envy on the part of the artists who have aspirations to immense scale but little chance of being able to work in such dimensions. (Frederick Kiesler wrote about the direct influence of the mountain landscape on the architectural forms of Machu Pichu). The artists' attempts to improve upon and compete visually with their non-art surroundings have contributed to the new concern with public art. Morris, Smithson, Andre, among others, have plans for immense earth mounds, trenches and walls, a "City of Sand" and a "City of Ice," that would be experienced like landscape rather than optically isolated as art. Ideally, some of their projects would in fact create a new landscape made of sculpture rather than decorated by sculpture, along the lines of Tony Smith's long visualized "artificial landscape without cultural precedent."

16

Such projects are obviously public not only in scale but in scope. Governmental or corporate assistance is necessary for their realization. A pilot project is planned at the moment for a Texas airport which would employ earth as the medium for the four sculptures to be made in the clear zones at the beginning of the landing strips. This past fall, Claes Oldenburg made his Placid City Monument for the New York City sculpture show; it consisted of a trench dug between the Metropolitan Museum and Cleopatra's Needle (an obelisk). The pit was dug and then filled again by union gravediggers. As a monument, it probably attracted more public attention than all of the equestrian statues in Central Park. Its invisibility made it all the more visualizable. A still more conceptual monument was "made" years ago by Marcel Duchamp with the note: "Find inscription for Woolworth Building as a readymade."

17

Morris has projected a sculpture of steam jets; Andre made a "monument" out of sand dropped into a conical pile from one floor above; LeWitt has hidden elements of his serial projects within other elements where their existence must be taken completely on faith, as will his buried cube at the airport mentioned above. Hermeticism, dematerialization, total intellectualization has an increasing appeal. The complex concept buried in an impressive mass of purely physical bulk or else dispersed into thin air, but remembered, relates to the idea of archeology itself. The pyramids started out as architecture, but once the tombs were closed, they became sculpture. Over the ages they have become objects rather than functional enclosures, but a part of their fascination lies in their unseen cores, in the uses for which they were originally intended. Someone defined the major characteristic of sculpture as "just being there," a statement also made by Robbe-Grillet about Samuel Beckett's plays.

18

By its very restrictiveness, a primary art opens new areas of esthetic experience. It even tends to be over-stimulating. Above all, it has to be considered, not only seen but looked at or not only acknowledged but thought about. It will not provide instant departures for the familiar picture-finding, landscape-spotting, memory-inducing that often passes for enjoyment of abstract art. Many viewers are lost without these crutches of associative relationship to other objects or sights, so the new art is often called "boring" or said to test the spectator's commitment. The fact is that the process of conquering boredom can be boring. Most people prefer to stay with the viewer's digest. ("Honi soit qui mal y pense.")

19

Good art is never boring no matter how spare it is. This art is as committed as any other idiom. When it fails, it is as boring as any other kind. Its frequently cited impersonalism is just a new kind of personalism. It challenges the concept of boredom, monotony, and repetition by ruling out hitherto considered essentials and demonstrating that intensity does not have to be melodramatic.

20

"No formal sequence is ever really closed out by the exhaustion of all its possibilities in a connected series of solutions. The revalidation of old problems in new circumstances is always possible and sometimes actual." (George Kubler, *The Shape of Time*.) "Many machines grow more complex as they develop, because their functions and powers increase. But as each kind of machine approaches the limits of its inherent possibilities as a type, it tends to revert to simplicity, to emphasize economy of means, and to achieve what engineer and artist would agree in calling beauty of design and function." (A. L. Kroeber, *Anthropology: Cultural Patterns and Processes*.)

Lawrence Alloway

The Expanding and Disappearing Work of Art

The minimum requirement of esthetic identity in a work of art has been legibility as an object, a degree of compactness (so that the object is united, composed, stable). In the sixties, a number of noncompact art forms (diffuse or nearly imperceptible) have proliferated. It is the expansion or diminution of art as a solid structure that I want to describe. The interface (cross-over point, junction) of art and other things has blurred. (This tendency has been discussed as "The *Dematerialization* of Art."[1]) New control methods devised by artists lead to recognition-problems for spectators.

I propose a cluster of seven items: (1) the function of the cliché, (2) the mode of intimacy, (3) permissive configurations, (4) exteriority, (5) occupancy of places, (6) conceptualization, and (7) diffuse systems.

1. Clichés.
The use of the cliché in the context of art connects public signs with personal systems. Clichés dissolve formal boundaries (as in Roy Lichtenstein). Alain Robbe-Grillet: "The integration in a plastic work of, on the one hand, the objects belonging to an acquisitive society and, on the other, the comic strips."[2]

Reprinted from *Auction,* III/2 (October, 1969) and Lawrence Alloway's *Topics in Modern Art Since 1945* (Norton, 1975), by permission of the author.

238

2. The mode of intimacy.

2.1. Claes Oldenburg: "I am for an art that unfolds like a map, that you can squeeze, like your Sweety's arm, or kiss, like a pet dog. Which expands and squeaks like an accordion, which you spill dinner on, like an old table cloth." "I am for an art that grows up not knowing it is art at all, an art given the chance of having a starting point of zero." "If I could only forget the notion of art entirely, I really don't think you can." "I have got my sentiment for the world all mixed up with art."[3]

2.2. Oldenburg's Ray Gun Manufacturing Co. (his studio used like a store) became the Ray Gun Theatre: crowded audience and performers. Partial views and ambiguous duration.

2.3. George Brecht's, Robert Watts' Events known only incompletely to those taking part. Allan Kaprow: "The Activity Happening selects and combines situations to be participated in, rather than watched or just thought about."[4]

3. Permissive configurations.

3.1. Soft sculpture and scatter. Robert Morris on the opposition to "preconceived enduring forms and orders for things." "Object-type art," rigid, predicated on right-angled relationships. "Oldenburg was one of the first to use . . . materials other than rigid industrial ones."[5] Alan Saret's galvanized wire, 1967-68; Barry Le Va's "distributions," 1966-68; Bruce Nauman. An imagery of harnesses, straitjackets, ragtrade leftovers, fallen fences. Use of felt.

3.2. Carl Andre: "Random piling, loose stacking, hanging, give passing form to the material. Chance is accepted and indeterminancy is implied since replacing will result in another configuration." Andre, referring to his brick piece in the Jewish Museum, 1965: "naturally occurring particles which I simply display in a natural unmodified manner."[6]

4. Reflecting and transparent materials.

4.1. Formerly celebrated as symbols of modernity ("new materials of new world") but, as visual fact, plastics and polished metal are incessantly renewed by light-changes. The spectator as witness of unexpected disintegrations and shifts of the object.

4.2. Work of art as "an instrument for seeing rather than merely an object" (Michael Kirby's expression). "Years of practice in ignoring the surrounding environment"[7] reflected in the glass in front of pictures (used as a trap by Francis Bacon). Exteriorated works,[8] as Michael Heizer calls them, tolerate environmental changes, are larger than their physical dimension as parts of the outside are incorporated. Limits not set by the work's outer face. "Awareness must clearly include the real space" (Kirby) around the work, including light sources and movements. Sculpture as "instruments" that are stimuli to perception (Samaras' mirror rooms).

5. *Earthworks* (title of science-fiction novel by Brian Aldiss, 1965); also land art.

5.1. "Remote places such as the Pine Barrens of New Jersey and the frozen wastes of the North and South poles could be coordinated by art forms that would use actual land as a medium."[9] Smithson's proposal makes the scale of Heinz Mack's (ideal) Sahara project feasible. Area as place (site) mapped and sampled (nonsite). Smithson's New Jersey rockpile as specimens in trays. Dennis Oppenheim: Decompositions, in which the matter used is an ingredient of the place (in a gallery it could be gypsum, for instance); place reduced to constituent matter. Removal in progressive steps as a "decomposition" of the place's substance. In both Smithson and Oppenheim the material is (a) brute sample and (b) metaphor of state.

5.2. Pressure of outdoor scale defeats monumental art, which is never big enough. (David Smith, Barnett Newman's *Broken Obelisk*). Nature not a receptive medium for big objects to be thrust on, but one term in a relationship. Hence the term *Ecologic Art*. Michael Heizer's "negative objects" in deserts in Nevada or California: "indeterminate" and "inaccessible"[10] Systems that are alternatives to monumentality.

5.3. Smithson's "Monuments of Passaic" substitute Passaic, New Jersey for Rome, Italy.[11] Retitling as art-conferral act: sandbox as "The Desert," sewage outlet as "the Fountain Monument, etc."

6. *Conceptual art* as part of a reaction against art as process-record (history of the creative act as facture) towards art as end-state (signs of manufacture and production minimized). Increase in forms of conceptualization from premonitory gestures in the fifties to present activity.

6.1. Sol LeWitt: "In conceptual art the idea or concept is the most important aspect of the work." "In other forms of art the concept may be changed in the process of execution." Idea/end-state compatibility, even symmetry.

6.2. Art in a framework of language. Verbal substitution and translatability. "Some ideas are logical in conception and illogical perceptually." (Le Witt) "The function of conception and perception are contradictory (one pre- the other post-fact)." "Ideas may also be stated with number, photographs or works or any way the artist chooses, the form being unimportant."[12] Propositional art. Art separated from perceptual hardware.

6.3. Douglas Huebler: The existence of the work of art is certified by its documentation in the "form of photographs, maps and descriptive language."[13] Sites on maps indicated by markers; fourteen towns along forty-second parallel marked by the "exchange of certified postal receipts." Matching areas in Boston and New York as "exchange shapes."

6.4. Where process may appear is after the completion of the work. Exhibition announcement: "Dennis Oppenheim's Sculpture is Alive and Growing at John Gibson's." Compare Robert Rauschenberg's (accidental) dirt paintings of circa 1953 with grass and moss.

7. Art and distribution

7.1 Art as a communication system: Ray Johnson's New York Correspondence School. Collages, verbal and/or visual, and straight found material mailed to various people, sometimes to send on, sometimes to hoard. Content: somewhere between gossip and oracle, joke and enigma. Envelope as well as the enclosures significant.

7.2. The Andy Warhol continuum. Silk-screened photographs in paintings, interviews in magazines or on TV, films, rock 'n' roll group, *A*, all points of a unified sensibility using the techniques of home movies and tape recording. Warhol thrives on disintegrating thresholds, unlike Rauschenberg who is hung up on hardware and concrete things.

My point was to argue for a rehabilitation of the relation of environment to works of art. And to assume an expansionist rather than a reductive esthetics. Conceptual art has its clerks as abstract expressionism has its truckdrivers, but no movement is tested by its failures. The animation of the spectator, by signs, by scale, by substitutions, by deceptive familiarity, by durational change, by wide focus, is part of the argument.

Walter de Maria

Meaningless Work

Meaningless work is obviously the most important and significant art form today. The aesthetic feeling given by meaningless work cannot be described exactly because it varies with each individual doing the work. Meaningless work is honest. Meaningless work will be enjoyed and hated by intellectuals—though they should understand it. Meaningless work cannot be sold in art galleries or win prizes in museums—though old fashioned records of meaningless work (most of all paintings) do partake in these indignities. Like ordinary work, meaningless work can make you sweat if you do it long enough. By meaningless work I simply mean work that does not make you money or accomplish a conventional purpose. For instance putting wooden blocks from one box to another, then putting the blocks back to the original box, back and forth, back and forth and so on, is a fine example of meaningless work. Or digging a hole, then covering it is another example. Filing letters in a filing cabinet could be considered meaningless work, only if one were not a secretary, and if one scattered the file on the floor periodically so that one didn't get any feeling of accomplishment. Digging in the garden is not meaningless work. Weight lifting, though monotonous, is not meaningless work in its aesthetic sense because it will give you muscles and you know it. Caution should be taken that the work chosen should not be too pleasurable, lest pleasure become the purpose of the work. Hence sex,

Reprinted from *An Anthology* (Heinar Friedrich, 1969), by permission of the author. Copyright © 1963 by La Monte Young and Jackson Mac Low.

though rhythmic, cannot strictly be called meaningless—though I'm sure many people consider it so.

Meaningless work is potentially the most abstract, concrete, individual, foolish, indeterminate, exactly determined, varied, important art-action-experience one can undertake today. This concept is not a joke. Try some meaningless work in the privacy of your own room. In fact, to be fully understood, meaningless work should be done alone or else it becomes entertainment for others and the reaction or lack of reaction of the art lover to the meaningless work cannot honestly be felt.

Meaningless work can contain all of the best qualities of old art forms such as painting, writing and so on. It can make you feel and think about yourself, the outside world, morality, reality, unconsciousness, nature, history, time, philosophy, nothing at all, politics, without the limitations of the old art forms.

Meaningless work is individual in nature and it can be done in any form and over any span of time—from one second up to the limits of exhaustion. It can be done anywhere in any weather conditions. Clothing, if any, is left to the individual. Whether the meaningless work, as any art form, is meaningless, in the ordinary sense of that term, is of course up to the individual. Meaningless work is the new way to tell who is square.
Grunt
Get to work

March, 1960

Robert Smithson

A Sedimentation of the Mind

The earth's surface and the figments of the mind have a way of disintegrating into discrete regions of art. Various agents, both fictional and real, somehow trade places with each other—one cannot avoid muddy thinking when it comes to earth projects, or what I will call *abstract geology*. One's mind and the earth are in a constant state of erosion, mental rivers wear away abstract banks, brain waves undermine cliffs of thought, ideas decompose into stones of unknowing, and the conceptual crystallizations break apart into deposits of gritty reason. Vast moving faculties occur in this geological miasma, and they move in the most physical way. This movement seems motionless, yet it crushes the landscape of logic under glacial reveries. This slow flowage makes one conscious of the turbidity of thinking. Slump, debris slides, avalanches all take place within the cracking limits of the brain. The entire body is pulled into the cerebral sediment, where particles and fragments make themselves known as solid consciousness. A bleached and fractured world surrounds the artist. To organize this mess of corrosion into patterns, grids, and subdivisions is an esthetic process that has scarcely been touched.

The manifestations of technology are at times less "extensions" of man (Marshall McLuhan's anthropomorphism), than they are aggregates of elements. Even the most advanced tools and machines are made of the raw matter of the earth. Today's highly refined technological tools are not much

Reprinted from *Artforum* (September, 1968), by permission of Nancy Holt (Smithson).

different in this respect from those of the caveman. Most of the better artists prefer processes that have not been idealized, or differentiated into "objective" meanings. Common shovels, awkward looking excavating devices, what Michael Heizer calls "dumb tools," picks, pitchforks, the machine used by suburban contractors, grim tractors that have the clumsiness of armored dinosaurs, and plows that simply push dirt around. Machines like Benjamin Holt's steam tractor (invented in 1885)—"It crawls over mud like a caterpillar." Digging engines and other crawlers that can travel over rough terrain and steep grades. Drills and explosives that can produce shafts and earthquakes. Geometrical trenches could be dug with the help of the "ripper"—steel toothed rakes mounted on tractors. With such equipment construction takes on the look of destruction; perhaps that's why certain architects hate bulldozers and steam shovels. They seem to turn the terrain into unfinished cities of organized wreckage. A sense of chaotic planning engulfs site after site. Subdivisions are made—but to what purpose? Building takes on a singular wildness as loaders scoop and drag soil all over the place. Excavations form shapeless mounds of debris, miniature landslides of dust, mud, sand and gravel. Dump trucks spill soil into an infinity of heaps. The dipper of the giant mining power shovel is 25 feet high and digs 140 cubic yards (250 tons) in one bite. These processes of heavy construction have a devastating kind of primordial grandeur and are in many ways more astonishing than the finished project—be it a road or a building. The actual *disruption* of the earth's crust is at times very compelling, and seems to confirm Heraclitus's *Fragment 124,* "The most beautiful world is like a heap of rubble tossed down in confusion." The tools of art have too long been confined to "the studio." The city gives the illusion that earth does not exist. Heizer calls his earth projects "The alternative to the absolute city system."

Recently, in Vancouver, Iain Baxter put on an exhibition of *Piles* that were located at different points in the city; he also helped in the presentation of a *Portfolio of Piles.* Dumping and pouring become interesting techniques. Carl Andre's *"grave* site"—a tiny pile of sand, was displayed under a stairway at the Museum of Contemporary Crafts last year. Andre, unlike Baxter, is more concerned with the *elemental* in things. Andre's pile has no anthropomorphic overtones; he gives it a clarity that avoids the idea of temporal space. A serenification takes place. Dennis Oppenheim has also considered the *"pile"*—"the basic components of concrete and gypsum . . . devoid of manual organization." Some of Oppenheim's proposals suggest desert physiography—mesas, buttes, mushroom mounds, and other "deflations" (the removal of material from beach and other land surfaces by wind action). My own *Tar Pool* and *Gravel Pit* (1966) proposal makes one conscious of the primal ooze. A molten substance is poured into a square sink that is surrounded by another square sink of coarse gravel. The tar cools and flattens into a sticky level deposit. This carbonaceous sediment brings to mind a tertiary world of petroleum, asphalts, ozocerite, and bituminous agglomerations.

PRIMARY ENVELOPMENT

At the low levels of consciousness the artist experiences undifferentiated or unbounded methods of procedure that break with the focused limits of rational technique. Here tools are undifferentiated from the material they operate on, or they seem to sink back into their primordial condition. Robert Morris (*Artforum*, April, 1968) sees the paint brush vanish into Pollock's "stick," and the stick dissolve into "poured paint" from a container used by Morris Louis. What then is one to do with the *container?* This entropy of technique leaves one with an empty limit, or no limit at all. All differentiated technology becomes meaningless to the artist who knows this state. "What the Nominalists call the grit in the machine," says T. E. Hulme in *Cinders,* "I call the fundamental element of the machine." The rational critic of art cannot risk this abandonment into "oceanic" undifferentiation, he can only deal with the limits that come after this plunge into such a world of noncontainment.

At this point I must return to what I think is an important issue, namely Tony Smith's "car ride" on the "unfinished turnpike." "This drive was a revealing experience. The road and much of the landscape was artificial, and yet it couldn't be called a work of art." ("Talking with Tony Smith" by Samuel Wagstaff Jr., *Artforum*, December 1966.) He is talking about a sensation, not the finished work of art; this doesn't imply that he is anti-art. Smith is describing the state of his mind in the "primary process" of making contact with matter. This process is called by Anton Ehrenzweig "de-differentiation," and it involves a suspended question regarding "limitlessness" (Freud's notion of the "oceanic") that goes back to *Civilization and Its Discontents.* Michael Fried's shock at Smith's experiences shows that the critic's sense of limit cannot risk the rhythm of de-differentiation that swings between "oceanic" fragmentation and strong determinants. Ehrenzweig says that in modern art this rhythm is "somewhat onesided"—toward the oceanic. Allan Kaprow's thinking is a good example—"Most humans, it seems, still put up fences around their acts and thoughts—" (*Artforum*, June 1968.) Fried thinks he knows who has the "finest" fences around their art. Fried claims he rejects the "infinite," but this is Fried writing in *Artforum*, February 1967 on Morris Louis, "The dazzling blankness of the untouched canvas at once repulses and engulfs the eye, like an infinite abyss, the abyss that opens up behind the least mark that we make on a flat surface, or *would* open up if innumerable conventions both of art and practical life did not restrict the consequences of our act within narrow bounds." The "innumerable conventions" do not exist for certain artists who *do* exist within a physical "abyss." Most critics cannot endure the suspension of *boundaries* between what Ehrenzweig calls the "self and the nonself." They are apt to dismiss Malevich's *Non-Objective World* as poetic debris, or only refer to the "abyss" as a rational metaphor "within narrow bounds." The artist who is physically engulfed tries to give evidence of this experience through a limited (mapped) revision of the original unbounded state. I agree with Fried that limits are not part of the primary process that Tony Smith was talking about. There is different experience before the physical abyss than before the mapped revision. Nevertheless, the quality of Fried's *fear* (dread) is high, but his experience of the abyss is low—a weak metaphor—"like an infinite abyss."

The bins or containers of my *Non-Sites* gather *in* the fragments that are experienced in the physical abyss of raw matter. The tools of technology become a part of the earth's geology as they sink back into their original state. Machines like dinosaurs must return to dust or rust. One might say a "de-architecturing" takes place before the artist sets his limits outside the studio or the room.

BETTER HOMES AND INDUSTRIES

> *Great sprays of greenery make the Lambert live-in room an oasis atop a cliff dwelling. In a corner, lighted by skylights and spotlights, "Hard Red," an oil by Jack Bush, all planting by Lambert Landscape Company.*
> —Caption under a photograph
> *House and Garden,* July 1968

In *Art in America,* Sept.-Oct. 1966, there is a *Portrait of Anthony Caro,* with photographs of his sculpture in settings and landscapes that suggest English gardening. One work, *Prima Luce 1966,* painted yellow, matches the yellow daffodils peeking out behind it, and it sits on a well-cut lawn. I know, the sculptor prefers to see his art indoors, but the fact that this work ended up where it did is no excuse for thoughtlessness about installation. The more compelling artists today are concerned with "place" or "site"—Smith, de Maria, Andre, Heizer, Oppenheim, Heubler—to name a few. Somehow, Caro's work picks up its surroundings, and gives one a sense of a contrived, but tamed, "wildness" that echoes to the tradition of English gardening. Around 1720 the English invented the antiformal garden as protest against the French formal garden. The French use of geometric forms was rejected as something "unnatural." This seems to relate to today's debate between so-called "formalism" and "anti-formalism." The traces of weak naturalism cling to the background of Caro's *Prima Luce*. A leftover Arcadia with flowery overtones gives the sculpture the look of some industrial ruin. The brightly painted surfaces cheerfully seem to avoid any suggestion of the "romantic ruin," but they are on closer investigation related to just that. Caro's industrial ruins, or concatenations of steel and aluminum may be viewed as Kantian "things-in-themselves," or be placed into some syntax based on So and So's theories, but at this point I will leave those notions to the keepers of "modernity." The English consciousness of art has always been best displayed in its "landscape gardens." "Sculpture" was used more to *generate a set of conditions*.

Clement Greenberg's notion of "the landscape" reveals itself with shades of T. S. Eliot in an article "Poetry of Vision" (*Artforum*, April 1968). Here "Anglicizing tastes" are evoked in his descriptions of the Irish landscape. "The ruined castles and abbeys," says Greenberg, "that strew the beautiful countryside are gray and dim," shows he takes "pleasure in ruins." At any rate, the "pastoral," it seems, is outmoded. The gardens of history are being replaced by sites of time.

Memory traces of tranquil gardens as "ideal nature"—jejune Edens that suggest an idea of banal "quality"—persist in popular magazines like *House Beautiful* and *Better Homes and Gardens*. A kind of watered down Victorianism, an elegant notion of industrialism in the woods; all this brings to mind some kind of wasted charm. The decadence of "interior decoration" is full of appeals to "country manners" and liberal-democratic notions of gentry. Many art magazines have gorgeous photographs of artificial industrial ruins (sculpture) on their pages. The "gloomy" ruins of aristocracy are transformed into the "happy" ruins of the humanist. Could one say that art degenerates as it approaches gardening? These "garden-traces" seem part of time and not history, they seem to be involved in the dissolution of "progress." It was John Ruskin who spoke of the "dreadful Hammers" of the geologists, as they destroyed the classical order. The landscape reels back into the millions and millions of years of "geologic time."

FROM STEEL TO RUST

As "technology" and "industry" began to become an ideology in the New York Art World in the late '50s and early '60s, the private studio notions of "craft" collapsed. The products of industry and technology began to have an appeal to the artist who wanted to work like a "steel welder" or a "laboratory technician." This valuation of the material products of heavy industry, first developed by David Smith and later by Anthony Caro, led to a fetish for steel and aluminum as a medium (painted or unpainted). Molded steel and cast aluminum are machine manufactured, and as a result they bear the stamp of technological ideology. Steel is a hard, tough metal, suggesting the permanence of technological values. It is composed of iron alloyed with various small percentages of carbon; steel may be alloyed with other metals, nickel, chromium, and others, to produce specific properties such as hardness and resistance to rusting. Yet, the more I think about steel itself, devoid of the technological refinements, the more *rust* becomes the fundamental property of steel. Rust itself is a reddish brown or reddish yellow coating that often appears on "steel sculpture," and is caused by oxidation (an interesting nontechnological condition), as during exposure to air or moisture; it consists almost entirely of ferric oxide, Fe_2O_3 and ferric hydroxide, $Fe(OH)_3$. In the technological mind rust evokes a fear of disuse, inactivity, entropy, and ruin. Why steel is valued over rust is a technological value, not an artistic one.

By excluding technological processes from the making of art, we began to discover other processes of a more fundamental order. The break-up or fragmentation of matter makes one aware of the sub-strata of the earth before it is overly refined by industry into sheet metal, extruded I-beams, aluminum channels, tubes, wire, pipe, cold-rolled steel, iron bars. I have often thought about nonresistant processes that would involve the actual sedimentation of matter or what I called "Pulverizations" back in 1966. Oxidation, hydration, carbonatization, and solution (the major process of rock and mineral disintegration) are four methods that could be turned toward the making of art. The smelting process that goes into the making of steel and other alloys separates "impurities" from an original ore, and extracts metal in order to make a more "ideal" product. Burnt-out ore or slag-like rust is as basic and primary as the material smelted from it. Technological ideology has no sense of *time* other than its immediate "supply and demand," and its laboratories function as blinders to the rest of the world. Like the refined "paints" of the studio, the refined "metals" of the laboratory exist within an "ideal system." Such enclosed "pure" systems make it impossible to perceive any other kinds of processes other than the ones of differentiated technology.

Refinement of matter from one state to another does not mean that so-called "impurities" of sediment are "bad"—the earth is built on sedimentation and disruption. A refinement based on all the matter that has been discarded by the technological ideal seems to be taking place. The coarse swathes of tar on Tony Smith's plywood mock-ups are no more or less refined than the burnished or painted steel of David Smith. Tony Smith's surfaces display more of a sense of the "prehistoric world" that is not reduced to ideals and pure gestalts. The fact remains that the mind and things of certain artists are not "unities," but *things* in a state of arrested disruption. One might object to "hollow" volumes in favor of "solid materials," but no materials are solid, they all contain caverns and fissures. Solids are particles built up around flux, they are objective illusions supporting grit, a collection of surfaces ready to be cracked. All chaos is put into the dark inside of the art. By refusing "technological miracles" the artist begins to know the corroded moments, the carboniferous states of thought, the shrinkage of mental mud, in the geologic chaos—in the strata of esthetic consciousness. The refuse between mind and matter is a mine of information.

THE DISLOCATION OF CRAFT— AND FALL OF THE STUDIO

Plato's *Timaeus* shows the demiurge or the artist creating a model order, with his eyes fixed on a nonvisual order of Ideas, and seeking to give the purest representation of them. The "classical" notion of the artist copying a perfect mental model has been shown to be an error. The modern artist in his "studio," working out an abstract grammar within the limits of his "craft," is trapped in but another snare. When the fissures between mind and matter multiply into an infinity of gaps, the studio begins to crumble and fall like The House of Usher, so that mind and matter get endlessly confounded. Deliverance from the confines of the studio frees the artist to a degree from the snares of craft and the bondage of creativity. Such a condition exists without any appeal to "nature." Sadism is the end product of nature, when it is based on the biomorphic order of rational creation. The artist is fettered by this order, if he believes himself to be creative, and this allows for his servitude which is designed by the vile laws of Culture. Our culture has lost its sense of death, so it can kill both mentally and physically, thinking all the time that it is establishing the most creative order possible.

THE DYING LANGUAGE

The names of minerals and the minerals themselves do not differ from each other, because at the bottom of both the material and the print is the beginning of an abysmal number of fissures. Words and rocks contain a language that follows a syntax of splits and ruptures. Look at any *word* long enough and you will see it open up into a series of faults, into a terrain of particles each containing its own void. This discomforting language of fragmentation offers no easy gestalt solution; the certainties of didactic discourse are hurled into the erosion of the poetic principle. Poetry being forever lost must submit to its own vacuity; it is somehow a product of exhaustion rather than creation. Poetry is always a dying language but never a dead language.

Journalism in the guise of art criticism fears the disruption of language, so it resorts to being "educational" and "historical." Art critics are generally poets who have betrayed their art, and instead have tried to turn art into a matter of reasoned discourse, and, occasionally, when their "truth" breaks down, they resort to a poetic quote. Wittgenstein has shown us what can happen when language is "idealized," and that it is hopeless to try to fit language into some absolute logic, whereby everything objective can be tested. We have to fabricate our rules as we go along the avalanches of language and over the terraces of criticism.

Poe's *Narrative of A. Gordon Pym* seems to me excellent art criticism and prototype for rigorous "nonsite" investigations. "Nothing worth mentioning occurred during the next twenty-four hours except that, in examining the ground to the eastward third chasm, we found two triangular holes of great depth, and also with black granite sides." His descriptions of chasms and holes seem to verge on proposals for "earthwords." The shapes of the chasms themselves become "verbal roots" that spell out the difference between darkness and light. Poe ends his mental maze with the sentence—"I have graven it within the hills and my vengeance upon the dust within the rock."

THE CLIMATE OF SIGHT

The climate of sight changes from wet to dry and from dry to wet according to one's mental weather. The prevailing conditions of one's psyche affect how he views art. We have already heard much about "cool" or "hot" art, but not much about "wet" and "dry" art. The *viewer*, be he an artist or a critic, is subject to a climatology of the brain and eye. The wet mind enjoys "pools and stains" of paint. "Paint" itself appears to be a kind of liquefaction. Such wet eyes love to look on melting, dissolving, soaking surfaces that give the illusion at times of tending toward a gaseousness, atomization or fogginess. This watery syntax is at times related to the "canvas support."

The world disintegrates around me.

—Yvonne Rainer

By Palm Desert springs often run dry.

—*Van Dyke Parks,*
Song Cycle

The following is a proposal for those who have leaky minds. It could be thought of as The Mind of Mud, or in later stages, The Mind of Clay.

THE MUD POOL PROJECT

1. Dig up 100 ft. sq. area of earth with a pitchfork.
2. Get local fire department to fill the area with water. A fire hose may be used for this purpose.
3. The area will be finished when it turns to mud.
4. Let it dry under the sun until it turns to clay.
5. Repeat process at will.

When dried under the sun's rays for a sufficiently long time, mud and clay shrink and crack in a network of fissures which enclose polygonal areas.

Fredric H. Lahee,
Field Geology

The artist or critic with a dank brain is bound to end up appreciating anything that suggests saturation, a kind of watery effect, an overall seepage, discharges that submerge perceptions in an onrush of dripping observation. They are grateful for an art that evokes general liquid states, and disdain the desiccation of fluidity. They prize anything that looks drenched, be it canvas or steel. Depreciation of aridity means that one would prefer to see art in a dewy green setting—say the hills of Vermont, rather than the Painted Desert.

Aristotle believed that heat combined with dryness resulted in fire: where else could this feeling take place than in a *desert* or in Malevich's head? "No more 'likenesses of reality,' no idealistic images, nothing but a desert!", says Malevich in *The Non-Objective World*. Walter de Maria and Michael Heizer have actually worked in the Southwestern deserts. Says Heizer, in some scattered notes, "Earth liners installed in Sierras, and down on desert floor in Carson-Reno areas." The desert is less "nature" than a concept, a place that swallows up boundaries. When the artist goes to the desert he enriches his absence and burns off the water (paint) on his brain. The slush of the city evaporates from the artist's mind as he installs his art.

Heizer's "dry lakes" become mental maps that contain the vacancy of Thanatos. A consciousness of the desert operates between craving and satiety.

Jackson Pollock's art tends toward a torrential sense of *material* that makes his paintings look like splashes of marine sediments. Deposits of paint cause layers and crusts that suggest nothing "formal" but rather a physical metaphor without realism or naturalism. *Full Fathom Five* becomes a Sargasso Sea, a dense lagoon of pigment, a logical state of an oceanic mind. Pollock's introduction of pebbles into his private topographies suggests an interest in geological artifices. The rational idea of "painting" begins to disintegrate and decompose into so many sedimentary concepts. Both Yves Klein and Jean Dubuffet hinted at global or topographic sedimentary notions in their works—both worked with ashes and cinders. Says Dubuffet, regarding the North and South Poles, "The revolution of being on its axis, reminiscent of a dervish, suggests fatiguing, wasted effort; it is not a pleasant idea to consider and seems instead the provisional solution, until a better one comes along, of despair." A sense of the earth as a map undergoing disruption leads the artist to the realization that nothing is certain or formal. Language itself becomes mountains of symbolic debris. Klein's IKB globes betray a sense of futility—a collapsed logic. G.E.M. Anscombe writing on "Negation" in *An Introduction to Wittgenstein's Tractatus* says, "But it is clear then an all-white or all-black globe is not a map." It is also clear that Klein's all-blue globe is not a map, rather it is an anti-map, a negation of "creation" and the "creator" that is supposed to be in the artist's "self."

THE WRECK OF FORMER BOUNDARIES

The strata of the earth is a jumbled museum. Embedded in the sediment is a text that contains limits and boundaries which evade the rational order, and social structures that confine art. In order to read the rocks we must become conscious of geologic time, and of the layers of prehistoric material that is entombed in the earth's crust. When one scans the ruined sites of prehistory one sees a heap of wrecked maps that upsets our present art historical limits. A rubble of logic confronts the viewer as he looks into the levels of the sedimentations. The abstract grids containing the raw matter are observed as something incomplete, broken and shattered.

In June, 1968, my wife, Nancy, Virginia Dwan, Dan Graham, and I visited the slate quarries in Bangor-Pen Angyl, Pennsylvania. Banks of suspended slate hung over a greenish-blue pond at the bottom of a deep quarry. All boundaries and distinctions lost their meaning in this ocean of slate and collapsed all notions of gestalt unity. The present fell forward and backward into a tumult of "de-differentiation," to use Anton Ehrenzweig's word for entropy. It was as though one was at the bottom of a petrified sea and gazing on countless stratographic horizons that had fallen into endless directions of steepness. Syncline (downward) and anticline (upward) outcroppings and the asymmetrical cave-ins caused minor swoons and vertigos. The brittleness of the site seemed to swarm around one, causing a sense of displacement. I collected a canvas bag full of slate chips for a small *Non-Site*.

Yet, if art is art it must have limits. How can one contain this "oceanic" site? I have developed the *Non-Site*, which in a physical way contains the disruption of the site. The container is in a sense a fragment itself, something that could be called a three-dimensional map. Without appeal to "gestalts" or "anti-form," it actually exists as a fragment of a greater fragmentation. It is a three-dimensional *perspective* that has broken away from the whole, while containing the lack of its own containment. There are no mysteries in these vestiges, no traces of an end or a beginning.

CRACKING PERSPECTIVES AND GRIT IN THE VANISHING POINT

Parallactic perspectives have introduced themselves into the new earth projects in a way that is physical and three-dimensional. This kind of convergence subverts gestalt surfaces and turns sites into vast illusions. The ground becomes a map.

The map of my *Non-Site #1 (an indoor earthwork)* has six vanishing points that lose themselves in a pre-existent earth mound that is at the center of a hexagonal airfield in the Pine Barren Plains in South New Jersey. Six runways radiate around a central axis. These runways anchor my thirty-one subdivisions. The actual *Non-Site* is made up of thirty-one metal containers of painted blue aluminum, each containing sand from the actual site.

De Maria's parallel chalk lines are twelve feet apart and run a half a mile along the Dry Lake of El Mirage in the Mojave Desert. The dry mud under these lines is cracking into an infinite variety of polygons, mainly six-sided. Under the beating sun shrinkage is constantly going on, causing irregular outlines. Rapid drying causes widely spaced cracks, while slow drying causes closely spaced cracks. (See E. M. Kindle's "Some Factors Affecting the Development of Mud Cracks," *Jour. Geol.* Vol. 25, 1917, p. 136). De Maria's lines make one conscious of a weakening cohesion that spreads out in all directions. Nevada is a good place for the person who wants to study cracks.

Heizer's *Compression Line* is made by the earth pressing against the sides of two parallel lengths of plywood, so that they converge into two facing sunken perspectives. The earth surrounding this double perspective is composed of "hardpan" (a hard impervious sediment that does not become plastic, but can be shattered by explosives.) A drainage layer exists under the entire work.

THE VALUE OF TIME

For too long the artist has been estranged from his own "time." Critics, by focusing on the "art object," deprive the artist of any existence in the world of both mind and matter. The mental process of the artist which takes *place* in time is disowned, so that a commodity value can be maintained by a system independent of the artist. Art, in this sense, is considered "timeless" or a product of "no time at all"; this becomes a convenient way to exploit the artist out of his rightful claim to his temporal processes. The arguments for the contention that time is unreal are a fiction of language, and not of the material of time or art. Criticism, dependent on rational illusions, appeals to a society that values only commodity type art separated from the artist's mind. By separating art from the "primary process," the artist is cheated in more ways than one. Separate "things," "forms," "objects," "shapes" with beginnings and endings are mere convenient fictions: there is only an uncertain disintegrating order that transcends the limits of rational separations. The fictions erected in the eroding time stream are apt to be swamped at any moment. The brain itself resembles an eroded rock from which ideas and ideals leak.

When a *thing* is seen through the consciousness of temporality, it is changed into something that is nothing. This all-engulfing sense provides the mental ground for the object, so that it ceases being a mere object and becomes art. The object gets to be less and less but exists as something clearer. Every object, if it is art, is charged with the rush of time even though it is static, but all this depends on the viewer. Not everybody sees the art in the same way, only an artist viewing art knows the ecstasy or dread, and this viewing takes place in time. A great artist can make art by simply casting a glance. A set of glances could be as solid as any thing or place, but the society continues to cheat the artist out of his "art of looking," by only valuing "art objects." The existence of the artist in time is worth as much as the finished product. Any critic who devalues the *time* of the artist is the enemy of art and the artist. The stronger and clearer the artist's *view* of time the more he will resent any slander on this domain. By desecrating this domain, certain critics defraud the work and mind of the artist. Artists with a weak view of time are easily deceived by this victimizing kind of criticism, and are seduced into some trivial history. An artist is enslaved by time, only if the time is controlled by someone or something other than himself. The deeper an artist sinks into the time stream the more it becomes *oblivion;* because of this, he must remain close to the temporal surfaces. Many would like to forget time altogether, because it conceals the "death principle" (every authentic artist knows this). Floating in this temporal river are the remnants of art history, yet the "present" cannot support the cultures of Europe, or even the archaic or primitive civilizations; it must instead explore the pre- and post-historic mind; it must go into the places where remote futures meet remote pasts.

James Seawright

Phenomenal Art:
Form, Idea and Technique

I'd like to talk about certain aspects of the kind of work I do. It's a kind of work a number of other people are doing too, and one which I believe will sooner or later become predominant in the concerns of artists. I will try to substantiate such a rash claim as I go on, but first I would like to clear up something about the "phenomenal art" of my title. I use the term to describe, in an approximate way, works that undergo actual change with the passage of time. I want you, however, to eliminate from consideration works that produce phenomena which are the result of some change in the relationship between the work and the viewer: changes of perspective, visual illusions, that sort of thing. What I want to talk about are sculptures or objects or systems—whatever you want to call them—that undergo changes of their own, active changes, in time, changes that are inherent in them, that they were constructed to produce physically. These changes, or phenomena, might be changes of illumination, of spatial relationships, or of sound production. I don't wish to suggest that there is any philosophical notion of phenomenalism involved, nor do I think that any particular aesthetic attitude is necessary in order to consider this type of work from the point of view of the artist. As far as I'm concerned, my own works produce phenomena actively, and I am interested in the form and structure in which these phenomena are organized, the origin of the ideas that underlie the phenomena, and the methods of producing and controlling the phenomena.

Let us consider a structure that incorporates real lamps. To whatever physical properties the structure may have must be added the properties of the phenomena produced by turning the lights on or off, individually or in groups, in some temporal sequence. The lamps may be controlled in a binary fashion—that is to say, they may be either "on" or "off"—or they may exhibit intermediate levels of brightness. Conceivably, the color of the light can be controlled as well, although this is not easily done in practice. I think it is possible to make an analogy between the totality of the phenomena produced by this structure of lamps and, let's say, a piece of music, or the performance of a piece of music. You can, of course, carry the analogy too far. A sculptor who builds a device producing some kind of time-dependent phenomenon is probably going to solve the problems related to it in a way entirely different from the way a composer of music would use, because he will more likely be using mechanical means to control the lamps or whatever the parts are that produce the phenomena. I wouldn't rule out the *possibility* of having an "orchestra" or a group of people operating some kind of phenomena-producing device, but it would never occur to me to use this method in the majority of cases, because of the easy availability of a mechanism to do the job. More significant than the use of mechanisms to control phenomena is the fact that one can take advantage of the mechanism's ability to control itself; in other words, one can use automatic or self-regulating mechanisms, which have properties both very like and very unlike what human beings consider to be organization and order.

Let's suppose that we want to compose a pattern of phenomena, such as a series of light changes. If we have a mechanism to produce them, or if we have to construct one, we must be able to describe what we want in some kind of language intelligible to the mechanism. This requires a consideration of the result we want in a way not generally experienced by artists heretofore. A good example of this is found in music. Composers today usually represent a score by means of symbols, each one of which carries a tremendous amount of information. Through the evolution of music there has been a tendency to think of the notation of a musical event in a score as an adequate representation of the actual event, but this is not true unless you can rely on the performer's understanding of all the implications of the symbol and of the ways his body and instrument will behave when he attempts to carry out the action called for by the symbol. When you produce a piece of electronic music, you no longer have the performer's experience and skill to help in interpreting the real meaning of the symbolic instructions, and you must cause the electronic equipment to reproduce your exact intentions by giving instructions even down to the most absurd detail. If the particular things you want done are extremely complex or full of nuance, and thereby difficult to explain in every detail, it might be preferable to produce works of art in which phenomena other than sounds (or in addition to sounds) are the content of the work and in which these phenomena are produced under the control of other people. You would then be able to utilize the individual judgements of these persons who are in control, and this might be, in effect, an extension of your own taste.

But let us say that you do use a mechanism to produce a series of phenomena. Once you learn how to make the mechanism and how to shape information into a form it can understand or embody, you will see that there is a certain equivalency between the body of information you put into the mechanism as a program of instruction and the totality of the phenomena produced. This equivalency, simply a transformation of one kind of information into another, suggests the possibility of using bodies of information that already exist. Rather than try to compose in advance every detail of the performance you want to have, you might be able to find a "bulk" form or a "bulk" kind of performance (that is, a body of information already possessing some degree of organization) and then attempt to change its structure and to reorganize or modify its instructions into suitable material for performance.

Now let's look at a specific example—several shots of a piece, *Photocrystal II,* taken at random, showing whatever it happened to be doing at the moment. Here, the phenomena of the lights going on and off represent the direct transformation of the movements of a mechanism into the motions and patterns of the lights. The pattern of movements is cyclical, but it takes twelve hours or so to go through the whole cycle. Within the cycle, there's a dynamic variation in what it does; there's a pattern in the rate at which activity follows inactivity. It seems to me that one of the crucial issues involved in working in a medium where the passage of time is significant is that you are obliged to exert some kind of control. Whether you're aware of it or not, whether you decide to let the lamps be switched on and off at random, let them all be on, or let them all be off, you have to make some decision about it. Even if you don't care— that in itself is a decision. In view of the possible ways that it can be done, this example represents one approach.

A kind of sacrifice is involved in controlling the totality of the phenomena produced, because if you start with a mechanism that has certain properties and you begin to tamper with one part of it by changing the length of a linkage or the number of teeth on a gear, you affect the whole cycle to some degree, however effectively you change the particular aspect you set out to change. This ability to shape or modify the "character" or behavior of one mechanism can be increased by compounding or bringing together several self-sufficient information-transforming mechanisms to produce or control the phenomena of a single work. There's also a secondary effect that I think is noteworthy: I was quite surprised to find at first that the mechanisms responsible for producing the phenomena were in some ways more interesting visually than the phenomena themselves—the kinetic, the sheer kinetic behavior of them, the linkages going all over the place. This, I think, is an illustration of the fact that you can't simply come from the outside with an idea and try to apply it by bending the technological resources that you may have (or can acquire) to suit it. The more I work, the more I believe that the best ideas grow out of an understanding of the processes being used, rather than out of a preconceived notion of the effects to be achieved.

The next example, *Watcher*, is a piece in which a deliberate effort was made to use several different, independent programmed mechanisms whose information content is directly transformed into phenomena. The actual mechanisms are all fully visible and contribute to the total visual effect. There's at least one relationship or subsystem in the work in which sensors detect or receive information that constitutes one set of phenomena, and transform it into still another form, another set of phenomena. This amounts to a transformation of the light phenomena into electronically generated sounds, which originate in the structure. The information required to specify the characteristics of the sounds is received by the photocells, which scan the bank of lamps. You certainly have no way of predicting, in a practical way, where they are going to be pointing at any given time—if you bend one photocell a little bit too much, it sees another lamp, and so forth—but it's quite interesting to note how well the character of the sound seems to correspond to and enhance the idea of cause and effect.

I'd like to go back now and reiterate one or two things. I very much want to get across my thought that the interrelationship between form, idea, and the techniques used applies in a special way to this kind of work. I certainly can see that this is a statement one has always been able to make about various kinds of art, but in time-dependent work, where the concern is primarily with the phenomena themselves, it's almost inevitable that the forms evolved for treating these phenomena, whether organizing them or structuring them, will be analogous to the forms that have evolved in a much older performing art, such as music. The necessity of organizing in a cyclical way certainly takes away some element of development, some element of drama, perhaps, in beginning with something and building into something else, so that it is very hard to say where form stops and ideas begin.

There are other factors involved, which also represent compromises. Once you decide to define something, to limit it, to package it—once you say, "All right, I'm going to make something that works and is a sculpture, and I'll put it in a gallery, and people will look at it"—you can no longer legitimately say, "Well, I don't really care what people think about it; I simply made it because I wanted to, and that's that." You really have to consider what people think, because you run into the most incredible spectrum of reactions from people, which seems to arise out of the ambiguous position the object occupies in their experience. Once you allow work to be shown, that, in addition to affecting viewers in the way works of art usually do, is able to capture and engage their attention by performing, you are more or less committed—at least this is my feeling—to making the process as efficient as possible. Thus, when you get reactions like "How does it work?" or "To what extent is it necessary to know how it works?" or even "What is it?" you realize that something is getting in the way of their simply regarding the work. I don't feel that my pieces are just demonstrations of complicated processes, techniques that you have to know about, and so forth, but in any case I can't really judge this, because I *do* know how they work. And I feel that the ideas themselves and the way they are presented have grown out of knowing, or at least thinking about, the processes or the techniques that interested me at the time.

The next piece, *Tetra,* is an even better example of what I'm talking about. To describe it physically: it stands about seven feet tall; the hublike thing is actually a cluster of four little motors with large spoked wheels attached to them, arranged symmetrically as the vertices of a tetrahedron; the whole thing is supported on a rod from the triangular base. This piece uses little motors that are called *selsyns.* These selsyns have the property of turning clockwise or counterclockwise a certain amount in order to remain exactly in step with other selsyns, to which they are connected electrically. They are used as remote indicators or as a means of transmitting a motion without an actual mechanical connection. Because, as in any electric motor, the force that operates them is a magnetic attraction between their fixed and moving parts, the selsyns have a certain elasticity. For instance, when rotors, or wheels having rotational inertia, are attached to the shafts of the selsyns, the rotation of one wheel will not produce an instantaneous response in the others, but will set up a condition in which a restoring force tries to bring them back into alignment.

This piece grew out of experiments with the little selsyns. The reason four were used is that four was the largest number that seemed to work reasonably well before the effects grew too weak (the selsyns were originally designed to be used only in pairs). The questions of the geometrical organization of the piece are obviously related to the use of four selsyns. The spoked wheels in the piece were determined by the nature of the selsyns that turn them. For these selsyns the wheels can't be too heavy; a spoked wheel gives the appearance of being quite large without being too heavy. So far, so good. If you turn one wheel with a breath of air or a touch, the other three try to follow, but because of their inertia they swing back and forth as they try to get back in alignment, and a kind of oscillation takes place before they finally reach equilibrium again.

When the piece reached this stage, I began to run into artifacts, or consequences, of the process involved. For instance, these little selsyns were originally intended to be used in aircraft, and in order for them to be small and light, they were designed to use 400-cycle AC power instead of the normal 60 cycles. So I had to build a 400-cycle power supply. The kind of 400-cycle power supply that is cheapest and simplest to build is stable only if the power demand on it is constant. But when the wheels were turned and the selsyns were put out of alignment, that is, when the restoring force or tension was created, the power demand increased, and the frequency of the power supply increased. This happened to be clearly audible as a sound, because of slight vibrations of all the mechanical parts. So you see, all kinds of things that I certainly could not have anticipated appeared at every step. And I had to decide whether to go with it or fight against it. The spokes could have been made longer in order to resonate the sound better. But suppose the pitch of the sound had not increased when there was a tension, and had gone down instead? What do any of these things mean in perceptual terms?

I'm not going into all of this to extol the virtues of the piece. That's totally beside the point. The point is that the problem of making the piece work, of making it function in some active way, necessarily involves you in an area of concepts that I think is central to our times, and that is technology. There's a difference between the understanding of a technological process and the understanding of anything else, I think. Perhaps it's just that technology *can* be understood. I believe that artists will be simply unable to resist the power that the medium seems to offer, once they are working with it or become more exposed to it. For instance, to go back once again to the illustration, my feeling about the piece is that, in a very rudimentary or primitive way, it possesses an actual *sensitivity*. If you do something to it, it reacts. Reactivity. It possesses a behavior. It possesses an unpredictability. And yet it's just nuts and bolts. In order to reconcile this somehow, I think you have to recognize that technology is offering us the power to animate things, literally, and the opportunity to intensify or amplify the intention to signify animate phenomena that has always existed with artists. This is an irresistible power indeed.

Let me show you another example. This is another kind of development; it goes beyond the last piece in that an effort was made here to construct a kind of automaton. The piece, *Searcher,* either seeks or avoids light, depending on the state of internal circuits, and the changes that occur in its circuits constitute a program. There is, however, an unpredictability involved, since it's a powerful source of light itself and will be either frustrating or encouraging its own efforts to react to light. This behavior is susceptible to modification according to the way in which the piece is adjusted. The wide variations in the overall pattern of behavior that this piece will exhibit in a room full of people, at night, or in bright daylight make it clear that environmental influences are strong. When a person walks in front of it, and it happens to be in a certain state (of internal connection), it will follow that person around the room with its light beam. It's impossible not to think that this isn't what it's "supposed to do" except that it will ignore the person the next time, even if he tries to induce an expected reaction by some provocative movement. But now his reaction to the piece is beginning to color the relationship between it and himself. This kind of encounter isn't really as theatrical as it sounds, because the artist has much less control. But as the artist, you are setting up a generalized set of options and throwing them, so to speak, at an audience. What you observe, you try to refine for the next piece.

I was interested in carrying this still further. The two pieces *Captive* and *Scanner* are both basically the same as *Searcher.* They operate exactly the same way but they have completely different configurations, and when I had all three together for the first time in the same room, it became quite obvious that, whether there were people around or not, there was plenty of interaction between the pieces. And I thought that was very entertaining: an environment of interaction in which it was possible to participate without dominating.

I would like to conclude talking about the latest thing I have done. This is an environment-piece which I was commissioned to design for the Kansas City Performing Arts Foundation. It was called *Electronic Peristyle.* It consists of a circle twenty-one feet across, bordered by columns; within this space there is a false floor with the supporting structures underneath. In the center is a control unit. The idea was to bring the viewer into the things, isolating external influences and, as far as possible, letting only the actual movements of the viewer be the information transformed and used to generate the phenomena. The phenomena were patterns of sound, light, and wind emanating from the columns.

A person can enter the circle, and his movements will be detected and recorded in the center unit as patterns of data in digital form. The center unit functions as a limited kind of computer, performing certain operations with the data as program steps and then decoding the data into electronically generated sounds and light patterns and, occasionally, wind effects. The way the effects, or phenomena, are organized is designed to allow the viewer to see that he is influencing what is going on, although it is initially unclear as to how he can anticipate what effect his actions will have. The longer he is involved, however, the more he is able to see what he is controlling and what he isn't.

The piece is really a very, very crude approach to what I think it is possible to do. The piece observes the viewer in a very simple way: it detects whether he passes one of a number of points. It determines practically nothing about his reactions and presents him with very limited inducements for continued interest. But the possibilities for development and refinement are almost unlimited, for the quantity of information that can be managed in this type of arrangement is quite staggering, and yet it isn't really a very expensive proposition. It is, moreover, something that was practically impossible a few years ago.

I believe, however, that there may be a limit as to how far one can go in a quasi-theatrical direction. The more people that get in this sort of piece, the less chance there is for any comprehension of the phenomena as they relate to the individual viewer in the framework of the system. It really works best with only one person. If there are two people in there, they have to cooperate, or else they become simply adversaries. While working with a number of people has some interesting possibilities for future pieces, it just leads to problems in this one, and I don't see any practical way to solve them. It's as if the more elaborate and complicated the system, the less room there is in it for the irrationality of human interactions. It's almost a metaphor of modern life.

My belief that the involvement with technologically related processes and active works will come to dominate artists' concerns really boils down to the fact that the possibilities are nearly unlimited. The only thing that approximates the magnitude of the possibilities is the suddenness with which they have become available. The possibilities are not just the possibilities of imagination, or of ideas applied to new materials; these have always been expressible in open-ended terms. But the possiblities of control over the physical world, of extending our personal attitudes into the active behavior of works—these are what technology gives us. And yet the technique that this statement implies is not really a technique of manual skills or factual knowledge, but a technique of understanding conceptually the many disciplines that make up technology. For me, there is a continuing problem of trying to learn about something that I wasn't taught, something that I didn't know I should know about. It means learning, simply studying all the time to find out how things work and what this knowledge may imply in another area of concern. I'm not necessarily advocating that artists or people in general do this, but I think it likely that people who already have this kind of understanding or attitude will think increasingly of themselves as artists producing work which they believe to be art, or else looking for this kind of work to regard as art. The proliferation of scientific and technical training that has come about in the last two or three decades is beginning to produce artists from its ranks, rather than through our traditional routes. I think that in time, if there is to be time, this will become the new tradition. Art is, after all, only a record of people in a time, and this is the time of technology.

James Wines

De-Architecturization

Public art since the nineteenth century has seldom functioned as anything more than peripheral embellishment for urban spaces. This limitation has been a result, in part, of the treatment of areas and objects adjacent to architecture as minor accessories for the main event and, in part, from a pervasive formalist tradition determining the relationship between art and buildings. In private (gallery) art there has been a demanding precedent for innovation and a built-in responsibility to discredit outworn traditions. Public art, on the other hand, has continued to function as a subsidiary (or "branch-office") specialization of real art—without sufficient status to exert a seminal influence on new ideas. Also, it has never been implicit that public art should ever be anything more than a reinforcement of some compositional totality. For example, the parochial view that works of art can be "placed" on a site is an acknowledgement that: 1) they already exist, in plan or fact, independent of context, and 2) they are relative to site only by default or by the act of "installation." Successful public art is not private art transplanted.

The problem is further compounded by the absence of a critical dialogue sensitive to public meaning. Rather than recognize the differences between public and private sensibilities, most critics develop rationales to perpetuate

Reprinted from *Arts in Society*, XII/3 (Fall-Winter, 1973), by permission of the author.

the objectified, portable, monument in one form or another. In this respect criticism has been remiss in its obligations to elevate standards and to provide an expanded frame of reference. This contention is well illustrated by a 1970 essay entitled "Monumental Art in Cincinnati" by Lawrence Alloway. He states:

> However a work can "go public" without ostensible public content, just as a work of art acquires meanings and values in addition to those that may have been part of the artist's original intention. The monumental art reaches its public by a different route than earlier public art. Such works acquire a social meaning from acquisition for civic display. Instead of a work beginning with a pre-arranged public meaning, it takes on its public role experimentally, after installation.

Although Mr. Alloway was specifically discussing an assembly of large scale sculptures displayed in a metropolitan setting, his attribution of some unintended osmotic dimension to result from this juxtaposition avoids the real issue of whether this dimension should be "acquired" or inherent from the outset. His observations are useful only to the extent to which the value systems of private art may be superimposed on a public situation. Mr. Alloway's assertions may be conditionally true, and yet his premises are myopic. Earlier in the essay he offers a limited reference to another dimension of public meaning by conceding a traditional "commemorative function" for public art; whereas the illustration of a popular iconography is only one of innumerable alternatives for meaning. The monument and its totemic purposes is clearly dead. The potential for a new art responsive to urban environment is significantly alive.

During the past one hundred years the syntactic cohesion of an art language applicable to painting, sculpture and architecture has been considerably reduced, if not eliminated altogether. The evolution of a medieval city center obviously required an inclusionist vocabulary—a common terminology essential to the integration of complex spatial, structural, and iconographic elements. With the obsessive objectification of art in the late nineteenth century, this language polarized art and architecture into separate entities. Their relationships to each other became increasingly awkward, so that now the very appearance of public art has become a self-conscious intrusion, an accessory to architecture—ultimately more at home in a museum. This reliance on a circumscribed and portable testimony to the fact of art is a critical limitation that precludes any really valid understanding of public and/or environmental art. In a sense the problem recalls Joseph Kosuth's response to the formalist criticism of the late 1960s.

> Being an artist now means to question the nature of art. If one is questioning
> the nature of painting, one cannot be questioning the nature of art. If an artist
> accepts painting (or sculpture) he is accepting the tradition that goes with it.
> That's because the word *art* is general and the word *painting* specific. Painting
> is a kind of art.

Similarly, if one insists upon art as an object, one cannot accept art as periphery. Art *in* space is not art *as* space. It is also instructive to note that Kosuth's concept of *art* retained the "exhibition context" as a perimeter around his definition. Successful public and environmental art cannot rely on the assumptions of a structured containment. It follows, therefore, that exclusionist language of private art (whether formalist or anti-formalist) is not interchangeable with the inclusionist language appropriate to the public experience.

The comparable deficiencies in architecture are also the result of an exclusionist vocabulary and a formalist tradition. Indeed, architecture during the past sixty years has been restrained at every turn by Bauhaus maxims-cum-economy and reconciled to a level of innovation that is more technical than fundamental. Unlike the visual arts of the twentieth century, architecture has not undergone a total inversion or destruction of its aesthetic convictions; but, instead, has continued to thrive on those modest inventions which generally serve to confirm propriety. For example, architecture cannot claim a revolutionary figure of the stature of Duchamp. Even its most respected creative forces—Wright, Corbusier, Mies, Kahn—are appreciated primarily for their uncanny ability to manipulate form and process as extensions of tradition and not as purveyors of some cataclysmic change. There is no one personality who, like Duchamp, questioned every premise, every asssumption, and who finally rejected historical precedent in order to establish an entirely new set of definitions. It is rationalized that architecture is essentially a problem-solving art and does not lend itself to the dramatic conceptual break-throughs associated with visual art. There is truth in the axiom, but a prejudicial restraint as well. One of the unqualified doctrines of modern architecture is the "form follows function" ethic, wherein every juxtaposition of shape, every spatial transition, every element of structure must be rationalized in terms of a preconceived set of practical motivations. Even though function itself is often the product of some specious rationale, it is always considered to be the unequivocal hypothesis by which all buildings and the spaces around them may be evaluated. Function is supposed to be absolute, and the only manipulative ingredient in architecture is form. Un-

fortunately, these formalist guidelines have often become a convenient abso-
lution from responsibility for the pithy matters of concept and change.

"De-architecturization" represents an alternative to the formalist relationship between public art and architecture. Superficially the term seems to
suggest a subversive destruction of habitat or a blanket rejection of architecture's system of values. Actually, what is being suggested is a difference in
attitude toward urban art, space, and facade. Urban art should be a sema-
phore of information (however ambiguous) and not an accessory to a building
or the reinforcement of some compositional totality. If art uses circumstances
and space as media, a new level of communication is established between urban environment and urban dweller. If the city itself is the media—the raw
material (or the ultimate "found object")—then art becomes a condition of
inversion, or de-architecturization.

De-architecturization is an umbrella term applicable to a number of
subdivided concepts. These ideas may apply to both environmental art and
architecture, or a hybrid fusion of both. The categorical distinctions are irrelevant since most of the really interesting examples defy classification—except
insofar as they comment on traditional frames of reference to establish a
point of departure. Briefly described these concepts are:

> *Inclusion* describes an integration of plastic elements when it becomes
> necessary to incorporate some existing structure into a new work of art or
> architecture. A more interesting dimension to this idea (and the one that
> concerns us here) is to reject the elements that physically exist in favor of
> "thoughts about things" that are implied to exist.
>
> *Inversion* has many interpretations. Its basic premise in this context is to utilize
> the rhetorical language of form to subvert its original meaning. The work of
> Duchamp, which commented on both art and life without a conditional
> commitment to where one began and the other left off, is a supreme example of
> art as inversion. It has been said of Duchamp's work that it cannot be compre-
> hended without an acute awareness of art history. But this assessment refers to
> his art as the negation of this legacy, rather than its confirmation.
>
> *Indeterminacy and chance* have been seldom allowed to influence the design of
> the city environment. As we have observed, the formalist achievement is a
> condition of working from the relatively unknown toward the absolute. Theories
> of chance suggest that the process be reversed and that art is conclusive only at
> that moment when it has reached its highest level of indecision.
>
> *Entropy,* as a measure of phenomenology, may bring to mind the unpleasant
> specter of disaster. In science entropy concerns the irreversible degradation of

matter and energy in the universe. With respect to art, the psychological and cultural intensity of this natural catastrophe suggests an "aesthetic of chance" approaching heroic and ritual dimensions. The artist's conventional response to nature has usually been attracted to those stable and inert manifestations which offer reassurance of an objectified, rational, world—evidence of the importance of man's own physicality. As science has substituted its theories of relativity, infinity, dematerialization, and implosion, the artist and architect have been gradually forced to accept a less orderly view of their environment. For some, this realization has been a signal to oppose chaos with an even more formalized aesthetic; or, as in the case of many urban pragmatists, to resist by the recycling of energy into ever more useful purpose. For others, entropy has been an inspiring contradiction to the mechanistic view of the world. It has always been assumed that architecture and urban development should be the product of some resolute preconception. The alternative to this hypothesis was proposed by the late sculptor Robert Smithson who concluded that, "Architects tend to be idealists, not dialecticians. I propose a dialectics of entropic change."

In the discussion of examples of de-architecturization, the standard separations between the visual arts and architecture must be forfeited in order to address the central issues more effectively. For example, the concept may be applied to situations where the only tangible evidence is energy-electronic resources or informational interchange. It may state itself metaphorically, metaphysically, or metamorphically. The methods include performance, social statement, political action, as well as construction process, psychological inversion, and phenomenological change. If the work of Duchamp may be considered pivotal to the art of our time, then surely the attitudes and ideas of de-architecturization owe a considerable debt to this legacy. His work successfully established that intellectual equivocation becomes a heightened level of aesthetic response when all of the crafted and emotionalized baggage is removed from art. By forfeiting the mythology of the artist's "hand" and the specific nature of objects he seemed to imply that these objects were never meant to be looked *at* or contain an intrinsic message *in* themselves; but rather, to function as semaphores in space which changed the spectator's attitudes toward the immediate surroundings. The objects, in other words, are without value beyond their existence as the vortexes of certain environments. These environments (for him, interior exhibition spaces) represented psychological perimeters full of commonplace reassurances that could be inverted. The periphery became the art and the object only a shadow. There is confirmation of this view in a statement by Duchamp concerning the development of the *Large Glass.*

Simply I thought of the idea of a projection of an invisible fourth dimension, something you couldn't see with your eyes. Since I found that one could make a cast shadow from a three dimensional thing, any object whatsoever—just as the projecting of the sun on the earth makes two dimensions—I thought that, by simple intellectual analogy, the fourth dimension could project an object of three dimensions, or to put it another way, any three dimensional object which we see dispassionately is a projection of something four dimensional, something we're not familiar with.

An ultimate dimension of this rationale (and a prophetic comment on the nature of indeterminacy) occurred when the *Large Glass* was broken enroute to an exhibition. "It's better with the breaks, a hundred times better. It's the destiny of things," was Duchamp's response to this alteration-by-chance. By incorporating the unforeseen contingency, by systematically destroying the hallowed techniques of art, by subverting the formalist ideals, and by assaulting the valued object, Duchamp evolved an idea art of negatives and inversions approximating de-architecturization.

By definition, the term *de-architecturization* refers to an act of reversing and/or removing some quality or element from architecture. The character and effect of this process may be perceived only because architecture exists as an unqualified hypothesis in the mind of the viewer. By way of parallel, Duchamp's inversions of art were successful to the degree that this audience maintained preconceptions of exactly what constitutes genuine art and his work was predicated upon sabotaging these spectator habits. Accordingly, to examine de-architecturization, we must establish a frame of reference, a static view of architecture as a point of departure. In recent history the Bauhaus heritage has provided the most consistent and influential criteria for architecture (in the popular notion of the word) and the form-function e-quations have become the most acceptable measure for all designed structures and the spaces around them. The Bauhaus represents impeccable taste and a spartan economy—virtues of comparison by which the excesses and ornamentation of the past may be condemned and the blandness of the present justified. It is, therefore, this architecture-as-formalism, architecture-as-unassailable-idealism that exists as the raw material for de-architecturization.

Although our concern here is the state of contemporary urban art, it is interesting to examine a selection of historical precedents for de-architecturization—particularly in the light of an anti-formalist legacy which is seldom acknowledged by recent criticism. A casual chronology will be maintained for idea transition.

Inclusion has persisted in urban structuring and visual art throughout the centuries. In architecture it usually refers to the adjustment of a design concept to accomodate existing (and often intractable) physical elements. In painting and sculpture the process is often manifested in the accumulation of random and disparate media ingredients that may be regarded by the artist as plastic or informational resources, (collage, decollage, assemblage). Michelangelo's incorporation of the ruins of the Thermae Diocletian into the Church of Santa Maria Degli Angeli is an extraordinary example of inclusion. Although the Renaissance was noted for its respectful treatment of antiquities and the preservation of cultural heritage, there is little precedent for this creative adjustment of a new structure to a deteriorating ruin. Commisioned by Pope Pius IV to transform the Thermae into a Carthusian church in Rome, the artist broke the line of the original wall of the baths, but totally preserved the concave vault as an integral part of the facade—demonstrating a great sensitivity to the combination of erosion and indeterminacy in tension with carefully designed structure.

The Trevi Fountain, growing organically out of the base of the Palazzo Poli in Rome is another unique contribution to the history of de-architecturization. As an informational resource the Trevi is exceptional. It is not an object, it is a place; and, as a place, it informs us about a still larger place (and hence the entire city). It is inseparable from its environs, and the metamorphic transformation of the Poli facade into rock formations is a bold inversion of architecture. Indeed, the fountain contains no units of sculpture to be judged in isolation from context, no "masterpieces" to be extracted and preserved. The Trevi is a composite of details roughly contained within architectural perimeters. There is an implication that an evolutionary process has been temporarily arrested and that the "edge" of art in this case is an expanding and undefined periphery.

The breakdown of the edge of art (in fact and implication) is part of an historical continuum. Juan Downey, in a 1973 essay entitled "Invisible Architecture" has traced the reduction of volume in architecture from ancient Egypt through the present, and into the future. The chronology begins with the Pyramids (maximum volume—minimum interior) and proceeds steadily toward a minimum of structure in favor of a maximum of space enclosure. His examples, in progression, are the column-beam technology of Greece, the Roman arch, the Florentine palazzo around a courtyard, the Crystal Palace Exposition Hall, the curtain-wall tower, the geodesic dome, the inflatable, and on into speculations about energy architecture. In art, Lucy Lippard's book *Six Years: The Dematerialization of the Art Object* summarized; "During the 1960s the anti-intellectual, emotional/intuitive processes of art making characteristic of the last two decades began to give way to the ultra-conceptual art that emphasizes thinking process almost exclusively." Whereas Mr. Downey's observations dwell on structure and evolution, Ms. Lippard's essays deal primarily with a series of cerebral events or art as philosophy/criticism. With respect to public/urban/environmental art, the dialogue is more about situation, attitude, periphery, and the nature of space. Perhaps the dialectic differences are comparable to the scientific community's efforts to interpret the "edge of the universe." The pragmatists insist on a mathematical definition of the phenomenon; the analysts are resigned that the determinant mind cannot embrace the indeterminate universe and value speculations over solutions; and the philosophers maintain that the issue is inaccessible since man is a microcosm of the universe and hence the embodiment of the forces he is trying to explain. In any event the "edge" remains elusive and the questions are still more interesting than the answers. In part, this may parallel the current widespread disenchantment with the art object.

The past twenty years have witnessed a de-materialization in art to a point where most conventional definitions are no longer relevant or necessary. Although the once significant pioneering of Smith, Giacometti, Calder, Caro, and others contributed to the destruction of the monolith, their work preserved the fundamental objectivity of formalist sculpture. The shift of art to cerebralization has served to destroy this qualification as requisite—except insofar as the physical evidence (models) of conceptual ideas must be tailored for exhibition in an art gallery where the sanction of *context* predetermines the reaction of the spectator to *content*. Dealing with open spaces and the cityscape is quite a different matter. Distractions abound, perimeters are nonexistent except by implication, visual access is uncontrolled, and the focality of the exhibition sanctuary is unavailable. The genuine pioneering of earth art (usually interpreted as a concurrent by-product of conceptualism) is most directly responsible for the new dimensions in environmental art. Artists like Heizer, Oppenheim, and Smithson enlarged the scope of the visual field to include those far points of infinity formerly assumed to the province of urban planning and architecture. Also Heizer's trenches and Smithson's *Asphalt Rundown* forecast ideas of negation and the inversion of circumstances which, although dealing with the physical properties of land surface, are important to de-architecturization. The prevailing aspect of recent urban structure is the antithesis of negation. Cities are a composite of relentless density and mass with virtually no sense of land occupancy beyond the cost per square foot. Inversion, under these conditions, refers to an art that can change the pedestrian-motorist's attitudes toward this prevailing oppression.

An urban environment responsive only to the demands of construction costs, land values, and services seems destined to conform to predictable standards well into the foreseeable future. Art effecting changes of attitude toward public spaces and city facade can be achieved by means that are more gestural than emphatic. The procedure might be compared to the confrontations between emerging "idea" artists of the early 1960s and the impenetrable fortress of abstract expressionism (then water-logged in its third generation). The "Erased DeKooning" of Rauschenberg became an affront to the sacrosanct object d'art; but also an inversion of its own revered methodology. By that time DeKooning had become a venerable capital stock and Rauschenberg's deliberate elimination-of-art-as-art was significant in the chronology of art as information versus art as form and symbol. This gesture of cancellation was not directed at DeKooning; rather, at the rituals of cultural fetishism, at DeKooning as an institution. Similarly, art as the inversion of architecture is best achieved through a commentary on an institutionalized value system.

Inversion is both informational and procedural and, when applied to the architectural (or public) environment, may seem to subvert certain rational prerogatives. A superb turn-of-the-century example is the Gaudi viaduct and retaining wall in the Parc Guell supported by its row of leaning columns. It must be remembered that Gaudi's motivations were the approximation of nature in architecture and the development of structural systems to arrive at these equations. His work was the product of a Mediaevalist sensibility and the commentary level was more often the result of a religious ideology, rather than architectural theory. There was never a perverse endeavor to arrive at conclusions which would threaten the spectator's sense of equilibrium or destroy a formalist aesthetic. The results of the casual masonry and precarious articulation of Guell Viaduct did, however, achieve an extraordinary composite of implied organic growth and impending collapse.

An urban art project currently being developed by SITE, Inc. for a courtyard space in the new Intermediate School 25 in lower Manhattan, is another illustration of the inversion process. The proposal suggests a transformation of situation by reversing the evolutionary development of a structured space. The volume of the imposing stairwell is to be physically reduced and fragmented by gradually enlarging the size of the aggregate in the cement mix until the outward flow of the adhesive mass disintegrates into a casual distribution of stones and boulders at the far end of the courtyard. The I.S. 25 project is not intended to evoke a ritual place or propose a materiality aesthetic. It is a hybrid catalyst breaking down the habitual focus on art and architecture as separate entities. The reduction of the stair tower seems to arrest an action which would normally result in either the restoration or the removal of the building. This implied suspension of forces requires the spectator to reconcile his intuitions concerning the security of the structure against what appears to be tentative and/or subversive. The project is the result of speculations about art as periphery and architecture as information.

Theories of *indeterminacy* and *chance* have attracted disciples in most of the arts—painting, multi-media, performance, poetry—but seldom in architecture and urban design. The reasons for this may be attributed to the pragmatic responsibilities of space planning and the widely-held conviction that these obligations include a pre-ordained structuring of the behavior patterns of the pedestrians. Directional walkways, benches, potted trees, and public sculptures are the standard devices used to insure a conditioned response. Cityscape surprises are rare and usually discouraged by the architecture profession and particularly by their corporate and government clients who are anxious to maintain regulatory rituals for society. Although visual art has been ostensibly free of such control factors, the trappings of recognition—galleries, museums, frames, pedestals, spotlights—are still very much in evidence. The happenings and event structures of Allan Kaprow in the 1960s became an influential attack on the traditional role of the audience-participant and the apparatus of recognition. In 1965 Kaprow stated,

> The work of art (dematerialized art), must now receive its meaning and qualities from the unique expectant (and often anxious) focus of the observer, listener, or intellectual participant. But in greater number of cases the responsibilities have at least been reapportioned to include certain outsiders who may or may not be told beforehand exactly what their duties are. The artist and his artist-public are expected to carry on a dialogue on a mutual plane, through a medium which is insufficient alone and in some instances is nonexistent before this dialogue, but which is given life by the parties involved.

This cerebralized participation was earlier defined by Duchamp, but never carried to the magnified scale of Kaprow's work (except perhaps in his designs for the surrealist exhibitions in Paris in 1938 and New York in 1942, which were essentially gallery spaces). It is important to remember that Duchamp's ideas affected context—but the controlled and antiseptic context of the museum, gallery, and private collection. His inversions and destructions have to be evaluated in terms of an object heredity and, although relevant to undefined space, must be addressed within carefully bounded perimeters. His was a French vision and intellect, and epicurean love of the particular. The American sensibility (especially Kaprow's) is comfortable with broad and epic dimensions and it is only fitting that if Duchamp's conceptual estate is to be considered a healthy influence it must be re-evaluated within this expanded frame of measure. Kaprow's *Yard Environment* of 1961, an architectural space filled to overflowing with automobile tires, exemplifies this change of scale reference. Participants in the event were expected to both view and navigate the area, each according to his own perceptual and physical capacity. By comparison, Duchamp's objects were intellectual icons which made the periphery seem indeterminate. Kaprow's assemblages involve corporeal and material congestions that make the periphery seem more rational.

Another aspect of the indeterminate sensibility is a quality of impending threat. This need not be considered a negative force—particularly in art. Kaprow has further defined the element of chance as a "dramatic affair involving both our need for security and our need for discovery and risk." The precariously balanced lead and steel structures of Richard Serra which might topple at the slightest touch and the repellent materiality of Robert Morris' distribution pieces composed of dirt and refuse are examples that come to mind (and yet, each is conditionally associated with the gallery-museum enclosure). Some recent works by Dennis Oppenheim are more particularly involved with urban space and ideas commensurate with de-architecturization. His 1971 *Protection Piece* was located in the rigidly formalist space of Battery Park in New York City. He stationed twelve chained police dogs on a plot of park land to keep people off a space that they would normally occupy, creating a sphere of inaccessibility. Oppenheim describes the piece as . . . "infecting the land with an air of preciousness, yet there was nothing there. . . . The piece is really about pure concentration, protection, making by keeping away."

Entropy, applied to art activity, is most directly associated with the work of the late Robert Smithson. As noted earlier, entropy may be interpreted as an inevitable deteriorating force to be resisted, or a pleasant relief from an over-structured view of natural phenomena. Smithson admitted to a fascination with disaster, a feeling that this attraction constituted a basic human need. "There is a desire for spectacle," he observed, "I know when I was a kid I used to love to watch the hurricanes come and blow trees down and rip up sidewalks. There is a kind of pleasure one receives on that level." As a result, his interests centered on catastrophe, mining regions, and plundered topography. He was suspicious of the idealism of architecture, comparing the evolution of the cityscape to economics. "It seems as if architects build in an isolated, self-contained, a-historical way. They never seem to allow for any kind of relationships outside of their grand plan. And this seems to be true in economics too. Economics seem to be isolated and self-contained and conceived of as cycles, so as to exclude the whole entropic process." As an alternative to this attitude he preferred the example of a park in Anchorage, Alaska created by inhabitants from the consequences of an earthquake, or the recent eruptions in the Vestmann Island outside of Iceland when an entire community of buildings was submerged in black ashes—comparable to his *Partially Buried Woodshed* project in Kent State, Ohio, where he piled twenty cartloads of dirt on this fragile structure until the central beam cracked. Aside from the obvious references to natural calamity on a physical level, Smithson equated his earthworks to the erosions of mental process. In an essay for *Artforum* entitled "Sedimentation of the Mind" he wrote of his works as a kind of "abstract geology." Slump, debris, slides, avalanches, all take place within cracking limits of the brain. The entire body is pulled into the cerebral sediment, where particles and fragments make themselves as solid consciousness.

Smithson's work is central to an art dialectic of entropy; however, some of the most remarkable examples of degradation-as-urban-aesthetic are provided by graffiti-covered walls and subway trains. Although these clandestine inscriptions and the more recent mural-scale calligraphy are considered by many citizens to be pernicious attacks on public property, they have become intrinsic to the vitality of metropolitan life. Sociologically motivated by the desire for identity in an oppressively determinate environment, the graffitti art has proliferated to a degree where it no longer represents a pattern of destruction; but rather, an inevitable acceptance of the tension between the forces of authoritarian design control and the irreversible desire of certain members of the community to humanize this tyranny. All efforts by an establishment law system have failed to thwart these indigenous artists and, in the meantime, pedestrians have gradually learned to accept the spontaneously scribbled epigraph as readily as the official directives of traffic control and public advertising. In fact, a more liberalized public taste now prefers the casual crudeness of graffiti to the sterile elegance of Helvetica.

A more amusing example of entropy versus the structured system has been demonstrated by the various adversaries involved in the cause and prevention of graffiti. During a certain period in 1970 the New York journals offered daily reports on each new development in the conflict. On one hand, an outraged mayor and his task force declared war on the vandals—with claims from law enforcement that the culprits would be dealt with severely and from science that a new paint remover had been perfected to obliterate every vestige of urban scrawl. The spray paint manufacturers were subsequently interviewed to reveal the surprising information that their pigments now contained an indelible component guaranteed to resist any known solvent. And finally, the graffitists themselves were questioned only to discover that they had organized into militant phalanxes and were determined to paint on at any risk. The collision course of these three obdurate combatants has never been favorably mediated or resolved, as evidence of a continuing entropic process and greatly to the benefit of a more diverse city environment.

> Thus, for us now, the idea of a "perfect work of art" is not only irrelevant because we do not know what are the conditions for such a phantasm, but it is, if desired, presumptuous and unreal.
>
> —Allan Kaprow

At the core of a formalist architecture and urban design lies an abiding belief in the integrity of some superior plan—an aspiration towad the "final solution"—and the assumption that by sufficient effort the goal may be attainable. The history of final solutions (whether sociological, military, or aesthetic) has been characterized more by repression than by liberation. Also, in view of a pervasive technology, automation, and the alienation of the individual, formalism only succeeds in compounding the problems. Every detail of contemporary life is a confirmation of the industrial autocracy and it becomes redundant in the extreme for urban facade and public space to function as persistent reminders. Ambiguity, although usually considered anathema to architecture, is indeed the only quality that makes city life tolerable. The combination of practical expedience, rapid mobility, and depersonalization has forced the individual to withdraw increasingly into the privacy of the mind. As a result, the old art and architecture of form and symbol has become less relevant than an art and architecture of information and thought.

The concept of de-architecturization is open to innumerable interpretations—inclusionism, inversion, indeterminacy, entropy, destruction, biomorphic change—and represents an interesting alternative to the familiar translation of a gallery object to outsized scale for use in the public environment. The age of monuments (whether art, architecture, or urban spaces) is finished and most attempts to perpetuate the tradition are pretentious and extraneous no matter how well conceived. We presently lack the cultural estate and the unifying ideology necessary to lend any significance to these heroic icons. As architecture accumulates greater height and mass, art continues to suffer as a superfluous vehicle of decoration, (a competitive role that is doomed from the outset in terms of scale and plastic relationships). Art cannot compete with the size and urgency of architecture, nor should it try. De-architecturization is a catalyst suggesting that public art does not have to respond to formalist doctrine; but rather, may evolve from the informational reservoirs of the city environment, where phenomenology and structure become the fabric of existence. Perhaps the only requisite ingredient is a reaction to the complacent state of architecture. A large proportion of the art produced in this century has been art about art. De-architecturization is art about architecture.

Milton Babbitt

The Composer as Specialist

This article might have been entitled alternatively, and perhaps less conten-
tiously, "The Composer as Anachronism." For I am concerned with stating
an attitude towards the indisputable facts of the status and condition of the
composer of what we will, for the moment, designate as "serious,"
"advanced," contemporary music. This composer expends an enormous
amount of time and energy—and, usually, considerable money—on the
creation of a commodity that has little, no, or negative commodity value. He
is, in essence, a "vanity" composer. The general public is largely unaware of
and uninterested in his music. The majority of performers shun it and resent
it. Consequently, the music is little performed, and then primarily at poorly
attended concerts before an audience consisting in the main of fellow
professionals. At best, the music would appear to be for, of, and by
specialists.

Towards this condition of musical and societal "isolation" a variety of
attitudes has been expressed, usually with the purpose of assigning blame,
often to the music itself, occasionally to critics or performers, and very
occasionally to the public. But to assign blame is to imply that this isolation is
unnecessary and undesirable. It is my contention that, on the contrary, this
condition is not only inevitable, but potentially advantageous for the
composer and his music. From my point of view, the composer would do well

Reprinted from *High Fidelity* (February, 1958), where it appeared under a different title ("Who
Cares If You Listen?"), by permission of the author and publisher.

to consider means of realizing, consolidating, and extending the advantage.

The unprecedented divergence between contemporary serious music and its listeners, on the one hand, and traditional music and its following on the other, is not accidental and—most probably—not transitory. Rather, it is a result of a half-century of revolution in musical thought, a revolution whose nature and consequences can be compared only with, and in many respects are closely analogous to, those of the mid-nineteenth-century revolution in mathematics and the twentieth-century revolution in theoretical physics. The immediate and profound effect has been necessity for the informed musician to re-examine and probe the very foundations of his art. He has been obliged to recognize the possibility, and actuality, of alternatives to what were once regarded as musical absolutes. He lives no longer in a unitary musical universe of "common practice," but in a variety of universes of diverse practice.

This fall from musical innocence is, understandably, as disquieting to some as it is challenging to others, but in any event the process is irreversible; and the music that reflects the full impact of this revolution is, in many significant respects, a truly "new" music. Apart from the often highly sophisticated and complex constructive methods of any one composition, or group of compositions, the very minimal properties characterizing this body of music are the sources of its "difficulty," "unintelligibility" and—isolation. In indicating the most general of these properties, I shall make reference to no specific works, since I wish to avoid the independent issue of evaluation. The reader is at liberty to supply his own instances; if he cannot (and, granted the condition under discussion, this is a very real possibility), let him be assured that such music does exist.

First. This music employs a tonal vocabulary which is more "efficient" than that of the music of the past, or its derivatives. This is not necessarily a virtue in itself, but it does make possible a greatly increased number of pitch simultaneities, successions, and relationships. This increase in efficiency necessarily reduces the "redundancy" of the language, and as a result the intelligible communication of the work demands increased accuracy from the transmitter (the performer) and activity from the receiver (the listener). Incidentally, it is this circumstance, among others, that has created the need for purely electronic media of "performance." More importantly for us, it makes ever heavier demands upon the training of the listener's perceptual capacities.

Second. Along with this increase of meaningful pitch materials, the number of functions associated with each component of the musical event also has been multiplied. In the simplest possible terms, each such "atomic" event is located in a five-dimensional musical space determined by pitch-class, register, dynamics, duration, and timbre. These five components not only together define the single event, but, in the course of a work, the successive values of each component create an individually coherent structure, frequently in parallel with the corresponding structures created by each of the other components. Inability to perceive and remember precisely the values of any of these components results in a dislocation of the event in the work's musical space, an alteration of its relation to all other events in the work, and—thus—a falsification of the composition's total structure. For example, an incorrectly performed or perceived dynamic value results in destruction of the work's dynamic pattern, but also in false identification of other components of the event (of which this dynamic value is a part) with corresponding components of other events, so creating incorrect pitch, registral, timbral, and durational associations. It is this high degree of "determinacy" that most strikingly differentiates such music from, for example, a popular song. A popular song is only very partially determined, since it would appear to retain its germane characteristics under considerable alteration of register, rhythmic texture, dynamics, harmonic structure, timbre, and other qualities.

The preliminary differentiation of musical categories by means of this reasonable and usable criterion of "degree of determinacy" offends those who take it to be a definition of qualitative categories, which—of course—it need not always be. Curiously, their demurrers usually take the familiar form of some such "democratic" counterdefinition as: "There is no such thing as 'serious' and 'popular' music. There is only 'good' and 'bad' music." As a public service, let me offer those who still patiently await the revelation of the criteria of Absolute Good an alternative criterion which possesses, at least, the virtue of immediate and infallible applicability: "There is no such thing as 'serious' and 'popular' music. There is only music whose title begins with the letter 'X' and music whose title does not."

Third. Musical compositions of the kind under discussion possess a high degree of contextuality and autonomy. That is, the structural characteristics of a given work are less representative of a general class of characteristics than they are unique to the individual work itself. Particularly, principles of relatedness, upon which depends immediate coherence of continuity, are more likely to evolve in the course of the work than to be derived from generalized assumptions. Here again greater and new demands are made upon the perceptual and conceptual abilities of the listener.

Fourth, and finally. Although in many fundamental respects this music is "new," it often also represents a vast extension of the methods of the other.

musics, derived from a considered and extensive knowledge of their dynamic principles. For, concomitant with the "revolution in music," perhaps even an integral aspect thereof, has been the development of analytical theory, concerned with the systematic formulation of such principles to the end of greater efficiency, economy, and understanding. Compositions so rooted necessarily ask comparable knowledge and experience from the listener. Like all communication, this music presupposes a suitably equipped receptor. I am aware that "tradition" has it that the lay listener, by virtue of some undefined, transcendental faculty, always is able to arrive at a musical judgment absolute in its wisdom if not always permanent in its validity. I regret my inability to accord this declaration of faith the respect due its advanced age.

Deviation from this tradition is bound to dismiss the contemporary music of which I have been talking into "isolation." Nor do I see how or why the situation should be otherwise. Why should the layman be other than bored and puzzled by what he is unable to understand, music or anything else? It is only the translation of this boredom and puzzlement into resentment and denunciation that seems to me indefensible. After all, the public does have its own music, its ubiquitous music: music to eat by, to read by, to dance by, and to be impressed by. Why refuse to recognize the possibility that contemporary music has reached a stage long since attained by other forms of activity? The time has passed when the normally well-educated man without special preparation can understand the most advanced work in, for example, mathematics, philosophy, and physics. Advanced music, to the extent that it reflects the knowledge and originality to the informed composer, scarcely can be expected to appear more intelligible than these arts and sciences to the person whose musical education usually has been even less extensive than his background in other fields. But to this, a double standard is invoked, with the words "music is music," implying also that "music is *just* music." Why not, then, equate the activities of the radio repairman with those of the theoretical physicist, on the basis of the dictum that "physics is physics"? It is not difficult to find statements like the following from the *New York Times* of September 8, 1957: "The scientific level of the conference is so high . . . that there are in the world only 120 mathematicians specializing in the field who could contribute." Specialized music on the other hand, far from signifying "height" of musical level, has been charged with "decadence," even as evidence of an insidious "conspiracy."

It often has been remarked that only in politics and the "arts" does the layman regard himself as an expert, with the right to have his opinion heard. In the realm of politics, he knows that this right, in the form of a vote, is guaranteed by fiat. Comparably, in the realm of public music, the concertgoer is secure in the knowledge that the amenities of concert-going protect his firmly stated: "I didn't like it" from further scrutiny. Imagine, if you can, a layman chancing upon a lecture on "Pointwise Periodic Homeomorphisms." At the conclusion, he announces: "I didn't like it." Social conventions being what they are in such circles, someone might dare inquire: "Why not?" Under duress, our layman discloses precise reasons for his failure to enjoy himself: he found the hall chilly, the lecturer's voice unpleasant, and he was suffering the digestive aftermath of a poor dinner. His interlocutor understandably disqualifies these reasons as irrelevant to the content and value of the lecture, and the development of mathematics is left undisturbed. If the concertgoer is at all versed in the ways of musical lifemanship, he also will offer reasons for his "I didn't like it"—in the form of assertions that the work in question is "inexpressive," "undramatic," "lacking in poetry," tapping that store of vacuous equivalents hallowed by time for: "I don't like it, and I cannot or will not state why." The concertgoer's critical authority is established beyond the possiblity of further inquiry. Certainly he is not responsible for the circumstance that musical discourse is a never-never land of semantic confusion, the last resting place of all those verbal and formal fallacies, those hoary dualisms that have been banished from rational discourse. Perhaps he has read, in a widely consulted and respected book on the history of music, the following: "to call him (Tchaikovsky) the 'modern Russian Beethoven' is footless, Beethoven being patently neither modern nor Russian. . . ." Or, the following by an eminent "nonanalytic" philosopher: "The music of Lourié is an ontological music. . . . It is born in the singular roots of being, the nearest possible juncture of the soul and the spirit. . . ." How unexceptional the verbal peccadilloes of the average concertgoer appear beside these masterful models. Or, perhaps, in search of "real" authority, he has acquired his critical vocabulary from the pronouncements of officially "eminent" composers, whose eminence, in turn, is founded largely upon just such assertions as the concertgoer has learned to regurgitate. This cycle is of slight moment in a world where circularity is one of the norms of criticism. Composers (and performers), wittingly or unwittingly assuming the character of "talented children" and "inspired idiots," generally ascribed to them, are singularly adept at the conversion of personal tastes into general principles. Music they do not like is "not music," composers whose music they do not like are "not composers."

In search of what to think and how to say it, the layman may turn to newspapers and magazines. Here he finds conclusive evidence for the proposition that "music is music." The science editor of such publications contents himself with straightforward reporting, usually news of the "factual" sciences; books and articles not intended for popular consumption are not reviewed. Whatever the reason, such matters are left to professional journals. The music critic admits no comparable differentiation. He may feel, with some justice, that music which presents itself in the market place of the concert hall automatically offers itself to public approval or disapproval. He may feel, again, with some justice, that to omit the expected criticism of the "advanced" work would be to do the composer an injustice in his assumed quest for, if nothing else, public notice and "professional recognition." The critic, at least to this extent, is himself a victim of the leveling of categories.

Here, then, are some of the factors determining the climate of the public world of music. Perhaps we should not have overlooked those pockets of "power" where prizes, awards, and commissions are dispensed, where music is adjudged guilty, not only without the right to be confronted by its accuser, but without the right to be confronted by the accusations. Or those well-meaning souls who exhort the public "just to *listen* to more contemporary music," apparently on the theory that familiarity breeds passive acceptance. Of those, often the same well-meaning souls, who remind the composer of his "obligation to the public," while the public's obligation to the composer is fulfilled, manifestly, by mere physical presence in the concert hall or before a loudspeaker or—more authoritatively—by committing to memory the numbers of phonograph records and amplifier models. Or the intricate social world within this musical world, where the salon becomes bazaar, and music itself becomes an ingredient of verbal canapés for cocktail conversation.

I say this not to present a picture of a virtuous music in a sinful world, but to point up the problems of a special music in an alien and inapposite world. And so, I dare suggest that the composer would do himself and his music an immediate and eventual service by total, resolute, and voluntary withdrawal from this public world to one of private performance and electronic media, with its very real possibility of complete elimination of the public and social aspects of musical composition. By so doing, the separation between the domains would be defined beyond any possibility of confusion of categories, and the composer would be free to pursue a private life of professional achievement, as opposed to a public life of unprofessional compromise and exhibitionism.

But how, it may be asked, will this serve to secure the means of survival for the composer and his music? One answer is that after all such a private life is what the university provides the scholar and the scientist. It is only proper that the university, which—significantly enough—has provided so many contemporary composers with their professional training and general education, should provide a home for the "complex," "difficult," and "prob-lematical" in music. Indeed, the process has begun; and if it appears to pro-ceed too slowly, I take consolation in the knowledge that in this respect, too, music seems to be in historically retarded parallel with now sacrosanct fields of endeavor. In E. T. Bell's *Men of Mathematics,* we read: "In the eighteenth century the universities were not the principal centers of research in Europe. They might have become such sooner than they did but for the classical tra-dition and its understandable hostility to science. Mathematics was close e-nough to antiquity to be respectable, but physics, being more recent, was suspect. Further, a mathematician in a university of the time would have been expected to put much of his effort on elementary teaching; his research, if any, would have been an unprofitable luxury. . . ." A simple substitution of *musical composition* for *research,* of *academic* for *classical,* of *music* for *physics,* and of *composer* for *mathematician,* provides a strikingly accurate picture of the current situation. And as long as the confusion I have described continues to exist, how can the university and its community assume other than that the composer welcomes and courts public competition with the historically certified products of the past, and the com-mercially petrified products of the present?

Perhaps for the same reason, the various institutes of advanced research and the large majority of foundations have disregarded this music's need for means of survival. I do not wish to appear to obscure the obvious differences between musical composition and scholarly research, although it can be contended that these differences are no more fundamental than the differences among the various fields of study. I do question whether these differences, by their nature, justify the denial to music's development of assistance granted these other fields. Immediate "practical" applicability (which may be said to have its musical analogue in "immediate extensibility of a compositional technique") is certainly not a necessary condition for the support of scientific research. And if it be contended that such research is so supported because in the past it has yielded eventual applications, one can counter with, for example, the music of Anton Webern, which during the composer's lifetime was regarded (to the very limited extent that it was regarded at all) as the ultimate in hermetic, specialized, and idiosyncratic composition; today, some dozen years after the composer's death, his complete works have been recorded by a major record company, primarily—I suspect—as a result of the enormous influence this music has had on the postwar, nonpopular, musical world. I doubt that scientific research is any more secure against predictions of ultimate significance than is musical composition. Finally, if it be contended that research, even in its least "practical" phases, contributes to the sum of knowledge in the particular realm, what possibly can contribute more to our knowledge of music than a genuinely original composition?

Granting to music the position accorded other arts and sciences promises the sole substantial means of survival for the music I have been describing. Admittedly, if this music is not supported, the whistling repertory of the man in the street will be little affected, the concert-going activity of the conspicuous consumer of musical culture will be little disturbed. But music will cease to evolve, and in that important sense, will cease to live.

John Cage

The Future of Music

I told Jack Collins, with whom I study chess, that I had finished writing about the future of music. He said: Do you think there is one? Then he laughed and said, "I suppose if there is a future that music has one, too."

1974. As I think about the future of music, I notice that music—as an activity separated from other activities—doesn't enter my mind. Strictly musical questions are no longer serious questions.

Years ago, for instance, after I decided to devote my life to music, I noticed that people distinguished between noises and musical sounds. I decided to follow Varèse and fight for noises, to be on the side of the underdog. Other musicians made a similar decision. In 1933 or 4 the only piece for percussion alone was Varèse's *Ionization*. By 1942, there were over one hundred such works. Now they are countless. Almost anyone who listens to sound listens with ease to any sound no matter what overtone structure it happens to have. We no longer discriminate against noises.

Also, we can hear any pitch, whether or not it is part of a particular scale, of one temperament or another, occidental or oriental. Sounds that formerly seemed out of tune now seem, if anything, more distinguished than those in tune.

Some people still object to loud sounds. They're afraid of hurting their ears. Recently I had the opportunity to hear a very loud sound (it was the conclusion of a Zaj performance). I had been in the audience the evening before. I knew when the sound was coming. I moved very close to the loudspeaker from which it was to be heard and sat there for an hour, turning first one ear and then the other toward it. When the sound stopped, I noticed that my ears were ringing. The ringing continued through the night, through the next day, and through the next night. Early the following day I made an appointment with an ear specialist. On my way to his office, I noticed the ringing had more or less subsided. After a thorough examination, the doctor told me that my ears were normal, that the disturbance was temporary. As a result my attitude toward loud sounds has not changed. I shall listen to them with interest whenever the opportunity arises, keeping perhaps a proper distance.

Our experience of time has been greatly altered. We notice brief events that formerly might have escaped our notice and we enjoy very long ones, ones having lengths that would have been considered say, ten years ago, intolerable.

Nor are we concerned about how a sound begins, continues, and dies away. In this connection I recall a recent remark of Chou Wen-chung. During a panel discussion on recent piano music from the People's Republic of China, Chou Wen-chung said that Western musicians formerly insisted that a pitched sound should stay on its pitch and not waver from the moment it begins until it ends. On the other hand, Chinese musicians, he said, have the feeling that some change in its course in its pitch enlivens a sound, makes it "musical." Nowadays, anyone listens to any sounds, no matter how flexible or inflexible they are with respect to any of their characteristics. We have become attentive—on the lookout, so to speak—for sounds we haven't heard before. I remember being fascinated when Lejaren Hiller described his project, to use computer means to make a "fantastic orchestra." He planned to synthesize sounds having extraordinary characteristics; for example, sounds beginning as though plucked, continuing as from pipes, ending as though bowed.

We are open-minded about sound. And also about silence. Silence is not as generally upsetting as it used to be.

There is a general open-mindedness with regard to what sound follows another and when: an open-mindedness about melody. *Klangfarbenmelodie* has not taken the place of *bel canto*. It has extended our realization of what can happen. The same is true of aperiodic rhythm: it includes the possibility of periodic rhythm. In terms of counterpoint, we can recognize the presence of different known kinds (we can imagine inventing kinds of counterpoint as yet unknown); we can also recognize and enjoy the absence of counterpoint (that is to say, we cannot imagine two or more lines composed of sounds that couldn't or shouldn't be heard at the same time). Even if, say, two lines of sound, one very loud, the other very soft, were produced at the same time, we know that were we to listen very carefully, or, if necessary, from a different position in space, we could hear them both.

We can be extremely careful about harmony, as Lou Harrison, La Monte Young and Ben Johnston are, or we can be, as I often am, extremely careless about harmony. Or we can make do as our orchestras do with gray compromises about which sounds sounded together are harmonious.

Anything goes. However, not everything is attempted. I am thinking now of the division of a whole into parts. In the thirties when I was beginning to write music, fresh from my studies with Schoenberg, I was impressed by his insistence on musical structure, but disagreed with his view that tonality was its necessary means. I investigated time-lengths as a more comprehensive means, and, in the course of my investigation, I made, by means of permutations, tables of the numbers one through twelve, giving their divisions into prime numbers. These number-series could be understood either in terms of tonality or in terms of time-length or rhythmic structures. For instance, the series, 1-2-1, which appears in the table for the number 4, can be recognized as an A-B-A structure. It could be expressed tonally or rhythmically (or both). For the number 7 there are 64 different number-series. Only three of these 64 can be recognized as A-B-A, namely, 2-3-2, 3-1-3, and 1-5-1. Though some of the others have been exemplified musically, I am certain that many have not; and the possibilities increase for the higher numbers. There are 2,048 for the number 12. If we deal, as we may, with fractions, who knows what musical structures may be discovered? Interesting ones are being found by Elliott Carter and Conlon Nancarrow involving superimposed independent gradual transitions from one tempo to another; those by Nancarrow are particularly interesting. Dealing as he does exclusively with player pianos, he produces extremes of speed that are astonishing and exhilarating.

Though many composers continue to make musical structures (wholes that are divisible into parts), many others are exploring not structures but processes. The difference is that which obtains between an object (a table, for instance) and, say, the weather. In the case of the table, the beginning and end of the whole and of each of its parts are known. In the case of the weather, though we notice changes in it, we have no clear knowledge about its beginning or ending. We have, to be sure, some fear that we have through our technology brought about serious alterations in it, in the air we breathe, but we hope that even in the very distant future there will still be some of it to enjoy.

Were a limit to be set to possible musical processes, a process outside those limits would surely be discovered. And when we realize that processes can include objects (be analogous, that is, to environment), we see there are no limits. For some time now, I have preferred processes to objects for just this reason: processes do not exclude objects. It does not work the other way around. We are aware, of course, that within each object, a lively molecular process is in operation. But if we are to hear it, we must isolate the object in an isolation chamber. To focus our attention on an object, it is necessary to ignore all the rest of creation. We have a history of doing that. In changing our minds, therefore, we look for that attitude of mind that is nonexclusive, that can include all possibilities—those we know and those we do not yet imagine.

There is the question of feelings, whether like emotions they seem to spontaneously come from within, or, like likes and dislikes, they seem to be caused by sense experiences. In either case, we know that life is more fully lived when we are open to whatever—that life is minimized when we protect ourselves from it. Naturally, as I have said elsewhere, we don't set out to kill ourselves. We will continue to "wrestle with the Daimonic" (as M. C. Richards puts it), and a variety of disciplines will continue to be used to open the mind to events beyond its control. But more and more this concern with personal feelings of individuals, even the enlightenment of individuals, will be seen in the larger context of society. We know how to suffer or control our own emotions. If not, advice is available. There is a cure for tragedy. The path to self knowledge has been mapped out by psychiatry, by oriental philosophy, mythology, occult thought, anthroposophy, and astrology. We know all we need to know about Oedipus, Prometheus, and Hamlet. What we are learning is how to be convivial. "Here Comes Everybody." Though the doors will always remain open for the musical expression of personal feelings, what will more and more come through is the expression of the pleasures of conviviality (as in the music of Terry Riley, Steve Reich, and Philip Glass). And beyond that a nonintentional expressivity: a being together of sounds and people (where sounds are sounds, and people are people).

The difference between closed-mindedness and open-mindedness in music is made readable by the difference between any issue of *Perspectives of New Music* and any issue of *Ear,* a periodical published by Beth Anderson in California's Bay Area. Christian Wolff found the following, written by Charles Ives, and sent it on to me: "What music is and is to be may be somewhere in the belief of an unknown philosopher of half a century ago who said, 'How can there be any bad music? All music is from heaven. If there is anything bad in it, I put it there—by my implications and limitations. Nature builds the mountains and meadows and man puts in the fences and labels.' "

The fences have come down and the labels are being removed. An up-to-date aquarium has all the fish swimming together in one huge tank.

Musical open-mindedness has come about in this century in Western Europe (and many countries of Eastern Europe), in the Americas, in Japan, and Australia, and, perhaps, in New Zealand. As far as I know, it doesn't exist, except perhaps exceptionally, in India, Indonesia, and Africa, and it is politically excluded both in Russia and China (though I have been told that through the efforts of Italy's representatives in China, a concert of the music of Sylvano Bussotti took place in Peking in recent years).

The reasons for this musical open-mindedness are several. First of all: the activities of many composers. I will not name them all. But in this country alone, open-mindedness is implied by the work particularly of Ives, Ruggles, Cowell, and Varèse. Cowell used to tell me the story about Ruggles and the Florida class in the theory of harmony. The problem of modulating from one key to another described as being "very distant" was discussed. After an hour, the instructor asked Ruggles how he, Ruggles, would solve the problem. Ruggles began with his usual four-letter word and then added: I wouldn't make a problem out of it; I'd just go from one to the other without any transition.

A second reason for open-mindedness: changes in technology associated with music. Given the tape recorders, synthesizers, sound systems, and computers we have, we could not reasonably have been expected to keep our minds fixed on the music of earlier centuries, even though many of the schools, conservatories, and music critics still do. A third reason for open-mindedness: the interpenetration of cultures formerly separated. In the nineteenth century even Englishmen occupying India were few and far between who took Indian music seriously. Times have changed. At the present time, if a university takes music seriously, it does as Wesleyan University in Connecticut does: it brings together in one school as many different musical cultures of the world as it can afford (music of Africa, of India, of Indonesia, and Japan, together with European music, music of the American Indians, and new electronic music). A fourth reason for open-mindedness: there are more of us and we have many ways of getting together (the telephone, the media, travel by air). If one of us doesn't have an idea that will open the minds of the rest of us, another will. We begin to be keenly aware of the richness and uniqueness of each individual and the natural capacity each person has to open up new possibilities for another. In her recent book, *The Crossing Point,* M. C. Richards tells of her work with retarded children, how it is characterized not just by her helping them, but also by their helping her. Some years ago I was asked to speak to a group of doctors associated with a mental hospital in Connecticut. I had no clear idea in my mind what to say. But as I went down the corridors toward the room where I was to speak, I found myself among people "out of their minds." What had to be said to the doctors became clear: You're sitting on top of a gold mine! Share the wealth with the rest of us! The same is true of our prisons. When Buckminster Fuller did not know whether his wife Anne was to live or not (following an automobile accident), or, if she did live, whether she would be incapacitated or not, it was a letter from a former convict in a California penitentiary on the subject of life, love, and death, that gave him consolation. There are untouched resources in children and teen-agers that we do not have because we send them to school; and among the military whom we lose by sending them around the world and beneath its surface to bomb-proof offensive installations; and among the senior citizens whom we have persuaded to leave us in favor of sunshine, fun, and games. We have systematically deprived ourselves of all these people, probably because we didn't want them to bother us while we were doing whatever we were doing. But if there is any activity more than another which conduces to open-mindedness, it is our practice of bothering one another, of interrupting one another. Say we do not practice any spiritual discipline. The telephone then does it for us. It opens us to the world "outside."

George Herbert Mead, one of the "Chicago Philosophers," said that when one is very young he feels he belongs to one family, not to any other. As he grows older, he belongs to one neighborhood rather than another; later, to one nation rather than another. When he feels no limit to that to which he belongs, he has, Mead said, developed the religious spirit. The open-mindedness among composers (which has affected performers and listeners, too) is comparable and kin to the religious spirit. And the striking difference between a subscription audience at Avery Fischer Hall, and an audience that comes together freely in a loft, or church, or gallery in the Village, is the difference between using music to get away from life and using music to get into life. In the Lincoln Center lobby, during the intermission and after the concert, if anything at all is said about the music, it is in the nature of aesthetics and criticism. Downtown, the audiences don't criticize; they use the music. It is necessary for them in the enjoyment of their lives. *Nichi nichi kore ko nichi.* "Every day is a beautiful day." And this is said knowing full well that it is said as though by Daniel in the Lion's Den. Open-minded as the religious spirit is, it is not enough. Needed (and urgently) is a *social* sense of all Mankind as Family, of Earth as Home. I would be willing to say a "political" sense, if politics were understood as all of the actions of all of the people.

Music has not been idle. It has also prepared the way in this direction. The Renaissance-honored distinction in so-called serious music between composers, performers, and listeners are no longer everywhere maintained. The blurring of these distinctions has come about for several reasons. First of all: the activities of many composers, particularly Feldman and Wolff, who have introduced indeterminacy into their compositions, so that performers, rather than merely doing what they are told to do, have the opportunity to use their own faculties, to make decisions in a field of posibilities, to cooperate, that is, in a particular musical undertaking. Those listening to indeterminate music have been encouraged in their listening, since they have been joined in such music by the composers and performers, too.

Secondly, technology has brought about the blurring of the distinctions between composers, performers, and listeners. When I came to New York in the early forties, I was interested in making music for radio or film using sound effects rather than conventional instruments. I offered my services as a composer to several companies. But technicians who had made no study of musical composition at all were perfectly capable all by themselves of devising sound continuities for film and radio purposes. Later, in the early fifties, with David Tudor and, at times, Earle Brown, too, a team of workers assisted by Louis and Bebe Barron was formed to make music directly on magnetic tape. Subsequently Louis and Bebe Barron, though they had not studied musical composition, composed the music for a Hollywood science fiction film. Just as anyone feels himself capable of taking a photograph by means of a camera, so now and increasingly so in the future anyone, using recording and/or electronic means, feels and will increasingly feel himself capable of making a piece of music, combining in his one person the formerly distinct activities of composer, performer, and listener. However, combining in one person these several activities is, in effect, to remove from music its social nature. It is the social nature of music, the practice in it of using a number of people doing different things to make it, that distinguishes it from the visual arts, draws it toward theatre and makes it relevant to society, even society outside musical society. The popularity of recordings is unfortunate, not only for musical reasons, but for social reasons: it permits the listener to isolate himself from other people. What is needed is not that the several activities of different people come together in one person, but that the distinctions between the roles of different people are blurred, so that they themselves may come together.

A third cause for the blurring of the distinctions between composers, performers and listeners: the interpenetration of cultures formerly separated. There is no longer an essential difference between some serious music and some popular music—or, you may say, a bridge exists between them: their common use of the same sound systems, the same microphones, amplifiers and loudspeakers. In the cases of much popular and some oriental musics, the distinctions between composers and performers were never very clear. Notation, as Busoni said it did, did not stand between musician and music. People simply came together and made music. Improvisation. It can take place, so to speak, strictly, as within the *raga* and *tala* limitations of Indian music, or it can take place freely, merely in a space of time, as sounds do environmentally, whether in the country or in the cities. Just as aperiodic rhythm can include periodic rhythm, just as process can include object, so free improvisations can include strict ones, can even include compositions. The Jam Session. The Musicircus.

The interpenetration of cultures formerly separated is potentially a blurring of the differences between cultures, a coming together of their differences. Richard K. Winslow recently suggested changing my instrumental parts for *Etcetera* so that they would read Bowed Instrument, Wind Instrument, Double Reed, Single Reed, rather than Violin, Flute, Oboe, Clarinet, thus bringing to parts for pitched instruments something of the vagueness and freedom conventionally given to parts for percussion players. (If you don't have the percussion instrument called for, you substitute something else.) Oriental and occidental instruments together in ensemble. A duet between tuba and sitar! This is only possible when the actions to be made are not on the ground special to either, but on the ground common to both.

With our increase in population there has come about a great increase in musical activity. Formerly concerts of new music were few and far between. Now there is more going on than you can shake a stick at. (At least in New York City. That's why I was surprised last fall both in Paris and Rome to notice that in the questions of people interviewing me, it was repeatedly assumed that there is nothing further, nothing new, to do in music. I remember feeling that way myself, in the early thirties: my feeling was that of someone full of admiration for what had been accomplished in music, but who had not yet himself gotten to work.) For the most part, music that's now being made in New York, the new music, that is, is music that I for one want to hear. I notice that others feel as I do. The audiences are large, generally filling the spaces used; and I notice that more and more, as in the evenings with Philip Corner and his friends, the audiences themselves participate in the making of the music.

In 1949 or 50 Pierre Souvtchinsky told me that in order to have good art, you must have bad government. We in the U.S.A. have both. What we want is to keep the good art going, and to have at least good government, but preferably no government at all in its aspects of power and profit—just some smoothly running utilities organization. I would be willing to settle for that even if it brought about a decline in quality and quantity of our arts (which I don't believe it would).

We can say that this blurring of the distinctions between composer, performers, and listeners is evidence of an ongoing change in society, not only in the structure of society, but in the feelings that people have for one another. Fear, guilt, and greed associated with hierarchical societies are giving way to mutual confidence, a sense of common well-being, and a desire to share with another whatever one person happens to have or to do. However, these changed social feelings which characterize many evenings of new music do not characterize the society as a whole. We wonder therefore, how we can say *Nichi nichi* (something or other) *nichi*: Every Day is a Miserable Day.

For, as long as we continue stupidly to destroy the environment in which we live, we must each day remind ourselves that though it is beautiful, each day is miserable. And act accordingly. As long as we tolerate the division of mankind into power and profit organizations and nations all continuously at one another's throats, we must each day remind ourselves, that though it is beautiful, each day is miserable. And act accordingly.

I asked a Japanese friend of mine, Hiroshi Kawanishi, how to say in Japanese: Every Day is a Miserable Day. He laughed and said: "You can't say that." I then remembered what my father, the inventor, often said: "When anyone says can't, that shows you what you next must do." Revolution remains our proper concern. But instead of planning it, or stopping what we're doing in order to do it, it may be that we are at all times in it. I quote again from M. C. Richards' book, *The Crossing Point*.

> Instead of revolution being considered exclusively as an attack from outside upon an established form, it is being considered as a potential resource—an art of transformation voluntarily undertaken from within. Revolution arm in arm with evolution, creating a balance which is neither rigid nor explosive. Perhaps we will learn to relinquish voluntarily our patterns of power and subservience, and work together for organic change.

At the beginning of the *Essay on Civil Disobedience*, Thoreau has this quotation: "That government is best which governs not at all." He adds: "And when men are prepared for it, that will be the kind of government which they will have." Many musicians are ready. We now have many musical examples of the practicality of anarchy. Music with indeterminate parts, no fixed relation of them (no score). Music without notation. Our rehearsals are not conducted. We use that time to make our set-ups: to make sure that everything that is needed by any of the musicians is there, and that everything is in good working order. Musicians can do without government. Like ripe fruit (I refer to the metaphor at the end of Thoreau's *Essay*), they have dropped away from the tree.

Less anarchic kinds of music give examples of less anarchic states of society. The masterpieces of Western music exemplify monarchies and dictatorships. Composer and conductor: king and prime minister. By making analogies between musical situations we do have and desirable social circumstances which we do not yet have, we make music suggestive and relevant to the serious questions that face mankind.

Some politically concerned composers do not so much exemplify in their work the desired changes in society as they use their music as propaganda for such changes or as criticism of the society as it continues insufficiently changed. This necessitates the use of words. Sounds by themselves do not put messages across. And when they do not use words, politically concerned composers tend to revert to nineteenth-century musical practices. This is enforced in both Russia and China. And encouraged in England by Cornelius Cardew and the members of the Scratch Orchestra. They study pronouncements on art by Mao Tse-tung and apply them as literally and legalistically as they can. They therefore criticize the recent politically concerned music of Frederic Rzewski and Christian Wolff, simply because new ways to make music have been discovered by both of these composers. Rzewski's works (and some of Garrett List's, too) flow like the rapids of a river: they suggest irresistible change. Rzewski and List have found virtuosi who vocalize rapidly and over long periods of time uninterruptedly (not seeming to take any time off to breathe); Wolff's works invariably reveal to both performers and listeners energy resources in themselves of which they hadn't been aware, and put those energies intelligently to work.

Implicit in the use of words (when messages are put across) are training, government, enforcement, and finally the military. Thoreau said that hearing a sentence he heard feet marching. Syntax, N. O. Brown told me, is the army. The pen has formerly been considered more powerful than the sword. American shame and spiritual frustration result at least in part from the fact that even though the country's best pens and best voices throughout history have been raised in protest against our government's actions, and even though thorough plans have been clearly proposed for the improvement of environment and the well-being of all people—not just Americans, but all people—the American powers that be remain deaf and blind. We know from Buckminster Fuller and many others that the continued use of fossil fuels and atomic energy are against both environment and the lives of people in it. We should use above-earth energy sources: sun, wind, tides, and algae. Nixon and Kissinger don't seem to know this. Their triumphs, national and international, have to do with the foolish continued exploitation of below-earth resources, resources that cannot be replaced when they are used up. Fuller did not smile when I asked him about atomic energy. Inevitable in it is the slow but steady raising of Earth's temperature to a heat in which life would be unendurable. Since words, when they communicate, have no effect, it dawns on us that we need a society in which communication is not practiced, in which words become nonsense as they do between lovers, in which words become what they originally were: trees and stars and the rest of primeval environment. The demilitarization of language: a serious musical concern.

The first part of a new text by Norman O. Brown is on work. It was his reaction, I believe, to the somewhat complacent, though religious, spirit of the young in California communes. The willingness to settle for survival. Brown's concern is how to make a new civilization. Work is the first chapter. Ideas are in the air. In our polluted air there is the idea that we must get to work. Somehow, recently, in New York and in other cities, too, the air seems less polluted than it was. Work has begun.

For a musical work to be implemented in China, it must be proposed not by an individual but by a team. The necessity for teamwork in music has been emphasized by Pierre Boulez in a Canadian interview with him about the Research Institute he is forming in Paris. The evenings with Philip Corner and his friends, Carole Weber, Dan Goode, Charles Morrow, Julie Winter, and the participating "audience" are teamwork. They are learning how to work together without one person's telling another what to do, and these evenings are open to strangers. How many people can work together happily, not just efficiently—happily and unselfishly? A serious question which the future of music will help to answer.

When I received the announcement of the evenings with Philip Corner and his friends, I noticed that no names were given, not even Philip Corner's. However, the announcement was not typeset; it was handwritten. And I recognized Philip Corner's handwriting. The omission of names. Anonymity. People going underground. In order, like Duchamp, to get their work done.

People frequently ask me what my definition of music is. This is it. It is work. That is my conclusion.

However, just as I wrote it, the doorbell rang. It was the postman bringing me a present from William McNaughton, his editing of *Chinese Literature* (an anthology from the earliest times to the present day). The book includes many of McNaughton's own translations. On the endpaper of my copy is a dedication to me followed by fourteen Chinese characters, a reference to page 121, and McNaughton's signature. I turned to page 121 and read the following from his translation of *Chuang-tzu's Book:* "Everybody knows that useful is useful, but nobody knows that useless is useful, too." This is from Chapter 4 of *Chuang-tzu's Book.* A tree is described that gives a great deal of shade. It was very cold and had never been cut down simply because its wood was considered to be of no use to anyone.

I want to tell the story of Thoreau and his setting fire to the woods. I think it is relevant to the practice of music in the present world situation, and it may suggest actions to be taken as we move into the future.

First of all, he didn't mean to set the fire. (He was broiling fish he had caught.) Once it was beyond his control, he ran over two miles unsuccessfully for help. Since there was nothing he could do alone he walked to Fair Haven Cliff, climbed to the highest rock, and sat down upon it to observe the progress of the flames. It was a glorious spectacle, and he was the only one there to see it. From that height he heard bells in the village sounding alarm. Until then he had felt guilty, but knowing that help was coming his attitude changed. He said to himself: "Who are these men who are said to be the owners of these woods, and how am I related to them? I have set fire to the forest, but I have done nothing wrong therein, and it is as if the lightning had done it. These flames are but consuming their natural food."

When the townsmen arrived to fight the fire, Thoreau joined them. It took several hours to subdue the flames. Over one hundred acres were burned. Thoreau noticed that the villagers were generally elated, thankful for the opportunity that had given them so much sport. The only unhappy ones were those whose property had been destroyed. However, one of the owners was obliged to ask Thoreau the shortest way home, even though the path went through the owner's land.

Subsequently, Thoreau met a fellow who was poor, miserable, often drunk, worthless (a burden to society). However, more than any other this fellow was skillful in the burning of brush. Observing his methods and adding his own insights, Thoreau set down a procedure for successfully fighting fires. He also listened to the music a fire makes, roaring and crackling: "You sometimes hear it on a small scale in the log on the hearth."

Having heard the music fire makes and having discussed his fire-fighting method with one of his friends, Thoreau went further: suggesting that along with firemen there be a band of musicians playing instruments to revive the energies of weary firemen and to cheer up those who were not yet exhausted.

Finally he said that fire is not only disadvantage. "It is without doubt an advantage on the whole. It sweeps and ventilates the forest floor, and makes it clear and clean. It is nature's broom. . . . Thus, in the course of two or three years new huckleberry fields are created for birds and for men."

Emerson said that Thoreau could have been a great leader of men, but that he ended up simply as the captain for children of huckleberry picking parties. But Thoreau's writing determined the actions of Martin Luther King and Gandhi and the Danes in their light-hearted resistance to Hitler's invasion. India. Nonviolence.

The useless tree that gave so much shade. The usefulness of the useless is good news for artists. For art serves no material purpose. It has to do with changing minds and spirits. The minds and spirits of people are changing. Not only in New York, but everywhere. I have just returned from Portland in Oregon, from Detroit in Michigan. Friendship is in the air. The change is not disruptive. It is cheerful.

Steve Reich

Music as a Gradual Process

I do not mean the process of composition, but rather pieces of music that are, literally, processes.

The distinctive thing about musical processes is that they determine all the note-to-note (sound-to-sound) details and the overall form simultaneously. (Think of a round or infinite canon.)

I am interested in perceptible processes. I want to be able to hear the process happening throughout the sounding music.

To facilitate closely detailed listening a musical process should happen extremely gradually.

Performing and listening to a gradual musical process resembles:

pulling back a swing, releasing it, and observing it gradually come to rest;

turning over an hour glass and watching the sand slowly run through to the bottom;

placing your feet in the sand by the ocean's edge and watching, feeling, and listening to the waves gradually bury them.

Though I may have the pleasure of discovering musical processes and composing the musical material to run through them, once the process is set up and loaded it runs by itself.

Material may suggest what sort of process it should be run through

Reprinted from *Writings About Music* (New York University, 1974), by permission of the author. Copyright © 1968, 1974 by Steve Reich.

(content suggests form), and processes may suggest what sort of material should be run through them (form suggests content). If the shoe fits, wear it.

As to whether a musical process is realized through live human performance or through some electro-mechanical means is not finally the main issue. One of the most beautiful concerts I ever heard consisted of four composers playing their tapes in a dark hall. (A tape is interesting when it's an interesting tape.)

It is quite natural to think about musical processes if one is frequently working with electro-mechanical sound equipment. All music turns out to be ethnic music.

Musical processes can give one a direct contact with the impersonal and also a kind of complete control, and one doesn't always think of the impersonal and complete control as going together. By "a kind" of complete control I mean that by running this material through this process I completely control all that results, but also that I accept all that results without changes.

John Cage has used processes and has certainly accepted their results, but the processes he used were compositional ones that could not be heard when the piece was performed. The process of using the *I Ching* or imperfections in a sheet of paper to determine musical parameters can't be heard when listening to music composed that way. The compositional processes and the sounding music have no audible connection. Similarly in serial music, the series itself is seldom audible. [This is a basic difference between serial (basically European) music and serial (basically American) art, where the perceived series is usually the focal point of the work.]

What I'm interested in is a compositional process and a sounding music that are one and the same thing.

James Tenney said in conversation, "Then the composer isn't privy to anything." I don't know any secrets of structure that you can't hear. We all listen to the process together since it's quite audible, and one of the reasons it's quite audible is that it's happening extremely gradually.

The use of hidden structural devices in music never appealed to me. Even when all the cards are on the table and everyone hears what is gradually happening in a musical process, there are still enough mysteries to satisfy all. These mysteries are the impersonal, unintended, psychoacoustic by-products of the intended process. These might include submelodies heard within repeated melodic patterns, stereophonic effects due to listener location, slight irregularities in performance, harmonics, difference tones, and so forth.

Listening to an extremely gradual musical process opens my ears to *it*, but *it* always extends further than I can hear, and that makes it interesting to listen to that musical process again. That area of every gradual (completely controlled) musical process, where one hears the details of the sound moving out away from intentions, occurring for their own acoustic reasons, is *it*.

I begin to perceive these minute details when I can sustain close attention and a gradual process invites my sustained attention. By *gradual* I mean extremely gradual; a process happening so slowly and gradually that listening to it resembles watching a minute hand on a watch—you can perceive it moving after you stay with it a little while.

Several currently popular modal musics like Indian classical and drug-oriented rock and roll may make us aware of minute sound details because in being modal (constant key center, hypnotically droning and repetitious) they naturally focus on these details rather than on key modulation, counterpoint and other peculiarly Western devices. Nevertheless, these modal musics remain more or less strict frameworks for improvisation. They are not processes.

The distinctive thing about musical processes is that they determine all the note-to-note details and the overall form simultaneously. One can't improvise in a musical process—the concepts are mutually exclusive.

While performing and listening to gradual musical processes one can participate in a particular liberating and impersonal kind of ritual. Focusing in on the musical process makes possible that shift of attention away from *he* and *she* and *you* and *me* outwards towards *it*.

Richard Foreman

Glass and Snow

Composer Philip Glass and filmmaker Michael Snow are in the vanguard of a small group of artists who have been building upon that contemporary aesthetic which sees the work of art as primarily a structure articulating its "mode of being-present."

> The painter or sculptor is making an object which is clearly "placed" at each encounter—placed contextually within the going contents of the brain, the perceptual fringe, the memory overlay, the ideological overlay.

To a greater or lesser extent, it forces a reorganization of at least certain areas of the consciousness. The power of these minimal, systemic, primary structure space objects lies in the confrontation of the purely *present* (the art-object) with the consciousness mechanism of the spectator, which is no longer purely present as it is encrusted with a web of associational conditioning. As a result, the art-object is unavoidably "object," "other," a realm of "elsewhere," no matter what strategies the artist resorts to in the attempt to create a work that exalts the fact of its presence in the here and now. The viewer's basic task as a "consciousness" is to choose, to say "yes" or "no," to make decisions as to whether or not the newly encountered object-of-presentness has created a unique and valuable experience in his consciousness.

The music of Glass, the films of Snow, do not evoke this same degree of

Reprinted from *Arts Magazine* (February, 1970), by permission of the author and the publisher.

implied "ego-centeredness" as the fulcrum and pivot of the art-experience.

Philip Glass's compositions are all based upon the premise of a performing group of five to eight musicians. All amplified instruments (electric organs, viola, cello, soprano saxophones) play in unison throughout each piece. Only one of his pieces has had to be written up in parts; in every other, each player plays exactly the same notes at the same time, or an intervallic displacement of those notes. In *Music in Fifths* a simple phrase is played by all the musicians in unison; the phrase has a bottom and a top line, identical but for the fact that a fifth separates each simultaneous note. The phrase is repeated in performance between two and eight times—Glass plays and also conducts—depending on the tightness of unison playing and the overall length of the piece. At the point when he feels the group is ready to change, Glass cues the ensemble to proceed to the next section, in which an additional few notes are added to the end of the original phrase. This second phrase is repeated until the performers have again attained the same tightness of unison playing, whereupon new notes are added to this second stage form, and so on through perhaps thirty or so phrases of addition. The piece itself may last from twenty minutes upwards. In recent pieces, such as *Music in Similar Motion* and *Music in Eight Parts*, the introduction of intervallic displacement of some parts leads to a treatment of musical texture in terms of the overall structure. But the method is constant in Philip Glass's music: simple addition allowing for the expansion and contraction of musical phrases, and simultaneous unison playing.

I would relate the "additive" nature of Glass's structure to his own growing vision of his music as primarily a kind of "performance piece" rather than a disembodied sound phenomenon that stands by itself. The compositional exploration of addition and unison playing leads directly to a consciousness that the performers themselves are cellular units who maintain their identity, just as the musical phrase is added to but never manipulated and reshuffled. Unison playing reveals each player as a unit "added" to the next, contrary to the normal situation where performers intertwine their musical lines in such a way that they lose their identity in the service of a composition that exists as a kind of transcendental structure.

This method of composition then is a total rejection of serial method, for process here is the subject rather than the source of the music. The web of lucidly clear, reiterated yet slightly "shifting" sound created by Glass is not to be understood as a disembodied "force" of sound, snatched by the artist out of some normally "unheard" level of sound "elsewhere." The few commentators who have so far written of Glass's music err in linking it to Eastern music (which might indeed be thought of as a sound continuum snatched from elsewhere). Though there is a certain similarity in the texture of shifting sound, Glass's compositions are rather to be understood as performance situations in which musicians (and spectators) put themselves in a certain "place," located through the coordinates of the specific phrase. Then this place—which is not an evocative composed "elsewhere" but rather the here-and-now of a chosen method of procedure—slowly opens, becomes slowly filled and informed with the shared "space" of consciousness which is founded at each moment as the spectator "allows" the piece to exist.

Michael Snow's films are all basically the exploration of a given "idea of presentation " set to work on a particular object. The black and white *New York Eye & Ear Control* examines all the compositional variations available in the placement and manipulation of a positive and negative silhouette of a walking woman in various scenic and social environments; an opposition is created between these basically static images and an intense dynamic sound track. *Wavelength* is a single, slow, forty-five minute zoom down the length of Snow's studio. The light, color and textural variations of the image serve as filmic events on an equal basis with several events involving people. All these events briefly punctuate, at five or ten minute intervals, the unceasing zoom, which ends on a photo of the ocean tacked to the wall at the far end of the studio. An electronic sine wave rises in pitch as the film proceeds with a synchrone sound (street noises, conversations). In *Standard Time* the camera has been set in the center of a room, and it proceeds to pivot, filming the room in smooth circular sweeps. There is some variation in the length and speed of the sweeps, and toward the end a cat, a girl and a turtle are briefly glimpsed; all of this against a sound track of a radio discussion fading in and out in counterpoint to the sweeps of the camera. In *One Second in Montreal* a series of still photos of Montreal covered with snow (A pun? There are flashes of wit in all Snow's films, for all their rigor and shattering intelligence.) fill the screen for a subtly varying period. In the silence one watches what is alive, *now,* in the presented film (the image gently shakes, dirt flashes lightly against each frame . . .), as opposed to other films where one watches that life pictured and alluded to as "elsewhere." As each cut to the next photo is anticipated, one watches the anticipation modulating one's watching. In ←—→, perhaps the most powerful of Snow's films, the camera has been set up in a classroom. Four windows look out upon trees and houses. The camera pans back and forth through approximately 180 degrees with the continuous machine sound in accord with the varying speed of the camera movements, and with a "clunk" at the limit of each pan. The speed of the back and forth movement increases, and, within the panning, there are sometimes jump cuts to pop people into the frame. Sometimes these people disappear after a few frames, sometimes they remain longer and the camera pans back and forth across some ongoing activity in which they are engaged. The camera pans get faster and faster until the image itself blurs, and the pure motion of the pan takes over and becomes the available visual material. At top speed, the pan suddenly becomes an equally fast vertical camera motion, and, as that motion is slowly reduced in speed, we see the camera filming the same room—up and down, up and down. At the end the camera is motionless, and after the titles appear with a brief coda of superimposition of the various camera movements, the film ends with a mysterious blue-white blur.

As in Glass's music, Snow is working in these films not to re-create the image of an intuited or sensed reality that is normally unavailable to consciousness; rather he is taking the material (the view of the room, in Glass's case the musical phrase) and subjecting it to a series of reiterated manipulations in which its elements are held in unchanging relation (there is no cutting in the camera motion, the notes from the phrase are not rearranged). The changes that are slowly introduced respect the integrity of the found image or structure and are specifically designed to show how they sustain themselves under the impact of *time*. Going back and forth over the image or the musical, time is a heavy truck knocking them a little this way, a little that way . . . repeatedly impressing a bit of dirt from the road.

As time rolls over the musical phrase or the selected image, it is also rolling over the spectator; it is a "process" selected as a rule for composition and perception. The initial moment of the spectator's encounter with this art is perhaps not unlike the encounter in spatial art, where consciousness feels the necessity to give a "yes" or "no" to the work. In most previous time-art the work begins and the spectator decides to hold his "yes-no" decision in abeyance. He sees the work is going to develop in time and that development is crucial to a final determination of exactly what the work has done to his consciousness. Glass's music and Snow's films generally succeed in establishing a different kind of relationship to the work of art. The spectator very soon intuits that these structures are *not* developing in the usual way. He is *not* going to be gratified by a series of modulations which will so manipulate and exercise the range of his feeling-tone resources that he will be re-awakened to the full range of his "savoring." This function of stimulating the spectator to "flex his feeling apparatus" is the source of gratification in most Western art; our "yes" or "no" is really determined by whether or not our "feeling" center has been momentarily "re-presented" to the consciousness so that its boundaries can once again be reached.

Glass and Snow have created works which, in a sense, baffle our attempt to derive pleasure in the name of that characterological configuration which is "myself." Rather than creating images of an "elsewhere" that asks our sense of emotional self to wake up and go for a moment to its frontier, their art makes its *process* rather than it resultant object into the mode of "being-present." The reiteration of process is always in the now, and we do not confront its occurring in the same way that we confront an object. We rather test ourselves, our own consciousness continuing in time against the piece's continuing in the same shared time. The only object that is "elsewhere" is the self which experiments with creating different modes of its own problem of "doing something with the attention" as it confronts the on-going structure of the work.

The capacity that the work's process of "being-present" brings to consciousness is not the capacity to "feel," to experience a variation of an internal "yes" or "no"; but rather a capacity of attention in which the internal "noticing" seems cleansed of the need to constantly check whether or not it is pleasure or pain. The noticing of process itself becomes exhilarating—the matching of one's internal on-going time with the piece's "suffering" of a time which is the common possession of piece and spectator.

To clarify this, one should not overlook the importance of the slight variations which occur within the repetitions of this art. Those who claim that Glass and Snow are creating an art basically hypnotic in intent are missing the point. The spectator discovers his consciousness as a nonsubjective faculty— as a Hegelian "spirit" behind all being rather than as a means of being his exclusive self—precisely as he registers the matching and slight mis-match-composition as the piece "drifts" precisely onward in time. Exposure to the piece makes present the factors of memory lag and overlap, a feeling for the slow distortion of process by the time alone, and a kind of tuning to the truth of quantum theory as a basic organizational principle; Glass's music seems to "prove" that change is but the biological or spiritual "blooming into the next stage" after a certain optimal fulfillment of a previous form has been achieved (that is, change when the ideal of unison playing has been attained). In Snow's←— —→, it is as if the initial premise of the back and forth camera motion is a means of letting both the spectator and the room photographed be open to energies which—reflected in the continual *alterations* of speed, etc. that impinge upon the initial movement— are the secret energies of growth and transformation.

Whereas most of the advanced art which has led to the moment of Philip Glass and Michael Snow has created Zen-like moments of confrontation between the impenetrable object and "what we are now," the art of Glass, Snow, and perhaps a few others (composers Steve Reich, LaMonte Young,

Terry Riley; filmmakers Ken Jacobs, Joyce Wieland, Ernie Gehr, Hollis Frampton; and also Yvonne Rainer in dance, Ken Kelman and myself in theatre) is rather a setting into motion of a process that vibrates in such a way that what grows in us is not greater knowledge of the self and its resources but the capacity to let the universe of consciousness (the non-I consciousness) work through us, to be more attuned to the ontological truths and categories.

Most art of the West has taken the form of objects that channeled our consciousness into the work . . . encouraged it to read into the work, to project into it what we are as individuals and "persons" in the full Christian sense of the word. Recent advanced spatial art has put a stop to that; we run into the surface of such work and are thrown back upon ourselves. But in a sense, the work is then a mirror that still returns us to the self that has just "suffered" (in the best, wisdom-giving sense of the word) a collision. The new time-art of Glass and Snow, because it does go on in time and because the drift of regular change built into the work keeps us from settling back to use the work as a mere reflecting-glass (useful as that might be in itself) opens a new dimension in art. No longer images and relics brought back by artists from the spiritual "beyond," it is the building of a house within which the spectator, in order to simply *notice* the work itself, *must* replace himself so that he is no longer confronting an object, but putting "himself-as-self" elsewhere, so that naked presence is the mode and matter of the artistic experience.

Merce Cunningham

The Impermanent Art

There has been a shift of emphasis in the practice of the arts of painting, music and dancing during the last few years. There are no labels yet but there are ideas. These ideas seem primarily concerned with something being exactly what it is in its time and place, and not in its having actual or symbolic reference to other things. A thing is just that thing. It is good that each thing be accorded this recognition and this love. Of course, the world being what it is—or the way we are coming to understand it now—we know that each thing is also every other thing, either actually or potentially. So we don't, it seems to me, have to worry ourselves about providing relationships and continuities and orders and structures—they cannot be avoided. They are the nature of things. They are ourselves and our materials and our environment. If a dancer dances—which is not the same as having theories about dancing or wishing to dance or trying to dance or remembering in his body someone else's dance—but if a dancer *dances*, everything is there. The meaning is there, if that's what you want. It's like this apartment where I live—I look around in the morning and ask myself, what does it all mean? It means: this is where I live. When I dance, it means: this is what I am doing. A thing is just that thing. In painting, now, we are beginning to see the painting and not the painter nor the painted. We are beginning to see how a painted space is. In music, we are beginning to hear free of our well-tempered ears.

In dance, it is the simple fact of a jump being a jump, and the further fact of what shape the jump takes. This attention given the jump eliminates

Reprinted from *Seven Arts* (Indian Hills, CO, 1955), by permission of the author. Copyright 1955 by Merce Cunningham.

the necessity to feel that the meaning of dancing lies in everything but the dancing, and further eliminates cause-and-effect worry as to what movement should follow what movement, frees one's feelings about continuity, and makes it clear that each act of life can be its own history: past, present and future, and can be so regarded, which helps to break the chains that too often follow dancers' feet around.

There doesn't seem to be the need to expound any longer on the idea that dance is as much a part of life as anything else. Since it takes place in one form or another almost constantly, that is evidence enough. The play of bodies in space—and time. When I choreograph a piece by tossing pennies—by chance, that is—I am finding my resources in that play, which is not the product of *my* will, but which is an energy and a law that I too obey. Some people seem to think that it is inhuman and mechanistic to toss pennies in creating a dance instead of chewing the nails or beating the head against a wall or thumbing through old notebooks for ideas. But the feeling I have when I compose in this way is that I am in touch with a natural resource far greater than my own personal inventiveness could ever be, much more universally human than the particular habits of my own practice, and organically rising out of common pools of motor impulses.

Since dance as a part of life seems self-evident enough—a few words about what dance is not. "Not this, not that." Dance is not social relationships. Though it may influence them. Dance is not emoting, passion for her, anger against him. I think dance is more primal than that. In its essence, in the nakedness of its energy it is a source from which passion or anger may issue in a particular form, the source of energy out of which may be channeled the energy that goes into the various emotional behaviors. It is that blatant exhibiting of this energy, that is, of energy geared to an intensity high enough to melt steel in some dancers, that gives the great excitement. This is not feeling about something, this is a whipping of the mind and body into an action that is so intense, that for the brief moment involved, the mind and body are one. The dancer knows how solidly he must be aware of this centering when he dances. And it is just this very fusion at a white heat that gives the look of objectivity and serenity that a fine dancer has.

Our ecstasy in dance comes from the possible gift of freedom, the exhilarating moment that this exposing of the bare energy can give us. What is meant is not license, but freedom, that is, a complete awareness of the world and at the same time a detachment from it.

In the thinking about contemporary dance, I am concerned here with the concert dance, I find that it is the connection with the immediacy of the action, the single instant, that gives the feeling of man's freedom. The body shooting into space is not an idea of man's freedom, but is the body shooting into space. And that very action is all other actions, and is man's freedom, and at the same instant his nonfreedom. You see how it is no trouble at all to get profound about dance. It seems to be a natural double for metaphysical paradox.

In reference to the current idea that dance must be expressive of something and that it must be involved with the images deep within our conscious and unconscious, it is my impression that there is no need to push for them. If these primordial, pagan or otherwise archetypical images lie deep within us, they will appear, regardless of our likes and dislikes, once the way is open. It is simply a matter of allowing it to happen. The dancer's discipline, his daily rite, can be looked at in this way: to make it possible for the spirit to move through his limbs and to extend its manifestations into space, with all its freedom and necessity. I am no more philosophical than my legs, but from them I sense this fact: that they are infused with energy that can be released in movement (to appear to be motionless is its own kind of intoxicating movement)—that the shape the movement takes is beyond the fathoming of my mind's analysis but clear to my eyes and rich to my imagination. In other words, a man is a two-legged creature—more basically and more intimately than he is anything else. And his legs speak more than they "know"—and so does all nature. So if you really dance—your body, that is, and not your mind's enforcement—the manifestations of the spirit through your torso and your limbs will inevitably take on the shape of life. We give ourselves away at every moment. We do not, therefore, have to try to do it. Our racial memory, our ids and egos, whatever it is, is there. If it is there, it is there; we do not need to pretend that we have to put it there. In one of my most recent solo works, called "Untitled Solo," I choreographed the piece with the use of "chance" methods. However, the dance as performed seems to have an unmistakable dramatic intensity in its bones, so to speak. It seems to me that it was simply a question of "allowing" this quality to happen rather than of "forcing" it. It is this "tranquility" of the actor or dancer which seems to me essential. A tranquility that allows him to detach himself and thereby *to present* freely and liberally. Making of himself such a kind of nature puppet that he is as if dancing on a string which is like an umbilical cord:—mother-nature and father-spirit moving his limbs, without thought.

My use of chance methods in finding continuity for dances is not a position that I wish to establish and die defending. It is a present mode of freeing my imagination from its own clichés and it is a marvelous adventure in attention. Our attention is, normally, highly selective and highly editorial. But try looking at events another way and the whole world of gesture, the whole physical world in fact, is as if jabbed by an electric current.

It has been a growing interest in "each thing-ness" that has led me to the use of chance methods in finding dance continuity.[1] In my case, and for one particular work, this involved an elaborate use of charts from which came the particular movements, the rhythm (that is, the division and the duration of the time they were done in), and the space they appear in and how they divide it. There were separate charts for each of the three elements—movement, time, and space. Then I tossed pennies to select a movement from the movement chart, and this was followed by tossing pennies to find the duration of that particular movement, and following that the space and direction of the movement were tossed for. This method might lead one to suspect the result as being possibly geometric and "abstract," unreal and non-human. On the contrary, it is no more geometric than the lines of a mountain are, seen from an airplane; it is no more abstract than any human being is, and as for reality, it is just that, it is not abstracted from something else, but is the thing itself, and moreover allows each dancer to be just as human as he is.

One of the things that has interested me for a long time, is how our balance works, not the fact that we can balance in many different ways and so find out how many ways, but just that we do balance at all, and how. On two legs or one. Dancing has two things in it: balance of the weight, and shift of that weight in space and time, that is, in greater or smaller areas, and over longer or shorter lengths of time. It depends upon the flexibility of the architecture of the body. The variety of that flexibility is limited only by the imagination of the dancer and you can see where that has brought us already. I suppose there are actually relatively few movements that we do, and it's probably most pleasant for the dancer in his searching for movement if he lights upon one of these in a straightforward simple way. Lack of fullness in a particular movement, or exaggeration of a movement outside the particular limits of its own shape and rhythm produces mannerism, I should think. And, equally so, the fullest possible doing of a particular movement with the minimum necessity of visible energy and the clearest precision in each element of that movement might possibly produce style. But when this is allowed to go out the window for further effect, prolongation of pose for bravura or other such delights of the performer's ego, then the first thing lost is serenity, and in the rush to catch up, the dancer stumbles, expressively if not physically.

Buckminster Fuller, the architect, once spoke of his feeling that man had migrated around the globe via two means: with the wind, that is under sail and perhaps eastward generally; and against the wind, that is across the land. This image of movement and resistance somehow makes me think of how an idea of mobile and static could be witnessed in the ways a dancer can be trained. The prime motivation can either be made a static one, that is by letting the position of the torso come first within the possibilities of its flexibility, and then to that adding the activity of its legs, or the prime motivation can be put in the legs, making a mobile situation upon which the back and upper limbs rest. This all presumes that a relationship runs up and down the spine into the arms and legs, to begin with, and that the base of the torso where the legs joint the back both stops the action of the limbs and allows it to continue. And the wondrousness of being free and clear with both of these bodily components at the same time!

But the pleasure of dance does not lie in its analysis, though one might sometimes be led to think otherwise. Dancing is a lively human activity which by its very nature is part of all of us, spectators and performers alike. It's not the discussion, it's the doing and seeing—of whatever kind. As an adolescent I took lessons in various forms of American popular stage dancing including tap and a kind of exhibition ballroom. But my teacher insisted there was not such a thing as just "tap," there was the "waltz clog," "the southern soft shoe," "the buck and wing," and all were different, and she would proceed to show us how they were different. The rhythm in each case was the inflecting force that gave each particular dance its style and color. The tempo for a slower dance, for instance, allowed for a certain weight and swing and stopping of the arms that wasn't indicated in a faster dance. These lessons eventually led to performances in various halls as the entertainers for local events and finally a short and intoxicating "vaudeville tour." I remember one of these situations when we (there were four of us), stood huddled and cold in a sort of closet that was the lone dressing room, behind the tiny platform that was the stage this time, and our teacher was in the front of the hall making last minute preparations. Finally she hurried back, took one look at the four of us, and smiled and said, "All right, kids, we haven't any make-up, so bite your lips and pinch your cheeks, and you're on." It was a kind of theatre energy and devotion she radiated. This was a devotion to dancing as an instantaneous and agreeable act of life. All my subsequent involvements with dancers who were concerned with dance as a conveyor of social message or to be used as a testing ground for psychological types have not succeeded in destroying that feeling Mrs. J.W. Barrett gave me, that dance is most deeply concerned with each single instant as it comes along, and its life and vigor and attraction lie in just that singleness. It is as accurate and impermanent as breathing.

Yvonne Rainer

A Quasi-Survey of Some "Minimalist" Tendencies in the Quantitatively Minimal Dance Activity Midst the Plethora

	Objects		Dances
		eliminate	
		or	
		minimize	

Objects	Dances
1. role of artist's hand	1. phrasing
2. hierarchical relationships of parts	2. development and climax
3. texture	3. variation: rhythm, shape, dynamics·
4. figure reference	4. character
5. illusionism	5. performance
6. complexity and detail	6. variety: phases and the spatial field
7. monumentality	7. the virtuosic feat and the fully extended body

substitute

1. factory fabrication	1. energy equality and "found" movement
2. unitary forms, modules	2. equality of parts, repetition
3. uninterrupted surface	3. repetition or discrete events
4. nonreferential forms	4. neutral performance
5. literalness	5. task or tasklike activity
6. simplicity	6. singular action, event,
7. human scale	7. human scale or tone

Although the benefit to be derived from making a one-to-one relationship between aspects of so-called minimal sculpture and recent dancing is questionable, I have drawn up a chart that does exactly that. Those who need alternatives to subtle distinction-making will be elated, but nevertheless such a device may serve as a shortcut to ploughing through some of the things that have been happening in a specialized area of dancing and once stated can be ignored or culled from at will.

It should not be thought that the two groups of elements are mutually exclusive ("eliminate" and "substitute"). Much work being done today—both in theater and art—has concerns in both categories. Neither should it be thought that the type of dance I shall discuss has been influenced exclusively by art. The changes in theater and dance reflect changes in ideas about man and his environment that have affected all the arts. That dance should reflect these changes at all is of interest, since for obvious reasons it has always been the most isolated and inbred of the arts. What is perhaps unprecedented in the short history of the modern dance is the close correspondence between concurrent developments in dance and the plastic arts.

Isadora Duncan went back to the Greeks; Humphrey and Graham[1] used primitive ritual and/or music for structuring, and although the people who came out of the Humphrey-Graham companies and were active during the thirties and forties shared socio-political concerns and activity in common with artists of the period, their work did not reflect any direct influence from or dialogue with the art so much as a reaction to the time. (Those who took off in their own directions in the forties and fifties—Cunningham, Shearer, Litz, Marsicano, et al.—must be appraised individually. Such a task is beyond the scope of this article.) The one previous area of correspondence might be German expressionism and Mary Wigman and her followers, but photographs and descriptions of the work show little connection.

Within the realm of movement invention—and I am talking for the time being about movement generated by means other than accomplishment of a task or dealing with an object—the most impressive change has been in the attitude to phrasing, which can be defined as the way in which energy is distributed in the execution of a movement or series of movements. What makes one kind of movement different from another is not so much variations in arrangements of parts of the body as differences in energy investment.

It is important to distinguish between real energy and what I shall call "apparent" energy. The former refers to actual output in terms of physical expenditure on the part of the performer. It is common to hear a dance teacher tell a student that he is using "too much energy" or that a particular movement does not require "so much energy." This view of energy is related to a notion of economy and ideal movement technique. Unless otherwise indicated, what I shall be talking about here is "apparent" energy, or what is seen in terms of motion and stillness rather than of actual work, regardless of the physiological or kinesthetic experience of the dancer. The two observations—that of the performer and that of the spectator—do not always correspond. A vivid illustration of this is my *Trio A:* Upon completion, two of us are always dripping with sweat while the third is dry. The correct conclusion to draw is not that the dry one is expending less energy, but that the dry one is a "nonsweater."

Much of the Western dancing we are familiar with can be characterized by a particular distribution of energy: maximal output or "attack" at the beginning of a phrase[2], recovery at the end, with energy often arrested somewhere in the middle. This means that one part of the phrase—usually the part that is the most still—becomes the focus of attention, registering like a photograph or suspended moment of climax. In the Graham-oriented modern dance these climaxes can come one on the heels of the other. In types of dancing that depend on less impulsive controls, the climaxes are farther apart and are not so dramatically "framed." Where extremes in tempi are imposed, this ebb-and-flow of effort is also pronounced: in the instance of speed the contrast between movement and rest is sharp, and in the adagio, or supposedly continuous kind of phrasing, the execution of transitions demonstrates more subtly the mechanics of getting from one point of still "registration" to another.

The term *phrase* can also serve as a metaphor for a longer or total duration containing beginning, middle, and end. Whatever the implications of a continuity that contains high points or focal climaxes, such an approach now seems to be excessively dramatic and more simply unnecessary.

Energy has also been used to implement heroic more-than-human technical feats and to maintain a more-than-human look of physical extension, which is familiar as the dancer's muscular set. In the early days of the Judson Dance Theatre someone wrote an article and asked, "Why are they so intent on just being themselves?" It is not accurate to say that everyone at that time had this in mind. (I certainly didn't; I was more involved in experiencing a lion's share of ecstacy and madness than in "being myself" or doing a job.) But where the question applies, it might be answered on two levels: 1) The artifice of performance has been reevaluated in that action, or what one does, is more interesting and important than the exhibition of character and attitude, and that action can best be focused on through the submerging of the personality; so ideally one is not even oneself, one is a neutral "doer." 2) The display of technical virtuosity and the display of the dancer's specialized body no longer make any sense. Dancers have been driven to search for an alternative context that allows for a more matter-of-fact, more concrete, more banal quality of physical being in performance, a context wherein people are engaged in actions and movements making a less spectacular demand on the body and in which skill is hard to locate.

It is easy to see why the *grand jeté* (along with its ilk) had to be abandoned. One cannot "do" a *grand jeté*; one must "dance" it to get it done at all, that is, invest it with all the necessary nuances of energy distribution that will produce the look of climax together with a still, suspended extension in the middle of the movement. Like a romantic, overblown plot this particular kind of display—with its emphasis on nuance and skilled accomplishment, its accessibility to comparison and interpretation, its involvement with connoisseurship, its introversion, narcissism, and self-congratulatoriness— has finally in this decade exhausted itself, closed back on itself, and perpetuates itself solely by consuming its own tail.

The alternatives that were explored now are obvious; stand, walk, run, eat, carry bricks, show movies, or move or be moved by some *thing* rather than oneself. Some of the early activity in the area of self-movement utilized games, "found" movement (walking, running), and people with no previous training. (One of the most notable of these early efforts was Steve Paxton's solo, *Transit,* in which he performed movement by "marking" it. "Marking" is what dancers do in rehearsal when they do not want to expend the full amount of energy required for the execution of a given movement. It has a very special look, tending to blur boundaries between consecutive movements.) These descriptions are not complete. Different people have sought different solutions.

Paul Sharits

Words Per Page

Can we begin in the present? If film is to be "an art," it will measure itself in terms of the maturity, rigor and complexity of the "other arts" (advanced painting, dance, sculpture, music, and so on). Although the specific problems of film (temporal) are not the same as the problems of, say, sculpture (spatial), there seem to be some general aesthetic interests shared by contemporary arts (one of which is, "paradoxically," *self-definition*—"painting as the subject of painting," etc.). Being "contemporary" is not a simplistic matter of being "abstract" rather than "realistic" in subject choice; probably any "content" is valid—what is more problematic is attitude and systems of forming. Certain attitudes (nonintellectual, nonreflective, self-indulgent, noncritical, "intuitive-emotional") seem a bit out of place in the 1970s. Certain forms of organization ("the story," "metaphor-allegory," reference to "psychological states") seem to be somewhat expended. Older forms need not be negated but can become transformed through radical restructuring (Bresson and Dreyer) or through a purification wherein, say, "the story" may become "direct autobiography" (Jonas Mekas' *Diaries*) and then "investigation" or "measurement'" or "document" (wherein the less interesting the subject is, the more interesting the procedure of recording becomes: methodology as subject matter; "the story" as a map of actual behavior). I would like you, in this "course," to regard your art as *research,* research in contempo-

This essay was originally presented in 1970 as an introduction to a course in film production at Antioch College. Reprinted from *Afterimage,* no. 4 (Autumn, 1972), by permission of the author. Copyright © 1972 by Paul Sharits.

rary communication and "meaning" systems. Anticipating objections that this may be "sterile" and/or "nonexpressive," I would like to suggest that current research methodologies such as general systems, information and communication theory, structuralism, cybernetics, and others which are more involved with "form/function" than with "content/substance" are not isolated nonhumanistic fads. Because they are increasingly significant in anthropology, linguistics, sociology, economics, natural sciences, community planning, communication and transportation systems, engineering, medicine, psychology, and so forth, they are *defining our environment* and, as such, they must have some significant implications for culturally relevant art.

Before saying anything more about film, it is necessary to point out a few general concepts that have emerged in the last several years in painting and new three-dimensional work. The idea of "wholeness" is obviously not new, but recently it has taken on a meaning different than the accepted "organic unity" principle, which Eisenstein stated so lucidly: " . . . in an organic work of art, elements that nourish the work as a whole pervade all the features composing this work. A unified canon pierces not only the whole and each of its parts, but also each element that is called to participate in the work of composition. One and the same principle will feed any element, appearing in each in a qualitatively different form. Only in this case are we justified in considering a work of art organic, the notion 'organism' being used in the sense which Engels spoke of it in his 'Dialectics of Nature':"The organism is certainly a *higher unity*." ("The composition of *Potemkin*") This idea of a unity of tensional relationships ("collisional montage"), and Kandinsky's, Mondrian's, and Malevich's ideas of "dynamic" asymmetrical balance are quite different from Pollock's influential nonrelational unity of the entire visual field; Pollock's "overallness," directness, flatness gives his works the "presence" of autonomous objects. In all cases, in the structural "self-sufficiency" of early nonobjective art and in the literalness of recent work, an attempt is made to segregate the works from "reality," so that the works take their place as a part of rather than representative of that reality; the works define rather than mimic actuality. "Objecthood" is achieved by: intensification of materiality (repetitive stress of "flaws" in a process, over-use of a variable, accumulation, intersection, allowing materials to shape themselves, and so forth); equal internal division of parts to create a sense of isotropism and to allow an easy enough gestalt so that the whole seems nonrelational; use of a priori systems of serial or nonhierarchical or chance or random or numerical ordering. Often serial structuring has the dynamic effect of shifting organization of the whole out of the work so that the perceiving mind is actively engaged in perceptual and conceptual creation. Before rejecting the viability of systematic approaches, because they sound "mechanical" and "nonemotional," think of the power of Bach's *Art of the Fugue*; at the very least, a priori decisions regarding ordering or nonordering have heuristic value in that surprising forms may emerge from their use which could never be preconceived or developed intuitively. Along with these phenomenological means, new ontological approaches have been highly developed. "Self-reference," through both formal tautology (as in Stella's edge-referring internal surface division in his "striped" paintings) and conceptual tautology (as in Johns's early "target," "map," and "flag" paintings) generate convincingly self-sufficient works.

When André Bazin asks "What is Cinema?" he answers by describing the interesting ways in which cinema has been *used* to tell stories, enlarge upon theatre, cinematize "human themes." If we dispense with such nonfilmic answers, do we have anything left? I believe that we can turn away from the cinema that began with Lumière (*using* cinema to create illusions of nonfilm movement), and which developed through Méliès, Griffith, Eisenstein, and so on up to today's Bergman, Fellini, and others, and we can ask a new set of questions that greatly *expand* the possibilities of the system. There is no doubt that there is a great deal of value in the nonfilmic tradition of cinema, in the accepted descriptions of cinema as illusionistic representation and as "documentary"; but any further developments of these areas, without acute reappraisal of their metaphysical premises, will lead most probably to mere elaborations and effete indulgences in a time of massive cultural transvaluation. This is not to say that cinema *should be*, say, "nonrepresentational." Film, "motion picture" and "still" film, unlike painting and sculpture, can acheive an autonomous presence without negating iconic reference because the phenomenology of the system includes "recording" as a physical fact. And the linear-temporal physicality of motion pictures allows for a kind of "representation" suggested by Barthes in his essay "The Activity of Structuralism":

> The aim of all structuralist activity, in the fields of both thought and poetry is to reconstitute an "object," and, by this process, to make known the rules of functioning, of "functions," of this object. The structure is therefore effectively a representation of the object, but it is a representation that is both purposeful and relevant, since the object derived by imitation brings out something that remained invisible or, if you like, unintelligible in the natural object. The structuralist takes reality, decomposes it, and recomposes it again... *something new* is brought into being, and this new element is nothing less than intelligibility: the representation is intellect added to the object. . . (the structuralist activity derives) from a *mimesis,* founded not on the analogy of substances (as in "realist" art), but on the analogy of functions. . . .

Not denying the viability of this proposition, I would extend this "mimeticism" (by involution) and suggest that the "recording" of the structure-process of recording can free cinema from referring to anything beyond itself; cinema can then *legitimately* become "meaningless" *syntax.* It is, of course, too soon to define limits; numerous areas provoke interest and potentiality—some involve first-order mimeticism and some do not. The question "What is cinema?" is rather *open.* At moments, when faced with the overwhelming, confusing clutter of physical and conceptual definitions of *cinema*, that set of random anthropomorphic accumulations which is only understandable in its contradictoriness and is only recognizable in its proliferation of ersatz complexities, it seems best to abandon attempts at functional redefinition and simply make a fresh start. The word *language,* with its muddled definitions, is a worse point of departure for an understanding of human communication than is the more precise concept of "linguistics." Perhaps the vague term *cinema* should be abandoned with all its anthropomorphic, pseudopsychological presuppositions and, instead, the less fashionable term *cinematics* should be used as a base for our fresh systems. A lot could be gained from a study of linguistics if one wished to build a comprehensive and usable "cinematics" model. As a process, film is related to language in that both are, on many levels, linear systems; for example, "the sound wave emanating from the mouth of a speaker is physically a continuum" (Malmberg, *Structural Linguistics and Human Communication*)—this is easily demonstrated by looking at the way speech is patterned on an optical soundtrack of a film. And, as Ferdinand de Saussure pointed out, "The signifier, being auditory, is unfolded solely in time from which it gets the following characteristics: (a) it represents a span, and (b) the span is measurable in a single dimension; it is a line." (*Course in General Linguistics*). I am not prepared to make or support at this time the hypothesis that "cinematics" is a viable analogue of "linguistics," but I am convinced that thought in this direction is not without value; it is easy to see how the concepts in the following quotation are relevant to such a case: "A structure, according to everyday usage, is made up of parts or elements having a certain mutual relationship, as opposed to a mere accumulation of mutually independent items. If human language is said to be structured, this should be understood in such a way that any language is built up of so-called discrete elements (that is, sharply delimited from each other and without any possible gradual passage from one to the other). Language consequently is analyzable into minimal independent units, which are restricted in number and the functions of which are determined by their relations to the other units with which they are combined, within a system of communication possibilities (a paradigm) and within the actual speech sequence, the chain (or the syntagm) . . . . If linguistics is called structural, this consequently implies that its main concern is the description and analysis of its functional units (its discrete elements) and of the relationship between these" (Malmberg). We see that it is highly problematic which of the parameters of "cinema" can be legitimately regarded as "elements"; in fact, it is clear that our definition of what we shall regard as our "morphemes" and "phonemes" will predetermine what paradigms we can create. How can we discover "elements"? Certainly not by conceptual logic alone. William Burroughs suggested that his "cut-up" writing method could reveal the essence of a political speech more easily than a careful analysis of the unaltered speech; that is, cut the thing apart and scan over the random reassembly of words and phrases and the deeper logic of the statement becomes glaringly apparent. A method of empirically probing the cinema system, aside from looking at the system one part at a time, is to allow several redundant and permuting parts to "rub against each other" in time; emergents from such systematic interactions can be regarded as "natural" macroscopic representations of "microscopic" "cinematic" elements. So-called "defective parts," which in "cinema" are regarded as "mistakes" are probably the most adequate parts to deal with in "cinematics" approach; obviously, flaws reveal the fabric and "cinematics" is the art of the cinema's fabric. (For the sake of brevity, I have decided not to develop the "cinematics" model any further in this introduction; so, I will most often use the conventional term *cinema*, rather than "cinematics" when referring to our "subject"; however, before leaving "cinematics," it is worth noting that because this approach is structural-informational, because it provides a means of creating powerfuly *direct* perceptions, it is as fruitful an approach for the politically motivated filmmaker as it is for pure researchers. Godard has begun to understand this in newer works such as *One Plus One*, where he seems to be cautiously moving away from traditional narrative-dramatic molds towards the sort of compellingly blunt recording style Warhol has invented. But these are not convincing examples for the truly radical political filmmaker because while Godard's films "contain" political sentiments they are not ultimately politically *activating,* because they are viewed not by the "masses," who need to be activated, but by a group of persons who are no doubt already convinced of at least the possibility that a form of revolution is occurring. Truly effective political statements have not been made yet; however, the important experimental filmmakers working in Russia after the Revolution of 1917, by scrutinizing what they believed to be the *syntax* of film, came closest in making *radicalizing* films.)

Stan Brakhage's massive work is too expansive in its implications and richness to discuss here except to mention that his use of the camera as a behavioral extension, his forceful modulation of disjunctive, "distractive" "mistakes" (blurs, splices, flares, frame lines, flash frames) and his decomposition-reconstitution of "subjects" in editing, because of their cinematically self-referential qualities (they reveal the system by which they are made), bring cinema up to date with the other advanced arts. And, in another manner, Andy Warhol has demonstrated in his early work that *prolongations* of subject (redundant, nonmotion pictures) because they deflect attention finally to the material process of recording-projecting (to the *succession* of film *frames*, and by way of consciousness of film grain, scratches, and dirt particles, to the sense of the *flow* of the celluloid *strip*), it is perhaps as revealing of the "nature of cinema" as is consistent interruption of "normative" cinematic functions.

At one point some artists felt that painting had evolved irretrievably away from "reference." Delaunay even believed that he was not only making "nonobjective" but also "shapeless" (pure-color) paintings. Because his semantic culture set did not recognize, as we recognize today, that regularly bounded color fields can be regarded as subsets of the concept "shape," he was unaware of the referential nature of his forms. Definitions of "reality" change. It is hard today to make distinctions between what is "nonobjective" and what is "symbolic" and/or "referential." "Reference" is no longer an adequate axis of differentiation, but there are those who still hold simplistic notions about the "intrinsic realism" of film (Kracauer). Further, most critics and historians still regard the *tentative* experience of perceiving a film as "more real," in their definitions of cinema, than holding in their hand a nontentative strip of celluloid that has a measurable length and width and that has a measurable series of "frames," degrees of opacity, and so on. It is interesting to consider some phenomenological differences between painting, music, and film: in viewing painting, our experience is changing while the painting's existence is enduring; in music, both our experience and the existence of the music are changing; however, in film we have a case where we can experience both a changing and an enduring existence—we can look at the "same" film as an *object*, before or after projection (and it is not a "score"; it is "the film"), and as temporal *process*, while it is being "projected" on the stable support of the screen. This equivocality of object/projection is further complicated when we admit that there are occasions when we are looking at a screen and we don't know whether we are or are not seeing "a film"; we cannot distinguish "the movie" from "the projection." Let us say that the room is dark and the screen is white; we may believe that the projector is simply throwing light on the screen, because there is no indication that a film is being shown; yet, in fact, the projector may be casting *images* of a succession of clear-blank frames onto the screen, projecting not "light" but *a picture* which represents motion (the motion of the strip of film being projected); so, unless we are in the projection booth and thus experience both the film as object and as projection, this "viewing" would be incomprehensible. Even Cage's "silent" piece for piano does not present this problem because we can see the performer "nonperforming" the music without having to look "behind the scene."

There are even deeper implications issuing from the apparent dualism of film's "being" in that those who acknowledge only the projected "movie" as a source of their metaphysics tend to impose a value hierarchy that recognizes the frame and the strip of film only as potential distractions to the flow of a "higher" process, that temporal abstraction, "the shot." Notice that in the normative cinema we neither see the motion of the film strip (unless the strip is scratched) nor are we aware of a succession of frame units (unless the projector is "improperly framed"). The cameramen who shoot such "movies" utterly and disdainfully ignore the frame structure of their medium; when the cameraman "frames" a "shot" he is thinking in image boundary abstractions rather than acknowledging the basic modularity of his image support. On the other hand, a filmmaker like Man Ray, in his *Return to Reason,* directs attention to *the fact* of film's frame structure in his rayogram constructed passages where there is *discontinuity* from frame to frame. Brakhage, in *Mothlight*, allows the natural length of his "subjects" to determine their duration on the screen—in the unforgettable passage where it seems as if a long thin leaf is *passing us* (rather than it seeming as if the camera is tracking over the leaf), we get an immediate fix on the film strip *process* which is in fact occurring; this remarkable film "feels frameless" and congruently, *has no frame lines!*

This problematic equivocality of film's "being" is perhaps cinema's most basic ontological issue. George Landow's films coherently frame these issues, particularly *Film in Which There Appear Sprocket Holes, Edge Lettering, Dirt Particles, Etc.,* wherein one becomes involved in the perceptual differentiation of the dirt/scratches as image (those which refer to the printed frame) and the dirt/scratches that are actually on the surface of the particular print, the particular *strip* of film passing through the projector. One is reminded of Vermeer's multiple mappings of mapping procedures in *The Painter in His Studio.*

To begin getting a clear perspective on these complex questions, it would be valuable to regard cinema as an informational system, rather than starting with a priori metaphysical theories or with a fully developed aesthetic or with the kind of exclamatory presumptions that Vertov's "Kino Eye" concept typifies (the drawing of morphological analogies between the human body and the nonhuman instruments). Let us investigate the system as it exists in a descriptive, concrete modality of comprehension. It would be a mistake to be initially concerned with the *intentions* that formed the system, the naive pseudo-aesthetic that "caused" the technological development of photography ("capturing a likeness of the world") and cinematography ("capturing a likeness of the world in motion")—after all, the system exists today, with or without our "intention" that it do this or that. The system simply exists, and a taxonomy of its basic elements seems a more appropriate beginning for analysis than propounding rashly abstract, speculative "reasons" *for* its existence. This latter case, in its simple overgeneralizing, has led, from the very beginning, to premature, so-called "languages of the film," "grammars of the film." Such a beginning accounts for the normative postulate that "the shot" is one of cinema's irreducible particulars. As if their remarks were analytically suggestive, "informed cineastes" speak of "mise en scène." My hypothesis does not exclude the formation of higher abstraction classification; I only suggest that there is nothing to be gained by starting with highly abstract and highly questionable presuppositions. Lumière was so emphatic in his belief in "the shot" that he constructed both the internal structure and external boundaries of his films with one and the same shot.

A listing of elements is confounded by the object/projection "dualism"; but at least a crude breakdown of the modes that the system can embody can be made; this seems necessary before "elements" can be located. There are at least: processes of intending to make a film; processes of recording light patterns on raw stock (films can be made that bypass this mode); processes of processing; processes of editing; processes of printing; processes of projecting; and processes of experiencing. The problem of whether or not "concepts" like "intention" are "elements" complicates the issue; that is to say, even those "things" that are observable, such as "emulsion grains," can be shown to be essentially "concepts." Remembering this difficulty, a partial list of elements that can be observed should be made as a (tentative) fundamental frame of reference. We can observe cameras, projectors, and other pieces of equipment and their parts and their parts' functions (shutters, numerous circular motions of parts, focus, and so on). We can observe the support itself, its emulsions before and after "exposure," sprocket holes, frames, and so on. We can observe the effects of light *on* film and, likewise, we can note the effects of light *passing through* the film and illuminating a reflective support. There is a remarkable structural parallel, which is suggestive of new systems of filmic organization, between a piece of film and the projections of light through it; both are simultaneously corpuscular ("frames") and wave-like ("strip").

Warhol, in his early "static" films, by disregarding the normative idea that a film is composed of parts and that its time-scale (its duration) is the sum of those heterogeneous parts, made the important discovery that the internal structure of a film (the natural duration of its "subject") could define, be congruent to, be a parallel of, the perimeter of a film's shape; this is a temporal analogy to Jasper Johns's making the edge of his "flag" works congruent with their surface area image. Ironically, this freed film from its "scale" being dependent upon arbitrary subject-orientated judgments; now we see that even when there are internal subdivisions in a film, the "edge" of the film can be *generated by*, rather than arbitrarily *contain*, the internal structure of the film; a sort of natural ("necessary") wholeness is possible. As P. Adams Sitney has pointed out, the edges of the temporal shape of some new films are highly emphasized; this is because a film's shape, its time-surface area is comprehensible as a discrete unit. The factor of "wholeness" is central to this discreteness. In time, this wholeness is sensed in homogeneous structured works as a *constantly simultaneous gestalt,* whereas in developmental works, senses of linear direction *through* nonsimultaneous, nonredundant time gives a sense of coherent overall duration-shape (in other words, the "edges" of the duration-shape of a film are not just the beginning and ending measurements but have as much to do with defining the shape [s] of the time after the film begins being projected and all during the projection until the film stops being projected); in these works, which appear to have the kind of cohesiveness wherein shape and edge are indistinguishable, one cannot speak of "beginning" and "end" because that implies a fragmentation of the film's shape and a truly one-part temporal shape cannot be apprehended as such if we can make it *three* discrete shapes ("beginning," "ending," and "middle"). What an irony it is that such a discrete shape does not have the boundaries of beginning and ending! Somehow, these new films achieve the quality of being revelatory fragments of a larger system that is patterned after the prototype of the film itself. Warhol's "actual scale," in works like *Sleep* and *Empire*, because it documents cyclic ideas such as sleep/wakefulness/ sleep and night/day/night obviously implies larger cyclic systems; another homogeneous work, Snow's *Dripping Water,* does not imply a cycle of any kind because there is no predictable measure of where the dripping began or ended or whether it even began or will end—so, since there is no definable boundary such as an "end," this noncyclic work implies that it is a segment of a larger noncyclic system. One can conceive of many forms of homogeneous and nonhomogeneous overall time-shapes. In what senses can these shapes be regarded as cinematic? Snow understood the vectorial implications of the projector light beam and this seems to account at least in part for *Wavelength's* directional structure. Physically, the conic shape is directive toward the projector lens; yet, we sense the internal projectiveness of the beam directing itself toward the screen, as if magnitude was its target. In 1966 I became aware of the projector beam, in a piece called *Unrolling Movie Screen,* and to a certain extent allowed the beam's projective and volumetric vectorial characteristics to inform the overall structuring of the piece. The piece involved the projection of a film loop called *Instructions,* which depicts one conventional way a roll of soft white tissue can be used; using rolls of that white tissue, I gradually, physically actualized the light beam while I delivered an informal lecture on the logical necessity of developing movie screens that would realize the projected image at every point, from the projector lens to the screen. The piece ended when the screen finally became a volumetric, tautological metaphor of the projection beam. One could say that because time itself is "an arrow," it is impossible to avoid vectorial directionality in articulating temporal media and that one inevitably ends up with a sort of story form. But this "story," if it is such a form, is a physical or procedural one and what it tells us is analogous to what we are actually perceiving while it is being projected. Besides, approaching film from these new frames of reference, we are free to conceive of not only forward-oriented vectors but any vectorial direction; negative vectors come to mind easily but they are something which are not intrinsic to narrative development logic. *Last Year at Marienbad* and other works that shift temporal arrangements out of linear order nevertheless do not ever achieve retrograde vectorial structures.

One thing we can say for sure about the release print of a film is that it is a long single "line" of film stock and that during its projection, even though it may be structured according to retrograde vectorial concepts and even be experienced as temporally negative, it is, in fact, a *straight line* in our actual overall isotropic time field. And the frames on the strip, as well as the image frame on the screen, is regular and repeating. So a homogeneously structured film would be as valid an amplification of the nature of film as would be a vectorial oriented work. In fact, from this angle it would seem that film experiences that had *any* variation would disrupt this sense of linear homogeneity and would in effect be anti-filmic. However, by considering one of cinema's most basic syntagms, "the fade," we discover a most natural way of reintroducing structural directionality without negating either the continuous nature of the strip (the fade *emphasizes* the linear quality of the strip) or the flat, modular nature of the individual film frames (because the flat screen, being the most direct projection/image of the frame's morphology, constantly refers our attention across its even surface in all directions to its edge, that is, rather than looking *through* a "frame" into a picture, we find ourselves looking at an image of the film frame). My work of the past five years has been based on the importance of the fade; it provided a believable model for the vectorial construction of those works. My interest in creating temporal analogues of Tibetan mandalas, evoking their circularity and inverse symmetrical balance, led me to making what are basically two-vector, symmetric works in which the first part's foward-directed structure is countered by the second part's retrograde direction. A complex form of this vectorial approach, which issues a sense of isotropic homogeneity rather than a sense of developmental directiveness, can be obtained by overlapping or regularly intersecting two opposing vectors (that is, superimpose a forward progression "over" a backwards progression); the whole work is, so to speak, a conceptual "lap dissolve" and will have the curious quality of constant but *directionless* motion. In 1968 I abandoned the mandala-like structures and am now working with a single vector form, rather than dualistically balanced vectors; I have come to believe that while they provide discrete experiences, the latter are too closed and death-evoking in their overstressing of "beginning" and "ending" and, in this sense, are models of closed systems.

Once the screen frame is regarded as a projection of a total film frame, we must begin to think about *appropriate* scale relationships, such as distance of camera from subject to distance of screen and projected subject and viewer and, consequently, the size of the image to the size of its frame, and the size of the screen-as-image to the size of the wall on which it is projected. These features are normally regarded as arbitrary. Surface division of the projected frame has also been regarded as arbitrary; the flat film frame does not have the deep space most "shots" containing diagonals evoke, yet directors do not hesitate in using diagonal shapes in their compositions; rarely do these diagonals refer to the rectangular shape of the frame. If the film frame is a valid subject of footage, then footage should be considered a valid subject within the screen frame. A continuous scratch across frame lines down the length of film refers not only to the footage as a flowing strip but is also a valid internal division in its congruent relation to the verticality of the right and left edges of the frame image. An intensified splice not only refers to the horizontality of the top and bottom edge of the frame, but it also interrupts the flow of our experiencing a film in such a way that we are reminded that we are watching the flowing of footage through a projector. When a film "loses its loop," it allows us to see a blurred strip of jerking frames; this is quite natural and quite compelling subject material. When this nonframed condition is intentionally induced, a procedure I am currently exploring, it could be thought of as "anti-framing." I am developing another approach to simultaneously reveal both the frame and strip nature of film (both of which are normally hidden due to the intermittant shutter system) by removing the gripper arm and shutter mechanism from the projector.

Light and color are obviously primary aspects of cinema. However, even in fine cinema works color has not very convincingly realized its temporal potentialities. Some works use color as a "functional/symbolic" tool, in an Eisensteinian sense, or for psychological reference and physical effect, or for definition and clarification of images in the picture. In a lot of lesser works, color is decorative and ornamental or is used nonphilosophically merely for its stimulatory values; this latter use of color to produce essentially nonfilmic "psychedelic effects" is conceptually uninteresting and is better suited to video works where color more intense than cinema's reflected screen color can be obtained. This area has elicited very little systematic concern from filmmakers and film critics. In many cases a great deal of attention is paid to getting "proper color balance" for no good *cinematic* purpose; this technical "attentiveness" is not what I mean by "systematic concern." The vast problems of cinematic light and color structuring call for a separate discussion.

Perhaps the most engaging problem of cinema is the relationship sound may have to visual image. Although Warhol and Snow have used synchronous sound in convincing ways, an uncritical acceptance of this traditional mode of correlation usually leads to work in which both sound and image are mutually weakened; this is true in both the "lip synch" of anthropomorphic works and in the simplistic paralleling of sound and image effects in non-narrative works. Eisenstein's idea of "vertical montage" is a classical point from which one can consider nonsynchronous uses of sound. It may be that through a controlled continuous collision of sound and image an emergent psychophysiological heterodyne effect could be generated. Both light and sound occur in waves, and in optical sound composite prints are both functions of interrupted light, that is, both are primarily vibratory experiences whose "continuous" qualities are illusional. The major difference, aside from obvious differences in physical qualities between the two systems, is that the soundtrack operates in terms of continuous passage over the projector soundhead while the image intermittantly jerks in discrete steps through the film gate—there are no frame lines in the soundtrack. From this angle, it is apparent that drawing direct relationships between systems that have significant structural differences is an illusional oversight. There is also no intrinsically filmic relational logic supportive of the use of "mood music," whether it be the electronic music *backgrounds* for so-called "abstract movies" or Bergman's use of Bach fragments to act as psychological *backups* to certain key visual passages in his film *Through a Glass Darkly*. The variations on sound systems that are basically supportive of visual images are innumerable and vary widely in their levels of conceptual relationship to visual images. Whether or not the audio and visual systems should be discrete and powerful enough in themselves so that they achieve mutual autonomy is a serious question. What possibilities are there for developing both sound and image from the same structural principle and simply presenting them side-by-side as two equal yet autonomous articulations of one conception? Of course, sound need not be considered as a primary aspect of cinema; the wealth of films that succeed on visual levels alone is enough to justify silence. Aside from a few eccentricities, the first projectors had no sound option; the sound variable could be regarded as an arbitrary addition to an already complete visual system. (If we regard works that have no sound tracks as "silent films," then why don't we regard listening to music without visual accompaniment as "blind music"?) Only a few types of sound can be regarded without doubt as cinematic: the case in which the sound of a synch sound camera might be recorded and projected in synch with the visual "recording"; the case in which the drone sound of a projector projecting a visual "projection" might be heard; and the case in which one hears the sound of sprockets acting as a commentary on the length each frame of visual image has in time.

In the end, the cinematic process as the "subject matter" of a new cinema, as in a work like Ken Jacobs's brilliant *Tom, Tom the Piper's Son,* which is literally a film of a film, or as in more filmically concrete or conceptually filmic works, has already proven its viability. When a focus on highly general and prematurely fixed narrative or narrative-like forms is blurred in shifting perception to more distinctly contemporary focal lengths, then that "blur" measures wide angle lengths *from* "reality," telephoto lengths *to* micromorphological understandings of "cinema" and, lengths *of* temporal modulation in what is ultimately an omnidirectional grammar. Certainly an analysis of the focusing process itself is necessary; but "focusing" does not necessarily mean "reductiveness." It may be that by "limiting" oneself to a passionate definition of an elemental, primary cinema, one may find it necessary to construct systems involving either no projector at all or more than one projector and more than one flat screen, and more than one volumetric space between them. A focused film frame is not a "limit."

Allen Ginsberg

"When the Mode of the Music Changes the Walls of the City Shake"

Trouble with conventional form (fixed line count & stanza form) is, it's too symmetrical, geometrical, numbered and pre-fixed—unlike to my own mind, which has no beginning and end, nor fixed measure of thought (or speech—or writing) other than its own cornerless mystery—to transcribe the latter in a form most nearly representing its actual "occurrence" is my "method"—which requires the Skill of freedom of composition—and which will lead Poetry to the expression of the highest moments of the mind-body—mystical illumination—and its deepest emotion (through tears—love's all)—in the forms nearest to what it actually looks like (data of mystical imagery) & feels like (rhythm of actual speech & rhythm prompted by direct transcription of visual & other mental data)—plus not to forget the sudden genius-like Imagination or fabulation of unreal & out of this world verbal constructions which express the true gaiety & excess of Freedom—(and also by their nature express the First Cause of the world) by means of spontaneous irrational juxtaposition of sublimely related fact, by the dentist drill singing against the piano music; or pure construction of imaginaries, hydrogen jukeboxes, in perhaps abstract images (made by putting together two things verbally concrete but disparate to begin with)—always bearing in mind, that one must verge on the unknown, write toward the truth hitherto unrecognizable of one's own sincerity, including the avoidable beauty of doom, shame and

Reprinted from *Second Coming*, no. 2 (1961), by permission of the author. Copyright © 1961 by Allen Ginsberg.

embarrassment, that very area of personal self-recognition (detailed individual is universal remember) which formal conventions, internalized, keep us from discovering in ourselves & others—For if we write with an eye to what the poem should be (has been), and do not get lost in it, we will never discover anything new about ourselves in the process of actually writing on the table, and we lose the chance to live in our works, & make habitable the new world which every man may discover in himself, if he lives—which is life itself, past present & future.

Thus the mind must be trained, i.e. let loose, freed—to deal with itself as it actually is, and not to impose on itself, or its poetic artifacts, an arbitrarily preconceived pattern (formal or Subject)—and *all* patterns, unless discovered in the moment of composition—all remembered and *applied* patterns are by their very nature arbitrarily preconceived—no matter how wise & traditional—no matter what sum of inherited experience they represent—The only pattern of value or interest in poetry is the solitary, individual pattern peculiar to the poet's moment & the poem *discovered* in the mind & in the process of writing it out on the page, as notes, transcriptions—reproduced in the fittest accurate form, at the time of composition. ("Time is the essence" says Kerouac.) It is this personal discovery that is of value to the poet & to the reader—and it is of course more, not less, communicable of actuality than a pattern chosen in advance, with matter poured into it arbitrarily to fit, which of course distorts & blurs the matter . . . Mind is shapely, art is shapely.

II

The amount of blather & built-in misunderstanding we've encountered—usually in the name of good taste, moral virtue or (at most presumptuous) civilized value—has been a revelation to me of the absolute bankruptcy of the Academy in America today, or that which has set itself up as an academy for the conservation of literature. For the Academy has been the enemy and Philistine host itself. For my works will be taught in the schools in twenty years, or sooner—it is already being taught for that matter—after the first screams of disgruntled mediocrity, screams that lasted three years before subsiding into a raped moan.

They should treat us, the poets, on whom they make their livings, more kindly while we're around to enjoy it. After all we are poets and novelists, not Martians in disguise trying to poison man's mind with anti-earth propaganda. Tho to the more conformist of the lot this beat & Buddhist & mystic & poetic exploration may seem just that. And perhaps it is. "Any

man who does not labor to make himself obsolete is not worth his salt."—
Burroughs.

People take us too seriously & not seriously enough—nobody interested in what *we* mean—just a lot of bad journalism about beatniks parading
itself as highclass criticism in what are taken by the mob to be the great journals of the intellect.

And the ignorance of the technical accomplishment & spiritual interests is disgusting. How often have I seen my own work related to Fearing &
Sandburg, proletarian literature, the 1930s—by people who don't *connect* my
long line with my own obvious reading: Crane's "Atlantis," Lorca's *Poet in
NY,* Biblical structures, psalms & lamentations, Shelley's high buildups,
Apollinaire, Artaud, Mayakovsky, Pound, Williams, & the American metrical
tradition, the new tradition of measure. And Christopher Smart's *Rejoice in
the Lamb.* And Melville's prose-poem *Pierre.* And finally the spirit &
illumination of Rimbaud. Do I have to be stuck with Fearing (who's alright
too) by phony critics whose only encounter with a long line has been anthology pieces in collections by Oscar Williams? By intellectual bastards and
snobs and vulgarians and hypocrites who have never read Artaud's *Pour
en finir avec le jugement de Dieu* and therefore wouldn't begin to know that
this masterpiece, which in thirty years will be as famous as *Anabasis* is the
actual model of tone for my earlier writing? This is nothing but a raving back
at the false Jews from Columbia who have lost memory of the Shekinah &
are passing for middleclass. Must I be attacked and contemned by these
people, I who have heard Blake's own ancient voice recite me the Sunflower a
decade ago in Harlem? and who say *I* don't know about "poetic tradition"?

The only poetic tradition is the Voice out of the burning bush. The rest is
trash, & will be consumed.

If anybody wants a statement of values—it is this, that I am ready to die
for Poetry & for the truth that inspires poetry—and will do so in any case—
as all men, whether they like it or no—. I believe in the American Church of
Poetry.

And men who wish to die for anything less or are unwilling to die for
anything except their own temporary skins are foolish & bemused by illusion and had better shut their mouths and break their pens until they are
taught better by death—and I am sick to death of prophesying to a nation
that hath no ears to hear the thunder of the wrath & joy to come—among
the "fabled damned" of nations—& the money voices of ignoramuses.

We are in American Poetry & Prose still continuing the venerable tradition of compositonal self-exploration & I would say the time has not
come, historically, for any effort but the first sincere attempts at discovering

those natural structures of which we have been dreaming & speaking. Generalizations about these natural patterns may yet be made—time for the Academies to consider this in all technical detail—the data, the poetry & prose, the classics of original form, have already been written or are about to be—there is much to learn from them and there may be generalizations possible which, for the uninitiated, the nonpoets, may be reduced to "rules & instructions" (to guide attention to what is being done)—but the path to freedom of composition goes through the eternal gateless gate which if it has "form" has an indescribable one—images of which are however innumerable.

There is nothing to agree or disagree with in Kerouac's method—there is a statement of fact (1953) of the method, the conditions of experiment, which he was pursuing, what he thought about it, how he went about it. He actually did extend composition in that mode, the results are apparent, he's learned a great deal from it & so has America. As a proposed method of experiment, as a completed accomplishment, there is nothing to agree or disagree with; it is a fact—that's what he was interested in doing, that's what he did—he's only describing his interest (his passion) for the curious craftsman or critic or friend—so be it. Why get mad and say he's in "error"? There's no more error here than someone learning how to build a unicorn table by building one. He's found out (rare for a writer) *how* he really wants to write & he is writing that way, courteously explaining his way.

Most criticism is semantically confused on this point—should & shouldn't & art is & isn't—trying to tell people to do something other than that which they basically & intelligently want to do, when they are experimenting with something new to them (and actually in this case to U.S. literature).

I've had trouble with this myself, everybody telling me or implying that I shouldn't really write the way I do. What do they want, that I should write some other way I'm not interested in? Which is the very thing that doesn't interest me in their prose & poetry & makes it a long confused bore?—all arty & by inherited rule & no surprises no new invention—corresponding inevitably to their own dreary characters—because anyway most of them have no character and are big draggy minds that don't *know* and just argue from abstract shallow moral principles in the void? These people are all too abstract, when it comes down to the poetry facts of poetry—and I have learned in the past two years that argument, explanation, letters, expostulation are all vain—nobody listens anyway (not only to what I say, to what I *mean*), they all have their own mental ax to grind. I've explained the prosodaic structure of *Howl* as best I can, often, and I still read criticism, even favorable, that assumes that I am not interested in, have no, form—they just don't recognize any form but what they have heard about before & expect & what they want (they, most of them, being people who don't write poetry even & so have no idea what it involves & what beauty they're violating).—And it is also tiresome & annoying to hear K or myself or others "Beat" described because of our art as Incoherent, we are anything but. After all.

But so far we have refused to make arbitrary abstract generalizations to satisfy a peculiar popular greed for Banality. I perhaps lose some of this ground with this writing. I occasionally scream with exasperation (or giggles); this is usually an attempt to communicate with a blockhead. And Kerouac sometimes says "Wow" for joy. All this can hardly be called incoherence except by ororverbal madmen who depend on longwinded defenses of their own bad prose for a livelihood.

The literary problems I wrote of above are explained at length in Dr. Suzuki's essay "Aspects of Jap Culture" (*Evergreen Review*) & placed in their proper aesthetic context. Why should the art of spontaneity in the void be so, seem so, strange when applied in the U.S. prosepoetry context? Obviously a lack of intuitive spirit and/or classical experience on the part of these provincial frauds who have set themselves up as conservators of tradition and attack our work.

A sort of philistine brainwashing of the public has taken place. How long the actual sense of the new poetry will take to filter down, thru the actual writing and unprejudiced sympathetic reading of it, is beyond my power to guess & at this point beyond my immediate hope. More people take their ideas from reviews, newspapers & silly scholarly magazines than they do from the actual texts.

The worst I fear, considering the shallowness of Opinion, is that some of the poetry & prose may be taken too familiarly, and the ideas accepted in some dopey sociological platitudinous form—as perfectly natural ideas & perceptions which they are—and be given the same shallow treatment, this time sympathetic, as, until recently, they were given shallow unsympathy. That would be the very woe of fame. The problem has been to communicate the very spark of life, and not some opinion about that spark. Most negative criticism so far has been fearful overanxious obnoxious opinionation about this spark—and most later "criticism" will equally dully concern itself with favorable opinions about that spark. And that's not art, that's not even criticism, that's just more dreary sparkless blah blah blah—enough to turn a poet's guts. A sort of cancer of the mind that assails people whose loves are eaten by their opinions, whose tongues are incapable of wild lovely thought, which is poetry.

The brainwashing will continue, tho the work be found acceptable, and people will talk as emptily about the void, hipness, the drug high, tenderness, comradeship, spontaneous creativity, beat spiritual individuality & sacramentalism, as they have been talking about man's "moral destiny" (usually meaning a good job & full stomach & no guts and the necessity of heartless conformity & putting down your brother because of the inserviceability of love as against the legal discipline of tradition because of the unavailability of God's purity of vision & consequent souls angels—or anything else worthwhile). That these horrible monsters who do nothing but talk, teach, write crap & get in the way of poetry, have been accusing us, poets, of lack of "values" as they call it is enuf to make me vow solemnly (for the second time) that pretty soon I'm going to stop even trying to communicate coherently to the majority of the academic, journalistic, mass media & publishing trade & leave them stew in their own juice of ridiculous messy ideas. SQUARES SHUT UP & LEARN OR GO HOME. But alas the square world will never and has never stopt bugging the hip muse.

That we have begun a revolution of literature in America, again, without meaning to, merely by the actual practice of poetry—this would be inevitable. No doubt we knew what we were doing.

[1961]

Richard Kostelanetz

An ABC of Contemporary Reading

PREFACE

Ezra Pound's purpose in *ABC of Reading* (1934) was predisposing people to comprehend modernist poetry. As a longer, more resonant sequel to his earlier essay on "How To Read" (1928), this book could have been called "ABC of Understanding." Pound wanted, with all the intelligence and passion at his command, to sensitize his readers to appreciate the new literature he loved and incidentally made. On behalf of this goal, he recommends, explains, badgers, makes incisive discriminations and raises critical issues, in addition to offering guidelines, identifying precursors to the new poetry, and reprinting choice examples.

In preparing an analogous essay, four decades later, I find that specific recommendations and explanations appear in critical surveys and anthologies published under my name. The badgering I would prefer to avoid.

As in Pound's day, there are pernicious establishments that must be overcome, chiefly because their strictures lamentably narrow the minds of many literate readers. Whereas Pound made a concerted effort to pulverize

Reprinted from *Margins* (1977) by permission of the author. Copyright © 1977 by Richard Kostelanetz. Passages previously appeared in *The New York Arts Journal, Poetry Australia,* and the exhibition catalog, *Language & Structure in North America* (Kensington Arts, 1975).

artistic deadwood in his time, I would prefer to think that current semblances are by now disintegrating of their own rot.

By developing themes through a succession of *pensées,* this essay offers some general principles that will, I hope, sensitize perception and instill more percipient attitudes. At best, some of these guidelines will stick in one's head, for among my purposes are saving the reader's time, cordially ushering him into a new world of literary experience, ideally accelerating his acclimatization.

One presupposition that ought to be acknowledged at the beginning is that literature exists in a universe of other arts; thus, recent painting and music are relevant to recent writing (and vice versa).

The principal reason for writing an "ABC of *Contemporary* Reading" is that vanguard literature today is considerably different from what Pound had in mind. Thus, criticism of imaginative writing must start again from the ABCs.

"AVANT-GARDE"

The term *avant-garde* refers to those out in front, forging a path that others will take. Initially coined to characterize the shock troops of an army, the term passed over into art. Used precisely, it should refer, first of all, to work that transcends current conventions in crucial respects, that will take considerable time to find its maximum audience, and that will probably inspire future, comparably advanced endeavors.

One characteristic of avant-garde art is that, in the course of entering new terrain, it violates entrenched rules; it seems to descend from "false premises" or "heretical assumptions." Another characteristic is that it is initially hard to comprehend, not because it is intrinsically inscrutable, but because it challenges the perceptual systems of artistically educated people; that is why an audience perceives it as different, if not revolutionary, as well as why, if audiences accept the work, it will stretch their perceptual capabilities. A third, closely related characteristic is that it usually offends people, especially artists, before it persuades. It would rather be disreputably unforgettable than commendably forgotten. (Art that offends but does not advance into new terrain is likely to be forgotten.)

As a temporal term, *avant-garde* characterizes art that seems to be "ahead of its time"—that is beginning something, while "decadent" art, by contrast, stands at the end of a prosperous development. The vanguard, the leading edge of art, is the front of the train; the derrière-garde, the caboose.

Most passengers ride cars in the middle.

The "past" that the avant-garde aims to surpass is not the tradition of art but the currently decadent fashions. Harold Rosenberg: "Avant-garde art is haunted by fashion." Those most antagonized by the avant-garde are not the general populace, which does not care, but the guardians of culture, who do care, whether they be bureaucrats or established artists (or their epigones), because they feel, as they say, "threatened." Avant-garde activity has a dialectical relationship with fashion, for the emerging lucrative tendencies can usually be characterized as a synthesis of advanced elements (the anti-thesis of fashion) with more familiar stuff.

The term *avant-garde* can also refer to individuals creating such path-forging art; but even by this criterion, the work itself, rather than the artist's intentions, is the measure of the epithet's legitimacy. Thus, an artist or writer is "avant-garde" only at crucial points in his creative career, and only his most advanced works will be considered genuinely avant-garde. The word may also refer to artistic groups, if and only if all of its members are crucially contributing to an authentically step-ahead activity. *Avant-garde* defines work that old fogeys dismiss and younger artists debate.

The term is sometimes equated with cultural antagonism, for it is assumed that the avant-garde leads artists in their endless war against the philistines. However, this philistine antagonism is a secondary characteristic, as artists' social position and attitudes stem from the fate of their creative efforts, rather than the reverse.

Though vanguard activity may dominate discussion among professionals (and semi-professionals), it never dominates the general making of art. Most work created at any time, in every art, honors long-passed models. Even today, in the United States, most of the fiction written, published and reviewed is nineteenth-century in form; most painting today is similarly decadent.

Certain conservative critics have recently asserted that "the avant-garde no longer exists," because, as they see it, the suburban public laps up all new art. However, it is both false and ignorant to use a secondary attribute in lieu of a primary definition; and if an art critic in particular fails to use *avant-garde* as primarily an art-historical term, then he is exploiting the authority of his position to spread needless confusion. The fact that the avant-garde is widely discussed, as well as written about, scarcely makes it fashionable or lucrative—not by a long shot.

The conservative charge is factually wrong as well, as nearly all avant-gardes in art are ignored by the middle class public (and its agents in the culture industries), precisely because innovative work is commonly perceived as peculiar; and the commonness of that perception is one patent measure of the work being art-historically ahead of its time.

It is also erroneous to think of current avant-gardes as extending or elaborating previous avant-gardes. It is misleading, for instance, to classify Jasper Johns as only a descendant of the dadaists, for his best art is really something else. Conversely, the term *avant-garde* most truly applies to work that is so different in intention and experience that the old classifications are rendered irrelevant.

One reason why the artistic innovations of the future cannot be described today is that the avant-garde, by definition, transcends prediction.

ORIGINALITY

It is simply untrue to say that "there is nothing new under the sun," for always there have been and always there will be certain works that are formally so original that, if they were presented to a jury of ten experts, the sages would agree that, yes, this has not been done before.

Nonetheless, even innovative art resembles more conservative work in revealing the influence of one or another example of previous art; but what separates the innovative from the conservative is the extent of difference. Though Mallarmé's *Un Coup de Des* (1897) reflects certain preoccupations of earlier French poetry, it is also drastically different in certain respects, such as the disjunctiveness of its syntax and its use of the entire space of the printed page; and few literate people have ever denied the spectacular originality of Joyce's *Finnegans Wake.*

Pound speaks of literary inventors as "men who found a new process, or whose extant work gives us the first known example of a process." By these criteria, Pound himself was an inventor; so were Faulkner and Beckett and Gertrude Stein at crucial points in their creative lives. Invention, in science as in art, is the creation of something decisively unlike anything that went before.

This kind of originality is, to repeat, indubitably verifiable; indeed it, is almost measurable.

The community of art, by common consent, bestows a kind of patent upon genuine invention. Thus, the artist who uses it without change (and without acknowledgment) is customarily accused of plagiarism. If a later artist turns the innovation to personal uses, then his or her work is initially characterized as imitative or derivative. Such reminders do not invalidate the new work; instead, they give it an art-historical context.

As everyday life is marked by recurrence and predictability, we turn to art for invention and surprise.

PROGRESS

I once thought, as a practicing critic, that literature need not be new to be good. Criticism of the new was merely a specialty of mine; it was only one of several strong critical interests.

I later believed that a work might be better if it were new as well as good; its innovative quality became an increment, so to speak, upon its artistic base.

I then judged that a work was not consequential unless it were new, because only by realizing innovation did it earn a place in the history of art. By this time, I was avoiding questions of quality.

By now it is clear to me that simply by being radically innovative a work is worthwhile. Only what is new deserves serious consideration; only by realizing innovation can a work be truly significant.

Though art may not get increasingly better, our critical comprehension of how art is created and perceived does indeed improve.

There is no ultimate plateau to either art or perception. Only Ad Reinhardt could assuredly accept his contention that he had made "the last painting which anyone can make." The attempt to transcend time seems doomed, because everything done yesterday can be surpassed in one way or another. There is no end, only change.

EXPERIMENTAL

Avant-garde writing resembles experimental science in that both incorporate, to quote *Webster's*, "an action or process undertaken to discover something not yet known." In a broad sense, all imaginative writing could be considered experimental, as writers are continually making literature that, short of plagiarism, does not already exist.

However, only those forays that courageously court the unknown—that go well beyond established conventions—finally deserve the honorific epithet. Francis Bacon, the father of experimental science, noted in *The New Organon* (1620): "It would be unsound and self-contradictory to expect things which have never been done can be done except by means which have never been tried."

Bertolt Brecht once said: "Only new contents permit new forms." But it is more true to say that new forms permit, as well as generate, new contents—only with new means, with new methods, can the poet or the scientist discover new ends. In reality, new contents are better handled with older forms, precisely because unfamiliar experiences are more easily understood and communicated in familiar formats. Conversely, if the writer wants to experiment with unprecedented forms, it might be wise to select a familiar subject.

What art and science also share is the principle that the most consequential experiments are usually those that are acknowledged by peer workers—at least some of them; and one practical measure of the value of a current experiment is its capacity to inspire further consequential experiment.

At first I planned to say that, "An artistic experiment may be successful on its own terms, but irrelevant to any larger contents, simply because it fails to generate any further exploration." However, reconsidering that statement against specific examples, I was unable to think of any step-ahead artistic experiment that did not eventually have some sort of perceptible impact upon future art.

One measure of "success" in literary creation is whether its language creates its own world, and one measure of experimental success is whether or not this language has appeared in print before. At best, a writer reinvents language anew for every work or every phase of his career. One factor making Gertrude Stein more significant than Thomas Wolfe, say, is that she invented not one style but several.

In both art and science, there is no future in doing what has already been done. Pound: "Willingness to experiment is not enough, but unwillingness to experiment is mere death."

Marcel Duchamp's reputation is based upon the quality not of his craftsmanship but of his inventions.

INFLUENCE

Imitation is the surest sign of artistic influence, for imitation signifies that another artist has successfully assimilated the original creative advance. And if this happens once, it will probably happen again, each imitation breeding yet further imitations, as the resonant innovation eventually spreads beyond the artist's personal milieu.

By influencing how art is made, the initial inventor ultimately influences how art is perceived by a widening audience; so that by changing the creative procedures of many artists, the influential innovator eventually revamps the perceptual sensibilities of an entire audience. Piet Mondrian quite literally changed how we see, Edgar Varèse how we hear. In the course of its development, an artistic invention generates energies that have an impact that is often implicit, indirect, and subliminal.

Language shapes one's perception of the world; and if language is changed, so is thought. Through the creation of new forms in art comes re-creation in life.

THE LIFE OF FORMS

Biological metaphors appropriately characterize the career of innovative forms. That is, a form is born, it develops and matures before passing through a period of senility, which ushers its eventual death. Once this process has begun, it may be halted; but it cannot be reversed.

Collage, which was probably the single greatest formal invention of twentieth century art, reached its artistic demise in the sixties. That is not to say that collage disappeared—quite the contrary is true—but that the recent works indebted to collage techniques were no longer so strikingly original. What initially made collage so fertile was not just the enormous number of possibilities but its usefulness in all the arts. Once artists discovered the principle of splicing materials that would not normally be found together, the potential for realizing resonant juxtapositions seemed limitless. As the syntax of collage became familiar, it was popularized in posters, in ads, and even in popular music.

However, there came a time when collage could no longer generate original art; it could no longer instill the sense of awesome surprise that even the sophisticated viewer experiences in the presence of something authentically new. I estimate that this turning point occurred around 1960, because I cannot think of a single consequential work composed since then, in any art, that is formally based on collage.

The last great use of collage in poetry, for instance, occurred in Pound's *Cantos*, whose own history recapitulated the evolution of its principal form— innovative when Pound began it (1915), and yet by its end (1970) standing as a compendium of ways in which poetry need no longer be written. The last major collage in fiction was William Burroughs' *Naked Lunch* (1958).

In art, unlike life, death is one symptom of success.

SCIENTIFIC REVOLUTIONS

One of the most inadvertently illuminating essays about avant-garde art is Thomas S. Kuhn's *The Structure of Scientific Revolutions* (1962), because it provides a neat and accurate model for understanding a radical change in artistic style. As Kuhn has it, a certain paradigm dominates a scientific field at a particular time, and by *paradigm* he means "universally recognized scientific achievements that for a time provide model problems and solutions to a community of practitioners."

By analogy, representationalism in painting and diatonic tonality in music were paradigms, while rhyme and meter in verse had a similar function within the community of poetry. Not only does this dominant paradigm characterize certain dimensions of all endeavors within an intellectual field, but it also offers general guidelines for deploying the materials of an art.

Into a settled field comes a new work that is so radically different, so revolutionary, that it conflicts with the reigning paradigms. As Kuhn describes this process, a revolutionary work is one that "necessitated the community's rejection of one time-honored scientific theory in favor of another incompatible with it. Each produced a consequent shift in the problems available for scientific scrutiny and . . . each transformed that scientific imagination in ways that we shall ultimately need to describe as a transformation of the world within which scientific work was done." In modern painting, two analogies for a scientific revolution were, of course, cubism and collage; in music, two revolutions were dissonant counterpoint and then Schoenberg's twelve-tone system; in poetry, free verse and then associational syntax.

It is Kuhn's thesis that the history of science is not cumulative and linear, with contributions inevitably following upon each other. Rather, each field of science has witnessed a discontinuous series of drastic reorientations. The histories of modern art and writing have, of course, precisely the same structural shape.

AUTONOMY OF ART

Modern art exists in a domain apart from human life, just as scholarship inhabits yet another autonomous domain. Both art and scholarship are collective enterprises whose achievements and traditions survive individual births and deaths.

Thus, each new work of art is primarily about matters that belong exclusively to art. It is only incidentally about life, just as Life is primarily about Life and only incidentally about Art. "Feelings" belong to Life; "forms," to Art.

Most philosophy in our time is primarily about the intellectual enterprise bearing that name and secondarily about Life; for each new work of philosophy (even social philosophy) is designed to comment initially upon issues in that intellectual field. New philosophical research is, like a new painting, valued primarily for its contributions to a conscious tradition of concern and only incidentally for its relevance to common knowledge. Pure mathematics is yet more consciously confined to its own traditions.

Certain dadaists, among other artists, claimed to put life above art, but the most tangible survivor of their counter-conventional effort was examples of innovative art. When Marcel Duchamp "abandoned art for life," his decision had meaning only within the traditions of visual art; Life went merrily along, unaffected. Only a community of artistically sensitive people can distinguish Non-Art from Life.

What is most valuable in a poem is not its "message" but qualities indigenous to poetry. The success of its communication depends upon both the reader's and the writer's love and intelligence not of Life but of Poetry. In approaching a new work of literature, we bring to it "all of our experience," which usually includes a good deal of reading. When content is more important than mediumistic qualities, then the reader is perceiving the work not as literature but as something else—as history, as sociology, as psychology, or as reportage.

Every work of imaginative writing incorporates, as its principal meaning, certain notions about literature; it embodies insight into the appropriateness and possibilities of literary works. A new piece of writing is more valuable and praiseworthy if these mediumistic ideas are original and suggestive. Literature, unlike journalism, survives not by saying something new, but by inventing something not seen before.

Formal ideas generate works of art; content fills them.

Every work draws a circle around itself, letting the reader know what does and does not belong to it. All writing is hermetic to idiosyncratic degrees—writers writing what can only be written.

"EXPERIENCE"

This difference between Art and Life explains why it is largely by reading, rather than living, that one learns not only to read but to write; and what distinguishes the writer from the non-writer is, first, his extensive experience with written forms and then his capacity to make mountains of literature out of molehills of life.

Rather than speak of literature as "experience mediated by language," to quote a common phrase, why not regard it as language mediated by experience, which particularly includes a familiarity with literary words?

This separation of Art from Life also accounts for such contradictions and contrasts as why an artist can succeed in art, while failing in life (or vice versa); or why he may show integrity in art and opportunism in life; or even why he may seem vibrant in life and dead in art, or intelligent in art and stupid in life, or eccentric in art and conventional in life.

Biographies of artists are irrelevant unless they focus upon how art, rather than something else, was produced by idiosyncratic creative methods. What makes Hemingway special was not the life he led but his works and how he wrote them.

CONSTRUCTIVISM

Two polarities of artistic creativity are expressionism and constructivism, each term defining a different attitude toward the making of imaginative things. In the former, the artist thinks he is primarily expressing himself, even though he is also using forms and materials that exist primarily apart from himself. Allen Ginsberg, for instance, regards his poetry as "GRAPH-ING the movement of the mind on the page." A further assumption is, to quote Ginsberg again, that, "if the poet's mind is shapely, his art will be shapely." Surrealism is an extreme extension of expressionism.

The constructivist artist believes, by contrast, that he is building things apart from himself, even though his creations are liable to reveal certain personal proclivities. As Piet Mondrian, a scrupulous constructivist, explained the difference, "One aims at the *direct creation of universal beauty,* the other at the *aesthetic expression of oneself."*

In painting's history, what distinguished cubism from constructivism was the former's interest in mundane reality (restructured, to be sure), while constructivism emphasized exclusively the presentation of invented forms. Thus, constructivist paintings are generally geometric and non-mimetic. In sculpture, the term *constructivism* refers to objects that are constructed, rather than cast or carved.

The constructivist assumes that, to quote Mondrian again, "It is possible to express oneself profoundly and humanly by plastics alone." In the visual material itself, in sum, are all the profundity and humanity the art is capable of expressing. The individual character of the work comes from qualities of style, rather than personality. The poet is not an ingredient in the poem but a catalyst of available materials. The artist is, in practice, the guy who moves the stuff around.

One quality distinguishing recent avant-garde writing from its predecessors is a constructivist tendency that is itself new to the history of literature.

STYLISTIC PLURALISM

In each art today, there exists not just one avant-garde but several, each of which stands decisively beyond earlier stylistic positions. The contemporary pursuit of possibility assumes the development of numerous alternative positions, rather than just a single one; for at the root of the modernist awakening lies a commitment to cultural opportunity and diversity.

One factor making this pluralism possible is the increased number of practitioners in every art; a second factor is the existence of several avant-garde traditions in every art. In literature, for instance, there is a line of linguistic invention whose modern English-language exemplars include Gertrude Stein, e.e. cummings, Hugh MacDiarmid (in his Scots dialect poems) and James Joyce (especially in *Finnegans Wake*).

An entirely different avant-garde tradition has emphasized structural alternatives—organizing the contents of literature in unprecedented ways. The exemplars here are Joyce again (especially in *Ulysses*), Pound, Faulkner, Stein (in her plays), and Samuel Beckett.

Another tradition is defined by the incorporation of materials previously regarded as nonliterary, such as the meaningless sounds of Alexei Kruchenyk's poetry, the theatricality of some recent visual art, the pictorialism of the visual poets, or the mathematical formulas in Alfred Jarry's "The Surface of God":

> —Let us note, in fact, that according to the formula
>
> $$\infty - 0 - a + a + 0 = \infty$$
>
> the length a is nil, so that a is not a line but a point.
> Therefore, *definitively:*
> GOD IS THE TANGENTIAL POINT BETWEEN ZERO AND INFINITY.

It would be false to say that just one of these traditions was necessarily more important or more valid or more fertile than the others, for all remain consequential. Not only do recent books make worthwhile advances within each of these strains, but some works contribute to two traditions; a rare few to all three.

These traditions remain perceptibly separate; each circumscribes a distinctly different way of generating (and appreciating) literary invention.

RICHARD KOSTELANETZ

POUND'S APHORISMS

What is at present most valuable in Pound's *ABC* is not its argument—the battle for modernist literature, which has been won and then transcended—but those sentences that have a continuing relevance:

> Great literature is simply language charged with meaning to the utmost possible degree.
> Literature is news that *stays* news.
> The sum of human wisdom is not contained in any one language, and no single language is *capable* of expressing all forms and degrees of human comprehension.
> Virgil was the official literature of the middle ages, but "everybody" went on reading Ovid.
> Artists are the antennae of the race.
> In all cases one test will be, "could this material have been made more efficient in some other medium?"
> You can spot the bad critic when he starts by discussing the poet and not the poem.
> Any general statement is like a cheque drawn on a bank. Its value depends upon what is there to meet it. . . . In writing, a man's "name" is his reference. He has, after time, credit.
> The student having studied geometry and physics or chemistry knows that in one you begin with simple forms, in another with simple substances.
> The honest critic must be content to find *very little* contemporary work worth serious attention; but he must also be ready to recognize that little, and to demote work of the past when a new work surpasses it.
> From the empiric angle, verse usually has some element roughly fixed and some other that varies, but which element is to be fixed and which varied, and to what degree, is the affair of the author.

MAJOR INNOVATIONS

The major esthetic innovations of recent art extend from three generative principles: minimalism, overload, and intermedia. The first term refers to the principle of reducing the amount of surface content in a work—painting with only one color, say, or sculpture with smooth rectangular shapes, or fictions with very few words, or poems with a severely limited vocabulary.

The contrary motive of overload informs such serial compositions as Milton Babbitt's *Relata I* (1964), which presents an awesomely large number of discrete musical events in remarkably few minutes, or James Joyce's *Finnegans Wake,* where several stories, in several languages, are rendered on a single page. Compression and extension, though superficially opposite, are similar in one respect: both techniques transcend the time/space scale of traditional literature, thereby making the reader more aware of perceptual duration.

Since experimental artists are continually trying to eschew the familiar measures of artistic communication—for example, not only how much plot but how many characters (and pages) a novel, say, should contain—the most interesting art of the past decade tends to be either much more, or much less, than works of art used to be. While the English fictioneer J. G. Ballard frequently compresses enough material for a novel into the length of a short story, Samuel Beckett's novels, on the other hand, have progressively fewer events; and the American poet Robert Lax in *Black & White* (1966) composes an extended poem with only four different words (three of which are announced in the title), punctuated only by white space. By current standards, the ideal of a one-page novel seems as valid and exciting as a fiction of ten thousand pages.

Intermedia, the third generative principle, is an encompassing term for the new art forms that were invented by marrying the materials and/or concepts of one traditional genre with another (or others), or by integrating art itself with something previously considered nonartistic. Out of the mating of theater with painting, sculpture, music and/or dance came that art called *happenings* or *mixed-means events,* while sculptures that incorporate an operational technology within the art, rather than as an anterior tool, comprise a genre that I call *artistic machines.* A related technique is the use of esthetic procedures indigenous to one medium as a basis for creative work in another medium.

In literature, out of the melding of language with design came what is called *visual poetry* or *word-imagery,* where the enhancing coherence of words is pictorial (rather than syntactical), while *sound poetry* comes from integrating musical values with initially verbal material. Since the possibilities of literary intermedia have scarcely been explored, it is reasonable to suspect that this may be the single greatest esthetic idea for our time—the sole contemporary peer of cubism and collage.

DIVERGENT AVANT-GARDES

What is innovative in art today tends either to purify the traditional properties of a medium or to miscegenate with other media. In painting, for instance, the first motive was epitomized by Ad Reinhardt, who regarded himself as doing "pure painting," uncontaminated by motives and materials indigenous to the other arts. A recent exemplar of the second, contrary tendency has been Robert Rauschenberg, who has incorporated mundane materials, three-dimensional objects and even operational technologies into his paintings.

In literature, the motive of mediumistic purification tends to predominate today, in part because fewer writers than, say painters are responsive to new developments in the other arts. Writers working in this purifying way try to engage the particular nature of their chosen medium and thus create works that cannot be translated into any other form:

> Poems that cannot be set to music,
> Theatrical experiences that are not susceptible to filming or televising,
> Novels that have no uses beyond the page of print,
> Poems that are not prose and cannot be facilely paraphrased.

This particular strain of experimental literature emphasizes those elements indigenous to the medium, ostensibly, the resources of language, as applied to sheets of paper.

When Pound spoke of purifying poetry, he declared, "The image is the poet's pigment." No, that is wrong. The true literary analogue for pigment is words.

The literary miscegenators, by contrast, emphasize the incorporation of visual and/or aural elements; they appropriate formal ideas developed in the other arts. Some have transcended the rectangular page in favor of other formats of visual or aural presentation, such as statuary or recording tape. Into literature come materials, dimensions and esthetic ideas that have not been used in print before.

Purification is no less valid than miscegenation; each direction seems equally capable of generating works of unprecedented excellence.

"ANTI-ART"

There is no such thing as "formless art," for any human creation that can be characterized in any way—as having one kind of organization, rather than another—has a perceptible form. The fact that this form may not be immediately definable in familar terms does not make this work of art "formless." Not at all. Most innovative art has an unprecedented form that, though it may not be immediately defined, can eventually be characterized in a certain way. Such characterizations are the initial problem in avant-garde criticism.

As a rule, when something looks incomprehensibly different and yet seems intrinsically coherent, even if in initially inexplicable ways, it is likely to be formally innovative.

There is no such thing as "anti-art," which is merely a journalistic term transiently thrown at new work that is so different that it implicitly repudiates the currently dominant styles. Here the use of the suffix *art* acknowledges an esthetic validity that, in practice, hastens the disappearance of the prefix. Even Marcel Duchamp's dogged attempts to produce a definitive anti-art were undermined first by his fellow artists, and then by the art public, and finally by the art historians and museum curators. Most radical work of the past decade was, at one time, called "anti-poetry," "anti-painting," or anti-whatever by someone who should have known better.

As the antagonistic posture has more currency in visual arts than elsewhere, some artist speak of their own work as "anit-form," but in their works the viewer can discover certain structures that reflect essentially formal decisions. John Cage's recent compositions have been dismissed as "not-music," even though they are filled with sounds; and Cage's penchant for aural disorder—thoroughly unpredictable relations—inspires others to dismiss him as "formless" and "chaotic," even though consistent disconnection creates its own kind of distinctive form.

"NOT ART"

"Not art" is similarly impossible, if the object in question can be regarded apart from utilitarian reality; and so is "unart." Indeed, anything under the sun can be considered "art" if either the creator or the beholder wishes to do so. Just as the spectator has as much authority as the artist in bestowing that usually honorific term, so neither artist nor spectator can conclusively deny the affirmations of the other.

Art is anything anyone anywhere can find artistic. "Literature" can be anything writers make, or readers make, of writing.

The epithet "not art" often functions as an excuse for stupidity—for dismissing what cannot be immediately understood; yet this term is intrinsically self-denying, because it acknowledges within itself the possibility of accepting any work of "not art" as Art. In my observation, what is dismissed as "not art" is not necessarily bad. Much of it *is* dreadful, to be sure; but "not art" that is not egregiously derivative or mundane is usually very original and, thus, quite interesting.

Alfred Kinsey once said, "The only sexual acts that are unnatural are the ones you can't do." Gertrude Stein: "Human nature is what any human will do." John Cage: "I have nothing to say and I am saying it and that is poetry," in part because it cannot be anything else (except perhaps "prose").

"ART" AS CONVENTION

The term *art* is a convenient convention, because "art" as such does not exist. I use the term as a catch-all to define works of esthetic quality, but others use it, I think erroneously, to identify an intangible essence that they think may (or may not) exist in the work at hand.

What exists, in fact, is not "art" but paintings and sculptures—or man-made works that are closer to previous paintings and sculptures than anything else. Nearly all writers I know regard themselves as making poems and fictions, say, rather than "art." The notion of "making art" seems very quaint—or spurious.

ALL MATERIALS

Back in 1938, the sculptor Naum Gabo wrote: "In sculpture as well as in technics, every material is good and worthy and useful, because every single material has its own esthetic value. In sculpture as well as in technics the method of working is set by the material itself. There is no limit to the variety of material suitable for sculpture."

Much the same could be said about literature—and often has been said. Only recently, however, have literary artists realized that this liberating assertion includes not only the content of literature but its fundamental materials—paragraphs, sentences, syntax, vocabulary, paper, and typography. There is no limit upon the ways in which *these* materials can be deployed.

Why, for instance, should words observe (at least roughly) conventional syntax to be considered "poetry" (rather than nonsense)? Need every line of poetry begin along the left-hand margin, as if lines of poetry had to be aligned like soldiers in the army? The fact that poetry has nearly always been printed that way is clearly not an inviolate reason. John Cage in his preface to *M* (1973): "I now write without syntax and sometimes with it."

Since the small rectangular page need not be the only medium for poetic language, there should be no limits upon the media incorporating words—film, videotapes, audiotape, photographic paper, and plastics are all available. Just as many materials can be cast in language, so language can be cast in any material. One should scarcely be surprised if qualities intrinsic in these "nonliterary" materials affect the words they contain. As literature is composed of language that articulates meaning, so alternative media contain their own capabilities for rendering words poetic.

MECHANICAL INVENTIONS

The history of stylistic innovation in modern literature is a record of mechanical inventions, each of which reflects verbal ingenuity.

The trick in writing comprehensible dialect, in realizing a spoken informal language in print, lies in developing a mechanical consistency not only in spelling and structure but also in integrating dialectical peculiarities with familiar language. Without mechanisms to produce roughly uniform results, the printed language would be incoherent and unreadable.

No good writing is purely mechanical, to be sure; for machines cannot yet write comprehensible prose. However, the infusion of technological ingenuity can induce stylistic distinction, apart from any craftsmanly talents. One reason why the invention itself is more important than "how well it is realized" is that the invention usually incorporates the implements conducive to its realization, much as rhyme and meter served post-Renaissance English poetry.

It was a genuinely mechanical trick for Gertrude Stein to scramble the structure of her sentences, or for John Dos Passos to omit certain parts of speech, or for Hemingway to eschew adjectives and adverbs whose presence could be assumed (his style reflecting the elliptical language of telegrams). In writing *Finnegans Wake,* James Joyce invented a style composed of many tongues, filled with freshly made-up words which, like all neologisms, are essentially mechanical inventions in language. Anthony Burgess, working on more modest levels, fluently incorporates Russian words into otherwise familiar English sentences in his novel, *A Clockwork Orange* (1962). All these devices produced, among other effects, a heightening of prose and an increase in suggestivity.

An initial advantage of mechanical invention is that it becomes, if consistently observed, a constraint that forbids conventional exposition. If the rather ordinary sentence that you are now reading were written, say, in dialect, the same idea would necessarily be expressed in a drastically different way. It might not even seem to be the same idea.

Some writers and critics resist the notion that mere mechanical inventions can change literary style, but they fail to perceive that written language itself is essentially a technology of human communication. And not unlike other technologies, verbal language is susceptible to inventive modifications.

RICHARD KOSTELANETZ

FINNEGANS WAKE

One reason why *Finnegans Wake* remains a monumental masterpiece is that its particular inventions have never been exceeded. Joyce's book also realizes, to an extraordinary degree, certain prime values of literary modernism; and one sure index of its excellence is that no other major modern work, except perhaps Gertrude Stein's *Geography and Plays* (1922), is still as widely unread and persistently misunderstood, decades after its initial publication.

Unlike journalism, which tries to render complex experience in a simple form, the *Wake* tells a simple story in a complex form. Its subject is familial conflict among two brothers and their two parents. Exploiting the techniques of literary symbolism, Joyce portrays numerous conflicts taking the same familial forms. The metaphors for the two brothers include competing writers, such as Pope and Swift, or countries, such as Britain and America, among other antagonistic pairs of roughly equal age and/or authority.

This interpretation of human experience hardly ranks as "original" or "profound," but thanks to the techniques of multiple reference, incorporating innumerable examples into a single text, the theme is extended into a broad range of experience. No other literary work rivals it in textural density; in no other piece of writing are so many dimensions simultaneously articulated.

Congruent with his method, Joyce coins linguistic portmanteaus (where one word incorporates parts of other familiar words), as well as inventing neologisms that echo various words; and the use of many languages serves to increase the range of multiplicity and allusion. He favors puns, which serve a similar function of incorporating more than one meaning within a single unit—the verbal technique reflecting the theme of history repeating itself many times over. The book's principal theme is entwined in its method. As Samuel Beckett put it, in 1929, "Here form *is* content, content *is* form."

As the demands of his all-encompassing technique forced Joyce to draw upon innumerable examples, the narrative generates a wealth of secondary themes, which are susceptible to remarkably profound particular analyses. Marshall McLuhan, for one, has demonstrated how some striking cultural perceptions can be read into (or out of) the *Wake*.

UNCONVENTIONAL CONSTRAINTS

The creation of art depends upon constraint, which puts a dialectical cast upon imagination. Examples of conventional constraints include meter in poetry and syntax in prose, both of which simultaneously inhibit and enhance the author's communication. One of the best ways to make original art is, by contrast, the use of an unconventional constraint.

It is unconventional, by contrast, to limit a poem to only a few words, as Lax does in *Black & White* (1971), or to abolish syntax in linear expression, as Gertrude Stein does in this opening to "IIIIIIIIII" (1922):

INCLINE

Clinch, melody, hurry, spoon, special, dumb, cake, forrester, fine, cane, carpet, incline, spread, gate, light, labor.

It is similarly unconventional to compose a poem entirely of numbers or to tell a story entirely in nonrepresentational images.

The practical advantage of such constraints is this: By forcing the writer to work in previously unfamiliar ways, an unusual compositional rule prevents the creation of familiar work. Not even William Faulkner, say, could "write like Faulkner" if his vocabulary were strictly limited to a few words, or if he cast his language exclusively in film or in sculpture. Nor could William Butler Yeats "write like Yeats." One thing such a severe constraint will surely do is produce unfamiliar effects.

Most artistic constraints, if scrupulously observed, generate their own particular range of possibilities, precisely because they make certain solutions more feasible than others. By discouraging the direct expression of personality, they are conducive to the realization of characteristic work. If the compositional constraint is a personal invention, then the resulting work will probably look and read like nothing else. Innovative ground rules will stretch the sensibilities of both writer and reader. And a truly experimental writer works not with just one constraint but with several.

"CHANCE"

One well-known contemporary constraint is the use of chance operations in composition, not only of music but in the other arts as well. A composer might throw dice, say, to determine in what order musical notes will appear, or a painter might toss paint in the air and let it splatter on the canvas. However, it is wrong to say that everything "is left to chance," as the painter chooses the color of his pigment, the size of his canvas, and the composer pre-selects his notes. Precisely because aleatory devices customarily function to divorce certain (though not all) decisions from the artist's control, they become an effective means for transcending ingrained compositional habits. However, unlike the constraints mentioned before, randomizing procedures are customarily not perceptible per se in the resulting work of art. One cannot hear chance or see it.

Aleatory methods can be used in many ways, and to many degrees; perhaps the most perceptible distinguishing marks are: disconnectedness among the parts, so that the elements seem isolated from each other, absence within the work itself of both a center and any hierarchy that would make one element dominate over the others, a related diffusion of material all over the available space and/or time (this factor joining nonhierarchy in contributing to a general flattening of the artistic field).

It is true that each (or even all) of these structural characteristics could be produced without chance methods—e.g., certain works of Gertrude Stein—but chance operations provide the most efficient means toward achieving these formal ends.

One sign of contemporary genius is the capacity to invent generative constraints. Although John Cage is customarily considered a prophet of artistic freedom, his real forte has been the creation of not one but several alternative constraints. His compositions in sound and print typically allow free choice in certain respects, while implicitly denying it in others.

"GIMMICKS"

Formal inventions are often dismissed as "gimmicks," but it is precisely such mechanisms that generate innovative forms and styles. The development of a good gimmick can change an artist's career; it can produce flowers in what was previously perceived to be a desert. A new concept, if radically pursued, can draw out of the artist capacities for innovation and intelligence that not even he knew he possessed.

The history of modern music is filled with gimmicks, such as the profusion of nonsynchronous folk tunes in Charles Ives's best-known music, John Cage's prepared piano, which became an even more convenient means for avoiding familiar pitches, or Andres Segovia's transcribing Bach's violin partitas for the guitar. Glenn Gould's peculiarly hunched-over way of physically approaching his piano was once dismissed as a gimmick, and what initially seemed a gimmicky way of applying paint to canvas produced Jackson Pollock's mature style.

In literature, many stylistic innovations and idiosyncrasies are indebted to syntactical gimmicks. Elements of literary craftsmanship no doubt contributed to the final product; but without the good gimmick there would be neither an innovation nor a distinctly individual style.

For Apollinaire, a crucial trick was merely the elimination of punctuation, which drastically changed the style and flow of his poetry. For Faulkner, it was, first, a penchant for exceedingly long sentences and then the use of different first-person narrators. One of e. e. cummings' pet gimmicks was the use of one part of speech to function in lieu of another. In places where nouns would normally be used, cummings put verbs, adjectives, adverbs, and even conjunctions. In drafting both poetry and prose, Ezra Pound always put two spaces between typewritten words, duplicating with technology a characteristic of his handwriting. Words   physically   separated   from each   other   are   perceived   differently. Tom Wolfe, in his preface to *The New Journalism* (1974): "I found that things like exclamation points, italics, abrupt shifts (dashes), syncopations (dots) helped give the illusion not only of a person talking but of a person thinking." The history of innovative writing is partly a record of gimmicks.

A fertile class of gimmicks in recent art is the use of nonartistic models, in either content or form: for example, paintings with popular iconography ("pop art"), a novel written in the form of encyclopedia notations (Richard Horn's *Encyclopedia*), poetry whose organization is permutational, rather than syntactical. The methods of nonartistic material can become both a constraint and a source of irony.

Unless a gimmick generates discernibly different art, it remains nothing more than "a gimmick."

INTELLIGENCE OF FORM

Embedded in structure is an intelligence that exists apart from the writer. A sloppily organized essay will appear stupid, notwithstanding the innate intelligence of its author, while a well-articulated exposition, with every part in the most propitious place, will be taken as evidence of authorial intelligence. Quite simply, someone who can efficiently organize a series of English sentences, whether in print or in speech, seems smarter than someone who cannot.

Form in this sense includes not only the organization of sentences and paragraphs, but the larger structures that inform the composition of the whole. These forms not only organize the representation of experience; they also generate imagination and/or intelligence simply by forcing the artist to honor the demands of his chosen structure. Mastery of the forms of intelligence enables a skilled actor to play a person who is far more intelligent than he is, and we have all met people who, because of their observant imitation of a certain manner, initially strike us as far more intelligent than we later discover they are.

RICHARD KOSTELANETZ

As essayists, say, usually seem more intelligent in those forms that are familiar to them, some of this sense of intelligence should be attributed to the efficacy of form, which embodies a capacity for authorial illusion. Whereas the editorial writer James Reston is succinct and often brilliant in a few hundred words, he seems prolix and confused in longer forms. The intelligence of a newspaper column sharpens Reston's mind, while longer forms defeat it.

One of the best ways to perceive the intelligence intrinsic in form is to ask why one and only one of a prolific author's many books should seem so much better than the others? For me, the best example of this is Doris Lessing's *The Golden Notebook* (1962), which strikes me as far superior to her earlier fictions (and perhaps her later novels as well). *The Golden Notebook* is indubitably more complex, more ambiguous, more penetrating. The reason is surely not its subject—the experience of a single woman—because that also appears in other Lessing fiction. Nor is the reason its length, because other Lessing novels are equally bulky. No, the primary reason for its superior intelligence is the form of four notebooks, which insures that experience is observed from a multiple perspective. That structural concept seems to generate a complexity of perception, and thus a profundity, that is absent from Lessing's other work. A traditional example of formal intelligence is rhyme and meter in poetry.

An operational truth is that if an intelligent artist whose mind is filled with ideas pays particular attention to forms, content will look after itself. Similarly, if a conventional (verbal) poet takes care of sound, sense will take care of itself. (Most "intelligent" modern painters progressed from a concern with content to an emphasis upon form.)

In beginning his work, the writer chooses not only his ends but the means (or machinery) that will heighten his materials and yet bring them to completion. This formal decision assumes the rejection of other available (or conceivable) possibilities. Formal invention embodies an intelligence that exists apart from its author and thus adds to his own mind.

The essay you are now reading was initially written with each section as a single paragraph, but breaking the paragraphs apart changed the form, the style, and even the content.

"DECLINE"

What is perceived to be "the decline of the novel" should not be blamed upon the absence of invention; in fiction, as in the other literary arts, the avant-garde tradition survives. Nor can this purported decline be blamed upon the diminution of an audience for fiction, for not only do Americans buy more best-selling trash than ever before, but the sales of Beckett, Barth and Bellow indicate an enlarging audience for what is perceived to be "serious literary fiction."

No, the "decline of the novel" is really based, first, upon the fact that all but a scarce few novels published today resemble previous works and, second, upon the sense that too many new novels take their cues not from the intrinsic possibilities of literature but from the other media. When novels try to imitate film or are written primarily to be "taken by the movies," the medium's independence and initiative are severely compromised.

On the other hand, the reported "decline of the short story" can be attributed, quite clearly, to the decrease in the number of media publishing it. At a time when more stories are written than ever before (thanks largely to courses in "creative writing"), fewer appear in print. Here, as elsewhere, cultural commentators are continually blaming art and artists for failures that are clearly caused by the intermediary agencies.

One reason why form is "pure" is that it is noncommercial. Nearly all publishers buy content over form.

NEGLECTED DIMENSIONS

One continuing characteristic of experimental art is a concern with dimensions that were neglected in previous work.

If conventional filmmaking cultivates a moving camera and montage (the editing of film so that the same subject is perceived from different angles), Andy Warhol's *Empire*, by contrast, emphasizes a stationary camera and the pure continuity of unedited film. It was common knowledge, of course, that the camera could be stationary and that film had uninterrupted continuity, but no filmmaker prior to Warhol had isolated these dimensions quite so prominently. In music, both John Cage and Morton Feldman created works that emphasized silence in place of intentional sounds. If the old literature depends upon syntax and semantics for its principal means of connection, the new literature depends upon something else; that difference is one measure of its originality.

One reason why a creative artist neglects certain dimensions is irremediable personal incompetence. Schoenberg told his pupil Cage that the young composer had no talent for harmony, while Gertrude Stein's college instructors were forever criticizing her grammatical infelicities. What Cage and Stein share with other artistic inventors is this principle: Ignore incompetences in order to concentrate upon something else. Cage chose duration in lieu of harmony; Stein invented a variety of alternative grammars.

The following passage from Gertrude Stein's "IIIIIIIII" is unified not by syntax or semantics but by other qualities indigenous to language:

> Secret in a season makes the pining wetter. So much hooding, so best to saw into right places the clang and the hush. The held up ocean, the eaten pan that has no cut cake, the same only different clover is the best, is the best.

And this familiar "tongue twister" emphasizes the musical qualities of language, sound exceeding sense:

> If a Hottentot taught a Hottentot tot to talk ere the tot could totter, ought the Hottentot tot be taught to say ought or naught or what ought to be taught 'er?

In a classic statement of contemporary poetics, Clark Coolidge declared, "As Stein has most clearly and accurately indicated, words have a universe of qualities other than those of descriptive relation: Hardness, Density, Sound-Shape, Vector Force, and Degrees of Transparency/Opacity." And Coolidge's own poetry implicitly admonishes readers to pay attention to dimensions of language that they might otherwise ignore. His poems cannot be read in any other way.

The apparent elimination of "subject matter" is no total loss for literary art, for language with "nothing to say" is language looked at, not through. Poetic devices have intrinsic value, apart from meaning. Rosmarie Waldrop: "Even the Dadaists by saying nothing have extended the field of the sayable." The French poet Pierre-Albert Birot once suggested that if everything can be said in prose, then poetry should be saved for saying nothing. In my judgment, poetry should be saved for things that cannot be said in prose, including "nothing."

MEDIUMISTIC INTEGRITY

One ideal of modernism that frequently gets forgotten is mediumistic integrity. According to this rule, painting should emphasize effects that are indigenous to the medium of two-dimensional painted canvases, just as sculptures should emphasize their three-dimensionality. A poem should emphasize techniques and purposes that are strictly poetic, while abjuring what is prosaic and fictional. Once the photographic camera had been perfected, what painting gained by avoiding representational verisimilitude was mediumistic integrity—painters painting what could only be painted.

The indigenous materials of live theater are light, space, action, and sound (which includes words). The essential material of literature is language. The German poet-critic Helmut Heissenbuttel finds in the longer poems of Ezra Pound and Charles Olson "a world of language and nothing but language," but that is even more particularly true of certain prose works by Gertrude Stein, William Faulkner, and James Joyce.

This ideal notwithstanding, creators in one art frequently appropriate formal ideas that were initially developed in another art. The collage techniques of Ezra Pound's *Cantos* echoed earlier inventions in painting, while the acoherence of John Ashbery's poetry acknowledges musical atonality, and some of Clark Coolidge's poems echo the choreographer Merce Cunningham's unusual sense of space. Yet in all three examples, the resulting works are not painterly or musical but indubitably poetic. The critical question is whether or not the poetic medium was the most propitious choice for articulating the work's indigenous material.

Northrop Frye once described literature as "intermediate between music and painting; its words form patterns which approach a musical sequence of sounds at one of its boundaries, and form patterns which approach the hieroglyphic or pictorial image at the other. The attempt to get as near to these boundaries as possible form the main body of what is called experimental writing." Certain contemporary avant-garde writers try harder than their precursors to emulate the conditions of abstract painting and abstract music.

Even though foreign boundaries are approached, experimental work nonetheless primarily echoes its original genre. What is called "sound poetry" is primarily poetry, rather than music, and "visual poetry" is similarly closer to poetry than to graphic design.

Marcel Duchamp learned mathematics to make not science but art.

Words have status and meaning initially as words. This cannot be denied or erased. Divorced from both syntax and semantics, language is cleansed and reborn, for unprecedented creative purposes.

If you think it is easy to write counter-syntactical language that is nonetheless poetically coherent, try it sometime.

SOUND POETRY

Sound poetry must be heard to be "read," just as visual poetry must be seen. The experience of sound poetry's asensical strain is comparable to hearing poetry in a foreign language, largely because a sound poem is successful to the degree that it invents a language that is "foreign" and yet coherent to everyone:

> 'Twas brillig, and the slithy toves
>   Did gyre and gimble in the wabe:
> All mimsy were the borogoves,
>   And the mome raths outgrabe.
>
> —Lewis Carroll, "Jabberwocky" (1855)

> Kroklokwafzi? Semememi!
> Seiokrontro—prafriplo
> Bifzi, bafzi; hulalemi:
> quasti basti bo . . .
> Lala lalu lalu lalu la!
>
> —Christian Morgenstern, "Das Grosse Lalula" (1905)

One reason why this is poetry is that it resembles traditional poetry more than anything else; it clearly is not prose. Nor can it be paraphrased. Raymond Federman: "Nothing is more poetic than nonsense." It is "pure" because it is not "about" anything except itself.

COMMUNICATION

An artist does not "speak to us" through art; he "speaks" only when he addresses his audience directly, in person. Instead, the artist makes a work of art, and it is this object (not the artist) that "expresses." It says something to an audience, while the artist is off elsewhere, ideally, making something else. (Artists create not just arguments for thought but objects for contemplation, simultaneously.)

What the work actually communicates may be quite different from what the artist thinks (or says) he intended. In case of disputes, the ultimate source of evidence is not the artist but his work. If the painter tells us that his green landscape is "depicting a skyscraper," we consider his advice but ultimately respect his art. Trust not the teller but the tale, because the teller can lie in ways the tale cannot.

The issue in perception (as well as criticism) is not "what the artist is trying to say," but what the work is saying.

Contemporary literature at its best has clear surfaces; so that the reader can easily discern, at minimum, what's happening. Writing becomes opaque, by contrast, when its communication is confused, contradictory, unclarified, or incomplete. The reader senses the existence of secrets that the author is withholding. Opacity in art is sometimes confused with "mystery," but the latter term should not serve as an excuse for the absence of clarity. Mystery in art ideally exists in addition to clarity, not in lieu of it; that epithet is a convenient way of identifying those dimensions of a work that are perceived to exist, but are not immediately understood. Northrop Frye identifies this quality "of art as coming not from concealment but from revelation, not from something unknown or unknowable in the work, but something unlimited from it."

Language is literary when it does more than communicate.

CRITICS

Serious, consistent critics can be divided into conservatives and radicals. The former prefer works that formally resemble the milestones of the past; they relish acknowledgment of traditional artistic verities and the fulfillment of expectation.

Radical critics, by contrast, prefer works that are formally unlike anything they have seen before. They appreciate not only the disruption of artistic expectations but also a fundamental challenge to their sense of art. Since art changes as rapidly as life, they assume that the most relevant new art will be as different from the past as their own experience is different; the most valuable new work will represent an innovative interpretation of a perceptible artistic issue or of an acknowledged tradition.

While the conversatives bow before familiar deities, the radicals tend to feature names that are either controversial or unknown.

Radicals are more inclined than conservatives to do their own creative work, to become cultural middlemen (agents, anthologists, curators), to write polemical critiques of cultural dissemination—the first, because radical critics tend to be closer than conservatives to the creative processes of contemporary art; the second, because their biases make them aware of first-rate work that does not enter the cultural marketplace; and the last, because they inevitably wonder why the art they admire is not earning its just rewards.

The conservative critic likes epithets such as "masterpiece," which purportedly connects a new work to the ages, while the radical prefers more temporal language. Conservative critics, by definition, are those who continually object to the emerging avant-gardes.

A "critic" lacking a coherent viewpoint is really a "reviewer." A "critic" unresponsive to innovation is ultimately not a critic but a caretaker.

Truly experimental art incorporates a measure of risk, as well as a capacity to offend. By contrast, any work that is instantly, universally acceptable cannot possibly be experimental. The same values apply to arts criticism.

AUTHOR AND ART

Every work of human imagination no doubt reflects (and reveals) peculiarities of its creator, but what these might be is hard to identify without prior acquaintance with the person. As a rule, if viewers are not personally acquainted with a living artist, they cannot justifiably claim any knowledge of the artist's intentions, his ideas or his mental proclivities. Doing so is not only fallacious but presumptuous. Similarly, knowing an artist apart from his work is no sure guide to guessing what his art might be.

All human creations, no matter how superficially "impersonal," reflect human decisions; Ortega y Gasset's "dehumanization of art" is really a contradiction in terms. Ad Reinhardt: "Once [Robert Motherwell] said of abstract-expressionism that the abstract part was the art part and the expressionism was the human part. . . . But that's a disgraceful dichotomy. The abstract part is human by itself. Abstract art is only made by humans. No animals or vegetables make it." "Inhuman literature," by definition, would have to be something that human beings cannot do.

Style reflects not "the man," as some would have it, but the author's decisions about the materials of articulation.

An innovative style is less personal than characteristic, though idiosyncracies no doubt reflect personality.

A prime deceit of literary politicking is making the writer (and his or her professional associations) more important than what he or she writes. It joins advertising and promotion in creating a cult of personality. However, what one actually reads is not an author but his or her words.

One assumption of personal poetry is the superior humanity of the poet, but neither reading nor writing poetry necessarily makes a human being more humane. Indeed, every writer knows that the demands of his trade are often humanly deleterious, and rare is the poet who was not at one time in his life hideously insensitive, for the sake of his art, to his immediate surroundings. The best measure of superior humanity is good works in the world, not well-meant poetry.

GENRES

Here and elsewhere, I have usually regarded the corpus of human writing as divided into the traditional genres of poetry, fiction, drama, and the essay. Genre is the literary equivalent of the biological *genus*—a subordinate class with common distinguishing characteristics.

Although much experimental writing tries to knock down the separating barriers, these terms still strike me as valid and useful. Not only is most writing, even experimental writing, conceived with reference to a particular generic category—we speak of "experimental fiction" or an "avant-garde poet"—but nearly all experimental literature clearly belongs to one genre rather than another.

In brief, the common distinguishing characteristics of poetry are personalized expression that favors conciseness and the observing of severely restrictive forms; "fiction" creates a world of self-referring activity and thus favors narrative; "drama" consists of scenarios to be realized in performance; "theatre" is sound, light and action before a live audience; and "essays" confront particular subjects with a high degree of ideation and explicitness.

It is true that some new literature tries to blur the distinctions, especially when the motives and techniques of one genre are integrated with another— for example "narrative poetry" and "lyric fiction." Part of the interest in works of this kind is precisely the tension between the demands of particular genres and the artist's propensities for invention. (A similar tension informs experiments with sentence structure and even with diction.)

Nonetheless, no matter how hard the artist tries to balance the demands of one genre against another, the resulting work clearly falls into one or another category.

ESSAYS

Essays differ from poetry and fiction in striving for direct engagement with personal experience and worldly realities. Poetry and fiction proceed from interior understanding, essays from exterior knowledge. The subject of an essay is more explicit than implicit, as the essayist never loses sight of his chosen concerns. *Essay* is commonly used as an honorific term to characterize expositions that, for reasons of style, do more than merely expose.

In essays, unlike fictions, the author speaks directly, rather than symbolically or metaphorically; he favors definition and communication over implication and ambiguity. Since an essay tries to communicate an author's understanding, one measure of "success" is the reader's comprehension of the author's thoughts.

Since essays are inspired by experience, rather than by literary precedents, essayistic form should ideally follow function; optimally, the essayist should reinvent a form for every new function. One reason why this opportunity has rarely been taken is that people writing about their own experience nearly always observe conventional structures, rarely considering how else their subjects might be approached. The question to ask, each time an essay is written is, what form would be most appropriate for communicating the author's experience?

A detailed chart is an essay; so is the front page of a newspaper. Both of them offer disconnected details that need not be read consecutively. These essays are designed to be "dipped into" and perused; they cannot be read from beginning to end, simply because they have neither beginning nor end.

MEDIA

The experience of comprehending words incorporated into a variety of communications media makes one realize how they differ as extensions of literary language:

Individual pages, prints and paintings have the common quality of best presenting words in visual space, where layout, lettersize and white space affect the presentation and thus the comprehension of language.
Audio tape presents words in time, so that rhythm and silences affect the listener's experience of language.
In sculpture, shape and substance are the crucial factors in enhancing language.
Videotape and film resemble each other in presenting words in automatic visual sequence (though these two media differ in other respects).
Books incorporate the human process of turning the page which means that they deal not only with sequential continuity but with cross-referencing. In books, unlike film or videotape, the reader can, on his own initiative, refer back to an earlier moment or skip ahead to a later one.
The introduction of a new communications medium, like film or videotape, can at its beginnings produce an instant avant-garde, creating art unlike anything seen before.

SPATIAL FORM

The American critic Joseph Frank perceived, over three decades ago, that the predominant form of modernist writing is spatial, as opposed to linear. Even in traditionally narrative genres, such as fiction, the representation of time is often so fragmented and disordered that the reader has trouble following the plot the first time through. In Frank's analysis, advanced fiction was emulating the predominant form of modernist poetry, which favors a "spatial interweaving of images and phrases independently of any time-sequence or narrative action." As novels structured in this way recompose the chronology of the stories they tell, they force the reader to develop perceptual processes quite different from those honed on traditional fiction. Frank advises that, "By continually fitting fragments together and keeping allusions in mind by reflexive reference, [the reader] can link them to their complements."

Though some old-fashioned readers (and teachers) try, at least mentally, to reorder the parts into the semblance of linear sequence, this effort is usually futile. Not only do certain temporal relationships remain persistently ambiguous, but the effort seems false to the epistemology of the work. Precisely because such writing neglects the linear representation of time, it tends to portray life in process, without specific beginning or ends; in this respect it is truly utopian. The experience of other media suggests that the printed page may place as great a limitation upon the "imaginative writing" as syntax.

Since "what happens next" is not a consequential matter, it would instead be wiser for the reader to disregard chronological concerns—to take the story as it is, letting it engage him directly, and even reading around the book, rather than through it—just as he no longer needs a detailed representation of space to understand a cubist painting. Major works of contemporary literature create an impression, an aura, an "afterimage," apart from the details of plot and subject, and it is these general qualities that the reader particularly remembers.

A painting need not be "read" from "beginning to end." Nor need most modern music compositions. Nor need the pages of *Finnegans Wake*, typically, be read in numerical sequence.

Indeed, this essay need not necessarily be read sequentially, though I think there are certain advantages to doing so.

Here and elsewhere, modernist fiction prepares its readers to make those perceptual readjustments necessary to comprehend subsequent new fiction. In reading such works (unlike detective stories), what is principally remembered is not narrative sequence by a sense of thematic interests and images, of both characters and the atmosphere in which they move, in addition to prose style and overall structures—qualities that the reader comprehends bit by bit. It is those qualities, rather than sequential narrative, that the modernist novel tries especially to communicate; so that *spatial form* becomes a means entwined in the end.

"POST-MODERN"

It is becoming fashionable to speak of current art as *post-modern,* which implies that we are now into a period that should be understood as coming *after* "modernism." However, this new term is scarcely appropriate, because a genuine post-modernism would represent either a departure from modernism or a repudiation of it. Harold Rosenberg defined the latter possibility as "a relaxation, a stopping short, or even a return to a state preceding modernist excitement." He cannot discern it. Nor can I. Theoretically, this "post-modernism" should be a development so clear-cut that historians of art and literature could draw a verifiable line between the two periods—a line as definite as that separating "modernism" from classical art. However, this dividing line is not drawn and, in my judgment, cannot be.

Besides, *post* is a petty prefix, both today and historically; for major movements are defined in their own terms rather than by their relation to something else. The only *post* in my dictionary of art history is "post-impressionism," which the editors, Peter and Linda Murray characterize as "a vague term" to define "either a return to a more formal conception of art or a new stress on the importance of the subject." My music dictionary has *post-romanticism* to define patently decadent, post-Wagnerian developments (say, Mahler). No genuinely avant-garde artist would want to be "post" anything.

It is more apt to regard advanced art and writing today as extensions of modernism. In addition to drawing upon earlier innovation, it also honors the modernist values of experiment, mediumistic integrity, complexity, subtlety, difficulty. Artworks that are currently considered "innovative" neither close modernism nor transcend it.

Some art implicitly repudiates modernism, but it is customarily classified as "reactionary." None of it is consequential enough to earn a place in the pantheon of art history. It is not "post-modern" but nowhere.

EDUCATION

Literature is a "teaching machine" that particularly prepares its students to read more literature. (Machine—"a structure consisting of a framework and various fixed and moving parts for doing some kind of work.") Literature depends for its pedagogic success upon the fact that running words before one's eyes is, for many people, first of all a pleasure.

Since literary innovation completely revamps our tastes in previous literature, one by-product of experimental writing is a reinterpretation of the literary past, largely to emphasize certain previously neglected precursors. New works shine different lights on past writings. After one has appreciated

Finnegans Wake, for instance, Lewis Carroll seems the most interesting of Victorian writers. After the reader has submerged himself deeply in contemporary avant-garde writing, the Russian futurists seem more interesting than most of the English romantics, art criticism more fertile than literary criticism, Moholy-Nagy and Kurt Schwitters more suggestive than artists who specialized in only one medium, and the essays of both Ezra Pound and T. S. Eliot more pertinent than their poetry. One also prefers Gertrude Stein to William Faulkner, e. e. cummings to Robert Frost, Wyndham Lewis to D. H. Lawrence, and Dada to surrealism. *Alice in Wonderland* is still literature, while *Middlemarch* is by now sociology or history.

Literature teaches us not only how to read but how to reread. A *useful* book is, by definition, one that teaches us how to perceive words in ways we have not done before. Perceptual usefulness is a human virtue in art.

KNOWLEDGE

Knowledge of past art is the most essential preparation for perceiving originality in the present. Only by knowing thoroughly "what has already been done" can one acknowledge what is genuinely new. Only after one has read a carload of conventional novels and realized their limitations can one really appreciate true innovation.

The painter Robert Motherwell once remarked that the contemporary artist carries the history of modern art around in his head, and the possession of such mental baggage is essential not only for the avoidance of plagiarism but also for the development of discriminating avant-garde perception. To both artist and audience, knowledge of precursors is a prerequisite for the experience of historically authentic surprise. An illiterate, by contrast, is likely either to miss significant innovation or be conned by false advertising (which opportunistically exploits ignorance).

Apollinaire: "It is by the element of surprise, by the important place it assigns to surprise, that the new spirit is distinguished from all earlier artistic and literary movements." The spectator's pleasure in the experience of surprise is quite different from the satisfaction he gets from observing the fulfillment of a literary convention.

The difference between the artist's filling forms and inventing them is comparable to the difference between the spectator's appreciating a conventional realization and his experience of surprise.

Knowledge provides context that informs current experience. Without a knowledge of past works of art, it would be impossible to comprehend the significance of conceptual, inferential art (such as John Cage's *4'33''*, a presentation of no-sound in a context where music is expected) or Marcel Duchamp's history of meaningful inaction.

Especially to understand innovative writing, readers should know the other arts as well. One reason is that experimental writers like to discover whether an idea developed in another art can be applied to their own; that procedure exemplifies creative processes that are truly experimental. Unless one is familiar with minimalism, say, in painting, he is liable to miss its use and effect in writing.

Conversely, a knowledge of modernist writing helps one's appreciation of the other arts. *Finnegans Wake* is probably the most appropriate precursor, as well as the most effective sensitizer, to multiple serialization in contemporary music.

TECHNIQUES

In artistic endeavor much depends upon techniques that are acquired in experience. For writing, the most useful education initially involves a mastering of basic procedures: how to write sentences, construct paragraphs, observe forms, organize perceptions, and so forth. This can be done in an academic setting, in a situation of apprenticeship, or by concentrated personal study. The operational assumption is that these techniques enable an aspiring artist to impose the intelligence of effective forms upon "talent" and "invention."

An aspiring poet is someone who is assimilating the traditions and techniques of poetry. Artistic growth is measured initially by an increasing mastery of extant forms, and then by an ability to generate personal structures.

At minimum, technique is an arsenal of options in lessening the inevitable resistances between an artist's imagination and his chosen medium, between the mental desire and its material realization. An idiot can be a good athlete, even in sports requiring intelligence (for example, football), if he assimilates those techniques that will, with a maximum of physical effort and psychological concentration, enable him to perform intelligently. Mastery of superior technique can also enable inferior minds to produce intelligent writing, precisely because form marshals their mental material.

As different sports emphasize different techniques, so do different literary genres; and even within the techniques indigenous to a certain genre, different styles or "positions" emphasize particular techniques. Whereas one kind of fiction depends upon characterization, another emphasizes heightened prose, a third formal invention. "Technique," according to Gertrude Stein, "is not so much a thing of form and style as the way that form and style came and how it can come again." (Technique is thus a mechanism, a generative system that exploits human talent to produce certain ends.)

Without a mastery of these fundamental techniques, the aspiring artist, like the aspiring athlete, can hardly begin to play the game successfully. Both the artist and the athlete will otherwise feel oppressed by desires that cannot find expression, at least not in forms they find satisfactory. What happens after the mastering of basic techniques is the true measure of inspiration and artistry.

As one learns to write initially by reading, so it is by rereading that one learns to rewrite, as well as how not to rewrite, and by rewriting one learns the possibilities of language.

PHILISTINISM

In protesting resistances to the dissemination of their work, experimental writers are advised to blame the amorphous public; but it is really more appropriate to excoriate publishers, who stand between art and its likely public. And decidedly innovative writers can also blame certain other writers. In a remarkably perspicacious reformulation of this predicament, the art critic Leo Steinberg noted that,

> Whenever there appears an art that is truly new and original, the men who denounce it first and loudest are artists. Obviously, because they are the most engaged. No critic, no outraged bougeois, can match an artist's passion in repudiation. . . .Therefore, instead of repeating the charge that only academic painters spurn the new, why not reverse the charge? Any man becomes academic by virtue of, or with respect to, what he rejects.

If critics dislike a new artist, he may indeed be not particularly good; but if artists dislike him as well and, better yet, publicly denounce his work, then it is probably exceptionally original. Nothing measures the power of a new style more surely than the extent to which the professional establishment dislikes it.

In my observation, it is not professional editors but other poets who *resist* (rather than just neglect) the publication of experimental literature. That explains why the current avant-gardes in poetry and fiction are completely excluded from so many periodicals and anthologies edited by practicing poets and novelists.

The commissars of cultural commerce, who control the channels of communication, subscribe to the principle of precedent, whose fundamental role is that nothing succeeds more surely than semblances of past success. And there is nothing, but nothing, that the scrupulous avant-gardist wants to resemble least.

REPUTATION

An artist initiates his "reputation" by creating works to be observed, and the first person to like his art becomes the initial engine in a burgeoning process. Should this admirer be influential, say, because his spoken opinions are persuasive or because he has access to a publicizing medium, then others will reiterate this initial praise, which will, in turn, be communicated to expanding circles of possible admirers.

At this point, the reputation will probably have its detractors, especially if the new work is perceived to be different or threatening. Though these disparaging critics may make considerable noise, their negative opinion does not really hamper the development of a reputation. Indeed, vociferous hate inadvertently gives a new art publicity, which induces people to pay attention to what they would otherwise ignore.

By this point, the further growth of an artist's eminence depends less upon who hates his work than upon who likes it, and whether the latter can communicate their enthusiasm to yet larger circles of possible admirers. The measure of a reputation's decline is not the existence of detractors but the absence of advocates. As long as someone tells someone else of an artist's work, his reputation will survive.

SELECTIVITY

The cruelest process in art is the selectivity that governs its communication. Out of the many who practice, only a few are acclaimed.

Publishers select from the manuscripts available to them; book reviewers select from the publications that are sent to them.

Bookstore managers, even in more literary shops, select from the titles offered them, and customers select from the merchandise available in the stores.

Readers select when they read or reread one book on their shelves, rather than another, and select again when they recommend a book to other readers, who in turn discriminate among recommendations.

Historians of art and literature memorialize reputations by selecting from the hundreds that have some critical currency, and both readers and teachers exercise their preference in historians.

Though thousands of artists are working at a particular time, the annals of art history contain remarkably few names; and not only is membership in this top echelon continually changing, but the honor rolls get shorter and shorter as periods of art recede further into the past. This process is assumed to have a Darwinistic integrity—only the fittest survive—which may or may not be true. One fact separating the present from the past is the larger number of serious artists who currently regard themselves as avant-garde.

ACCURATE PERCEPTION

Since innovative art is likely to appear inscrutable, accurate perception is a prerequisite for further appreciation. Indeed, without the initial perception of What It Is, further comprehension is likely to be interdicted or confused. Pound opens his *ABC of Reading* with a memoir of Louis Agassiz telling a student to "describe" a small fish. The student checked a textbook and informed Agassiz of the fish's proper Latin name. "Agassiz again told the student to describe the fish. The student produced a four-page essay. Agassiz then told him to look at the fish."

In hearing people talk about innovative art—and even in reading newspaper reviews—one often feels as insistent as Agassiz. Even an attempt at accurate observation should precede the positing of judgments, for the ideal of thorough description should at mimimum force the observer to identify and perhaps assimilate essential esthetic properties that he might otherwise miss.

One practical function of unprecedented art is preparing the perceptual faculties for the puzzling forms in the changing scene around us. Constant change in art restimulates perception in a constantly transforming world, for art best influences society precisely by enhancing the understandings of its audience. People who are blinded by innovative art (or allow themselves to be) are liable to be similarly ignorant about what is most original in contemporary life.

BIBLIOGRAPHY

Kenneth Burke, *Counterstatement* (1931)

John Cage, *Silence* (1961), *A Year from Monday* (1967), *M.* (1973)

Donald Drew Egbert, *Social Radicalism in the Arts* (1970)

T. S. Eliot, *Selected Essays* (1932)

RICHARD KOSTELANETZ

Ralph Ellison, *Shadow and Act* (1964)

Joseph Frank, *The Widening Gyre* (1963)

Northrop Frye, *Anatomy of Criticism* (1957), *Fables of Identity* (1963)

E. H. Gombrich, *Art and Illusion* (1961)

Clement Greenberg, *Art and Culture* (1961)

Ihab Hassan, *Paracriticisms* (1975)

Dick Higgins, *Foew&ombwhnw* (1969)

James Joyce, *Finnegans Wake* (1939)

Michael Kirby, *The Art of Time* (1969)

Richard Kostelanetz, *Breakthrough Fictioneers* (1973), *The End of Intelligent Writing* (1974),
   Essaying Essays (1975)

George Kubler, *The Shape of Time* (1962)

Thomas S. Kuhn, *The Structure of Scientific Revolutions* (1962)

Lucy R. Lippard, *Changing* (1971)

Vladimir Markov, *Russian Futurism* (1968)

Marshall McLuhan, *Understanding Media* (1964)

L. Moholy-Nagy, *Vision in Motion* (1947)

Piet Mondrian, *Plastic Art and Pure Plastic Art* (1938)

Renato Poggioli, *The Theory of the Avant-Garde* (1968)

Ezra Pound, *ABC of Reading* (1934), *Selected Essays* (1960)

Ad Reinhardt, *Art as Art: Selected Writings* (1975)

Harold Rosenberg, *The Tradition of the New* (1959)

Gertrude Stein, *Geography and Plays* (1922), *Lectures in America* (1935)

Ludwig Wittgenstein, *Tractatus Logico-philosophicus* (1921)

Rosmarie Waldrop, *Against Language* (1971)

Jerome Rothenberg

Pre-Face

PRIMITIVE MEANS COMPLEX

That there are no primitive languages is an axiom of contemporary linguistics where it turns its attention to the remote languages of the world. There are no half-formed languages, no underdeveloped languages. Everywhere a development has taken place into structures of great complexity. People who have failed to achieve the wheel will not have failed to invent and develop a highly wrought grammar. Hunters and gatherers innocent of all agriculture will have vocabularies that distinguish the things of their world down to the finest details. The language of snow among the Eskimos is awesome. The aspect system of Hopi verbs can, by a flick of the tongue, make the most subtle kinds of distinction between different types of motion.

What is true of language in general is equally true of poetry and of the ritual-systems of which so much poetry is a part. It is a question of energy and intelligence as universal constants and, in any specific case, the direction that energy and intelligence (=imagination) have been given. . . . Poetry, wherever you find it among the "primitives" (literally *everywhere*), involves an extremely complicated sense of materials and structures. Everywhere it involves the manipulation (fine or gross) of multiple elements. If this isn't always apparent, it's because the carry-over (by translation or interpretation) necessarily distorts where it chooses some part of the whole that it can meaningfully deal with. The work is foreign and its complexity is often elusive, a question of gestalt or configuration, of the angle from which the work is seen. . . .

It's very hard in fact to decide what precisely are the boundaries of "primitive" poetry or of a "primitive" poem, since there's often no activity differentiated as such, but the words and/or vocables are part of a larger total "work" that may go on for hours, even days, at a stretch. What we would separate as music and dance and myth and painting is also part of that work, and the need for separation is a question of "our" interest and preconceptions, not of "theirs." Thus the picture is immediately complicated by the nature of the work and the media that comprise it. And it becomes clear that the "collective" nature of primitive poetry (upon which so much stress has been placed despite the existence of individualized poems and clearly identified poets) is to a great degree inseparable from the amount of materials a single work may handle.

Now all of this is, if so stated, a question of technology as well as inspiration; and we may as well take it as axiomatic for what follows that where poetry is concerned, *primitive* means complex.

PRIMITIVE AND MODERN: INTERSECTIONS AND ANALOGUES

Like any collector, my approach to delimiting and recognizing what's a poem has been by analogy: in this case (beyond the obvious definition of poems as words-of-songs) to the work of modern poets. Since much of this work has been revolutionary and limit-smashing, the analogy in turn expands the range of what "we" can see as primitive (tribal/oral) poetry: an expansion that can work equally well at the other end of the process, opening up new possibilities for our own work as well. It also shows some of the ways in which primitive poetry and thought are close to an impulse toward unity in our time, of which the poets are forerunners. The important intersections (analogies) are:

(1) the poem carried by the voice: a "pre"-literate situation of poetry composed to be spoken, chanted or, more accurately, sung; compare this to the "post-literate"

written poem as score
public readings

poets' theaters
jazz poetry

situation, in McLuhan's good phrase, or where-we-are-today;

(2) a highly developed process of image-thinking: concrete or non-causal thought in contrast to the simplifications of Aristotelian logic, etc., with its "objective categories" & rules of non-contradiction; a "logic" of polarities; creation thru dream, etc.; modern poetry (having had & outlived the experience of rationalism) enters a post-logical phase;

(3) a "minimal" art of maximal involvement; compound elements, each clearly articulated, & with plenty of room for fill-in (gaps in sequence, etc.): the "spectator" as (ritual) participant who pulls it all together;

(4) an "intermedia" situation, as further denial of the categories: the poet's techniques aren't limited to verbal maneuvers but operate also through song, non-verbal sound, visual signs, & the varied activities of the ritual event: here the "poem"—the work of the "poet" in whatever medium, or (where we're able to grasp it) the totality of the work;

(5) the animal-body-rootedness of "primitive" poetry: recognition of a "physical" basis for the poem within a man's body—or as an act of body & mind together, breath &/or spirit; in many cases too the direct & open handling of sexual imagery & (in the "events") of sexual activities as key factors in

1960s folk-rock, etc.

Blake's multi-images
symbolism
surrealism

deep-image

random poetry
composition by field, etc.

concrete poetry

picture poems
prose poems

happenings
total theater

poets as filmmakers, etc.

dada
lantgedichte (sound poems)

beast language

line & breath
projective verse, etc.

sexual revolution, etc.

creation of the sacred;

(6) the poet as shaman, or primitive shaman as poet & seer thru control of the means just stated: an open "visionary" situation prior to all system-making ("priesthood") in which the man creates thru dream (image) & word (song), "that Reason may have ideas to build on" (W. Blake).

Rimbaud's voyant
Rilke's angel
Lorca's duende

beat poetry
psychedelic see-ins, be-ins, etc.

individual neo-shamanisms, etc. works directly influenced by the "other" poetry or by analogies to "primitive art": ideas of negritude, tribalism, wilderness, etc.

What's more, the translations themselves may create new forms and shapes-of-poems with their own energies and interest—another intersection that can't be overlooked.

David Antin

Video: Distinctive Features of the Medium

Video art. The name is equivocal. A good name. It leaves open all the questions and asks them anyway. Is this an art form, a new genre? an anthology of valued activity conducted in a particular arena defined by display on a cathode ray tube? the kind of video made by a special class of people—artists—whose works are exhibited primarily in what is called "the art world"—*artists' video*? An inspection of the names in an exhibition catalogue gives the easy and not quite sufficient answer that it is this last we are considering, *artists' video.* But is this a class apart? Artists have been making video pieces for scarcely ten years—if we disregard one or two flimsy studio jobs and Nam June Paik's 1963 kamikaze TV modifications—and video has been a fact of gallery life for barely five years. Yet we've already had group exhibitions, panels, symposia, magazine issues devoted to this phenomenon, for the very good reasons that more and more artists are using video and some of the best work being done in the art world is being done with video. Which is why a discourse has already arisen to greet it. Actually two discourses: one, a kind of enthusiastic welcoming prose peppered with fragments of communication theory and McLuhanesque media talk; the other, a rather nervous attempt to locate the "unique properties of the medium." Discourse 1 could be called *cyberscat* and Discourse 2, because it engages the issues that pass for "formalism" in the art world, could be called

Reprinted, abridged, from *Video Art* (Institute of Contemporary Art, University of Pennsylvania, 1975), by permission of the author. Copyright © 1975 by Institute of Contemporary Art. Initially published in an exhibition catalogue.

DAVID ANTIN

"the formalist rap." Though there is no necessary relation between them, the two discourses occasionally occur together as they do in the words of Frank Gillette, which offers a convenient sample:

D1

The emergence of relationships between the culture you're in and the parameters that allow you expression are fed back through a technology. It's the state of the art technology within a particular culture that gives shape to ideas.

D2

What I'm consciously involved in is devising a way that is structurally intrinsic to television. For example, what makes it *not* film? Part of it is that you look *into* the source of light, with film you look *with* the source of light. In television, the source of light and the source of information are one.[1]

Though it is not entirely clear what high class technology has to do with the rather pleasantly shabby technical state of contemporary video art, or what the significance is to human beings of the light source in two adjacent representational media, statements of this type are characteristic, and similar quotes could be multiplied endlessly. And if these concerns seem somewhat gratuitous or insufficient with respect to the work at hand, they often share a kind of aptness of detail, even though it is rarely clear what the detail explains of the larger pattern of activity in which these artists are involved. In fact, what seems most typical of both types of discourse is a certain anxiety, which may be seen most clearly in a recent piece by Hollis Frampton:

Moreover it is doubly important that we try to say what video art is at present because we posit for it a privileged future. Since the birth of video art from the Jovian backside (I dare not say brow) of the Other Thing called television, I for one have felt a more and more pressing need for precise definitions of what film art *is*, since I extend to film, as well, the hope of a privileged future.[2]

It would be so much more convenient to develop the refined discussion of the possible differences between film and video, if we could only forget the Other Thing—television. Yet television haunts all exhibitions of video art, though when actually present it is only minimally represented, with perhaps a few commercials or "the golden performances" of Ernie Kovacs (a television "artist"); otherwise its presence is manifest mainly in quotes, allusion, parody, and protest, as in Telethon's *TV History*, Douglas Davis's installation piece with the TV set forced to face the wall, or Richard Serra's

382

Television Delivers People. No doubt, in time there will be an *auteur* theory of television, which will do for Milton Berle and Sid Caesar what Sarris and Farber and *Cahiers du Cinéma* have done for John Ford and Nicholas Ray and Howard Hawkes. But the politics of the art world is, for good reasons, rather hostile to Pop, and that kind of admiring discussion will have to wait; even *Cahiers du Cinéma* has abandoned Hitchcock and Nicholas Ray for Dziga Vertov and the European avant-garde on sociopolitical, aesthetic grounds. But it's unwise to despise an enemy, especially a more powerful, older enemy, who happens also to be your frightful parent. So it is with television that we have to begin to consider video, because if anything has defined the formal and technical properties of the video medium, it is the television industry.

The history of television in the United States is well known. Commercial television is essentially a post-World War phenomenon, and its use was, logically enough, patterned on commercial radio, since control of the new medium was in the hands of the powerful radio networks, which constitute essentially a government-protected, private monopoly. This situation determined many of the fundamental communication characteristics of the new medium. The most basic of these is the social relation between "sending" and "receiving," which is profoundly unequal and asymmetrical. Since the main potential broadcasters, the powerful radio networks, were already deeply involved with the electronics industry through complex ownership affiliation, and since they also constituted the single largest potential customer for the electronic components of television, the components were developed entirely for their convenience and profit. While this may not seem surprising, the result was that the acts of picture-taking and transmission were made enormously expensive: Cameras and transmission systems were designed and priced out of the reach of anything but corporate ownership. Moreover, government regulations set standards on "picture quality" and the transmission signal, which effectively ensured that "taking" and "transmission" control would remain in the hands of the industry into which the federal government had already assigned the airwaves channel by channel. The receivers alone were priced within the range of individual ownership. This fundamental ordering—establishing the relations between the taker-sender and the receiver—had, of course, been worked out for commercial radio.

Only ham transmission—also hemmed in severely by government regulation—and special uses like ship-to-shore, pilot-to-control tower, and police band radio deal in the otherwise merely potential equalities of wireless telephony. That this was not technically inevitable, but merely an outcome of the social situation and the marketing strategies of the industry, is obvious. There is nothing necessarily more complex or expensive in the camera than there is in the receiver. It is merely that the great expense of receiver technology was defrayed by the mass production of the sets, whose multiplication multiplied the dollar exchange value of transmission time sold by the transmitter to its advertisers. So the broadcasters underwrote receiver development, because every set bought delivers its viewers as salable goods in an exchange that pays for the "expensive" technology.

For television also there is a special-use domain—educational, industrial, and now artistic—where the relation between the camera and receiver may be more or less equalized, but this is because transmission is not an issue and the distribution of the images is severely restricted. The economic fact remains—transmission is more expensive than reception. This ensures a power hierarchy—transmission dominates reception. And it follows from this asymmetry of power relations that the taker-transmitter dominates whatever communication takes place.

This is clearer when you consider the manners of telephony. A would-be transmitter asks for permission to transmit, rings the home of a potential receiver. It's like ringing a doorbell. Or a would-be receiver rings the home of a possible transmitter, asks him/her to transmit. This formal set of relations has become even more refined with the introduction of the *Answerphone* and the answering service, which mediates between the ring—an anonymous invitation to communicate—and the response, requiring the caller to identify himself and leaving the receiver with a choice of whether or not to respond. In telephony manners are everything, while in commercial television manners are nothing. If you have a receiver you merely plug in to the possibility of a signal, which may or may not be there and which you cannot modify except in the trivial manner of switching to a nearly identical transmission or in a decisive but final manner by switching it off. Choice is in the hands of the sender.

Now while this asymmetry is not inherent in the technology, it has become so normative for the medium that it forms the all-pervasive and invisible background of all video. This may not be so dramatically manifested in most artwork video, but that's because most artworks have very equivocal relations to the notion of communication and are, like industry, producer-dominated. Yet it has a formidable effect on all attempts at interactive video, which operates primarily in reaction to this norm. In this sense the social structure of the medium is a matrix that defines the formal properties of the medium—since it limits the possibilities of a video communication genre—and these limits then become the target against which any number of artists have aimed their works. What else could Ira Schneider have had in mind about the 1969 piece, *Wipe Cycle*, he devised with Frank Gillette:

> The most important thing was the notion of information presentation, and the notion of the integration of the audience into the information. One sees oneself exiting from the elevator. If one stands there for 8 seconds, one sees oneself entering the gallery from the elevator again. Now at the same time one is apt to be seeing oneself standing there watching *Wipe Cycle.* You can watch yourself live watching yourself 8 seconds ago, watching yourself 16 seconds ago, *eventually feeling free enough to interact with this matrix, realizing one's own potential as an actor.*[3] [my italics]

What is attempted is the conversion (liberation) of an audience (receiver) into an actor (transmitter), which Schneider and Gillette must have hoped to accomplish by neutralizing as much as possible the acts of "taking" and electronic transmission. If they failed to accomplish this, they were hardly alone in their failure, which seems to have been the fate of just about every interactive artwork employing significantly technological means. Apparently, the social and economic distribution of technological resources in this culture has a nearly determining effect on the semiotics of technological resources. More concretely, an expensive video camera and transmission system switched on and ready for use don't lose their peculiar prestigious properties just because an artist may make them available under special circumstances for casual use to an otherwise passive public. In fact, this kind of interactive video situation almost invariably begins by intimidating an unprepared audience, which has already been indoctrinated about the amount of preparedness (professionalism) the video camera deserves, regardless of the trivial nature of television professionalism, which is not measured by competence (as in the elegant relation of ends to means) but by the amount of money notably expended on this preparation. Yet while the most fundamental property of television is its social organization, this is manifested most clearly in its money metric, which applies to every aspect of the medium, determining the tempo of its representations and the style of the performances, as well as the visual syntax of its editing. The money metric has also played a determining role in neutralizing what is usually considered the most markedly distinctive feature of the medium: the capacity for instantaneous transmission.

In principle, television seemed to combine the photographic reproduction capacities of the camera, the motion capabilities of film, and the instantaneous transmission properties of the telephone. But just as the photographic reproduction capacity of the camera is essentially equivocal and mainly significant as mythology, so is the fabled instantaneity of television essentially a rumor that combines with photographic duplicity to produce a quasi-recording medium, the main feature of which is unlikeliness in relation to any notion of reality. The history of the industry is very instructive with respect to this remarkable outcome.

In the beginning, television made widespread use of live broadcasting both for transmitting instant news events that were elapsing in real time and for more or less well-rehearsed studio performances; and some of the most interesting events recorded by media were the result of the unpredictability of instantaneous transmission. Spokesmen for the industry never failed to call attention to this feature of instantaneity, and as late as 1968 a standard handbook for television direction and production by Stasheff and Bretz asserted:

> Perhaps the most distinctive function of television is its ability to show distant events at the moment when they are taking place. The Kefauver hearings, with a close-up of the hands of gangster Frank Costello; the Army-McCarthy hearings; the complete coverage of the orbital shots; the presidential nominating conventions; the Great Debates of 1960; the live transmissions from Europe and Japan via satellite—this is television doing what no other medium can do.[4]

Yet the same handbook casually points out a few pages later that between 1947 and 1957, kine-recordings, films taken directly from the TV screen, were in constant and heavy use, especially for delayed broadcast of East Coast programs on the West Coast, in spite of the much poorer image quality of the kines, and that by 1961 virtually all television dramatic programs were being produced on film. There were, apparently, from the industry's standpoint, great inconveniences in instantaneous transmission. The most obvious of these was that at the same instant of time the life cycles of New York and Los Angeles are separted by three full hours, and since the day for the industry is metrically divided into prime and nonprime viewing time, in accordance with whether more or fewer viewers may be sold to the advertisers, the money value of instantaneous transmission is inversely related in a complicated way to the temporal distance of transmission. But this is only the most obvious manner in which the money metric worked to eliminate instantaneity. A more basic conflict exists between the structure of the industry and the possibility of instantaneity and unpredictability.

Any series of events that is unfolding for the first time, or in a new way, or with unanticipated intensity or duration threatens to overrun or elude the framing conventions of the recording artists (the cameramen and directors). This element of surprise is always in conflict with the image of smoothness, which has the semiotic function of marking the producer's competence by emphasizing his mastery and control, his grasp of events. The signs of unpredictability and surprise are discontinuities and ragged edges that mark the boundaries of that competence by puncturing or lacerating that grasp. The image of smoothness depends always upon the appearance of the un-impeded forward course of the producer's intention, of facility, which means that there must be no doubt in the viewer's mind that what is transmitted is what the transmitter wants to transmit. And the only ways to achieve this were through (a) repeated preparation of the events (b) very careful selection of highly predictable events or (c) deletion of unexpected and undesirable aspects of events, which meant editing a recorded version of these events. Videotape came in 1956, and at the beginning Ampex was taping the Douglas Edwards newscasts and, not much later, the stage presentations of *Playhouse 90.* Once again, according to Stasheff and Bretz:

> . . .by 1957 a new TV revolution was under way. Undistinguishable from live TV on the home receiver, video tape quickly replaced the kine-recording done by the TV networks. Not only did the stations put out a better picture, but the savings were tremendous. . . . Live production, video-tape recording of live production, kine-recording, and film began to assume complementary roles in the pattern of TV production. Video-tape recording by 1961 became so commonplace that the true live production—reaching the home at the moment of its origination—was a rarity limited largely to sports and special events. *The live production on video tape, though delayed in reaching the home by a few hours or a few days, was generally accepted as actual live television by the average viewer.*[5] [my italics.]

Yet this did not place television in the same position as film, which from its origins appeared to be situated squarely in the domain of illusion. Film, after all, has made very few and very insubstantial claims to facticity. Amet's bathtub battle of Santiago Bay may have convinced Spanish military historians of its authenticity, but that was back in 1897 before the movie palaces together with the moviemakers dispelled any illusion of potential facticity. Flaherty looks as clearly fictional as Méliès now. But a genre that is marked "fictional" doesn't raise issues of truth and falsehood, and television never ceases to raise these issues. The social uses of television continually force the issue of "truth" to the center of attention. A President goes on television to declare his "honesty," a minister announces his "intentions," the evening news reports "what is being done to curb the inflation." The medium maintains a continual assertion that it can and does provide an adequate representation of reality, while everyone's experience continually denies it. Moreover, the industry exhibits a persistent positive tropism toward the appearance of the spontaneous and unrehearsed event in its perpetually recurring panel shows and quiz programs and in the apparently casual format of its late-evening news shows. According to Stasheff and Bretz:

> . . . the television audience will not only accept, but even enjoy, a production error or even a comedian who blows his lines and admits it or who asks his straight man to feed him a cue once again so that he can make another try at getting the gag to come out right. This leniency on the part of the audience is caused by the increased feeling of spontaneity and immediacy which minor crises create. The audience loves to admire the adroitness with which the performer "pulls himself out of a jam." [6]

The industry wishes, or feels obligated, to maintain the illusion of immediacy, which it defines rather precisely as "the *feeling* that what one sees on the TV screen is living and actual reality, at that very moment taking place." [7] The perfection of videotape made possible the careful manipulation and selective presentation of desirable "errors" and "minor crises" as marks of spontaneity, which became as equivocal in their implications as the drips and blots of third-generation abstract expressionists. It's not that you couldn't see the Los Angeles Police Department's tactical assault squad in real time, in full living color, in your own living room, leveling a small section of the city in search of three or four suspected criminals, but that what you would see couldn't be certainly discriminated from a carefully edited videotape screened three hours later. So what television provides video with is a tradition not of falseness, which would be a kind of guarantee of at least a certain negative reliability, but of a profoundly menacing equivocation and mannerism, determining a species of unlikeness.

At first glance artists' video seems to be defined by the total absence of any of the features that define television. But this apparent lack of relation is in fact a very definite and predictable inverse relation. If we temporarily ignore the subfamily of installation pieces, which are actually quite diverse among themselves but nevertheless constitute a single genre, the most striking contrast between video pieces and television is in relation to time. It may not be quite hip to say so without qualification, but it is a commonplace to describe artists' videotapes as "boring" or "long," even when one feels that this in no way invalidates or dishonors the tapes in question (Bruce Boice's comment that Lynda Benglis's video is "boring, interesting and funny";[8] or Richard Serra's own videotape, *Prisoners' Dilemma,* where one character advises another that he may have to spend two hours in the basement of the Castelli Gallery, which is "twice as long as the average boring videotape"). This perceived quality of being boring or long has little to do with the attitude of just about all the artists using video to the task at hand. John Baldessari has a tape called *Some Words I Mispronounce.* He turns to a blackboard and writes:

1. poor   4. Beelzebub

2. cask   5. bough

3. bade   6. sword

As soon as he completes the "d" of *sword* the tape is over. Running time is under a minute. It feels amazingly short. But it is longer than most commercials.

Robert Morris's *Exchange*, a series of verbal meditations on exchanges of information, collaborations, and interferences with a woman, accompanied by a variety of images taped and retaped from other tapes and photographs for the most part as indefinite and suggestive as the discourse, goes on until it arrives at a single distinct and comic story of not getting to see the Gattamelata, after which the tape trails off in a more or less leisurely fashion. Running time is forty-three minutes. Television has many programs that are much longer. The two artists' tapes are very different. Baldessari's is a routine, explicitly defined from the outset and carried out deadpan to its swift conclusion. *Exchange* is a typical member of what is by now a well-defined genre of artist narrative, essentially an extended voiceover in a carefully framed literary style that seeks its end intuitively in the exhaustion of its mild narrative energy. But they both have the same attitude toward time: The work ends whenever its intention is accomplished. The time is inherent time, the time required for the task at hand. The work is "boring," as Les Levine remarked, "if you demand that it be something else. If you demand that it be itself then it is not boring."[9] This is not to say that the videotapes may not be uninteresting. Whether they are interesting or not is largely a matter of judging the value of the task at hand, and this could hardly be the issue for people who can look with equanimity at what hangs on the wall in the most distinguished galleries. For whatever we think of the videotapes of Morris, or Sonnier, or Serra, these are certainly not inferior to whatever else they put in the gallery. Levine is right. Videotapes are boring if you demand that they be something else. But they're not judged boring by comparison with paintings or sculpture, they're judged boring in comparison with television, which for the last twenty years has set the standard of video time.

But the time standard of television is based firmly on the social and economic nature of the industry itself, and has nothing whatever to do with the absolute technical and phenomenological possibilities of visual representation by cathode ray tube. For television, time has an absolute existence independent of any imagery that may or may not be transmitted over its well-defended airwaves and cables. It is television's only solid, a tangible commodity that is precisely divisible into further and further subdivisible homogeneous units, the smallest quantum of which is measured by the smallest segment that could be purchased by a potential advertiser, which is itself defined by the minimum particle required to isolate a salable product from among a variable number of equivalent alternatives. The smallest salable piece turns out to be the ten-second spot, and all television is assembled from it.

But the social conventions of television dictate a code of behavior according to which the transmitter must assume two apparently different roles in transmission. In one he must appear to address the viewer on the station's behalf as entertainer; in the other on the sponsor's behalf as salesman. The rules of the game, which are legally codified, prescribe a sharp demarcation between the roles, and the industry makes a great show of marking off the boundaries between its two types of performances—the programs and the commercials. At their extremes of hard-sell and soft-show, one might suppose that the stylistic features of the two roles would be sufficient to distinguish them, but the extremes are rare, the social function of the roles are not so distinct, and the stylistic features seldom provide sufficient separation. Since the industry's most tangible presentation is metrically divisible time, the industry seems to mark the separation emphatically by assigning the two roles different time signatures. The commercial is built on a scale of the minute out of multiple ten-second units. It comes in four common sizes—10, 30, 60 and 120 seconds—of which the thirty-second slot is by far the commonest. The program is built on the scale of the hour out of truncated and hinged fifteen-minute units that are also commonly assembled in four sizes—15, 30, and 60 and 120 minutes—of which the half-hour program is the commonest, though the hour length is usual for important programs, two hours quite frequent for specials and feature films, and fifteen minutes not entirely a rarity for commentary. Television inherited the split roles and the two time signatures from radio, as well as the habit of alternating them in regularly recurrent intervals, which creates the arbitrary-appearing, mechanical segmentation of both media's presentations. But television carried this mechanical segmentation to a new extreme and presented it in such a novel way—through a special combination of its own peculiar technology and production conventions—that televsion time, in spite of structural similarity with radio time, has an entirely different appearance from it, bearing the relationship to it of an electronically driven, digital counter to a spring-driven, hand-wound alarm clock.

Television achieved its extreme segmentation of transmission time mainly through the intense development of multiple sponsorship. Old radio programs from the 1930s and 1940s tended to have a single sponsor. *The Lone Ranger* was sponsored for years by Silvercup Bread, *Ma Perkins* by Oxydol, *Uncle Don* by Ovaltine, and these sponsors would reappear regularly at the beginning, middle, and end of each program with pretty much the same commercial pitch. This pattern continued by and large into the early days of television with *Hallmark Theater, The Kraft Playhouse,* and so on. But current television practice is generally quite different. A half-hour program might have something like six minutes of commercial fitted to it in three two-minute blocks at the beginning, middle, and end of the program. But these six minutes of commercial time might promote the commodities of twelve different sponsors, or twelve different commodities of some smaller number of sponsoring agencies. The commodities could be nearly anything—a car, a cruise, a furniture polish, a breakfast food, a funeral service, a scent for men, a cure for smoking, an ice show, an X-rated movie, or a politician. In principle they could apply to nearly any aspect of human life and be presented in any order, with strategies of advocacy more various than the commodities themselves. In practice the range of commodity and styles of advocacy are somewhat more limited, but the fact remains that in half an hour you might see a succession of four complete, distinct, and unrelated thirty-second presentations, followed by a twelve-minute half of a presentation, followed by a one-minute presentation, one thirty-second presentation, and two ten-second presentations, followed by the second and concluding half presentation (twelve minutes long), followed by yet another four unrelated thirty-second presentations. But since this would lead to bunching of two two-minute commercials into a four-minute package of commercial at the end of every hour, and since viewers are supposed to want mainly to look at the programs—or because program-makers are rather possessive about their own commercials and want complete credit for them—the program-makers have recently developed the habit of presenting a small segment of their own program as a kind of prologue before the opening commercial, to separate it from the tail end of the preceding program, while the program-makers of the preceding program may attempt to tag onto the end of their program a small epilogue at the end of their last commercial, to affix it more securely to their own program. Meanwhile, the station may itself interject a small commercial promoting itself or its future presentations. All of these additional segments—prologues, epilogues, station promotions, and coming attractions—usually last no more than two minutes, are scaled to commercial time, and are in their functional nature promotions for either immediately succeeding or eventually succeeding transmissions. This means that you may see upward of fourteen distinct segments of presentation in any half-hour, all but two of which will be scaled to commercial time. Since commercial time is the most common signature, we could expect it to dominate the tempo of television, especially since the commercial segments constitute the only example of integral (complete and uninterrupted) presentation in the medium. And it does, but not in the way one would generally suppose.

It is very easy to exaggerate the apparent differences between commercial time and program time by concentrating on the dramatic program. Television has many programs that share a mechanically segmented structure with the packet of commercials. The most extreme cases are the news programs, contests, and the so-called talk shows. What is called news on television is a chain of successive, distinct, and structurally unrelated narrations called stories. These average from thirty seconds to two minutes in length, are usually presented in successions of three or four in a row, and are bracketed between packets of commercials from one to two minutes long. The "full" story is built very much like a common commercial. It will usually have a ten-to thirty-second introduction narrated by an actor seen in a chest shot, followed by a segment of film footage about one minute in length. There are alternate forms, but all of them are built on exactly the same type of segmentation. The narrating actor may merely narrate (read off) the event from the same chest shot seen against a background of one or two slides plausibly related to the event. The only continuity for the six- or seven-minute packet of programming called news consists of an abstract categorial designation (say, national) and the recurrent shots of the newsmen, actors who project some well-defined character considered appropriate for this part of the show, such as informed concern, alert aggressiveness, world-weary moralism, or genial confidence. This tends to be more obvious in the packets designated as sports and weather, where what passes for information consists of bits so small, numerous, and unrelated that they come down to mere lists. These may be held together respectively by more obvious character actors like a suave ex-jock and a soft-touch comic. Similarly, contest shows consist of structurally identical, separate events joined edge to edge and connected mainly by the continuous presence of the leading actor (the host). Television has also—through selection of the events themselves and manner of representation—managed to present most of its sports programs as sequences of nearly identical unrelated events. Baseball gets reduced to a succession of pitches, hits, and catches, football to a succession of runs, passes, and tackles, while the ensemble of events that may be unfolding lies outside the system of representation. If we count together all the programs that are constructed out of these linearly successive, distinct segments of commercial scale, the contrast between commercial and program becomes much less sharp.

Moreover, a closer inspection of both will show that there are really no clear stylistic distinctions between commercials and programs, because just about every genre of program appears also as a commercial. Dramas, comedies, documentaries, science talks, lists, all show up in thirty- and sixty-second forms. Even their distinctive integralness can be exaggerated, because often there is a clean partition between the programmatic parts of the commercial—its dramatic or imagistic material—and the details of the pitch that specify the name of the product and where you can get it. This separation is so common that it is possible to watch three thirty-second commercials in succession with some pleasure and find it difficult to remember the name or even the nature of the commodity promoted. This is not a functional defect in the commercial, the main function of which is to produce a kind of praise poetry that will elevate to a mild prominence one member out of the general family of commodities that television promotes as a whole tribe all of its transmitting day. Poems in praise of particular princes are addressed to an audience already familiar with the tribe, and commercials are constructed to particularize an already existing interest. Nobody unconcerned with body odors will care which deodorant checks them best. It takes the whole television day to encode the positive images of smoothness, cleanliness, or blandness upon which the massive marketing of deodorants and soaps depends. There is no fundamental distinction between commercial and program, there is only a difference in focus and conciseness, which gives the thirty-second commercial its appearance of much greater elegance and style. Both commercials and programs are assembled out of the same syntax: the linear succession of logically independent units of nearly equal duration. But this mechanically divisible, metrical presentation had none of the percussive or disjunctive properties of radio presentation. This is because of the conventions of camerawork and editing that television has developed to soften the shock of its basically mechanical procedures.

It is probably fair to say that the entire technology, from the shape of the monitor screen to the design of camera mounts, was worked out to soften the tick of its metronome. Almost every instrument of television technique and technology seems to have the effect of a shock absorber. As in film, the television presentation is assembled out of separate shots. But these shots are very limited in type and duration. Because of the poor resolution of the television image (525 bits of information presented on photosensitive phosphors) and the normal screen size, the bread-and-butter shots of television are almost all subforms of what film would consider a close-up. Common shot names illustrate this—knee shot, thigh shot, waist shot, bust shot, head shot, tight head shot. Or else they count the number of people in the frame—two shot, four shot, and so forth. Probably primarily for this reason shot durations are very limited in range—usually from two to ten seconds—and very predictable in function and type. The two- to three-second shot is almost always a reaction shot or a transition detail in a narrative, so it will usually be a head shot or detail of some activity. Distant shots of moving cars, or whatever, will usually run seven to ten seconds, like action in general. Shots of a second and under are very rare and only used for special occasions, but distinct shots over twenty seconds are practically nonexistent. We say *distinct* because television's camera conventions include a cameraman who is trained to act like an antiaircraft gunner, constantly making minute adjustments of the camera—loosening up a bit here, tightening up there, gently panning and trucking in a nearly imperceptible manner to keep the target on some imaginary pair of cross hairs. These endless, silken adjustments, encouraged and sometimes specifically called for by the director and usually built into the cameraman's training, tend to blur the edges of what the film director would normally consider a shot. To this we can add the widespread use of fade-ins and fade-outs and dissolves to effect temporal and spatial transitions,and the director's regular habit of cutting on movement to cushion the switch from one camera to another. This whole arsenal of techniques has a single function—to soften all shocks of transition.Naturally the different apparent functions of various genres of program or commerical will alter the degree of softening, so a news program will maintain a sense of urgency through its use of cuts, soft though they may be, while the soap opera constantly melts together its various close shots with liquid adjustment and blends scene to scene in recurrent dissolves and fades. This ceaseless softening combines with the regular segmentation to transform the metronomic tick-tock of the transmission into the silent succession of numbers on a digital clock.

Because of the television industry's special aesthetic of time and the electronics industry's primary adaptation of the technology to the needs and desires of television, the appearance of an art-world video had to wait for the electronics industry to attempt to expand the market for its technology into special institutional and consumer domains. The basic tool kit of artists' video is the portapak, with its small, mobile camera and one-half-inch black and white videotape recorder that can accommodate nothing larger than thirty-minute tapes. Combined with a small monitor and perhaps an additional microphone, the whole operation costs something in the vicinity of $2,000—a bit less than a cheap car and a bit more than a good stereo system. This is the fundamental unit, but it allows no editing whatever. The most minimal editing—edge-to-edge assembling of tapes into units larger than thirty minutes—requires access to at least another videotape recorder with a built-in editing facility, which means the investment of at least another $1,200. This is a primitive editing capacity, but increases the unit cost by 50 per cent to about $3,000. Yet precision editing and smoothness are still out of the question. Unlike film, where editing is a scissors-and-paste job anyone can do with very little equipment,and where you can sit in a small room and shave pieces of film down to the half-frame with no great difficulty, video pictures have to be edited electronically by assembling image sequences from some source or sources in the desired order on the tape of a second machine. The images are electronically marked off from each other by an electronic signal recurring (in the U.S.) thirty times a second. If you want to place one sequence of images right after another that you've already recorded onto the second tape, you have to join the front edge of the first new frame to the final edge of the other, which means that motors of both machines have to be synchronized to the thirtieth of a second and that there must be a way of reading off each frame edge to assure that the two recorded sequences are in phase with each other. Half-inch equipment is not designed to do this, and the alignment of frame edge with frame edge is a matter of accident.

Alignment of a particular edge with a particular frame edge is out of the question. If the frame edges don't come together, the tape is marked by a characteristic momentary breakup or instability of the image. You may or may not mind this, but it's the distinctive mark of this type of editing. Since this is absolutely unlike television editing, it carries its special mark of homemade or cheap or unfinicky or direct or honest. But the dominance of television aesthetics over anything seen on a TV screen makes this rather casual punctuation mark very emphatic and loaded with either positive or negative value. An installation with synchronized, multiple cameras, with capabilities for switching through cutting, fading, and dissolving, and some few special effects like black and white reversal, will cost somewhere in the $10,000 range, provided you stick to black and white and half-inch equip-ment. This is only a minor increase in editing control and a cost increase of one order of magnitude. If you want reliably smooth edits that will allow you to join predictably an edge to an edge, without specifying which edge, you will need access to an installation whose cost begins at around $100,000. One major art gallery has a reduced form of such a facility that permits this sort of editing, which costs about half that. Again we have an increase of control that is nearly minimal and a cost increase of another order of magnitude. Some artists have solved this problem by obtaining occasional access to institutions possessing this kind of installation, but usually this takes complete editing control out of the hands of most artists. There are also ways of adapting the one-inch system to precisionist frame-for-frame capacity, but that requires the investment of several thousand dollars more. A rule of thumb might specify that each increase in editing capacity represents an order of magnitude increase in cost. Color is still another special problem. Though it is hardly necessary, and possibly a great drawback in the sensible use of video for most artists' purposes (see Sonnier's pointless color work), it is by now television's common form and has certain normative marks associated with it. To use black and white is a marked move, regardless of what the mark may be construed to mean. So, many artists will seek color for mere neutrality. But it comes at a price. There are bargain-basement color systems, wonderfully cheesy in appearance, but the most common system is the three-quarter-inch cassette ensemble, which together with camera, videotape recorder, and monitor goes at about $10,000. If the portapak is the Volkswagen, this is the Porsche of individual artists' video. For editing control the system of escalation in color runs parallel to black and white. The model of ultimate refinement and control is the television industry's two-inch system, and since that's what you see in action in any model over the TV set, interesting or not, everyone takes it for the state of the art.

These conditions may not seem promising, but artists are as good at surviving as cockroaches, and they've developed three basic strategies for action. They can take the lack of technical refinements as a given and explore the theater of poverty. They can beg, borrow, or steal access to technical wealth and explore the ambiguous role of the poor relation, the unwelcome guest, the court jester, the sycophant, or the spy. This isn't a common solution; the studios don't make their facilitiles available so readily. But it includes works done by Allan Kaprow, Peter Campus, Les Levine, Nam June Paik, and numerous others. Artists can also raid the technology as a set of found objects or instruments with phenomenological implications in installation pieces. There are numerous examples from the work of Peter Campus, Dan Graham, Nam June Paik, Frank Gillette, and others. To a great extent the significance of all types of video art derives from its stance with respect to some aspect of television, which is itself profoundly related to the present state of our culture. In this way video art embarks on a curiously mediated but serious critique of the culture. And this reference to television, and through it to the culture, is not dependent on whether or not the artist sees the work in relation to television. The relation between television and video is created by the shared technologies and conditions of viewing, in the same way the relation of movies to underground film is created by the shared conditions of cinema. Nevertheless, an artist may exploit the relation very knowingly and may choose any aspect of the relation for attack.

Allan Kaprow

The Education of the Un-Artist, III

The models for the experimental arts of this generation have been less the preceding arts than modern society itself, particularly how and what we communicate, what happens to us in the process, and how this may connect us with natural processes beyond society.

The following examples—some dating from the early fifties but most of them recent—have been grouped according to five root types found in everyday life, the non-art professions, and in nature. These are: *situational* models (commonplace environments, occurrences and customs, often "ready-made"), *operational* models (how things and customs work and what they do), *structural* models (nature cycles, ecologies, and how things, places and human affairs are put together), *self-referring* or *feedback* models (those things or events that "talk" about or reflect themselves) and *learning* models (allegories of philosophical inquiry, sensitivity-training rituals and educational demonstrations).

A number of the artworks do not fit neatly into their assigned categories but can belong in two or three at once, depending on where one wants to put the emphasis. Baldessari's map piece, placed in the "self-referring" group, could also belong to the "operational" one; Beuys's sit-in, besides being "situational," could be called "operational" and "learning." And the High Red Center's *Cleaning Happening* could be extended from "operational" to

Reprinted from *Art in America* (January-February, 1974), by permission of the author and the publisher.

include both "learning" and "situational" models.

Within these large groupings, the works derive from more specific sources. Vostell's and Neuhaus's pieces are based on the guided tour; Haacke uses a polling device as the political tool it really is; Ruscha employs the format of a police report; Orgel parodies a domestic routine; Harrison's compact ecology system echoes many made in the science lab.

But exact pigeonholing is not essential now. What is essential is to look regularly for those ties to the "real" world, rather than to the art world, if the values of the new activities on any level is to be understood.

Situational Models:

Richard Meltzer occupied a small utility room in the basement of a university. He turned it into Meltzer's Clothing Store, where quantities of old clothes were hung or shelved in fixed proportions according to color, size, subject and, I believe, use. Anyone could take an article as long as it was replaced with something similar to a category, for instance, a violet tie for a sash of the same hue, or a pink sock and a blue one. That way the store retained its compositional integrity. There were dressing areas for men and women. (1962)

Paul Taylor, dressed in a business suit and standing in one spot, assumed simple poses in succession (hand on hip, foot extended, right turn) for the entire length of a dance, while an amplified recording of the telephone operator was heard telling the time every ten seconds. (1958)

For a Steve Paxton dance a group of people simply walked naturally across a stage, one after the other. (1970)

Josef Beuys conducted a sit-in for one hundred days in the recent international Documenta show at Kassel. He was available for anyone to discuss with him his current interests in political change and the role the arts might have in this change. He was officially on exhibit and, by implication, so was any future action that might ensue from the talks. (1973)

Merce Cunningham accompanied a tape of musique concrète by arranging a group of seventeen persons—mostly nondancers—to simply "do gestures they did normally." Chance procedures were applied to these movements regarding time and positions on stage. They were independent of the sounds coming over the loudspeakers. The gestures consisted of such things as "washing one's hands," "walking and viewing the country," "two people carrying a third," "touching," "eating," "falling asleep," "jitterbug step," and "running." (1953)

Allen Ruppersberg obtained the use of a rooming house in Los Angeles. He advertised it as *Al's Grand Hotel* and offered rooms for rent on six successive weekends. There was a bar, music, continental breakfast, maid service, souvenirs and price-adjusted rooms with double beds. The rooms contained such things as a large wooden cross (the "Jesus Room"), a picnic spread on a checkered cloth with *Life* magazine papering the walls (the "B Room"), and seven framed wedding photos, three-tier wedding cake, ten wedding presents, plastic ivy and flowers (the "Bridal Suite"). As at a popular resort, a catalog offered mementos of one's stay. (1971)

Sandra Orgel performed a collaborative piece at Woman House in Los Angeles. She appeared washed-out, wore a cheap housedress, her hair in curlers, floppy slippers, and a cigarette dangling from her mouth. She set up an ironing board and plugged in an iron. When it was hot she spat on it. Its hiss was the only sound. She methodically and silently pressed a bedsheet for about ten minutes and when it was finished she folded it and went out. (1972)

Ed Ruscha compiled a picture book of a drama on a desert freeway. An old Royal typewriter was thrown out of a speeding auto. Photo documents with measurements were carefully made of the strewn debris—an "official report" of the scene of the accident. (1967)

Joseph Kosuth arranged three clean-topped tables around the walls of a bare room. Three folding chairs at each table faced the walls. Fixed to walls were three numbered placards in enlarged type containing extracts from scholarly writings on the subject of models in scientific theory. Placed neatly on the tables before each chair was a notebook of related texts, opened for perusal. (1972)

In the Museum of Modern Art, Hans Haacke set up two adjacent lucite boxes with counting devices on each. An overhead sign asked the passerby to consider if New York Governor Rockefeller's silence on Nixon's Vietnam policy would stand in the way of a vote, if Rockefeller should run for reelection. A "yes" ballot was to go in the left box and a "no" ballot in the right one. (1970)

Operational Models:

Michael Heizer got a bulldozer and driver to hollow out of the desert a large crater. In a television interview afterwards the driver judged that he had dug a good hole. (1971?)

Barbara Smith produced a book with a Xerox copier. Beginning with a photo of her young daughter, the machine made a copy, copied the copy, copied that copy, and so on through a long series. As in biological generations, things changed. Because the Xerox machine automatically reduces each image copied by about ¼ inch, the girl's head gradually disappeared into a receding constellation of dots until it seemed a mere point in space. This occurred at the middle of the book. As the pages were turned, the reducing process reversed and soon a face was discernible advancing toward one. But at the end it was a somewhat different photograph of the same little girl! (This Xerox series was made in the same way but Smith simply turned around the order when assembling the book.) (1967)

Emmet Williams composed a book called *Sweethearts* that is more scanned than read. Each page is made up of spatially arranged permutations of the eleven letters in the title word. The book starts from the back cover and the pages are meant to be flipped with the left thumb so that a blurred but subliminally clear meaning is registered in the mind. This filmic treatment of a text recalls the "flip" photo and cartoon stories of our childhood in which a staccato sense of images in motion was achieved. (1966)

LaMonte Young's composition *Draw a Straight Line and Follow It* took place in a loft. He and a friend drew on the floor with a piece of chalk (as I recall, from two separated points, in the manner of surveyors). The process took some hours and every once in a while quiet comments were exchanged. (1960)

A group of men and women in a part of an Yvonne Rainer dance carried and stacked about a dozen mattresses, variously lying, diving and sitting on them. (1965)

George Brecht arranged a sundown event for cars in a parking lot. Each person had twenty-two rearrangeable cards indicating the equipment on his or her car that was to be activated within certain time-counts: radio, lights, wipers, doors, windows, motor, seatbacks, footbrake, glove compartment, trunk cover, engine hood, horn, and so forth. (1960)

As an agit-prop event, Japan's High Red Center group prepared a "Cleaning Happening." Dressed in immaculately white lab suits, mouths covered by sanitary hospital masks, they silently and precisely cleaned a busy street in Tokyo. (1968?)

Bernard Cooper devised a metal mouthpiece (a "Regulator") looking somewhat like an orthodontist's lip retractor. It was balanced on the front lower teeth. From this were hung one to six steel discs, each weighing five ounces. The user was instructed to say a word or two and notice what happened to the phonemes as the weights were added and the jaw pulled down. Conversations on the telephone, serious discussions, and public lectures were then recommended for users of the device. (1972)

Max Bense spread sixty-two common words at random on a page, words like *fish, nothing, wall, year, salt, way, night* and *stone*. He saw these as a "set of words" as in mathematical set theory. They could be recombined by the reader in almost endless "sets" as object-values rather than verbal ones. (1963)

Structural Models:

James Tenney programmed a computer to generate analogs to the structural characteristics of the sounds of cars he heard every day while driving through the Lincoln Tunnel in N.Y.C. The tape had a slightly hollow sound of wind around the ears. (1961)

Michael Snow had an apparatus made which, for hours, automatically swung a continuous running camera around two variable orbits. The rig was set up in a desolate section of Canada and the camera recorded whatever was in front of its lens: earth and sky. In viewing the film, one heard the sound of the rig's motors and saw the sun go down and come up in what felt like real time; the circling of the camera was like that of the earth around the sun. (1971)

For Thomas Schmidt's *Zyklus* the content of a full Coke bottle was slowly and carefully poured into an empty one, and vice versa, until (due to slight spillage and evaporation) no liquid remained. The process lasted nearly seven hours. (1966?)

Dieter Rot arranged to exhibit twenty-odd old suitcases filled with a variety of international cheese specialties. The suitcases—all different—were placed close together in the middle of the floor, as you might find them at a Greyhound bus terminal. In a few days the cheeses began to ripen, some started oozing out of the suitcases, all of them grew marvelous molds (which you could examine by opening the lids), and maggots were crawling by the thousands. Naturally, the smell was incredible. (1969)

Newton Harrison recently turned to farming. He made a model shrimp farm of four rectangular tanks of sea water of graduated degrees of salinity. Algae and young shrimp were put into the tanks; the algae were nourished by the sun and the shrimp ate the algae. As the sun evaporated the water the salinity of the tanks increased, making the water change color from green in the least salty, to bright coral in the most salty. The water level was then kept constant and the shrimp were eventually harvested. (1970)

Self-referring Models:

Helen Alm made a video tape of herself trying to relax. It was played back on a monitor and she sat in front of it and carried on a kidding dialogue with her playback self about the same thing: trying to relax. A tape was made of this doubling of Alm and was in turn played on a monitor for viewing by her and others. (1972)

John Baldessari selected a map of California. He determined where its printed letters C. A. L. I. F. O. R. N. I. A. would fall on the real space of the state. Travelling to each location on the map, he painted or made of rocks, yarn, flower seed, wood, and so on, a large corresponding letter on the landscape. Photo documents of these letter sites, mounted in a row, spelled back to the viewer California's map. (1969)

For a Robert Whitman theater piece, two women performed in front of a projected film of themselves. Another woman, in a full white dress, doubled as a second screen, on whom was projected a film of herself removing her clothes. She exactly matched the movements of her film self until she appeared nude, although everyone could also see her dress. (1965)

Michael Kirby put together a construction of aluminum struts and mounted photographs into a number of its spaces. As the spectator moved around it, it was discovered that each photo corresponded to the view of the room or window seen from its own vantage point. The piece functioned as a collection of "eyes," and when once it was moved to another site, all the photos naturally were retaken. (1966)

In a different piece, the devised scaffold was eliminated and a rectangle was conceived to lie both inside and outside of his apartment window. Photographs were taken from these four points, facing in and out, and were then mounted unobtrusively at their sight points as objectified views of their respective surroundings. (1969)

Dieter Rot noted that he was "advertising my typewriter" in the following poem:

olovebo
ollvåtl
oliveti
vèìvvtv
eåågeeå
oltvåtl
oliveti

The typewriter also misspells. . . . (1958)

Robert Morris made a small gray box. From inside it came barely audible hammering and sawing sounds. It was called *Box With Sounds of Its Own Making*. (1961)

Learning Models:

Robert Rauschenberg made a series of vertically joined blank white canvases. There was nothing else on them, so the viewer became aware of his shadow on the surface, the bumps in the fabric, and the flashes of colored light produced by the pulsing of his eyes. (1951, 1953)

Shortly after, John Cage presented his *4'33"*. Pianist David Tudor opened the piano keyboard cover and set a stop watch. Adjusting his stool he sat there for the prescribed time and played nothing. The sounds of the street, the elevator, airconditioning, squeaking chairs, coughing, giggling, yawning, became deafening. (1952, 1954)

Wolf Vostell provided a map for a trip on the Petite Ceinture bus line of Paris, and advised the traveller to look for torn posters, debris, ruins, and listen to noises and cries. . . . (1962)

Some years later, Max Neuhaus took friends on a number of tours of municipal electric generating plants, where they were able to listen to the pervasive whine of the enormous motors and feel the buildings through their feet. (1966, 1967)

In one of Ann Halprin's dances, a group of men and women slowly and ceremonially undressed and dressed themselves, all the while examining each other's movements. (1964?)

George Brecht sent small cards to friends, like this one (1960):

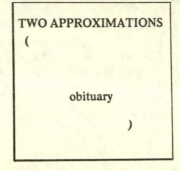

Vito Acconci placed himself blindfolded on a chair at the bottom of a cellar stair. Armed with a metal pipe or two, he proceeded to talk himself into a state of intense paranoia over the possibility of someone attempting to get past him into the cellar. Muttering constantly to build his nerve and slowly swinging his pipe at the imaginary challenger, Acconci punctuated his words with thuds of the pipe on the hard floor. A man in a group watching it all on a remote video monitor upstairs decided to try Acconci out and a dramatic scuffle ensued. (1971)

These examples mark a turning point in high culture. While artists have long been more or less consciously concerned with the nature of the physical universe, with ideas and with human issues—that is, with "life"—their primary models were life *in translation,* namely other artworks. Life itself was the secondary model; an artist didn't go to art school to study life, but art.

Now the procedure seems to be reversing. Large numbers of experimenters are bypassing the defined linguistic modes of poetry, painting, music and are going directly to sources outside of their professions. Acconci reads scholarly books on social behavior, and his work resembles case histories of abnormality presented as quasi-rites; Bernard Cooper's piece alludes to a familiar experience of trying to verbally respond to a dentist's small talk with one's mouth full of braces and tubes; Barbara Smith discovers a new kind of portraiture by taking advantage of the mechanical peculiarities of a standard office copier; and Cage applies to a concert situation Zen teachings and his acoustic perceptions in a scientifically soundproofed chamber.

None of this is to be found raw in prior art work. Instead, such activity calls for comparison with the models indicated (or causes us to look for them if they aren't immediately apparent in examples not described here). What follows now is a closer look at these non-art models and at what it has meant for artists to copy them.

Mirrors of the Mirror

Some imitations are made to deceive. Like the phony dollar bill, they are counterfeits—more or less well done. High art's prevailing prejudice against imitation suggests that even when palming off a copy for an original is *not* the intent, it is a kind of forgery anyway; that at the heart of the matter is an escape into another's identity and the impossibility of self-realization by such a practice.

It is too easy to get caught. After more than five hundred years of individualism, society's scrutinizing demand for proof of uniqueness quickly exposes the copy as if it were a fake and its artist a criminal. Faced with this great pressure, only rarely (and perhaps pathologically) will a person accept, for any length of time beyond apprenticeship, the role of disciple, copying faithfully a master's vision and style. In the past, the devotee may have felt so close to his guide that the efforts of each seemed almost mystically united. He strove for the impression that there was no difference between first- and second-hand. But in recent history, imitation, no matter how sincere, has appeared to most intellectuals dishonest in its very doubtlessness, as if, in a pluralistic culture, there were indeed one true way.

Yet there has been a strain of imitation allowed and even welcomed in the vanguard arts, in the form of take-off or quotation. Presented like a stage whisper between artist and public, the difference between the source and the copy was always explicit. It was essential to its meanings that everyone know both instantly; therefore what was copied was usually not fine art, but the daily world, its customs and artifacts. As an important early example, Alfred Jarry appropriated the style of his play *Ubu Roi* from a schoolboy marionette skit he probably helped author as a youth, a style familiar to anyone who has gone to summer camp or experienced preadolescent entertainments. In his novel *The Exploits and Opinions of Dr. Faustroll, Pataphysician,* the various jargons of popular science, legal and documentary records, "essential reading" listings, and occultism are juxtaposed into an absurd and mock-inflated portrait of the twentieth-century anti-hero. And in Jarry's sci-fi essay *How to Construct a Time Machine,* he uses the "how-to" form of technical manuals and sets the method for Duchamp's *Bride Stripped Bare,* and notes to the *Green Box.*

The cubists, for their part, included in their paste-ups bits and pieces of real newspaper, wallpaper, oil cloth and imitation woodgraining. Satie scored a typewriter, revolvers, airplane motor and siren in his music for the ballet *Parade*. The futurist Russolo built machines for his concerts that would reproduce the noises of the city: "whispers, thunders, bubblings, screeches, grindings . . . ." Blaise Cendrars reportedly copied every line of his book of poems, *Kodak,* from a series of pulp novels of the day. The Russians Tatlin and Rodchenko carried over the girdered and strutted look of the industrial scene into their constructions and monuments; and during 1918-1922, in St. Petersburg and Baku, there were those famous city-wide performances of factory steam whistles designed for apparently appreciative workers. In the same period, the dadas sprinkled their broadsides and posters with advertising slogans and reproductions. Picabia's best work was executed in the crypto-diagram manner of hardware catalogs and engineering texts. Most radically, Duchamp's Readymades replaced the artist's labor with a standardized object of ordinary use, simply by moving it, largely unchanged, into an art context.

Thus the passé but venerable notion of the artist as master illusionist was wryly hinted at, but deadpan, as though it were a slightly vulgar admission among friends. Mass production techniques, after all, had taken over this role by the last quarter of the nineteenth century (besides chromos, remember those mechanical music bands and cast iron classical building facades?), so illusions were more or less lifted from their metropolitan surroundings "readymade." They became the artist's cheap imitations of other imitations or multiples, but accomplished by none of the illusionistic skills once expected of a professional!

In our time, such re-presentations, parodies and quotes have continued in the writings of the Beats and in pop art; in the noise music of Cage, Neuhaus and others; in the "task" modes of dancers such as Yvonne Rainer; in the commonplace environments and enactments of happenings, body works, and activities; in the industrial materials, fabrication methods, and shapes of minimal sculpture; in schematically conceived paintings; in the electronic apparatus and scientism of tech-art; in computer-made and concrete poetry; in the propositional forms of conceptualism, and so on. (I've commented on this in Parts I and II of this essay). The irony here is that in releasing the ordinary object, sound or event from routine indifference, the act that does so also counts as novelty. For it is not the world that is being simply recreated but a comment made on the infinite reproducibility of its illusions.

Harold Rosenberg (in *The Anxious Object,* pp. 61-62) describes how illusionism of this recurrent sort, appearing stridently in pop art and new realism of the early 1960s, is due in part to urbanization.

> The city dweller's "nature," is a human fabrication—he is surrounded by fields of concrete, forests of posts and wires, etc.; while nature itself, in the form of parks, a snowfall, cats and dogs, is a detail in the stone and steel of his habitat. Given the enormous dissemination of simulated nature through window displays, motion picture and television screens, public and private photography, magazine advertisements, art reproductions, car and bus posters, five-and-ten art, it is plain that in no other period has the visible world been to such an extent both duplicated and anticipated by artifice. Surrounded by artistic copies of presidents, scenes, famous events, we become in the end largely insensitive to the distinction between the natural and the made-up.

This also may be true for the distinction between originals and copies. Do young people with long hair remember, or care, that it was the Beatles who were responsible for reviving a fashion that had endless echoes back into time? Who would insist that the Japanese have no right to a Western technology that allowed them to become a major economic and political power just because they copied it? Replication, modularity and serialism, aspects of mass production, have become the norms of daily life; they are part of the way we think.

Only in the fine arts does the quest for originality remain a vestige of individualism and specialization. It is the ideological token of the sufficient self. Yet popular acceptance of psychoanalysis makes everyone today an individual, while the phenomenal growth of leisure time in the economy implies that, potentially, anyone (not just artists or eccentrics) can pursue a personal lifestyle. And gradually increasing public and corporate support of pure research, arts education and the performing arts, promises more tangible rewards to the intellectual than isolation in the garret. These changing social circumstances have at least blunted, if not done away with, the special poignance that once moved artists to struggle to be idiosyncratic.

At any rate, originality as an index of integrity may be on the wane, expressing itself sometimes as nostalgic pose, more often as a kind of canned or repeatable individualism, which only thinly veils the anonymous sources of the new art's vitality. For in fact, artists are noticeably discarding unique, handmade qualities in favor of multiples made by machines or teams, ideas conceived by groups, or processes generated in the lab or environment.

> Jill Ciment found that for each of the numbers on a touch-tone telephone there is a different sound heard when a person is called. She then pushbuttoned the numbers of one hundred and eighty-five telephones that were "important during my life." The resulting tones were recorded on tape. The faintly thin, drawn-out whistles varied not only in pitch but in duration because of the stumbling time it took to carry out the process, while the dynamics remained constant.

Thus she composed an autobiography and group portrait of her past. (1972)

"On January 9, 1969, a clear plastic box measuring 1 x 1 x ¾ inches was enclosed within a slightly larger cardboard container that was sent by registered mail to an address in Berkeley, California. Upon being returned as "undeliverable" it was left altogether intact and enclosed within another slightly larger container and sent again as registered mail to Riverton, Utah—and once more returned to the sender as undeliverable.

"Similarly another container enclosing all previous containers was sent to Ellsworth, Nebraska; similarly to Alpha, Iowa; similarly to Tuscola, Michigan; similarly and finally to Hull, Massachusetts, which accomplished the 'marking' of a line joining the two coasts of the United States (and covering over 10,000 miles of space) during a period of six weeks of time.

"That final container, all registered mail receipts, and a map joined with this statement to form the system of documentation that completes this work"
—*Douglas Huebler*

Of course, there is still the original artist who can be applauded. The artist, has the *ideas* and conceives the prototype of his manufactures. But when Andy Warhol's popularity a few years ago was so great that he hired a stand-in to make appearances at universities (until he was fingered by one of the outraged intelligentsia), he left the nagging impression that an artist to-day might be as replicable as his art. In fact, for some time after the exposé, people wondered at parties if they were talking to the real Andy or another substitute. They seemed to enjoy that possibility.

While some criticism has been leveled at this apparent irreverence, not enough attention has been paid to our current taste for heroes made by, and experienced through, publicity channels. Rosenberg, in the piece quoted and again recently, has remarked on the way media create realities; as far as the fine arts are concerned, he has some reservations over the shift away from the created art object to the artist as creation, but points out that the phenomenon bears on the issue of illusionism.

In the semblance of the artist displayed in magazines and on TV, something particularly gratifying happens, as if, in support of McLuhan's view, each of us felt a close-up contact with the personality, closer even than a formal handshake could provide if that were possible, yet shared paradoxically with multitudes. It is at once intimate and public. And it is all the more real for its *reproducibility*. It is obvious that, in the flesh, the hero cannot be everywhere for everyone. Far better to commune with an immaterial fantasy in print, or served up at the touch of a dial in our living room.

Traditionally, the artist-genius, creator of the masterpiece, was the analogue of God-the-Father, creator of life. One artist, one original; one God, one Existence. But today there are countless artists and reproductions, countless gods and cosmologies. When "the one" is replaced by "the many," reality may be perceived as a menu of illusions, transformable and replenishable according to need (as the electric light turns night into day).

Lifelike That

The West's recurrent dreams of returning to rustic nature, or of exploring the future in outer space, are both accomplishable by the technology of the present. Besides the practicalities of rapid transportation and communication, without which getting to either would be impossible, there are quick medical services along the way in case of illness, guidelines about diverse lifestyles and techniques for physical and emotional survival, genetically advanced seedlings developed at major universities for the "new primitive" wishing to grow his own food, freeze-dried nourishment for the astronaut and, most critical of all, a cultural upbringing in which the presence of *options* is the birthright of the middle class.

Disney World engineers have on their drawing boards a highly sophisticated, planned city to be built in the vicinity of the recreation park. Not only would there be completely automated supply and waste systems, underground car and trainways, overhead footpath neighborhoods conceived in the expected variety of old-world styles, but a Fuller-type enclosing shell with controlled atmosphere more "naturally" pleasant than the tropical humidity of Florida. As the Disney song goes "It's a small, small world," and it can be wrapped in cellophane.

Then airline pilots have been trained for some time by flight simulators that reproduce in a laboratory all the conditions of flying. Sitting at controls that match an airliner's, they see outside the cockpit window a projected day or night scene that corresponds in detail and scale to one or another major airfield they'll have to land on or take off from. As they manipulate the controls, the scene recedes, enlarges, banks to left or right and streams below at greater or lesser speed, just as it would in the actual plane. Complete with earphones and vibrations, the replica is made to be, in effect, real.

In a related example, recent televised moon landings of exceptional clarity were interspersed with previously shot footage of simulations made on earth, so that, half-jokingly, some viewers conjectured that the whole business was a mock-up with only changes in caption.

The anthropologist Edmund Carpenter quotes a writer in his book *They Became What They Beheld:* "When (Robert) Kennedy's body was brought back to New York from Los Angeles, one of us was at the airport to see it arrive. Standing with a group of reporters, he noticed that they almost all watched the event on a specially rigged television screen. The actual coffin was passing behind their back scarcely any farther away than the small-screen version." In the same vein, Harold Rosenberg—always a keen observer of such occurrences—points out in one of his *New Yorker* articles (3/17/73) that "On television, POWs returning from Hanoi were shown passing the time watching POWs returning from Hanoi on television. A man rows across Main Street to buy a newspaper showing his town flooded. . . . "

Such examples, by their wide extent, reveal the implications of staple items like creamless sweet cream, meatless meat, synthetic wool, plastic bricks and astroturf. And *Life* magazine, true to its name, devoted one of its issues (10/1/65) to new discoveries in genetic code-breaking and led readers to speculate that test-tube babies are right around the corner. In this kind of civilization, dreams of nature's way, or life on the moon, are only different versions of human nature's artifice. Art, which copies society copying itself, is not simply the mirror of life. Both are made up. Nature is an echo system.

David Antin was asked to give a lecture on art. He talked impromptu and recorded it on tape. The tape was transcribed and all breath stops and phrases were indicated by spaces left in the lines of print. The transcript was then published as an article in an art magazine and subsequently as a poem in a book of his recent works. But when read silently or aloud it was just like David Antin speaking normally. (1971)

Terry Atkinson wrote an essay on the nature of conceptual art and posed the question "Are works of art theory part of the kit of conceptual art, and as such, can such a work, when advanced by a conceptual artist, come up for the count as a work of art?" The question was answered by Ian Burn and Mel Ramsden in another essay on this subject when they stated that their text "counts as an artwork." But when read silently or aloud both these essays were just like es-theticians writing about their subject. (1969, 1970)

For a happening of Robert McCarn's, four 8-foot-high, gray wooden crates were made, like ordinary shipping containers, and were stamped in yellow with the words *Fragile Works of Art*. They were forklifted onto a flatbed truck along with two pallets of sandbags, and driven (on prior agreement) some 800 miles to two museums and an art school gallery. Bills of lading were specially printed, a trucker's log was kept, and the proper forms and receipts were filled out upon delivery.

Some crates and sandbags were accepted (it was up to the recipient to accept or reject the shipment) and were then exhibited as art; one was accepted as a packing box for other art and was used accordingly; two were unloaded, opened (they were of course empty) and were then closed and sent back with the driver, McCarn. He and his friends carried out the process exactly the way any trucker might have done it. (1970)

Henry Flynt

Concept Art

Concept art is first of all an art of which the material is *concepts,* as the material of music is sound. Since *concepts* are closely bound up with language,
concept art is a kind of art of which the material is language. That is, unlike a
work of music, in which the music proper (as opposed to notation or analysis)
is just sound, concept art proper will involve language. From the philosophy
of language, we learn that a *concept* may as well be thought of as the "intension of a name"; this is the relation between concepts and language[1] The
notion of a concept is a vestige of the notion of a platonic form (the thing
which all tables have in common: tableness), which notion is replaced by the
notion of a name objectively, metaphysically related to its intension (so that
all tables now have in common their objective relation to *table*). Now the
claim that there can be an objective relation between a name and its intension
is wrong, and (the word) *concept*, as commonly used now, can be discredited
(see my monograph, *Philosophy Proper*). If, however, it is enough for one that
there be a subjective relation between a name and its intension, namely the
unhesitant decision as to the way one wants to use the name, the unhesitant
decisions to affirm the names of some things but not others, then *concept* is
valid language, and concept art has a philosophically valid basis.

Now what is artistic, aesthetic, about a work that is a body of concepts? This question can best be answered by telling where concept art came

Reprinted from *An Anthology* (1963), edited by La Monte Young, by permission of the author.
Copyright © 1961 by Henry A. Flynt, Jr.

411

from. I developed it in an attempt to straighten out certain traditional activities generally regarded as aesthetic. The first of these is *structure art,* music, visual art, and so on, in which the important thing is "structure." My definitive discussion of structure art is in my unpublished essay *Structure Art and Pure Mathematics;* here I will just summarize that discussion. Much structure art is a vestige of the time when music was believed to be knowledge, a science, which had important things to say in astronomy and so on. Contemporary structure artists, on the other hand, tend to claim the kind of cognitive value for their art that conventional contemporary mathematicians claim for mathematics. Modern examples of structure art are the fugue and total serial music. These examples illustrate the important division of structure art into two kinds according to how the structure is appreciated. In the case of a fugue, one is aware of its structure in listening to it; one imposes *relationships*, a categorization (hopefully that intended by the composer) on the sounds while listening to them, that is, has an *(associated) artistic structure experience.* In the case of total serial music, the structure is such that this cannot be done; one just has to read an *analysis* of the music, definition of the relationships. Now there are two things wrong with structure art. First, its cognitive pretentions are utterly wrong. Secondly, by trying to be music or whatever (which has nothing to do with knowledge), and knowledge represented by structure, structure art both fails, is completely boring, as music, and doesn't begin to explore the aesthetic possibilities structure can have when freed from trying to be music or whatever. The first step in straightening out structure music is to stop calling it *music,* and start saying that the sound is used only to carry the structure and that the real point is the structure—and then you will see how limited, impoverished, the structure is. Incidentally, anyone who says that works of structure music do occasionally have musical value just doesn't know how good real music (the Goli Dance of the Baoule; *Cans on Windows* by La Monte Young; the contemporary American hit song *Sweets for My Sweets,* by the Drifters) can get. When you make the change, then since structures are concepts, you have concept art. Incidentally, there is another, less important kind of art which when straightened out becomes concept art: art involving play with the concepts of the art such as, in music, *the score, performer versus listener, playing a work.* The second criticism of structure art applies, with the necessary changes, to this art.

The second main antecedent of structure art is mathematics. This is the result of my revolution in mathematics, presented in my *1966 Mathematical Studies;* here I will only summarize. The revolution occurred first because for reasons of taste I wanted to deemphasize discovery in mathematics, mathematics as discovering theorems and proofs. I wasn't good at such discovery, and it bored me. The first way I thought of to deemphasize discovery came not later than the summer of 1960; it was that since the value of pure mathematics is now regarded as aesthetic rather than cognitive, why not try to make up aesthetic theorems, without considering whether they are true. The second way, which came at about the same time, was to find, as a philosopher, that the conventional claim that theorems and proofs are discovered is wrong, for the same reason I have already given that *concept* can be discredited. The third way, which came in the fall-winter of 1960, was to work in unexplored regions of formalist mathematics. The resulting mathematics still had statements, theorems, proofs, but the latter weren't discovered in the way they traditionally were. Now exploration of the wider possibilities of mathematics as revolutionized by me tends to lead beyond what it makes sense to call *mathematics;* the category of *mathematics,* a vestige of Platonism, is an *unnatural,* bad one. My work in mathematics leads to the new category of *concept art,* of which straightened out traditional mathematics (mathematics as discovery) is an untypical, small but intensively developed part.

I can now return to the question of why concept art is *art.* Why isn't it an absolutely new, or at least a nonartistic, nonaesthetic activity? The answer is that the antecedents of concept art are commonly regarded as artistic, aesthetic activities; on a deeper level, interesting concepts, concepts enjoyable in themselves, especially as they occur in mathematics, are commonly said to *have beauty.* By calling my activity *art* therefore I am simply recognizing this common usage, and the origin of the activity in structure art and mathematics. However: it is confusing to call things as irrelevant as the emotional enjoyment of (real) music, and the intellectual enjoyment of concepts, the same kind of enjoyment. Since concept art includes almost perhaps it would be better to restrict *art* to apply to art for the emotions, and to recognize my activity as an independent, new activity, irrelevant to art (and knowledge).

Sol LeWitt

Paragraphs on Conceptual Art

The editor has written me that he is in favor of avoiding "the notion that the artist is a kind of ape that has to be explained by the civilized critic." This should be good news to both artists and apes. With this assurance I hope to justify his confidence. To continue a baseball metaphor (one artist wanted to hit the ball out of the park, another to stay loose at the plate and hit the ball where it was pitched), I am grateful for the opportunity to strike out for myself.

I will refer to the kind of art in which I am involved as conceptual art. In conceptual art the idea or concept is the most important aspect of the work.[1] When an artist uses a conceptual form of art, it means that all of the planning and decisions are made beforehand and the execution is a perfunctory affair. The idea becomes a machine that makes the art. This kind of art is not theoretical or illustrative of theories; it is intuitive, it is involved with all types of mental processes and it is purposeless. It is usually free from the dependence on the skill of the artist as a craftsman. It is the objective of the artist who is concerned with conceptual art to make his work mentally interesting to the spectator, and therefore usually he would want it to become emotionally dry. There is no reason to suppose however, that the conceptual artist is out to bore the viewer. It is only the expectation of an emotional kick, to which one conditioned to expressionist art is accustomed, that would deter the viewer from perceiving this art.

Reprinted by permission of the author.

Conceptual art is not necessarily logical. The logic of a piece or series of pieces is a device that is used at times only to be ruined. Logic may be used to camouflage the real intent of the artist, to lull the viewer into the belief that he understands the work, or to infer a paradoxical situation (such as logic vs. illogic).[2] The ideas need not be complex. Most ideas that are successful are ludicrously simple. Successful ideas generally have the appearance of simplicity because they seem inevitable. In terms of idea the artist is free to even surprise himself. Ideas are discovered by intuition.

What the work of art looks like isn't too important. It has to look like something if it has physical form. No matter what form it may finally have it must begin with an idea. It is the process of conception and realization with which the artist is concerned. Once given physical reality by the artist the work is open to the perception of all, including the artist. (I use the word *perception* to mean the apprehension of the sense data, the objective understanding of the idea and simultaneously a subjective interpretation of both.) The work of art can only be perceived after it is completed.

Art that is meant for the sensation of the eye primarily would be called *perceptual* rather than *conceptual.* This would include most optical, kinetic, light and color art.

Since the functions of conception and perception are contradictory (one pre-, the other postfact) the artist would mitigate his idea by applying subjective judgment to it. If the artist wishes to explore his idea thoroughly, then arbitrary or chance decisions would be kept to a minimum, while caprice, taste and other whimsies would be eliminated from the making of the art. The work does not necessarily have to be rejected if it does not look well. Sometimes what is initially thought to be awkward will eventually be visually pleasing.

To work with a plan that is pre-set is one way of avoiding subjectivity. It also obviates the necessity of designing each work in turn. The plan would design the work. Some plans would require millions of variations, and some a limited number, but both are finite. Other plans imply infinity. In each case however, the artist would select the basic form and rules that would govern the solution of the problem. After that the fewer decisions made in the course of completing the work, the better. This eliminates the arbitrary, the capricious, and the subjective as much as possible. That is the reason for using this method.

When an artist uses a multiple modular method he usually chooses a simple and readily available form. The form itself is of very limited importance; it becomes the grammar for the total work. In fact it is best that the basic unit be deliberately uninteresting so that it may more easily become an intrinsic part of the entire work. Using complex basic forms only disrupts the unity of the whole. Using a simple form repeatedly narrows the field of the work and concentrates the intensity to the arrangement of the form. This arrangement becomes the end while the form becomes the means.

Conceptual art doesn't really have much to do with mathematics, philosophy or any other mental discipline. The mathematics used by most artists is simple arithmetic or simple number systems. The philosophy of the work is implicit in the work and is not an illustration of any system of philosophy.

It doesn't really matter if the viewer understands the concepts of the artist by seeing the art. Once out of his hand the artist has no control over the way a viewer will perceive the work. Different people will understand the same thing in a different way.

Recently there has been much written about minimal art, but I have not discovered anyone who admits to doing this kind of thing. There are other art forms around called primary structures, reductive, rejective, cool, and mini-art. No artist I know will own up to any of these either. Therefore I conclude that it is part of a secret language that art critics use when communicating with each other through the medium of art magazines. Mini-art is best because it reminds one of mini-skirts and long-legged girls. It must refer to very small works of art. This is a very good idea. Perhaps "mini-art" shows could be sent around the country in matchboxes. Or maybe the mini-artist is a very small person, say under five feet tall. If so, much good work will be found in the primary schools (primary school primary structures).

If the artist carries through his idea and makes it into visible form, then all the steps in the process are of importance. The idea itself, even if not made visual is as much a work of art as any finished product. All intervening steps—scribbles, sketches, drawings, failed work, models, studies, thoughts, conversations—are of interest. Those that show the thought process of the artist are sometimes more interesting than the final product.

Determining what size a piece should be is difficult. If an idea requires three dimensions, then it would seem any size would do. The question would be what size is best. If the thing were made gigantic then the size alone would be impressive and the idea may be lost entirely. Again, if it is too small, it may become inconsequential. The height of the viewer may have some bearing on the work and also the size of the space into which it will be placed. The artist may wish to place objects higher than the eye level of the viewer, or lower. I think the piece must be large enough to give the viewer whatever information he needs to understand the work and placed in such a way that will facilitate this understanding. (Unless the idea is of impediment and requires difficulty of vision or access.)

Space can be thought of as the cubic area occupied by a three-dimensional volume. Any volume would occupy space. It is air and cannot be seen. It is the interval between things that can be measured. The intervals and measurements can be important to the work of art. If certain distances are important they will be made obvious in the piece. If space is relatively unimportant it can be regularized and made equal (things placed e-qual distances apart), to mitigate any interest in interval. Regular space might also become a metric time element, a kind of regular beat or pulse. When the interval is kept regular whatever is irregular gains more importance.

Architecture and three-dimensional art are of completely opposite na-tures. The former is concerned with making an area with a specific function. Architecture, whether it is a work of art or not, must be utilitarian or else fail completely. Art is not utilitarian. When three dimensional art starts to take on some of the characteristics of architecture, such as forming utilitarian areas, it weakens its function as art. When the viewer is dwarfed by the large size of a piece this domination emphasizes the physical and emotive power of the form at the expense of losing the idea of the piece.

New materials are one of the great afflictions of contemporary art. Some artists confuse new materials with new ideas. There is nothing worse than seeing art that wallows in gaudy baubles. By and large most artists who are at-tracted to these materials are the ones that lack the stringency of mind that would enable them to use the materials well. It takes a good artist to use new materials and make them into a work of art. The danger is, I think, in making the physicality of the materials so important that it becomes the idea of the work (another kind of expressionism).

Three-dimensional art of any kind is a physical fact. This physicality is its most obvious and expressive content. Conceptual art is made to engage the mind of the viewer rather than his eye or emotions. The physicality of a three-dimensional object then becomes a contradiction to its nonemotive in-tent. Color, surface, texture, and shape only emphasize the physical aspects of the work. Anything that calls attention to and interests the viewer in this physicality is a deterrent to our understanding of the idea and is used as an expressive device. The conceptual artist would want to ameliorate this emphasis on materiality as much as possible or to use it in a paradoxical way. (To convert it into an idea.) This kind of art then, should be stated with the most economy of means. Any idea that is better stated in two dimensions should not be in three dimensions. Ideas may also be stated with numbers, photographs, or words or any way the artist chooses, the form being unimpor-tant.

These paragraphs are not intended as categorical imperatives but the ideas stated are as close as possible to my thinking at this time.[3] These ideas are the result of my work as an artist and are subject to change as my experience changes. I have tried to state them with as much clarity as possible. If the statements I make are unclear it may mean the thinking is unclear. Even while writing these ideas there seemed to be obvious inconsistencies (which I have tried to correct, but others will probably slip by). I do not advocate a conceptual form of art for all artists. I have found that it has worked well for me while other ways have not. It is one way of making art: other ways suit other artists. Nor do I think all conceptual art merits the viewer's attention. Conceptual art is only good when the idea is good.

Dick Higgins

A Something Else Manifesto

When asked what one is doing, one can only explain it as "something else." Now one does something big, now one does something small, now another big thing, now another little thing. Always it is something else.

We can talk about a thing, but we cannot talk a thing. It is always something else.

One might well emphasize this. It happens, doesn't it? Actually, everybody might be in on this Something Else, whether he wants it or not. Everyman is.

For what is one confined in one's activity? Commitment on a personal level can be plural. One can be committed to both salads and fish, political action and photographic engineering, art and non-art. One does, we hope, what seems necessary, or at least, not extraneous, not simply that to which one has committed oneself. One doesn't want to be like the little German who hated the little Menshveik because the little German always did his things in a roll format, and when the little Menshevik did that kind of thing too, the little German got into a tizzy. If one is consistent and inconsistent often enough nothing that one does is one's own, certainly not a form, which is only a part of speech in one's language. One must take special care not to influence oneself. Tomorrow one will write Schubert's Fifth Symphony, cook some kohlrabi, develop a nontoxic epoxy, and invent still another kind of theater;

or perhaps one will just sit and scream; or perhaps. . . .

When you touch a fact it is a fact. No idea is clear to us until a little soup has been spilled on it.

So when we are asked for bread, let's give not stones, not stale bread. Maybe we have no bread at all, anyway. But why not give a little chicken?

Let's chase down an art that clucks and fills our guts.

Notes

The Aesthetics of the Avant-Garde — by Michael Kirby

1. In his brilliant book *The Banquet Years* subtitled *The Origins of the Avant-Garde in France 1885 to World War I* (Doubleday, 1961), p. 25, Roger Shattuck says, "Arbitrarily one can establish the origin of the avant-garde in 1863, when Napolean III consented to the Salon des Refuses."

2. From *The Influence of Culture on Visual Perception* by Marshall H. Segall, Donald T. Campbell, and Melville J. Herskovits (Bobbs-Merrill, 1966).

3. From *Eye and Brain: The Psychology of Seeing* by R. L. Gregory (McGraw-Hill, 1966).

4. From *Subcortical Mechanisms of Behavior: The Psychological Functions of Primitive Parts* by Robert A. McCleary and Robert Y. Moore (Basic Books, 1965).

The Function of Art — by L. Moholy-Nagy

1. *Culture* and *civilization* are used in this book as synonyms, though in German, for instance, a differentiation is made between the two: *civilization* is the term for the technological and *culture* for the humanistic sphere.

2. Alfred Korzybski, the leader of the general semanticists, states that if a "translation is made into the language of lower centers—namely into 'intuition,' 'feeling,' 'visualizations'—the higher abstractions gain the character of experience. By re-translating our higher order, verbal abstractions of relations and order into simplified but direct manifestations which can be visualized and felt, modern art affords immediate subcortical experience of essential structure." (Quoted by Oliver Bloodstein in *General Semantics and Modern Art,* in *etc.* vol. 1, no. 1, 1943) This suggests the intertwined nature of human experiences and their expression. I question only the biological justification of discriminating between "higher" and "lower" orders of experience. Biologically seen, they are of *equal* order and without their balanced, interpenetrated performance no satisfactory life exists.

Space-Time Problems — by L. Moholy-Nagy

1. Thomas Eakins, American painter, when collaborating with E. Muybridge in recording speed made similar photographs as early as 1881-84 as Charles Bregler reported in the *Magazine of Art,* January, 1943.

2. James Joyce captured this delicate quality, this becoming, in a passage of *Ulysses;* "a very short space of time through very short time of space."

Chance-Imagery   *by George Brecht*

1. Tristan Tzara, "Lecture on Dada" (1922). *The Dada Painters and Poets: An Anthology.* Edited by Robert Motherwell. The Documents of Modern Art series (Wittenborn, Schultz, Inc., 1951) p. 248. We will hereafter abbreviate this anthology to "Motherwell."

2. Sigmund Freud, *Psychopathology of Everyday Life. The Basic Writings of Sigmund Freud.* English translation by A. A. Brill. (New York: Random House, The Modern Library, 1938), p. 164.

3. Marcel Raymond, *From Baudelaire to Surrealism.* Quoted in Motherwell, p. xxix of the Introduction.

4. Andre Breton, "First Surrealist Manifesto." Quoted by Georges Hugnet in one of his two introductory essays for *Fantastic Art, Dada, Surrealism.* Edited by Alfred H. Barr, Jr. Third edition (New York: The Museum of Modern Art, 1947). Hereafter this book is referred to as "Barr."

5. Harriet and Sidney Janis, "Marcel Duchamp: Anti-Artist" (1945). Motherwell, Appendix C, p. 306.

6. Tristan Tzara, "manifesto on feeble love and bitter love." Motherwell, p. 92.

7. A. H Barr, Jr., "A list of devices, techniques, media." Barr, p. 65.

8. Gabrielle Buffet-Picabia, "Some Memories of Pre-Dada: Picabia and Duchamp" (1949), Motherwell, p. 266.

9. Jean (Hans) Arp, "Dada Was Not a Farce" (1949). Motherwell, p. 294.

10. Tristan Tzara, "Lecture on Dada" (1922). Motherwell, p. 294.

11. Sam Hunter, Catalog of the 1956 Pollock retrospective show. *Bulletin,* vol. xxiv, no. 2 of the Museum of Modern Art.

12. Jackson Pollock, "My Painting," *Possibilities* (N.Y.), no. 1:79, Winter 1947-48, pp. 78-83.

13. Jackson Pollock, "Jackson Pollock" (a questionnaire), *Arts and Architecture,* vol. 61, no. 2, February 1944, p. 14.

14. D. T. Suzuki, "Zen Buddhism," *Selected Writings of D. T. Suzuki.* Edited by William Barrett (New York: Doubleday & Co., Inc., Anchor edition, 1956), p. 234. Used by permission of Hutchinson & Co., Ltd., London.

15. *Ibid.,* p. 256.

16. Jean (Hans) Arp, "Notes from a Dada Diary," Motherwell, p. 222.

20. *Webster's New International Dictionary.* Second edition, copyright 1959 by G. & C. Merriam Co., publishers of the Merriam-Webster Dictionaries. Used by permission.

21. M. G. Kendall and B. Babington Smith, "Randomness and Random Sampling Numbers," *Journal of the Royal Statistical Society,* London, vol. CI, pt. 1, 1938, pp. 147-166.

22. G. Udny Yule and M. G. Kendall, *An Introduction to the Theory of Statistics.* Fourteenth edition (New York: Hafner Publishing Co., 1950).

23. Cited in M. G. Kendall, *The Advanced Theory of Statistics.* Fifth edition (New York: Hafner Publishing Co.), vo. I, p. 199.

24. The Rand Corporation, *A Million Random Digits with 100,000 Normal Deviates* (Glencoe, Ill.: The Free Press, 1955). A description of the method used for production of the random digits is contained in the introduction.

25. Interstate Commerce Commission, Bureau of Transport Economics and Statistics, *Table of 105,000 Random Decimal Digits* (Washington, D.C., May 1949). Copies are available free from the Commission. Refer to Statement No. 4914, File No. 261-A-1.

26. G. Udny Yule, "A Test of Tippett's Random Sampling Numbers," *Journal of the Royal Statistical Society,* vol. CI, pt. 1, 1938, p. 167.

28. Pierre Schaeffer, *A la recherche d'une musique concrete* (Paris: Editions du Seuil, p. 16.

29. Quoted by Frank Elgar; in Elgar and Maillard. *Picasso.* Frederick A. Praeger, Inc., New York, 1956.

30. Statement by Robert Motherwell in "The New Decade" exhibition catalog. Edited by John
I. H. Baur (New York: Whitney Museum of American Art, 1955).

On Form   *by Kenneth Burke*

1. Though my primary concern is with the application of these various subdivisions to
literature, if the reader is interested in their relation to music I could refer to *Chopin, The Man
and His Music* (Knopf, 1949), by the expert musicologist, Herbert Weinstock. See the chapter,
"An Introductory Note on Musical Form," where the author shows how the various subdivisions
of form (as schematized in my "Lexicon Rhetoricae") can be applied to the music of Chopin.

Style and the Representation of Historical Time   *by George Kubler*

1. G. A. Brecher, *Zeitschrift fur vergleichende Physiologie,* 18 (1932), 204-43. Roland Fischer,
"Aesthetics and the Biology of the Fleeting Moment," *Perspectives in Biology and Medicine,*
VIII (1965), 210-217.
2. Thus Meyer Schapiro: "Style is constant form" ("Style," *Anthropology Today,* Chicago:
CRM Books, 1953).
3. A. L. Kroeber, *Style and Civilizations* (Westport, CT.: Greenwood Press, 1973).
4. James Ackerman, "Theory of Style," *Journal of Aesthetics and Art Criticism,* XX (1962).

Art and Authenticity   *by Nelson Goodman*

1. And only for the sake of argument—only in order not to obscure the central issue. All talk
of mere looking in what follows is to be understood as occurring within the scope of this
temporary concession, not as indicating any acceptance of the notion on my part.
2. Germans learning English often cannot, without repeated effort and concentrated
attention, hear any differences at all between the vowel sounds in "sup" and "cop." Like effort
may sometimes be needed by the native speaker of a language to discern differences in color, and
so forth, that are not marked by his elementary vocabulary. Whether language affects actual
sensory discrimination has long been debated among psychologists, anthropologists, and
linguists; see the survey of experimentation and controversy in Segall, Campbell, and Herskovits,
The Influence of Culture in Visual Perception (Indianapolis: Bobbs-Merrill, 1966), pp. 34-48.
The issue is unlikely to be resolved without greater clarity in the use of "sensory," "perceptual,"
and "cognitive," and more care in distinguishing between what a person can do at a given time
and what he can learn to do.
3. In saying that a difference *between the pictures* that is thus relevant to my present
experience in looking at them constitutes an aesthetic difference between them, I am of course
not saying that everything (for example, drunkenness, snow blindness, twilight) that may cause
my experiences of them to differ constitutes such an aesthetic difference. Not every difference in
or arising from how the pictures happen to be looked at counts; only differences in or arising
from how they are to be looked at. Concerning the aesthetic, more is said later in this section and
in *Languages of Art,* (1968), section VI, 3-6.
4. For a detailed and fully illustrated account, see P. B. Coremans, *Van Meegeren's Faked
Vermeers and De Hooghs,* trans. A. Hardy and C. Hutt (Amsterdam: J. M. Meulenhoff, 1949).
The story is outlined in Sepp Schuller, *Forgers, Dealers, Experts,* trans. J. Cleugh (New York: G.
P. Putnam's Sons, 1960), pp. 95-105.
5. Not surprisingly, since a single quantum of light may excite a retinal receptor. See M. H.
Pirenne and F. H. C. Marriott, "The Quantum Theory of Light and the Psycho-Physiology of
Vision," in *Psychology,* ed. S. Koch (New York: McGraw-Hill, 1959), Vol. I, p. 290; also
Theodore C. Ruch, "Vision," in *Medical Psychology and Biophysics* (Philadelphia: W. B.
Saunders, 1960), p. 426.
6. That the forgeries purported to have been painted during a period from which no Vermeers
were known made detection more difficult but does not essentially alter the case. Some art

historians, on the defensive for their profession, claim that the most perceptive critics suspected the forgeries very early; but actually some of the foremost recognized authorities were completely taken in and for some time even refused to believe Van Meegeren's confession. The reader has a more recent example now before him in the revelation that the famous bronze horse, long exhibited in the Metropolitan Museum and proclaimed as a masterpiece of classical Greek sculpture, is a modern forgery. An official of the museum noticed a seam that apparently neither he nor anyone else had ever seen before, and scientific testing followed. No expert has come forward to claim earlier doubts on aesthetic grounds.

7. I deal with that question in *Languages of Art* (1968), section IV.

8. Attributed to Immanuel Tingle and Joseph Immersion (ca. 1800).

9. There may indeed be forgeries of performances. Such forgeries are performances that purport to be by a certain musician, and so forth; but these, if in accordance with the score, are nevertheless genuine instances of the work. And what concerns me here is a distinction among the arts that depends upon whether there can be forgeries of works, not upon whether there can be forgeries of instances of works. See further what is said below concerning forgeries of editions of literary works and of musical performances.

10. This is to be taken as a preliminary version of a difference we must seek to formulate more precisely. Much of what follows in this chapter has likewise the character of an exploratory introduction to matters calling for fuller and more detailed inquiry in later chapters (of *Languages of Art*).

11. Such identification does not guarantee that the object possesses the pictorial properties it had originally. Rather, reliance on physical or historical identification is transcended only where we have means of ascertaining that the requisite properties are present.

12. To be original a print must be from a certain plate but need not be printed by the artist. Furthermore, in the case of a woodcut, the artist sometimes only draws upon the block, leaving the cutting to someone else—Holbein's blocks, for example, were usually cut by Lützelberger. Authenticity in an autographic art always depends upon the object's having the requisite, sometimes rather complicated, history of productions, but that history does not always include ultimate execution by the original artist.

13. Of course, I am not saying that a correct(ly spelled) performance is correct in any of a number of other usual senses. Nevertheless, the composer or musician is likely to protest indignantly at refusal to accept a performance with a few wrong notes as an instance of a work; and he surely has ordinary usage on his side. But ordinary usage here points the way to disaster for theory (see *Languages of Art*, V, 2).

System Esthetics   *by Jack Burnham*

1. Quade, E. S. (November 1964) "Methods and Procedures" in *Analysis for Military Decisions* (Santa Monica: The Rand Corp., 1970), p. 153.

2. Galbraith, John Kenneth (1967) *The New Industrial State* (Boston: Houghton Mifflin Co., 1972), pp. 343-353.

3. Caudwell, Christopher (pseud.) (1937) *Illusion and Reality: A Study of the Sources of Poetry* (London: MacMillan and Co., 1963), p. 111.

4. Peckham, Morse (1965) *Man's Rage for Chaos: Biology, Behavior & the Arts* (New York: York: Schocken Books, 1967), p. 314.

5. Fried, Michael "Art and Objecthood," *Artforum*, Summer 1967, p. 15.

6. Bertalanffy, Ludwig von (1967) *Robots, Men and Minds* (New York: George Braziller, Inc., 1969), p. 69.

7. Anonymous "Ad Reinhardt, Painter, Is Dead, Reduced Color to Bare Minimum," in *The New York Times*, 1 September 1967, p. 33.

8. Judd, Donald (1965) "Specific Objects" in *Contemporary Sculpture* (New York: The Arts Digest, Inc.), p. 78.

9. Morris, Robert "Anti Form," *Artforum*, April 1968, p. 35.

10. Smithson, Robert "Towards the Development of an Air Terminal Site," *Artforum*, Summer 1967, pp. 36-40.

11. Fried, *op cit.*, p. 19.

Notes

12. Jacobs, Jay "More Les" *the ART gallery* (Ivoryton, Connecticut: Hollycraft Press, March 1968), p. 27.

13. Flavin, Dan (with an introduction by) *Dan Flavin: Pink and Gold,* exhibition catalog, (Chicago: The Museum of Contemporary Art, December, 1967).

14. Haacke, Hans (with statement by) *Hans Haacke,* exhibition catalog (New York: Howard Wise Gallery, January 1968).

15. Kaprow, Allan "The Happenings Are Dead—Long Live Happenings," *Artforum,* March 1966, pp. 36-39.

16. Gabo, Naum *Gabo: Constructions, Sculptures, Paintings, Drawings, Engravings* (Cambridge: Harvard University Press, 1957), p. 153.

Art as Internal Technology   *by José A. Argüelles*

1. Mircea Eliade, *Shamanism: Archaic Techniques of Ecstacy,* trans. Willard R. Trask (Princeton: Univ. of Princeton Press, 1964), p. xiv.

2. Paul Laffoley, inscription on painting, *The Visionary Point,* 1972.

3. Pierre Teilhard de Chardin, *The Future of Man,* trans. Norman Denny (New York: Harper & Row, 1969), p. 117.

4. Willard Van de Bogart, "Entropic Art," unpublished paper, 1973 (?) p.4.

5. *Ibid.,* p. 5.

6. Gene Youngblood, *Expanded Cinema* (New York: Dutton, 1970), p. 163.

7. Quoted in Arguelles, *Charles Henry and the Formation of a Psychophysical Aesthetic,* (Chicago: University of Chicago Press, 1972), p. 128.

8. Willard Van de Bogart, "Environmental Media Art," unpublished paper, 1973 (?).

The Expanding and Disappearing Work of Art   *by Lawrence Alloway*

1. Lucy Lippard and John Chandler, "The Dematerialization of Art," *Art International,* 12, 2, 1968.

2. Alain Robbe-Grillet, "Anti-humanism in Art," *Studio International,* 175, 899, 1968.

3. Claes Oldenburg, *Store Days.* Edited by Emmet Williams (Barton, Vt.: Something Else Press, Inc., 1967).

4. Allan Kaprow, "Pinpointing Happenings," *Art News,* 66, 6, 1967.

5. Robert Morris, "Anti Form," *Artforum,* 6, 8, 1968.

6. Quoted, Howard Junker, "Getting Down to the Nitty Gritty," *Saturday Evening Post,* 2 November 1968.

7. Michael Kirby, "Sculpture as a Visual Instrument," *Art International,* 12, 8, 1968. Reprinted in Kirby, *The Art of Time* (N.Y.: Dutton, 1969).

8. Quoted, *Options,* exhibition catalogue, Milwaukee Art Center, 1968.

9. Robert Smithson, "Towards the Development of an Air Terminal Site," *Artforum,* 5, 10, 1967.

10. Junker, *op. cit.*

11. Robert Smithson, "The Monuments of Passaic" (original title: "Guide to the Monuments of Passaic"), *Artforum,* 6, 4, 1967.

12. Sol LeWitt, "Paragraphs on Conceptual Art," *Artforum,* 5, 10, 1967.

13. Douglas Huebler, exhibition catalogue, New York, 1968.

A Sedimentation of the Mind   *by Robert Smithson*

1. The sinister in a primitive sense seems to have its origin in what could be called "quality gardens" (Paradise). Dreadful things seem to have happened in those half-forgotten Edens. Why does the Garden of Delights suggest something perverse? Torture gardens. Deer Park. The Grottos of Tiberius. Gardens of Virtue are somehow always "lost." A degraded paradise is perhaps worse than a degraded hell. America abounds in banal heavens, in vapid

"happy-hunting grounds," and in "natural" hells like Death Valley National Monument or The Devil's Playground. The public "sculpture garden" for the most part is an outdoor "room," that in time becomes a limbo of modern isms. Too much thinking about "gardens" leads to perplexity and agitation. Gardens like the levels of criticism bring one to the brink of chaos. This footnote is turning into a dizzying maze, full of tenuous paths and innumerable riddles. The abysmal problem of gardens somehow involves a fall from somewhere or something. The certainty of the absolute garden will never be regained.

The Impermanent Art   *by Merce Cunningham*

1. The actual technique of "choreography by chance" is the subject of an article by Remy Charlip in the January, 1954 issue of *Dance Magazine.*

A Quasi-Survey of Some "Minimalist" Tendencies ...   *by Yvonne Rainer*

1. In the case of Graham, it is hardly possible to relate her work to anything outside of theatre, since it was usually dramatic and psychological necessity that determined it.
2. The term *phrase* must be distinguished from *phrasing.* A phrase is simply two or more consecutive movements, while *phrasing,* as noted previously, refers to the manner of execution.

Video: Distinctive Features of the Medium   *by David Antin*

1. Judson Rosenbush, ed., *Frank Gillette Video: Process and Metaprocess.* Essay by Frank Gillette, interview by Willoughby Sharp (Syracuse, N.Y.: Everson Museum of Art, 1973), p. 21.
2. Hollis Frampton, "The Withering Away of the State of Art," *Artforum* (December 1974) p. 50.
3. Jud Yalkut, "TV As a Creative Medium at the Howard Wise Gallery," *Arts Magazine* (September 1961) p. 21.
4. Edward Stasheff and Rudy Bretz, *The Television Program: Its Writing, Direction, and Production* (New York: A. A. Wyn, 1951), p. 3.
5. *Ibid.,* p. 6.
6. *Ibid.,* p. 8.
7. *Ibid.,* p. 8.
8. Bruce Boice, "Lynda Benglis at Paula Cooper Gallery," *Artforum* (May 1973), p. 83.
9. Les Levine, "Excerpts from a Tape: 'Artistic'," *Art-Rite* (Autumn 1974), p. 27.

Concept Art   *by Henry Flynt*

1. The extension of the word *table* is all existing tables; the intension of *table* is all possible instances of a table. See Carnap's *Meaning and Necessity.*

Paragraphs on Conceptual Art   *by Sol LeWitt*

1. In other forms of art the concept may be changed in the process of execution.
2. Some ideas are logical in conception and illogical perceptually.
3. I dislike the term *work of art* because I am not in favor of work and the term sounds pretentious. But I don't know what other term to use.

Bibliography

The following bibliography is less comprehensive than selective, particularly in listing works on the edges of esthetics. The titles are divided into three admittedly approximate categories: Contemporary—reflecting an awareness of art and thought of the past two decades; Modern—dealing with the new art and ideas of the earlier part of the twentieth century; and Classical—relevant to all art. I have tended to acknowledge editions I have read. Dates in parentheses after the title identify the year of initial publication.

CLASSICAL

Abell, Walter. *The Collective Dream in Art.* Cambridge: Harvard Univ., 1957.

Aldrich, Virgil C. *Philosophy of Art.* Englewood Cliffs: Prentice-Hall, 1963.

Aristotle. *Poetics.* Many editions.

Beardsley, Monroe C. *Aesthetics.* N. Y.: Harcourt, Brace, 1958.

———. *Aesthetics from Classical Greece to the Present.* N. Y.: Macmillan, 1966.

———, and Schuller, Herbert M., eds. *Aesthetic Inquiry.* Belmont: Dickinson, 1967.

Berenson, Bernard. *Aesthetics and History in the Visual Arts.* N. Y.: Pantheon, 1948.

Brunius, Teddy. *Theory and Taste.* Uppsala, Sweden: Almquist, 1969.

Cassirer, Ernst. *An Essay on Man.* Garden City: Doubleday Anchor, 1944.

Bullough, Edward. *Aesthetics* (1907-20). Edited by Elizabeth Wilkinson. London: Bowes, 1957.

Coleman, Francis J., ed. *Aesthetics.* N. Y.: McGraw-Hill, 1968.

Collingwood, R. G. *The Principles of Art.* N. Y.: Oxford Univ., 1938.

Croce, Benedetto. "Aesthetics," in *Encyclopedia Britannica.* N.Y. & London: Encyclopedia Britannica, 1929.

Dickie, George. *Aesthetics: An Introduction.* Indianapolis: Pegasus, 1971.

Frye, Northrop. *Anatomy of Criticism.* Princeton: Princeton Univ., 1957.

Giedion, Sigfried. *Architecture and the Phenomena of Transition.* Cambridge: Harvard Univ., 1971.

Gilson, Etienne. *Forms and Substances in the Arts* (1964). N.Y.: Scribner's, 1966.

Hofstadter, Albert, and Kuhns, Richard, eds. *Philosophies of Art and Beauty.* N.Y.: Modern Library, 1969.

Hook, Sidney, ed. *Art and Philosophy.* N.Y.: New York Univ., 1966.

Hospers, John. *Meaning and Truth in the Arts.* Chapel Hill: Univ. of North Carolina, 1946.

Kant, Immanuel. *Critique of Judgement.* Trans. by James Creed Meredith. Oxford: Clarendon, 1952.

Kennick, W. E., ed. *Art and Philosophy.* N.Y.: St. Martin's, 1964.

Khatchadourian, Haig. *The Concept of Art.* N.Y.: New York Univ., 1971.

Levich, Marvin, ed. *Aesthetics and the Philosophy of Criticism.* N.Y.: Random House, 1963.

Longinus. "On the Sublime," *Classical Literary Criticism.* Trans. by T. M. Dorsch. Harmondsworth: Penguin, 1965.

Maritain, Jacques. *Creative Intuition in Art and Poetry.* N.Y.: Pantheon, 1953.

Munro, Thomas. *Oriental Aesthetics.* Cleveland: Case Western Reserve Univ., 1965.

———. *The Arts and Their Interrelations* (1949). Revised ed. Cleveland: Case Western Reserve Univ., 1967.

———. *Form and Style in the Arts.* Cleveland: Case Western Reserve Univ., 1970.

Nahm, Milton C. *Readings in the Philosophy of Art and Aesthetics.* Englewood Cliffs,: Prentice-Hall, 1975.

Osborne, Harold. *Aesthetics and Art Theory: An Historical Introduction.* N.Y.: Dutton, 1970.

Panofsky, Erwin. *Meaning in the Visual Arts.* Garden City: Doubleday Anchor, 1955.

Plato. *The Collected Dialogues.* Edited by Edith Hamilton and Huntington Cairns. Princeton: Princeton Univ., 1961.

Rader, Melvin, ed. *A Modern Book of Aesthetics* (1935). Third ed. N.Y.: Holt, 1960.

Rosenberg, Jakob. *On Quality in Art.* Princeton: Princeton Univ., 1967.

Santayana, George. *The Sense of Beauty.* N.Y.: Scribner's, 1896.

Saw, Ruth. *Aesthetics.* Garden City: Doubleday Anchor, 1971.

Schapiro, Meyer. "Style," in A. L. Kroeber, ed., *Anthropology Today* Chicago: Univ. of Chicago, 1953.

Schiller, Friedrich von. *On the Sublime, and Naive and Sentimental Poetry* (1795-96). N.Y.: Unger, 1966.

Sparshott, F.E. *The Structure of Aesthetics.* Toronto: Univ. of Toronto, 1963.

Vivas, Eliseo, and Krieger, Murray, eds. *The Problems of Aesthetics.* N.Y.: Holt, 1953.

Weitz, Morris, ed. *Problems in Aesthetics.* N.Y.: Macmillan, 1959.

Wofflin, Heinrich *Principles of Art History* (1915). Seventh ed. Trans. by M. D. Hottinger. N.Y.: Dover, 1950.

Wolheim, Richard. *Art and Its Objects.* N.Y.: Harper & Row, 1968.

MODERN

Adorno, Theodor. *The Philosophy of Modern Music* (1948). N.Y.: Seabury, 1973.

Argüelles, José A *Charles Henry and the Formation of a Psychophysical Aesthetic.* Chicago: Univ. of Chicago, 1972.

Arnheim, Rudolf. *Art and Visual Perception.* Berkeley: Univ. of California, 1954.

———. *Toward a Psychology of Art.* Berkeley: Univ. of California, 1966.

———. *Visual Thinking.* Berkeley: Univ. of California, 1969.

Auerbach, Erich. *Mimesis* (1946). Garden City: Doubleday Anchor, 1953.

Banham, Reyner. *Theory and Design in the First Machine Age* (1960). Second ed. N.Y.: Praeger, 1967.

Bann, Stephen, ed. *The Tradition of Constructivism.* N.Y.: Viking, 1974.

Barrett, William. *Time of Need.* N.Y.: Harper & Row, 1972.

Baudeliare, Charles. *The Mirror of Art.* Translated and edited by Jonathan Mayne. Garden City: Doubleday Anchor, 1956.

Beiderman, Charles. *Art as the Evolution of Visual Knowledge.* Red Wing: Charles Beiderman, 1948.

Bell, Clive. *Art.* London: Chatto & Windus, 1913.

Brown, Merle E. *Neo-Idealistic Aesthetics.* Detroit: Wayne State Univ., 1966.

Burke, Kenneth. *The Philosophy of Literary Form* (1941). N.Y.: Vintage, 1957.

Butor, Michel. *Inventory.* N.Y.: Simon & Schuster, 1968.

Cavell, Stanley. *Must We Mean What We Say?* N.Y.: Scribner's, 1969.

Chiari, Joseph. *The Aesthetics of Modernism.* N.Y.: Humanities, 1970.

Chipp, Hershel, ed. *Theories of Modern Art.* Berkeley: Univ. of California, 1968.

Collins, Peter. *Changing Ideals in Modern Architecture.* London: Faber & Faber, 1965.

Debussy, Claude; Busoni, Ferrucio; and Ives, Charles E., *Three Classics in the Aesthetics of Music.* N.Y.: Dover, 1962.

Dewey, John. *Art as Experience.* N.Y.: Minton, Balch, 1934.

Ducasse, Curt John. *The Philosophy of Art* (1929). N.Y.: Dover, 1966.

Dufrenne, Mikel. *The Phenomenology of Aesthetic Experience* (1953). Evanston: Northwestern Univ., 1973.

Ellman, Richard, and Fiedelson, Charles Jr., eds. *The Modern Tradition.* N.Y.: Oxford Univ. 1965.

Focillon, Henri. *The Life of Forms in Art* (1934). Second ed. N.Y.: Wittenborn, 1948.

Frank, Joseph. *The Widening Gyre.* New Brunswick: Rutgers Univ., 1963.

Fry, Roger. *Vision and Design* (1920). Harmondsworth: Penguin, 1937.

Frye, Northrop. *The Modern Century.* Toronto: Oxford Univ., 1967.

Gabo, Naum. *Of Divers Arts.* Princeton: Princeton Univ., 1962.

Giedion, Sigfried. *Space, Time and Architecture* (1941). Fourth ed. Cambridge: Harvard Univ., 1963.

Goldwater, Robert. *What is Modern Sculpture?* N.Y.: Museum of Modern Art, 1969.

Gombrich, Ernst H. *Art and Illusion* (1960). Second ed. Princeton: Princeton Univ., 1961.

Greenberg, Clement. *Art and Culture.* Boston: Beacon, 1958.

Greene, Theodore Meyer. *The Arts and the Art of Criticism.* Princeton: Princeton Univ., 1940.

Gregory, Richard L. *The Intelligent Eye.* N.Y.: McGraw-Hill, 1970.

———, and Gombrich, E.H., eds. *Illusion in Nature and Art.* N.Y.: Scribner's, 1973.

Grudin, Louis. *A Primer of Aesthetics.* N.Y.: Covici, Friede, 1930.

Hall, James B. and Barry Ulanov, eds. *Modern Culture and the Arts.* N.Y.: McGraw-Hill, 1967.

Harrell, Jean G., and Wierzbianska, Alina, eds. *Aesthetics in Twentieth-Century Poland.* Lewisburg: Bucknell Univ., 1973.

Hauser, Arnold. *The Philosophy of Art History* (1958). N.Y.: Meridian, 1963.

Herbert, Robert L., ed. *Modern Artists on Art.* Englewood Cliffs: Prentice-Hall, 1964.

Heyl, Bernard C. *New Bearings in Aesthetics and Art Criticism.* New Haven: Yale Univ., 1943.

Hulme, T. E. *Speculations.* London: Kegan, Paul, 1924.

Ingarden, Roman. *The Literary Work of Art* (1931). Evanston: Northwestern Univ., 1973.

Ives, Charles. *Essays Before a Sonata* (1920). N.Y.: Norton, 1964.

Jacobus, Lee A., ed. *Aesthetics and the Arts.* N.Y.: McGraw-Hill, 1968.

Kaelin, Eugene F. *Art and Existence.* Lewisburg: Bucknell Univ., 1970.

Kahler, Erich. *The Disintegration of Form in the Arts.* N.Y.: Braziller, 1969.

Kandinsky, Wassily. *Concerning the Spiritual in Art* (1912). N.Y.: Wittenborn, 1947.

Kenner, Hugh. *The Pound Era.* Berkeley: Univ. of California, 1971.

Kepes, Gyorgy. *Language of Vision.* Chicago: Theobald, 1944.

Kris, Ernst. *Psychoanalytic Explorations in Art* (1952). N.Y.: Schocken, 1964.

Langer, Susanne. *Philosophy in a New Key.* Cambridge: Harvard Univ., 1942.

———. *Feeling and Form.* N.Y.: Scribner's, 1953.

———. *Problems of Art.* N.Y.: Scribner's, 1957.

———, ed. *Reflections on Art.* Baltimore: Johns Hopkins Univ., 1958.

Lawder, Standish D. *The Cubist Cinema.* N.Y.: New York Univ., 1975.

Lewis, Wyndham. *Time and Western Man* (1927). Boston: Beacon, 1957.

Margolis, Joseph, ed. *Philosophy Looks at the Arts.* N.Y.: Scribner's, 1962.

Martin, J.L., et al., eds. *Circle: International Survey of Constructive Art* (1937). N.Y.: Praeger, 1971.

McLuhan, Marshall. *The Mechancial Bride.* N.Y.: Vanguard, 1951.

———, and Harley Parker. *Through the Vanishing Point.* N.Y.: Harper & Row, 1968.

Merleau-Ponty, Maurice. *The Primacy of Perception.* Evanston: Northwestern Univ., 1964.

Moffett, Kenworth. *Meier-Graefe as Art Critic.* Munich: Prestel-Verlag, 1973.

Moholy-Nagy, L. *Painting, Photography, Film* (1927). Cambridge: MIT, 1969.

———. *The New Vision* (1929). N.Y.: Brewer, Warren, 1932.

Morawski, Stefan. *Inquiries Into the Fundamentals of Aesthetics.* Cambridge: MIT, 1974.

Motherwell, Robert, ed. *The Dada Painters and Poets.* N.Y.: Wittenborn, 1948.

Munro, Thomas. "Present Tendencies in American Esthetics," in Marvin Farber, ed. *Philosophic Thought in France and the United States* (1950). Albany: SUNY, 1968.

O'Doherty, Brian. "Inside the White Cube," *Artforum* (Feb./March, 1976).

Ortega y Gasset, José. *The Dehumanization of Art* (1925). Garden City:

Doubleday Anchor, 1956.

Osborne, Harold, ed. *Aesthetics in the Modern World*. N.Y.: Weybright & Talley, 1968.

———. *Aesthetics*. London: Oxford Univ., 1972.

Parker, DeWitt H. *The Analysis of Arts*. New Haven: Yale Univ., 1924.

Pepper, Stephen C. *Aesthetic Quality: A Contextualist Theory of Beauty*. N.Y.: Scribner's, 1938.

Philipson, Morris, ed. *Aesthetics Today*. N.Y.: Meridian, 1961.

Poggioli, Renato. *The Theory of the Avant-Garde* (1962). Cambridge: Harvard Univ., 1968.

Pound, Ezra. *ABC of Reading* (1934). N.Y.: New Directions, 1960.

Read, Herbert. *The Philosophy of Modern Art* (1952). N.Y.: Meridian, 1954.

———. *Education Through Art* (1943). Third ed. London: Faber & Faber, 1961.

———. *Art and Alienation*. N.Y.: Horizon, 1967.

Rickey, George. *Constructivism: Origins and Evolution*. N.Y.: Braziller, 1968.

Ricoeur, Paul. *The Conflict of Interpretations* (1969). Evanston: Northwestern Univ., 1974.

Rosenberg, Harold. *The Tradition of the New*. N.Y.: Horizon, 1959.

———. *Art on the Edge*. N.Y.: Macmillan, 1975.

Rubin, William S. *Dada and Surrealist Art*. N.Y.: Abrams, n.d.

Sanchez Vasquez, Adolfo. *Art and Society* (1965). N.Y.: Monthly Review, 1973.

Scully, Vincent. *American Architecture and Urbanism*. N.Y.: Praeger, 1969.

Seitz, William C. *The Art of Assemblage*. N.Y.: Museum of Modern Art, 1961.

Shattuck, Roger. *The Banquet Years*. N.Y.: Harper, 1958.

Sherburne, Donald W. *A Whiteheadian Aesthetic* (1961). Hamden: Archon, 1970.

Sypher, Wylie. *Loss of the Self*. N.Y.: Random House, 1962.

———, ed. *Art History: An Anthology of Modern Criticism*. N.Y.: Vantage, 1963.

Weitz, Morris. *Philosophy Looks at the Arts*. Cambridge: Harvard Univ., 1950.

Whyte, L.L., ed. *Aspects of Form* (1951). Bloomington: Indiana Univ., 1961.

Wingler, Hans Maria. *Bauhaus: Weimar, Dessau, Berlin, Chicago*. Cambridge: MIT, 1969.

Wollheim, Richard. *On Art and the Mind*. Cambridge: Harvard Univ., 1974.

Worringer, Wilhelm. *Abstraction and Empathy* (1908). London: Routledge, 1953.

CONTEMPORARY

Antin, David. *Talking at the Boundaries.* N.Y.: New Directions, 1976.

Apollinaire, Guillaume. "The New Spirit and the Poets" (1917), in Roger Shattuck, ed., *Selected Writings of Apollinaire.* N.Y.: New Directions, 1949.

Argüelles, José A. *The Transformative Vision.* Berkeley: Shambhala, 1975.

Atkinson, Terry, et al. *Art and Language.* Cologne: DuMont Schauberg, 1972.

Bateson, Gregory. *Steps to an Ecology of Mind.* N.Y.: Ballantine, 1972.

Battcock, Gregory, *Why Art?* N.Y.: Dutton, 1977.

———, ed. *The New Art.* N.Y.: Dutton, 1966.

———, ed. *Minimal Art.* N.Y.: Dutton, 1968.

———, ed. *Idea Art.* N.Y.: Dutton, 1973.

Baxandall, Lee, ed. *Radical Perspectives in the Arts.* Harmondsworth: Penguin, 1972.

Benjamin, Walter. "The Work of Art in the Age of Mechanical Reproduction" (1936), *Illuminations.* N.Y.: Schocken, 1969.

Bense, Max. *Aesthetica.* Baden-Baden, Germany: Agis, 1965.

Bentall, Jonathan. *Science and Technology in Art Today.* London: Thames & Hudson, 1972.

Bergonzi, Bernard, ed. *Innovations.* London: Macmillan, 1968.

Berne, Stanley. *Future Language.* N.Y.: Horizon, 1976.

Birkoff, George D. *Aesthetic Measure.* Cambridge: Harvard Univ., 1933.

Brakhage, Stan. *Metaphors on Vision.* N.Y.: Film Culture, 1963.

Brown, Norman O. *Love's Body.* N.Y.: Random House, 1966.

———. *Closing Time.* N.Y.: Random House, 1973.

Buren, Daniel. *5 Texts.* N.Y.: John Weber Gallery, 1973.

Burnham, Jack. *Beyond Modern Sculpture.* N.Y.: Braziller, 1968.

———. *The Structure of Art.* N.Y.: Braziller, 1971.

———. *Great Western Salt Works.* N.Y.: Braziller, 1974.

Cage, John. *Silence.* Middletown: Wesleyan Univ., 1961.

———. *A Year from Monday.* Middletown: Wesleyan Univ., 1967.

———. *M.* Middletown: Wesleyan Univ., 1973.

———, ed. *Notations.* N.Y.: Something Else, 1968.

Cassou, Jean, et al. *Art and Confrontation.* Greewich: New York Graphics, 1968.

Celant, Germano, *Art Povera* (1968). N.Y.: Praeger, 1969.

Bibliography

Claus, Jurgen. *Kunst Heute.* Hamburg: Rowohlt, 1965.
———. *Expansion der Kunst.* Hamburg: Rowohlt, 1970.
Cunningham, Merce. *Changes: Notes on Choreography.* N.Y.: Something Else, 1968.
Danto, Arthur. "The Artworld," *Journal of Philosophy* (1964).
Davis, Douglas. *Art and the Future.* N.Y.: Praeger, 1973.
Dorner, Alexander. *The Way Beyond Art.* N.Y.: Wittenborn, 1947.
Duchamp, Marcel. *Salt Seller.* N.Y.: Oxford, 1973.
Ehrenzweig, Anton. *The Psychoanalysis of Artistic Vision and Hearing* (1953). N.Y.: Braziller, 1965.
———. *The Hidden Order of Art.* Berkeley: Univ. of California, 1967.
Eysenck, H. J. *Sense and Nonsense in Psychology* (1957). Harmondsworth: Penguin, 1958.
———. "Aesthetics and Personality," *Exakte Asthetic,* I (1965).
Federman, Raymond, ed. *Surfiction.* Chicago: Swallow, 1974.
Foreman, Richard. *Plays and Manifestos.* Ed. by Kate Davey. N.Y.: New York Univ., 1976.
Fried, Michael. *Three American Painters.* Cambridge: Fogg Art Museum, 1965.
Gablik, Suzi. *Progress in Art.* N.Y.: Rizzoli, 1977.
Gillette, Frank. *Between Paradigms.* N.Y.: Gordon & Breach, 1973.
Goodman, Nelson. *Languages of Art.* Indianapolis: Bobbs-Merrill, 1968.
———. *Problems and Projects.* Indianapolis: Bobbs-Merrill, 1972.
Graham, Dan. *"End Moments."* N.Y.: Privately published, 1969.
Groh, Klaus, ed. *If I Had a Mind.* . . .Cologne: DuMont Schauberg, 1971.
Hassan, Ihab, *Paracriticisms.* Urbana: Univ. of Illinois, 1975.
Henri, Adrian. *Total Art.* N.Y.: Praeger, 1974.
Higgins, Dick. *Foew&ombwhnw.* N.Y.: Something Else, 1969.
Hill, Anthony, ed. *DATA: Directions in Art, Theory and Aesthetics.* Greenwich: New York Graphic Society, 1968
Hogg, James, ed. *Psychology and the Visual Arts.* Baltimore: Penguin, 1969.
Huxley, Aldous. *The Doors of Perception.* N.Y.: Harper, 1954.
Judd, Donald. *Complete Writings 1959-75.* N.Y.: New York Univ., 1975.
Kaprow, Allan. *Assemblage, Environments, & Happenings.* N.Y.: Something Else, 1966.
———. "O.K.," in Ay-O, et al. *Manifestos,* N.Y.: Something Else, 1966.
———. "Education of the Un-Artist, Part I," *Art News* (Feb., 1971); Part II," *Art News* (May, 1972).

435

Kenner, Hugh. *The Counterfeiters.* Bloomington: Indiana Univ., 1968.

Kepes, Gyorgy, ed. *The Nature and Art of Motion.* N.Y.: Braziller, 1968.

Kirby, Michael. *Happenings,* N.Y.: Dutton, 1965.

————. *The Art of Time.* N.Y.: Dutton, 1969.

————, ed. *The New Theatre.* N.Y.: New York Univ., 1974.

Kostelanetz, Richard. *The Theatre of Mixed Means.* N.Y.: Dial, 1968.

————. *The End of Intelligent Writing.* N.Y.: Sheed & Ward, 1974.

————, ed. *The New American Arts* (1965). N.Y.: Collier, 1967.

————, ed. *John Cage.* N.Y.: Praeger, 1970.

————, ed. *Moholy-Nagy.* N.Y.: Praeger, 1970.

————, ed. *Breakthrough Fictioneers.* W. Glover, VT: Something Else, 1973.

————, ed. *Essaying 'Essays.* N.Y.: Out of London, 1975.

Krantz, Stewart. *Science & Technology in the Arts.* N.Y.: Van Nostrand Reinhold, 1974.

Kriwet, Ferdinand. "Decomposition of the Literary Unit," *Tri-Quarterly.* 20 (Winter, 1971).

Kubler, George. *The Shape of Time.* New Haven: Yale Univ., 1962.

Kuhn, Thomas S. *The Structure of Scientific Revolutions.* Chicago: Univ. of Chicago, 1962.

Kultermann, Udo. *Art and Life.* N.Y.: Praeger, 1971. [In England, as *Art-Events and Happenings.* London: Mathews Miller Dunbar, 1971.]

Kunst Bliebt Kunst. Cologne: Wallraf-Richartz-Museum, 1974.

Lippard, Lucy R. *Changing.* N.Y.: Dutton, 1971.

————. *From the Center.* N.Y.: Dutton, 1976.

———— ed. *Six Years: The Dematerialization of the Art Object.* N.Y.: Praeger, 1973.

Malina, Frank J. *Kinetic Art: Theory and Practice.* N.Y.: Dover, 1974.

Markov, Vladimir. *Russian Futurism.* Berkeley: Univ. of California, 1968.

McLuhan, Marshall. *Understanding Media.* N.Y.: McGraw-Hill, 1964.

McShine, Kynaston, ed. *Information.* N.Y.: Museum of Modern Art, 1970.

Meyer, Leonard B. *Music, the Arts, and Ideas.* Chicago: Univ. of Chicago, 1967.

Moles, Abraham. *Information Theory and Esthetic Perception* (1958). Urbana: Univ. of Illinois, 1966.

Moholy-Nagy, L. *Vision in Motion.* Chicago: Paul Theobald, 1947.

Monte, James, and Tucker, Marcia. *Anti-Illusion: Procedures/Materials.* N.Y.: Whitney Museum of American Art, 1969.

Munro, Thomas. "Aesthetics as a Science: Its Development in America," *Toward Science in Aesthetics.* N.Y.: Liberal Arts, 1956.

Neisser, Ulrich. *Cognitive Psychology.* N.Y.: Appleton-Century-Crofts, 1967.

Nodelman, Sheldon. "Sixties Art: Some Philosophical Perspectives," *Perspecta* (Yale Univ.), No. 11 (Jan., 1967).

Nuttal, Jeff. *Bomb Culture.* N.Y.: Delacorte, 1968.

Osborne, Harold. "The New Sensibility of the 1960s," *British Journal of Aesthetics,* XVI/2 (Spring, 1976).

Peckham, Morse. *Man's Rage for Chaos.* Philadelphia: Chilton, 1965.

Pierce, John R. *Symbols, Signals and Noise.* N.Y.: Harper & Row, 1961.

———. "Chance Remarks" (1949). *Science, Art and Communication.* N.Y.: Potter, 1968.

Popper, Frank. *Origins and Development of Kinetic Art.* London: Studio Vista, 1968.

———. *Art-Action and Participation.* N.Y.: New York Univ., 1975.

Rainer, Yvonne. *Work 1961-73.* N.Y.: New York Univ., 1974.

Reich, Steve. *Writings About Music.* N.Y.: New York Univ., 1974.

Reichardt, Jasia, ed. *Cybernetic Serendipity.* N.Y.: Praeger, 1968.

Reinhardt, Ad. *Art-As-Art: Selected Writings.* Ed. by Barbara Rose. N.Y.: Viking, 1975.

Robbe-Grillet, Alain. *For a New Novel* (1963). N.Y.: Grove, 1965.

Rose, Barbara. "A B C Art"," *Art in America* (Oct./Nov., 1965).

——— and Sandler, Irving, eds. "Sensibility of the Sixties," *Art in America* (Jan./Feb., 1967).

Rothenberg, Jerome, ed. *Technicians of the Sacred.* Garden City: Doubleday Anchor, 1968.

Ruesch, Jurgen and Kees, Weldon. *Nonverbal Communication.* Berkeley: Univ. of Calif., 1956.

Ryan, Paul. *Cybernetics of the Sacred* (1973). Garden City: Doubleday Anchor, 1974.

Schechner, Richard. *Public Domain.* N.Y.: Bobbs-Merrill, 1969.

———. *Essays on Performance Theory 1970-76.* N.Y.: Dramabook Specialists, 1977.

———, and Schuman, Mady, eds. *Ritual, Play, and Performance.* N.Y.: Seabury-Continuum, 1976.

Schillinger, Joseph. *The Mathematical Basis of the Arts.* N.Y.: Philosophical Library, 1948.

Schneider, Ira, and Beryl Korot, eds. *Video Art.* N.Y.: Harcourt, 1976.

Solt, Mary Ellen, ed. *Concrete Poetry: A World View.* Bloomington: Indiana Univ., 1969.

Sontag, Susan. *Against Interpretation.* N.Y.: Farrar, Straus, 1966.

———. *Styles of Radical Will.* N.Y.: Farrar, Straus, 1969.

Stein, Gertrude. *How to Write* (1931). N.Y.: Something Else, 1973.

———. *Lectures in America* (1935). Boston: Beacon, 1957.

———. *The Geographical History of America* (1936). N.Y.: Vintage, 1973.

Steinberg, Leo. *Other Criteria.* N.Y.: Oxford Univ., 1972.

Toynbee, Arnold, et al. *On the Future of Art.* N.Y.: Viking, 1970.

Treitler, Leo. "The Present as History," *Perspectives of New Music,* VII/2 (Spring/Summer, 1969).

Venturi, Robert. *Complexity and Contradiction in Architecture.* N.Y.: Museum of Modern Art, 1966.

Vostell, Wolf. *Aktionen.* Hamburg: Rowohlt, 1970.

Vries, Gerd de. *Uber Kunst/On Art.* Cologne: DuMont Schauberg, 1974.

Wittgenstein, Ludwig, *Philosophical Investigations.* Trans. G.E.M. Anscombe. N.Y.: Macmillan, 1953.

Woods, Gerald, et al., eds. *Art Without Boundaries.* N.Y.: Praeger, 1956.

Young, La Monte, ed. *An Anthology* (1963). Second ed. Munich: Heinar Friedrich, 1970.

Zekowski, Arlene. *Breaking Images.* N.Y.: Horizon, 1976.

Youngblood, Gene. *Expanded Cinema.* N.Y.: Dutton, 1970.

Contributors

LAWRENCE ALLOWAY (b. 1926, London) is professor of art at SUNY-Stony Brook, associate editor of *Artforum,* and art editor for *The Nation.* His books include *American Pop Art* (1974) and *Topics in American Art* (1975).

DAVID ANTIN (b. 1932, Brooklyn) is professor of art at the University of California at San Diego. His essays have appeared as widely as his poems. His most recent book, *Talking at the Boundaries* (1976), is a collection of poetic monologues.

JOSÉ ARGÜELLES (b. 1939, Rochester, MN) is a painter and illustrator who took his doctorate in the history of art at the University of Chicago in 1969. He wrote *Charles Henry and the Formation of a Psychophysical Aesthetic* (1972) and *The Transformative Vision* (1975), in addition to co-authoring, with his wife Miriam, *Mandala* (1972).

MILTON BABBITT (b. 1916, Philadelphia) is the Conant Professor of Music at Princeton University and was co-founding director of the Columbia-Princeton Electronic Music Center in New York. His major musical works include *Composition for Tenor and Six Instruments* (1960), *Vision and Prayer* (1961), and *Philomel* (1963).

ARNOLD BERLEANT (b. 1932, Buffalo) is professor of philosophy at C.W. Post Center of Long Island University. He is the author of *The Aesthetic Field* (1970), and many essays in esthetics and ethics, among other areas.

GEORGE BRECHT (b. 1923, Halfway, OR) lived in suburban New Jersey, working as an engineer, before studying composition with John Cage and moving to Europe and concentrating on his art. His works have been exhibited widely, especially in retrospectives of "Fluxus."

KENNETH BURKE (b. 1897, Pittsburgh) is a poet, critic, and philosopher. It is his unparalleled good fortune that all of his dozen books are currently in print. Among the better-known are *Counter-Statement* (1930), *The Philosophy of Literary Form* (1941), and *Language as Symbolic Action* (1966).

JACK BURNHAM (b. 1931) is professor of art at Northwestern University. Educated as a sculptor and architectural engineer, he graduated from Yale in 1961 with an M.F.A. His books include *Beyond Modern Sculpture* (1968), *The Structure of Art* (1971), and *Great Western Salt Works* (1974).

JOHN CAGE (b. 1912, Los Angeles) has authored three collections of miscellaneous, mind-bending writings: *Silence* (1961), *A Year from Monday* (1967), and *M.* (1973). His musical compositions are internationally renowned. A collection of writings by and about him is Richard Kostelanetz's *John Cage* (1970).

CARL D. CLARK (b. 1946, McKinney, TX) co-edits *Interstate* and works in theater, fiction, poetry and intermedia. His co-editor, LORIS L. ESSARY, is involved in experimental writing and theater.

MERCE CUNNINGHAM (b. sometime after WWI, Centralia, WA) is commonly regarded as the principal American avant-garde dance choreographer of the past three decades. He authored *Changes: Notes on Choreography* (1968) and is the subject of *Merce Cunningham* (1974), edited by James Klosty.

WALTER DE MARIA (b. 1935, Albany, CA) has exhibited his sculpture around the world. His essay reprinted here contributed to his involvement with "Fluxus."

MARCEL DUCHAMP (1887-1968) was one of the greatest polyartists of modernism, producing distinguished work in painting, sculpture, and language.

RICHARD FOREMAN (b. 1937, New York), a graduate of Brown and Yale universities, is the founder-director of the Ontological-Hysteric Theater,

Inc., of New York. Many of his writings for both the theater and the printed page were collected as *Plays and Manifestoes* (1976). He also directed a recent New York musical production of Bertolt Brecht's *Threepenny Opera.*

HENRY FLYNT (b. 1940, Greensboro, NC) describes himself as "a philosopher, socialist, economist and unsuccessful rock musician, among other things." His essay, "Concept Art," first published in 1962, coined the phrase and provided the original rationale. His philosophical writings were published as *Blueprint for a Higher Civilization* (1975).

ALLEN GINSBERG (b. 1926, Newark, NJ) has written numerous essays, in addition to poems known around the world.

NELSON GOODMAN (b. 1906, Somerville, MA) is professor of philosophy at Harvard University. Few members of his academic profession command as much influence, not only through essays, which appear largely in scholarly journals, but also through such books as *The Structure of Appearance* (1951, Second Ed., 1966), *Languages of Art* (1968), and *Problems and Projects* (1972). From 1929 to 1942, he operated an art gallery in Boston.

CLEMENT GREENBERG (b. 1908) is one of the world's best-known and most influential art critics. His early essays were collected as *Art and Culture* (1958). Currently living in Norwich, NY, he writes that he has recently "talked on art and juried it everywhere, more or less."

DICK HIGGINS (b. 1938, Cambridge, England, of American parents) founded the Something Else Press (1964-74). He has composed music, published poetry, staged mixed-means theatrical events, written essays, and much else. His works in various forms were collected as *Jefferson's Birthday/Postface* (1964) and *Foew&ombwhnw* (1969).

WILL INSLEY (b. 1929, Indianapolis) took his B. A. from Amherst and his B. Arch. at Harvard. He has exhibited his sculpture around the world and contributed his writings to many magazines. He lives in New York.

ALLAN KAPROW (b. 1927, Atlantic City, NJ) is professor of art at the University of California at San Diego. His books include *Assemblage, Environments & Happenings* (1966), and *Some Recent Happenings* (1966).

Since 1958, he has produced performance pieces around the world.

MICHAEL KIRBY (b. 1931, Oakland, CA) is chairman of the Graduate Drama Department, New York University, and editor of *The Drama Review*. A graduate of Princeton University and a sometime playwright, director, and sculptor, he is the author of *Happenings* (1965) and *The Art of Time* (1969).

RICHARD KOSTELANETZ (b. 1940, New York) has written and edited many books about contemporary art. His own works with words, numbers, and lines—prints, drawings, books, audiotapes, and video-tapes—have been widely exhibited.

GEORGE KUBLER (b. 1912, Los Angeles) is the Stirling professor of art at Yale University. His books include *Art and Architecture of Ancient America* (1962), *The Shape of Time* (1962), and *Portuguese Plain Architecture* (1972).

SOL LEWITT (b. 1928, Hartford, CT) received a B.F.A. from Syracuse University in 1949. A major retrospective of his visual work was held at the Gemeentemuseum, the Hague, in 1970. His most recent publications include prose essays and visual books.

LUCY R. LIPPARD (b. 1937, New Haven, CT) has compiled bibliographies, organized exhibitions, contributed essays to magazines, and written numerous catalogue introductions, in addition to publishing three books —*Pop Art* (1966), *Changes* (1971), *Six Years* (1973), and *From the Center* (1976).

MARSHALL McLUHAN (b. 1911, Edmonton, Alberta) is professor of English at the University of Toronto and director of its Centre for the Study of Culture and Technology. His books on esthetics include *Counterblast* (1969), *The Interior Landscape* (1969), *Through the Vanishing Point* (1968), *Understanding Media* (1964), *The Gutenberg Galaxy* (1962), and *The Mechanical Bride* (1951).

442

L. MOHOLY-NAGY (1895-1946) was perhaps the greatest polyartist of modernism. In addition to producing paintings, sculpture, stage designs, typography, photography, and films, he also wrote three major books—*Painting, Photography, Film* (1925), *The New Vision: From Material to Architecture* (1932), and *Vision in Motion* (1947). A collection of writings by and about him is Richard Kostelanetz's *Moholy-Nagy* (1970).

LINDA NOCHLIN (b. 1931, New York) is the Mary Conover Mellon Professor of Art History at Vassar College. Among her books are *Realism* (1972) and two anthologies, *Impressionism and Post-Impressionism* (1966) and *Realism and Tradition in Art* (1966).

MORSE PECKHAM (b. 1914) is the Distinguished Professor of English and Comparative Literature at the University of South Carolina. Among his books are *Beyond the Tragic Vision* (1962), *Man's Rage for Chaos* (1965), *Victorian Revolutionaries* (1970), and *The Triumph of Romanticism* (1970).

JACKSON POLLOCK (1912-1956) was one of the major painters of this age.

YVONNE RAINER (b. 1934, San Francisco) choreographs mixed-means performance pieces and makes films. Among the latter are *The Lives of Performers* (1972), *Film About a Woman Who . . .* (1974), and *Kristina Talking Pictures* (1976). Her writings were collected as *Work 1961/73* (1974).

STEVE REICH (b. 1936, New York) took his B.A. in philosophy at Cornell and his M.A. in music at Mills. His major musical compositions, played mostly by his own ensemble, have been widely performed and recorded: the most recent compilation is the three-disc album, *Drumming* (1974). *Writings About Music* (1974) is a collection of his essays.

AD REINHARDT (1913-1967) was one of the most extreme painters of the Western world. His prose writings were recently collected in *Art-as-Art* (1975) and his polemical cartoons (visual essays) in *Art Comics and*

Satires (1976).

HAROLD ROSENBERG (b. 1906, New York) is presently art critic for *The New Yorker* and professor in the Committee on Social Thought and the Department of Art at the University of Chicago. His essays have been collected as *The Tradition of the New* (1959), *Art on the Edge* (1975), *Discovering the Present,* among other titles.

JEROME ROTHENBERG (b. 1931, New York) authored *Poland/1931* (1974) and *Poems for the Game of Silence* (1970), among over a dozen other collections of his own poetry. He also edited several anthology-collages.

JAMES SEAWRIGHT (b. 1936, Mississippi) worked as a technician for the Columbia-Princeton Electronic Music Study and currently directs the Creative Arts Program at Princeton University. His sculptural machines and environments have been prominently exhibited.

PAUL SHARITS (b. 1943, Denver) presently teaches film at the Center for Media Study, SUNY-Buffalo. The Albright-Knox Gallery in Buffalo recently mounted a retrospective of his films, frozen film frames, drawings, and prints. Among his better-known films are *N:O:T:H:I:N:G* (1968), *S:TREAM:—S:S:ECTION:S:ECTION:S:S:ECTIONED* (1968-70), and *Apparent Motion* (1975).

ROBERT SMITHSON (1938-1973), initially known as a sculptor, also made films and wrote influential essays, establishing himself as a major theorist of recent essays. These essays will soon appear as a one-person book.

JAMES WINES (b. 1932, Chicago) is co-director of SITE, Inc., of New York City. The firm creates sculpture in the environment. Formerly a much-exhibited sculptor, he has recently been teaching at the School of Visual Arts in New York, lecturing, and contributing articles to magazines.